Oracle8™ Developer's Guide

Oracle8™ Developer's Guide

Carol McCullough-Dieter

IDG Books Worldwide, Inc.
An International Data Group Company

Foster City, CA ◆ Chicago, IL ◆ Indianapolis, IN ◆ New York, NY

Oracle8™ Developer's Guide

Published by
IDG Books Worldwide, Inc.
An International Data Group Company
919 E. Hillsdale Blvd., Suite 400
Foster City, CA 94404
www.idgbooks.com (IDG Books Worldwide Web site)

ISBN: 0-7645-3197-2

Printed in the United States of America

10 9 8 7 6 5 4 3 2 1

1B/QU/QT/ZZ/FC

Distributed in the United States by IDG Books Worldwide, Inc.

Distributed by CDG Books Canada Inc. for Canada; by Transworld Publishers Limited in the United Kingdom; by IDG Norge Books for Norway; by IDG Sweden Books for Sweden; by Woodslane Pty. Ltd. for Australia; by Woodslane (NZ) Ltd. for New Zealand; by TransQuest Publishers Pte Ltd. for Singapore, Malaysia, Thailand, Indonesia, and Hong Kong; by ICG Muse, Inc. for Japan; by Norma Comunicaciones S.A. for Colombia; by Intersoft for South Africa; by Le Monde en Tique for France; by International Thomson Publishing for Germany, Austria and Switzerland; by Distribuidora Cuspide for Argentina; by Livraria Cultura for Brazil; by Ediciones ZETA S.C.R. Ltda. for Peru; by WS Computer Publishing Corporation, Inc., for the Philippines; by Contemporanea de Ediciones for Venezuela; by Express Computer Distributors for the Caribbean and West Indies; by Micronesia Media Distributor, Inc. for Micronesia; by Grupo Editorial Norma S.A. for Guatemala; by Chips Computadoras S.A. de C.V. for Mexico; by Editorial Norma de Panama S.A. for Panama; by American Bookshops for Finland. Authorized Sales Agent: Anthony Rudkin Associates for the Middle East and North Africa.

For general information on IDG Books Worldwide's books in the U.S., please call our Consumer Customer Service department at 800-762-2974. For reseller information, including discounts and premium sales, please call our Reseller Customer Service department at 800-434-3422.

For information on where to purchase IDG Books Worldwide's books outside the U.S., please contact our International Sales department at 317-596-5530 or fax 317-596-5692.

For consumer information on foreign language translations, please contact our Customer Service department at 800-434-3422, fax 317-596-5692, or e-mail rights@idgbooks.com.

For information on licensing foreign or domestic rights, please phone +1-650-655-3109.

For sales inquiries and special prices for bulk quantities, please contact our Sales department at 650-655-3200 or write to the address above.

For information on using IDG Books Worldwide's books in the classroom or for ordering examination copies, please contact our Educational Sales department at 800-434-2086 or fax 317-596-5499.

For press review copies, author interviews, or other publicity information, please contact our Public Relations department at 650-655-3000 or fax 650-655-3299.

For authorization to photocopy items for corporate, personal, or educational use, please contact Copyright Clearance Center, 222 Rosewood Drive, Danvers, MA 01923, or fax 978-750-4470.

Library of Congress Cataloging-in-Publication Data

McCullough-Dieter, Carol.

    Oracle8 developer's guide/Carol McCullough-Dieter

      p. cm.

    Includes index.

    ISBN 0-7645-3197-2

    1. Oracle (Computer file) 2. Relational databases.
I. Title.
QA76.9.D3M39428   1999
005.75'85--dc21   98-52670
                                     CIP

ABOUT IDG BOOKS WORLDWIDE

Welcome to the world of IDG Books Worldwide.

IDG Books Worldwide, Inc., is a subsidiary of International Data Group, the world's largest publisher of computer-related information and the leading global provider of information services on information technology. IDG was founded more than 30 years ago by Patrick J. McGovern and now employs more than 9,000 people worldwide. IDG publishes more than 290 computer publications in over 75 countries. More than 90 million people read one or more IDG publications each month.

Launched in 1990, IDG Books Worldwide is today the #1 publisher of best-selling computer books in the United States. We are proud to have received eight awards from the Computer Press Association in recognition of editorial excellence and three from Computer Currents' First Annual Readers' Choice Awards. Our best-selling ...For Dummies® series has more than 50 million copies in print with translations in 31 languages. IDG Books Worldwide, through a joint venture with IDG's Hi-Tech Beijing, became the first U.S. publisher to publish a computer book in the People's Republic of China. In record time, IDG Books Worldwide has become the first choice for millions of readers around the world who want to learn how to better manage their businesses.

Our mission is simple: Every one of our books is designed to bring extra value and skill-building instructions to the reader. Our books are written by experts who understand and care about our readers. The knowledge base of our editorial staff comes from years of experience in publishing, education, and journalism — experience we use to produce books to carry us into the new millennium. In short, we care about books, so we attract the best people. We devote special attention to details such as audience, interior design, use of icons, and illustrations. And because we use an efficient process of authoring, editing, and desktop publishing our books electronically, we can spend more time ensuring superior content and less time on the technicalities of making books.

You can count on our commitment to deliver high-quality books at competitive prices on topics you want to read about. At IDG Books Worldwide, we continue in the IDG tradition of delivering quality for more than 30 years. You'll find no better book on a subject than one from IDG Books Worldwide.

John Kilcullen
John Kilcullen
Chairman and CEO
IDG Books Worldwide, Inc.

Steven Berkowitz
Steven Berkowitz
President and Publisher
IDG Books Worldwide, Inc.

Eighth Annual Computer Press Awards 1992

Ninth Annual Computer Press Awards 1993

Tenth Annual Computer Press Awards 1994

Eleventh Annual Computer Press Awards 1995

Credits

ACQUISITIONS EDITOR
John Osborn

DEVELOPMENT EDITOR
Barbra Guerra

TECHNICAL EDITOR
Piroz Mohseni

COPY EDITORS
Barry Childs-Helton
Nancy Crumpton
Anne Friedman

PROJECT COORDINATOR
Tom Debolski

PACKAGING COORDINATOR
Kathryn Hoover

BOOK DESIGNER
Jim Donahue

GRAPHICS AND
PRODUCTION SPECIALIST
Mario Amador

GRAPHICS TECHNICIANS
Sarah Barnes
Linda Barnes

QUALITY CONTROL SPECIALIST
Mick Arellano

ILLUSTRATOR
Jesse Coleman

PROOFREADING AND INDEXING
York Production Services

COVER DESIGN
©mike parsons design

COVER PHOTO
©Paul & Lindamarie Ambrose/FPG
International LLC

About the Author

Carol McCullough-Dieter began working with Oracle Designer before it existed. Well, it existed in several pieces: SQL*FORMS, CASE*TOOL, SQL*REPORTS, and so on. She helped perform beta testing of SQL*Forms on the MVS, AIX, and PC platforms in the late 1980s. Since then, she has developed and taught classes on advanced Forms design, SQL tuning, and advanced SQL*Plus. Carol presented papers at Oracle Openworld 98.

She currently works at the Pacific Disaster Center (www.pdc.org) on the island of Maui, Hawaii. She is the Database Administrator and is responsible for database administration as well as for the design, programming, and implementation of all Oracle applications. All the applications are Web-enabled and deliver dynamic Web pages on the PDC private, password-protected intranet sites.

She has written four other books (all published by IDG Books Worldwide): *Creating Cool Web Databases, Oracle7 For Dummies, Oracle8 For Dummies,* and *Oracle8 Bible.*

Her personal Web site is http://www.maui.net/~mcculc, and her e-mail address is mcculc@maui.net.

About the Contributing Authors

Marc de Oliveira received his M.Sc. in Computer Science from the University of Copenhagen in 1992 where he studied CASE tools as well as neural networks and cognitive science. He has been working with Oracle databases and tools since 1989 with primary interest in the Oracle CASE tools. He is currently employed by a large Danish pharmaceutical company. Through his own company, Pythia Information, he is the Scandinavian reseller of the Designer template package called Design-Assist. He is also chairman of the Designer Special Interest Group of the Danish Oracle User Group (OUGDK Designer SIG). You can contact him through e-mail at: Marc@deOliveira.dk, or visit his Web site at: http://www.deOliveira.dk/Pythia

Chester R. West was a presenter at the 1997 ODTUG Conference. Chet has been working with Designer and CASE Method for five years. He is a skilled systems analyst professional with experience in application lifecycle planning and development. His strengths include project management and Computer-Aided Software Engineering (CASE). Chet also has a knowledge of database and network design and administration, data migration from legacy systems and a strong background in application documentation procedures on both technical and non-technical levels. Chet is currently a CASE Engineer / Project Manager with Tactics, Inc.

Rachel Becker has been developing Oracle applications for nine years. She has designed systems for the education, utilities, healthcare, manufacturing, and financial markets. She has presented at ODTUG and IOUG conferences. She is a co-author of *Oracle Unleashed*. Currently, she is a senior consultant with Tactics, an Oracle development consulting firm in the Southeast. Rachel can be reached via e-mail at: rbecker@tacticsus.com.

Alec Goldis is president and cofounder of WebOracle, Inc. www.Weborcl.com (not Weboracle.com), a consulting and mentoring company, based in Atlanta, that helps companies to architect and build solutions using Windows NT. Get in touch with Alec at: alecg@Weborcl.com

Devin McRorie has been developing Oracle applications for 3 years. He has development experience in the aviation, manufacturing, and telecommunications industries. Currently, he is a consultant with Tactics, an Oracle development consulting firm in the Southeast. He can be reached at: dmcrorie@tacticsus.com. Tactics is available via the Web at: http//www.tactisus.com.

Kevin Budziszewski has been an Oracle developer and DBA since 1991. His project experience includes full life cycle development and technical consulting with Oracle Financials. While employed by Oracle, he acted as technical lead on several custom and Oracle Financials projects. In 1996, he formed TOGS, Inc. to pursue his interests in refining development methodologies. Kevin can be reached at KevinBud@togsinc.com or visit the TOGS Web site at www.togsinc.com.

To my children
Dustin, Jesse, Deja, Chrystal, and Blue.
You are the world — the future, the now, the always.
Love, Mom

Preface

Oracle Designer, Oracle Developer, Oracle WebServer, client/server implementation, and Web implementation. The *Oracle8 Developer's Guide* covers all these important designer tools and more.

How can one book span the information for all these products when other books of twice the size cover just one topic? *By sharpening the focus to the key elements of each tool that save you time, streamline your work, and simplify your implementation.* My goal is to deliver to you, under one cover, the best techniques for each tool using examples that you can pick up and use immediately.

Prerequisite Skills

I have made some assumptions about you, the reader, when writing this book. My goal is to provide Oracle programmers, designers, and application developers with a guide to the most useful and practical portions of each tool featured. I assume that you have these basic skills:

◆ **You use a mouse and a graphical user interface (GUI), such as Windows.** If you use e-mail or Word, you're in.

◆ **You know how to use a Web browser.** If you have "surfed the net" enough to know the difference between a search engine and a shopping cart, great! A basic understanding of HTML helps you even more.

◆ **You have some experience with relational database design.** If you know terms like "one-to-many" and are familiar with database diagrams, you are ready.

◆ **You know basic SQL.** While many of the tools boast that you need no SQL to produce an application, I will show SQL examples in the book that assume you are able to read and understand the code. If you are unfamiliar with SQL, I recommend purchasing my book, *Oracle8 Bible* (IDG Books Worldwide, 1998), which contains a complete SQL and PL/SQL reference section as well as tutorial style examples of how to write Oracle procedures, queries, functions, and DDL (data definition language) commands.

The book is intended primarily for levels of skill from intermediate to advanced. If this is your first exposure to Oracle Developer Toolset, you may benefit from a book that covers the basics of each tool in a more tutorial manner.

Reviewing the Book's Structure

This book uses several projects that are developed from beginning to end using Oracle's suite of tools. Every chapter contains sample code and illustrations describing techniques used in the projects.

The book is divided into four parts.

Part 1 – Oracle Designer

The Designer tool has had volumes written about it. How does it work? What can it do? Why won't it do this or that? You may wonder: How can a book of this size do justice to such a complex tool?

Along with my team of contributing authors, I have endeavored to present the latest new material about Designer release 2.1. The book contains concrete, usable, examples of code and design tips from experienced professionals. Some of the tricks you learn here cover undocumented features of Designer.

Here is just a partial list of the great information in store for you:

◆ How to use OPS$ automatic logon with Web modules

◆ How to create Oracle8 objects using Designer

◆ Advanced use of Form and Report generation

◆ Creating reusable modules and libraries

◆ Creating web server modules in Designer

◆ Placing and extracting user help text in the repository

◆ Calling PL/SQL procedures from the web

◆ Uncovering problems with Web-enabling client/server applications

◆ Designing for visual appeal without postgeneration changes

◆ Creating documentation with the Repository and MS-Word

I am confident you will find many new ideas and tips here that are not found anywhere else.

Part II – Oracle Developer

As you may know, Developer can be a world of its own. Some developers never use Designer to generate applications. Instead, they rely on the robust and complete tools contained in Developer for all their application work. Others design applications using Designer, generate an initial application and then customize the application. This approach can sometimes cause problems because it is difficult to recreate the application from the Designer. Therefore, often the maintenance of the application requires that the Designer portion get out of date in favor of quick maintenance in Developer.

Developer topics are many and it was difficult to narrow down the topics into the chapters that follow. My strategy was to focus on:

◆ The newest features of release 2.1 of Developer

◆ Web-enabling applications

◆ Oracle8 Objects within Forms

◆ Complex combinations of forms, charts, reports, and so on

You find some of the basics here as well. This book covers a lot of concrete examples that are carried throughout the chapters. The examples use common sample tables that are included on the CD-ROM. You can take any of the example applications and run them yourself. Go ahead: experiment, examine, explore, and discover.

The designer's job is delivering the best functionality while keeping the cost reasonable. If you are designing a marketable product, you must add the capability to jump on the latest trend without spending months retraining.

This book gives you a jump on developing with the very latest features of Developer. You will find a wealth of good ideas that are meant to be your springboard into new ideas for your own projects. Enjoy.

Part III — Other Fast-Track Tools

This part covers three great tools for delivering reports, query tools, and fully functioning applications to the Web:

◆ PL/SQL with HTML extensions

◆ Discoverer

◆ Enterprise Manager Web Publishing Assistant

Even though Designer and Developer can deliver applications in several ways to the Web, it is important to know the additional tools you have available to you. These tools are very different than Designer and Developer:

◆ They are either included with the Oracle8 Enterprise toolset, or available for a low cost.

◆ They are generally easy to learn.

♦ They give you options for generating stand-alone Web pages that do not require direct database access.

You may find some useful features that you thought you'd have to go to a third party to purchase. These tools can help you get a project onto the Web in record time. Read on for lots more great information.

Appendixes, Quick Reference, and Glossary

The fourth part contains diverse reference materials along with instructions on how to use the CD-ROM.

Appendix A points you to the location of the files on the CD-ROM included with the book. Here I've included instructions on how to install all the required tables and files needed to run the sample applications found in the book and on the CD-ROM. Appendix A is also located (in HTML format) on the CD-ROM at: D:\index.html

Appendix B provides a listing of Oracle-related and database-related Web sites with their corresponding URLs and a few annotations.

Appendix C lists all the SQL and HTML source code found scattered around the book. There is a table that describes each code file and what it is for. This appendix helps you study the code without skipping around the book and reading through long explanations that are scattered within the code in the chapters.

The Quick Reference chapter has sections on SQL, HTML, JSQL, and PL/SQL.

There is also a glossary of terms and an index near the end of the book.

Concept chapters

Each Part begins with a *concept chapter*. A concept chapter, as you expect, describes some of the theory and background of the subject. The concept chapter contains three important components:

♦ **An overview of concepts and theories.** Use the overview as background material to help you better understand later chapters.

♦ **A quick review of some basic techniques needed.** Subjects that are needed later in the Part are reviewed here. For example, PL/SQL programming techniques are covered briefly in the concept chapter for Part II (Designer).

♦ **Suggested reading for background information.** While this book is comparatively self-contained, you may want to read more on various subjects, such as HTML syntax. Good books are recommended.

These components are building blocks for using the tool logically. Following the concept chapter in each Part, appears the Quick Start chapter.

Quick Start chapters

The Quick Start chapters give a whirlwind tour of the tool. A simple application is used to guide you through the process of developing an application with the tool from start to finish. The Quick Start chapter provides a preview of the chapters that follow in each Part of the book.

Subsequent chapters illustrate more detailed examples on how to use the tool like an expert. Throughout the book, time-saving ideas are emphasized. In today's world of *rapid application development* (RAD) and prototyping, your efforts are wisely focused on the most efficient way to get from point A (initial concept) to point B (final product).

Most of the chapters use examples that illustrate how to use the concepts in practical ways. There are several projects used in the book to make the examples build from one chapter to the next.

Icon Guideposts

Icons used to point out important points are used throughout the *Oracle8 Developer's Guide.*

Look here for time-saving and other valuable tips. The essence of a chapter section gets boiled down into practical shortcuts and suggestions you can use in your own design and development work.

From time to time, you'll see this icon that is intended to steer you away from a problem or potential trouble spot.

For content found on the CD, look for the CD-ROM icon. This icon indicates a reference to the corresponding file names on the CD-ROM that accompanies this book.

Cross references to other chapters in the book help you find more information about related topics. This icon directs you to the specific section of the
related chapter.

Acknowledgments

My name is on the cover as author and I have written much of what follows here. However, my efforts were supported, enhanced, amplified, and improved by many others.

My husband, Pat, gave his time and energy to being my "ghost editor," reviewing all my work to correct spelling, grammar, and nonsensical sentences.

The first-class team of editors, artists, and production staff at IDG Books Worldwide — led by Barbra Guerra and John Osborn — was invaluable in creating the excellent quality of this book in its physical form.

I want to extend my heartfelt gratitude to the contributing authors. These professionals improved the quality and usefulness of this book beyond my expectations. To all of you: thank you for your generosity and your spirit of sharing; may it return to you one thousand fold.

Finally, a special thank you to all of my family and my co-workers at the Pacific Disaster Center for patiently tolerating my obsession with this book. Your support made the book a reality, plain and simple!

Contents at a Glance

Contents

Introduction

Projects Developed in This Book

The sample projects used in the book help you take abstract ideas and apply them to real-world problems. Three projects are developed from beginning to end in the book:

- **Toy Store Chain.** The toy store chain has stores in many locations. The chain determines an inventory number for each toy and sets the selling price of the toy. Each toy store has its own stock of toys, using the inventory number and selling price from the home office. The project involves a simple inventory system that is used in all the toy stores. The system has online forms for adding and removing toys from each store's inventory; updating each store's name, address, owner, and so on. Reports on inventories are designed to look at individual toys, toy categories, individual stores, or groups of stores.

- **Volunteer Net.** The volunteer net is a clearinghouse for volunteers and organizations that need their help. Each organization contributes details about its work and a "wish list" of tasks, money, equipment, and so on, that it needs. Each volunteer (or prospective volunteer) describes his or her skills, preferences, and availability. The project we build provides online forms for organizations and volunteers, including a cross-referencing report that matches volunteers to organizations.

- **Lending Library with Oracle8 Objects.** The lending library has a collection of books that are loaned to individuals. If a book is currently loaned out, people can be added to a reserve list for the book. Up to ten people can be on the reserve list for a book. If a book is not returned on time, the person is assessed a fine of 25 cents per day per book. The system includes online forms for the librarian's use. Functions include: loaning out books; receiving returned books; adding and reducing fines; viewing one person's activity (books on loan, books on reserve, outstanding fines). Reports on overall activity show the number of books and types of books loaned, and the total fines assessed. This project is implemented using Oracle8 Objects, Types, and Methods.

There are detailed database table designs, forms designs, function flowcharts, and code snippets that illustrate the concepts discussed as the projects evolve.

ON THE CD The CD-ROM contains sample tables, forms, reports, and case designs so that you can view the completed projects.

If you wish to try out the examples shown in the book, you must have the software listed in the next section available for your use.

Software for the Projects in This Book

This book is intended to be a handy desk reference with lots of suggestions, examples, and tips that you can use while developing your own Oracle Tools applications. The following software tools are examined and described in the book. Most of you will have some or all of these tools on your computer or network. If possible, have the tool featured in each Part of the book installed and available for your use:

- ◆ **Designer for Part I.** Release 2.1 is used in the book although most of the tips and techniques work equally well with release 2.0.

- ◆ **Developer for Part II.** The book uses Oracle Developer release 2.1. Most of the concepts and features are applicable to prior versions of Developer as well.

- ◆ **Fast-track tools for Part III**

    - ■ **Oracle WebServer for Part III.** The latest version of the software, Version 3.0 is used in the book. Many of the basic features are available in Version 2.0 and higher.

    - ■ **Discoverer.** Here is a tool that has been upgraded to include Web deployment.

    - ■ **Enterprise Manager.** In particular, the Web Assistant tool is covered.

Thoughts on Designing Online Database Systems

When designing for an online database application system, your system requires a great deal of interaction with the end user. This means that you must understand the business terminology so your data entry windows and menu buttons have meaningful labels. You need to understand the flow of events so the user can move through application windows in a more intuitive way. In addition, the fast pace of business and software requires you to respond quickly to changes in requirements and to deliver a completed system quickly. The more time you allow to elapse between gathering user requirements and delivering a completed system, the greater the likelihood that the system no longer meets your user's needs.

The two primary methods of implementing an online system today are client/server (two-tier) and triple-tier architectures.

Client/server (two-tier) design

A client/server system consists of two distinct components that function together as a unit. Figure I-1 shows the basic architecture used when implementing a client/server database system.

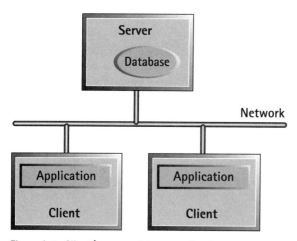

Figure I-1: Client/server architecture distributes much of the processing power to the client platform.

The client portion of the system interacts with the user, presenting information and gathering data. Much of the data validation and all of the navigation rely on a sophisticated client application. The client portion communicates transactions to the server. For example, the user might choose to add a new doll to the toy store chain's line of toys. The client application starts up a window displaying all the fields that are needed for this task. The user enters data. As the user moves from one field to another, the client application controls which fields are open for use and which are skipped over. The user completes her work and clicks the Save button. The client application validates all data, prepares a series of instructions for the Server and sends the instructions to the Server and waits for a response.

The server portion of the system retrieves the client's instructions and executes them. Continuing with the toy example, the server receives a transaction that inserts a row into the toy inventory table. The insert succeeds. The server sends a message to the client indicating that the task was a success.

The client hears the response from the server. In our example, the row was inserted so the client sends a message to the use saying that the record was saved in the database.

Client/server architecture requires that the client contain all the executable code for all applications in the system. If an application changes, then all clients must receive a new copy of the application. This means that maintenance and change control are more difficult than in the old-style centralized systems.

Triple-tier design

To me (an old programmer from the days when the computer was bigger than my car), the triple-tier architecture is a more flexible version of the old "dumb terminal" systems.

Figure I-2 illustrates the triple-tier concept. The client and server still exist, but are separated by a middle portion. The *client* (first tier) still interacts with the end user, presenting the data entry window, accepting data and sending status messages. However, in the triple-tier system, the client relies on standard software that the user already has in place on his or her computer, such as Windows 95 or Netscape Navigator. The client portion of the system is not actually stored on the client's computer at all (except temporarily, as in the case of Java applets). The client delivers a window or message to the user in a familiar format, such as a Web page. The client sends data from the user to the middle (second tier) portion of the system.

The *middleware* (second tier) resides on a remote computer (or network of computers). The second tier is like a translator. It sends information to the user in the format appropriate for a Web browser (for example). It receives information from the client and then translates it into commands appropriate for the database server. The commands are sent to the server.

The *server* (third tier) can reside on yet another computer, or possibly a network of computers. The server receives instructions, processes them in the database, and returns the results of the instructions to the middleware. The middleware prepares the results from the server in a user-friendly format and sends it to the client.

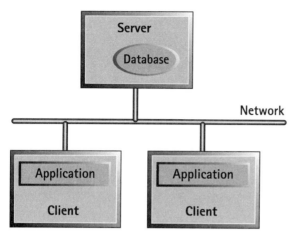

Figure I-2: The triple-tier concept.

The triple-tier system allows for many clients to use the system without requiring any maintenance of the applications on the client. When changes are made to an application, only the middleware is changed on the second tier. This reduces the work in maintenance by requiring the system administrator to distribute the change to a handful of computers rather than to hundreds or even thousands of clients.

With the growing popularity of the Internet, the triple-tier architecture enables businesses to deploy applications to literally millions of end users. One challenge that remains even with a triple-tier system is supporting diverse client platforms. However, with the advent of Java, this challenge has started to be resolved as never before. Java allows identical commands to execute on multiple hardware and operating systems with identical results. Java is to computer applications what a universal translator is to the United Nations – suddenly we can all talk to one another and be fully understood.

Rapid Application Development techniques

There are many variations on methodology for systems development. While these methodologies use different terminology and different diagrams to convey the system design, they all have at their core the same basic steps. These traditional methodologies of systems perform the following steps:

1. Gather user requirements.

2. Prepare initial design strategies.

3. Create detailed specifications to implement design.

4. Write applications according to specifications.

5. Show end results to users for approval.

6. Repeat steps 1 through 5 with any new user requirements.

Rapid Application Development (RAD) has become popular in the last few years because it allows you to develop and implement systems more quickly. One of the key elements of RAD is the prototype. The basic steps in RAD are:

1. Gather initial user requirements.

2. Prepare initial design strategies.

3. Create a *prototype*. A prototype is one or more applications or simulated applications that demonstrate the final system's functionality.

4. Gather more user feedback by demonstrating the prototype.

5. Add onto the prototype's functionality. Replace simulated applications with real applications.

6. Repeat steps 4 and 5 as long as needed.

The RAD methodologies lend themselves to businesses where user needs are new and not well defined. In addition, the RAD methodologies promote user involvement, so that the final system tends to be more closely aligned with the user's expectations.

TIP

The Oracle Development Tools can be used with either kind of systems design methodology or a mixture of both. In any case, a successful system design needs a consistent and predefined series of procedures or steps to follow.

Using Oracle Development Tools in the Design Cycle

There are as many ways to use Oracle Development Tools in your design process as there are designers. Here are some of the possibilities:

◆ **Use Designer to design the database entities and relationships.** Implement in a non-Oracle database with Java applications.

◆ **Use your own diagrammer to design the database.** Use Developer to create the applications and reports for the Oracle database. Use Developer's Web module to generate Web-enabled forms and reports for the same system.

◆ **Generate the applications and reports from Designer module definitions.** Generate the database from the Designer diagram tool.

◆ **Reverse engineer an existing Oracle database into Designer.** Use Designer to implement changes to the database.

◆ **Use Developer to promote standards across many systems designs by creating shared libraries of common elements and templates.**

As you explore these powerful tools, you will discover the portions of each tool that work best for your unique requirements. Experiment, think, be creative, ask other designers, join a user's group, and get results.

Part I

Oracle Designer

Chapter 1

Concepts of Designer

IN THIS CHAPTER

- ◆ Looking at Designer components
- ◆ Reviewing the designer tools in Designer version 2.1

THE DESIGNER PACKAGE was originally a CASE (Computer Aided Systems Engineering) design tool. I first saw it in 1989 when I used it for a project to define the shared database elements for a diverse collection of application systems. Since then, Designer has acquired more functionality and depth. It is the kind of tool a consultant can spend her entire career mastering. I do not claim to be the world expert on Designer. In fact, more chapters were written in this section by my esteemed coauthors than by me.

TIP

My goal in presenting the eight chapters in Part I is to give you ideas on how best to use this tool for speed and accuracy of design. A special emphasis is made on the latest version, 2.1, that contains many new features you may want to explore.

This chapter reviews the primary components of Designer version 2.1. We review briefly each of the Designer tools with hints of what future chapters hold in store for you.

Reviewing Designer Version 2.1 Toolset

Many tools make up Designer. You may choose to use whatever combination of tools you need for your particular project. The primary tool you use, once your repository is set up, is the Design Editor. This tool integrates much of your work, giving you a top-level view of your project's logic, modules, database objects, and so on. The next sections review all the tools in Designer. Figure 1-1 shows how the tools fit together.

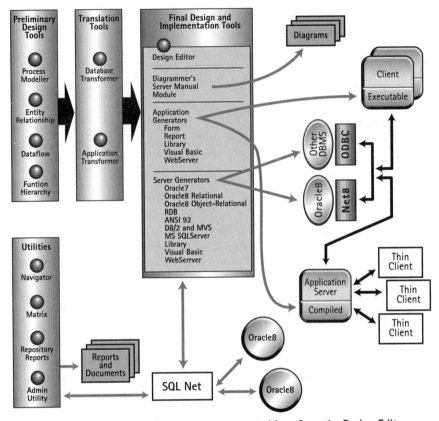

Figure 1-1: Designer's toolset has many components driven from the Design Editor.

Design Editor

The Design Editor uses a visual display to show you your database or your modules. You can drill down into the objects you see on the diagram to define the attributes of that object.

Chapter 3 goes through the steps you use to design your database system.
See that chapter for more details about the Design Editor.

You can generate the SQL you need to create the schema for your database design. The Design Editor supports a wide variety of databases, including Oracle8 objects. The Designer can also generate APIs for tables and other application modules.

When you design modules using the Design Editor, you can generate WebServer applications, Oracle Forms, and Oracle Reports directly from here.

A new feature enables you to create MS Help to support your Forms or Visual Basic applications. This feature cannot be used for WebServer applications.

Form Generator

The Form Generator has been improved to enable you to achieve 100 percent generated applications with better functionality and customization than ever. Here are just a few of the new features:

- **Subclassing.** You can tell Form Generator to create generated objects. Objects found in the object library can be either copied or subclassed. Define the location of the object library in the STOOLB preference.

- **Item prompts.** Form Builder has properties for mapping, formatting, and managing prompts.

- **Embedded custom code.** You can embed custom code in generated forms. Read the online help documentation to learn how the embedded code is layered between the generated code and the copied or subclassed library code.

- **Startup navigation.** Startup navigation code enables you to control which block the user navigates to when they start a form. This is one of the many new enhancements for controlling navigation in a generated form.

- **Data blocks for procedures.** This new feature supports the Designer feature of using a procedure instead of a base table in a data block. You can also base a data block on a subquery (less maintenance than a view).

- **Generated buttons.** Now you can define buttons for navigation, customized form actions, standard form actions, or for performing application logic. For example, to create a button that commits work, use the command CGAI$COMMIT, set in the button's Template/Library Object property.

- **Generated library objects.** The Library Generator enables you to create library objects when you generate, and these objects can be used inside generated forms.

Library Generator

The Library Generator is a new function of Designer. To create a library, create a module with the type of Library. If your library contains form functions, set the library's language property to "Forms." After creating the module, you can edit the module, if it is stored in the repository, with the Logic Editor. If the module is stored outside the repository, simply name the file and make sure that the file is in the proper path. This way it can be found by forms and other modules that need it.

Matrix Diagrammer

The Matrix Diagrammer enables you to look at the correlations between various objects in your repository. Figure 1-2 shows an example of the Matrix Diagrammer displaying a 3D matrix.

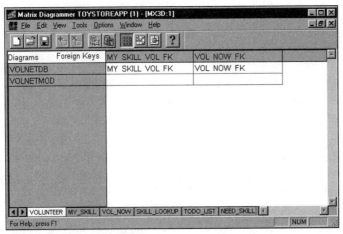

Figure 1-2: The Matrix Diagrammer enables 3D matrix diagrams for certain objects.

A new feature of the Matrix Diagrammer is the capability to create 3D matrices. See the online help "Element combinations for 3D matrices" for a complete list of objects that can be mapped in three dimensions.

Report Generator

The Report Generator creates a developer report or a Web-based report. You can specify the queries, breaks, templates, styles, and even calculated items. Figure 1-3 shows the Report Generator window.

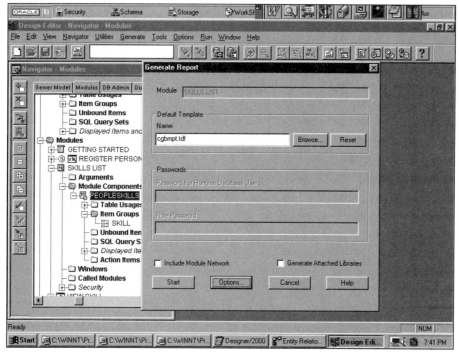

Figure 1-3: Define the essential elements of your report in the Report Generator.

The tools in Designer version 2.1 include new terminology, and Report Generator is no exception. Two important terms are:

◆ Master-detail reports are now called "Group Above" reports.

◆ Control-Break reports are now called "Group Left" reports.

This version also includes a new type of repository object, the Navigation Action Item, for defining navigation between report modules or between a report module and another type of module.

Another change in the Report Generator is the use of a new preference called DSPFMT. This preference replaces the old method for generating Web or PDF reports by attaching the CGWEBP.RDF or CGWEBH.RDF template to the report module. The following values can be set for report output:

◆ RDF. Create a Developer report in RDF format. This is the default.

◆ HTML. Create an HTML document.

◆ HTMLCSS. Generate a report with HTML, and use cascading style sheets.

◆ PDF. Generate a PDF-formatted report.

Repository Administration Utility

The Repository Administration Utility is set up to manage your repository. It includes functions to add users to the repository, upgrade to a newer version of the repository, and generate reports about information in the repository. This utility is your first stop when you are setting up Designer on your system.

TIP The repository owner and manager can be two different Oracle users; however, neither of these can be the SYSTEM user.

The main Repository Administration Utility window has been reorganized, with functions arranged as shown in Figure 1-4.

Figure 1-4: The Repository Administration Utility window looks better in version 2.1.

Some existing functions now have new buttons, such as the View Tablespaces, View Parameters, and View Objects buttons. Some new buttons have been added, such as the Compute Statistics button.

Repository Object Navigator

The Repository Object Navigator (RON) has become leaner and stronger with this version of Designer. Some of the tasks that were previously in the RON have been removed and placed in more appropriate tools. The remaining components of the RON are better and more logically arranged than before. Figure 1-5 shows the RON main window.

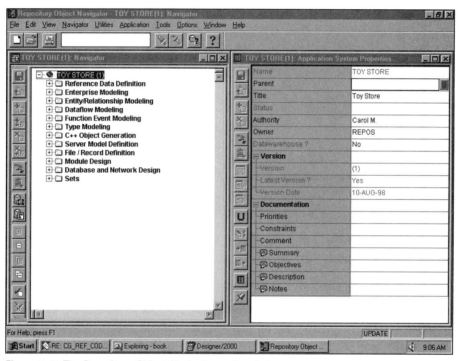

Figure 1-5: The Repository Object Navigator main window.

The Repository Object Navigator (RON) gives developers a tool in which they can choose to share modules with one another. Each developer can even customize the nodes and how objects are arranged in the Navigator.

The RON also contains a powerful search tool.

Chapter 8 covers the RON in detail, discussing how to customize it and how to use it for design recovery, module regeneration, and source management.

Repository Reports

You can run approximately 100 pre-defined reports to list details about your repository. You can also design your own reports.

While most reports have been preserved from earlier versions of Designer, some have been removed, renamed, or moved to another tool. Some reports have been removed in version 2.1 because the Matrix Diagrammer can show all the details that were once shown in the reports. The reports that have been removed are:

- Activity vs Business Unit
- Business Unit vs Activity
- Element to Element Matrix
- Externals in a Given Application
- Entities Used at a Given Business Unit
- Functions Executed at a Business Unit
- Functions Implemented by Modules
- Functions that Use a Given Attribute
- Modules and the Tables/Columns Used
- Modules that Implement a Given Function
- Modules Used by a Given Module
- Modules which Use a Given Module
- Modules which Use a Given Table/View

Some reports have been removed because the Server Generator validates for the conditions and does not enable them. The removed reports are:

- Database Trigger Quality Control
- Datastructure Quality Control
- Groups/Users Quality Control
- Package/Procedure Quality Control
- Table Quality Control

Another group of reports has been removed entirely – whether you like it or not. These are:

◆ Application Systems in a Version Group

◆ Attribute Names across Application Systems

◆ Attributes not Contained in any Datastore

◆ C++ Class Code Locations

◆ C++ File Contents

◆ C++ Object Model Definition

◆ Transferable Elements of an Application System

◆ Dataflows between a Function and an Ancestor

◆ Shareable Elements of an Application System

Hopefully, your favorite report can still be found in the Repository Reports tool!

Server Generator

The Server Generator enables you to generate SQL to create the schema you have designed in Designer. The Server Generator can also capture an existing database schema and load it into the Designer repository for your use. The Server Generator supports many different databases in both generating and capturing database structures.

Version 2.1 has even broader support than previous versions for capturing database structures from existing non-Oracle databases. You can now capture the structures of tables (including primary keys, foreign keys, and check constraints), indexes, views (if applicable), and domains (if applicable).

Personal Oracle Lite is not supported in Designer version 2.1.

Object-oriented structures such as object tables, object types, and object views can be captured with this release of Designer's Server Generator.

TIP Another new feature in this release is the capability of Server Generator to look at defined modules and generate lookup tables, or reference code tables that are loaded with the valid values as defined in the repository. This feature can save time over hard-coded values in your generated applications.

Visual Basic Generator

The Visual Basic Generator is another option when you create modules from your application design. One advantage of using Designer for generating VB forms is that you can use the same module design to generate Developer forms later.

 TIP A new feature of the VB Generator is the Design Capture Utility. Use the Design Capture Utility to grab existing Visual Basic applications and place them in your module design in the repository. This can be used simply to help you document existing VB applications. It can also be used as a method to transform your VB applications into Developer forms or reports.

 XREF See the "Generator Items" section in Chapter 5 for more details about the VB Generator.

WebServer Generator

The WebServer Generator supports the generation of Web-based applications that run on Oracle WebServer. This is different than running Developer forms on the Web, which requires you to run not only a Web server, but also the forms server as a go-between.

 XREF Chapter 2 outlines changes to the WebServer Generator that are new in release 2.1 of Designer.

Chapter 6 focuses on how to create Web applications using Designer and the WebServer Generator.

Broadcast Mechanism

The Broadcast Mechanism is a way to tell multiple users of the same repository about changes to repository objects. This helps when you are working with multiple designers on large projects or where projects have shared elements.

The Broadcast Mechanism notifies other users when something has been changed by setting an indicator next to the object in the other user's session. Once the other user knows an object has changed, he must requery the repository to view the most current version of the object.

Summary

This chapter reviews the many tools included in Designer version 2.1. You become familiar with the tools, their relationships with other tools, and with their latest improvements.

The most dramatic change in Designer is the use of the Design Editor, where you can view your entire design, from business rules to application modules using the Design Object Navigator.

Most of the tools described in the chapter have been improved to enable a more natural and intuitive flow of information from one phase of designing to the next. This version includes improved support for building non-Oracle databases and for retrieving the design of applications and databases from non-Oracle applications and databases.

In the next chapter, we look at how to increase your productivity by taking advantage of the best time- and work-saving techniques for using Developer tools.

Chapter 2

Quick Start for Designer

IN THIS CHAPTER

- ◆ Reviewing the new features in version 2.0 and 2.1
- ◆ Looking at tools and features that were dropped or renamed
- ◆ Checking into Web application generators
- ◆ Defining security for systems
- ◆ Reviewing Oracle8 object support

THIS CHAPTER REVIEWS the new features that will give you a head start in using Designer version 2.1.

There are a lot of different ways to use Designer. Some shops use all the tools, starting with designing the business logic and continuing all the way through generated applications. Other shops use Designer only for designing the logical and physical database. They use Designer to create the database schema but then rely on other tools to create application systems. Still others use the tool only for documenting and designing the application functions. Some use the reverse-engineering tool to give themselves a head start on redesigning a project. Depending on what your requirements and needs are, you may wish to skip around in this book and read appropriate chapters that are relevant to your needs.

Some of the newest features of Designer are described in the next sections. I also include cross-references to chapters that give you more detailed information about these features.

Changes and New Features in Designer Release 2.1

One important new feature of Designer is its fully integrated repository. This makes it much easier to integrate all phases of your design as you move from one phase to another. The Design Editor is your window into all areas of your repository. Use it to design business logic, reusable modules, security, and so on. This user interface includes data entry forms, reports, charts, other graphics, and portable program units that work directly with the database or directly with the user interface.

Designer comes with a number of tools. Table 2-1 lists the tools that either replace version 1 tools or are brand new in version 2 of Designer.

TABLE 2-1 NEW AND CHANGED TOOLS IN DESIGNER VERSION 2.1

New Tool Name	Replaced Tool Name
Server Model Diagrams	Data Diagrammer
Module Diagrams	Modules Diagrammer
Logic Editor	Module Logic Navigator
Preference Palette	Preferences Navigator
Design Editor Navigator	N/A
Database Navigator	N/A
Module Network Viewer	N/A
Broadcast Mechanism	N/A
Reusable Component Graphic Editor	N/A
Dependency Analyzer	N/A

Creating database security

Your project probably falls into one of these levels of security:

◆ **No security.** This level generally means that your end users are querying the database but not handling any data changes.

◆ **Database security.** This kind of security enables your users to view and modify database tables based on roles (usually). When a user is assigned to a role, the user inherits the appropriate privileges for a set of tables needed to work in the applications. Generally, this kind of security assumes that your user can perform all functions inside an application (module) so long as they have access to the application.

◆ **Module security.** This level of security further restricts your users' access to the database. This kind of security is often added on top of a database security scheme. Still, this level of security may contain holes because it is not possible to mimic the module security you want in the database security scheme. Therefore, you must determine how to prevent users from accessing your database from outside the applications.

To create database objects in your repository, use the DB Admin tab of the Design Editor Navigator. You can define security for your database objects here.

You can no longer grant access to an object definition (as you could in Designer 1.3.2); now you can grant only to an object implementation.

See Chapter 4 for details on how to set up the various levels of security while minimizing your exposure to unauthorized database access.

Using drag-and-drop features of the Design Editor

Figure 2-1 shows the Design Editor with the module diagram. A new feature of the editor is the capability to open the appropriate diagram editor by simply dragging the module or object icon from the list of objects into the main window of Design Editor. Design Editor knows which editing tool to start for your work.

Using new application generators

Application generation in Designer has gone through a major upgrade. Not only have the generators been upgraded to the latest version of the tools they support, but a much more extensive definition can be made in Designer for generation. You now can set up generation preferences in great detail. You can generate applications for:

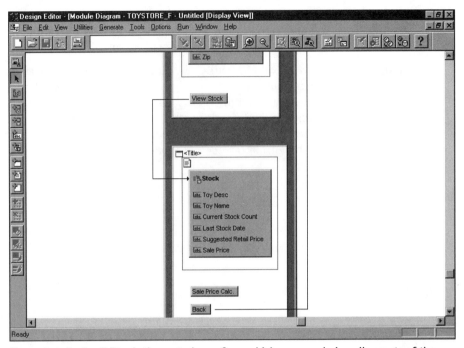

Figure 2-1: Design Editor is the central area from which you can design all aspects of the database system.

◆ Developer Forms

◆ Developer Reports

◆ Visual Basic

◆ Web Server

◆ MS help (within other generated applications)

Four new generators have been added:

◆ **Table API.** You can define specialized interfaces with tables. A new feature is the capability to create interfaces with programs in addition to interfaces with tables. You can also control the logic within a module that uses the Table API by defining what pre- and post-trigger actions occur.

- **Developer Common Libraries.** This generator enables you to create common libraries (PLLs) for your applications.

- **Reusable module components.** In a module definition, you can define a module component, which normally coincides with a base table usage. The reusable component enables you to define a module component once and reuse it in multiple module definitions. This promotes a common look and feel throughout your application. A typical module component contains a base table and all its lookup tables.

- **Report templates.** This new feature enables you to define report templates, which help you accomplish 100 percent generation for reports.

Two generators have also been removed:

- **Oracle SQL*Plus**

- **Oracle Graphics.** Developer has better support for Oracle Graphics, including 50 standard templates that make generating graphics much easier. However, you can no longer generate graphics from Designer.

XREF   Chapter 5 covers application generation. You will see advanced generation examples and some undocumented features that will improve your effectiveness.

Improving database support

The Designer repository requires an Oracle database. However, the database you actually generate need not be an Oracle database. In addition to Oracle 7 and 8, you can generate database definitions for:

- Personal Oracle Lite

- Rdb

- ANSI 92

- DB2/2 and MVS

- Microsoft SQL Server

- Sybase

Not all the features of Designer are available for all databases.

Oracle8 objects and object types can be designed in the new object extension for Designer. This enables you to define:

- **Oracle8 object types.** These define the composition of objects. Object types can include other object types as well as simple datatypes.

- **Oracle8 objects.** Design Oracle8 object tables that are composed of object types and simple datatype attributes.

- **Methods.** Design and write the PL/SQL supporting code for methods you need for your objects.

An interesting feature of the Oracle8 object support in Designer is that you can change the design during the generation to create:

- **An Oracle8 object database,** including objects, object types, and methods.

- **An Oracle8 object view database,** including objects, object types, and methods. In addition, this selection creates object views that enable you to access the objects as if they were relational tables. The required INSTEAD OF triggers are generated for you.

- **A flattened relational database,** which modifies, or "flattens" your objects into relational tables.

Generating Web applications

While the basic structure of Web module design has not changed much since Designer/2000 version 1.3.2, new features are available in version 2.1. These new features make the WebServer Generator a stronger tool. Some of these new features are:

- **Templates.** Now you can add a consistent look and feel to your Web applications with templates.

- **More preferences.** For example, you can define standard captions for buttons used to insert, update, delete, and so on.

- ◆ **HTML style sheet.** Support for the new HTML standard is included in this version of Designer.

- ◆ **User-defined application logic.** WebServer modules can incorporate user-defined application logic (in PL/SQL and JavaScript formats).

 Chapter 6 covers the Designer Web Application Generator.

Summary

This chapter describes new features and tools in Designer version 2.1.

Database security can be created at several different levels within the Designer. Database security and module-level security can be easily documented with Designer.

The Design Editor has been completely reworked so that it has more features and tools. Many of the tools in Designer have also been renamed.

The application generators have been expanded to support more kinds of applications.

Database support for many diverse databases has been expanded to include more databases. Oracle8 support includes creating Oracle8 object types, objects, and methods.

Generating Web applications is easier and more complete now. HTML-style templates are supported, as is JavaScript.

In the next chapter, we look at how to create database designs with Designer tools.

Chapter 3

Rapid Application Design

IN THIS CHAPTER

◆ Using the Design Editor for database tables

◆ Defining reusable modules for forms

◆ Generating forms and reports

◆ Retrofitting existing tables into Designer

◆ Creating Oracle8 object diagrams

DESIGNER CAN be used for many purposes; this application has so many facets that I cannot begin to show you everything you can do. Therefore, I have chosen to illustrate one technique that is frequently used by developers who are working in today's fast-paced marketplace.

 This chapter focuses on the fast way to generate your applications and database schema. Oracle's documentation recommends that you use the Design Editor for Rapid Application Design (RAD), and that is what this chapter covers.

We will build a new database schema and several applications to run with the schema. The schema focuses on a set of requirements to support a clearinghouse for charities and volunteers.

We will also see how to retrofit an existing database schema into the Design Editor. We take an existing database schema and move it into the repository.

The Charity Clearinghouse Example

This chapter uses examples to show you how to create many different objects within Designer. To put all these examples into context, we use an imaginary client (a volunteer organization) whose requirements are:

- ◆ **Gather information from charity and nonprofit groups.** This includes basic details about the organization and a list of projects that the organization needs volunteer help to complete.

- ◆ **Provide this information to volunteers.** Provide a simple query and report system for prospective volunteers.

- ◆ **Enable volunteers to register.** Give volunteers a data entry form to document their skills and their time schedule so that nonprofits can contact them.

- ◆ **Post a weekly pair of cross-reference reports on the Web.** One report lists people and displays charity projects that need their skills. The other report lists charity projects and the people who have matching skills.

When we create this system, we will work exclusively with Designer version 2.1. We will generate all the applications using Designer's generators.

Step-by-Step Rapid Application Design

The steps we will perform to create the database schema and the required forms and reports are:

1. Design modules and module networks that handle the tasks.
2. Design a relational database that stores all the data.
3. Create a reusable module for viewing the organizations table.
4. Connect modules, reusable modules, and database tables.
5. Generate and execute database schema.
6. Generate forms, reports, and WebServer applications.

The following sections go over these steps one at a time.

Step 1: Designing the modules

Modules are simply units of work that can be logically grouped. In the charity clearinghouse sample, the modules can be defined within the framework of the requirements. Figure 3-1 shows the modules that make up the sample system.

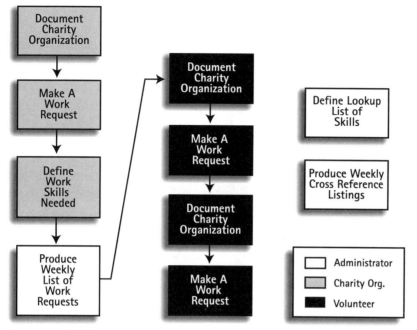

Figure 3-1: Modules arrange work into logical, interconnected components.

As you can see in Figure 3-1, this system has three groups of users:

♦ **Administrator.** This user handles behind-the-scenes maintenance of lookup tables and reports.

♦ **Charity organization.** This user logs data about his or her organization and documents the current requests for volunteer work that is needed.

♦ **Volunteer.** This user is a volunteer or potential volunteer who wants to make his or her skills available to the charities. This person documents his or her own work skills and (optionally) lists the dates he or she is available to work.

 The three divisions of users become three roles defined in the Database Administration section of the Design Editor.

When creating modules, work in the Design Editor. Click the Modules tab to display the Navigator objects for modules. For the sample application, begin in the Design Editor's Navigator, and create a new module for each box shown in Figure 3-1. Figure 3-2 shows the Create Module window that is invoked when you select the Module folder icon (found in the Design Editor Navigator) and then click the Create button (green plus sign).

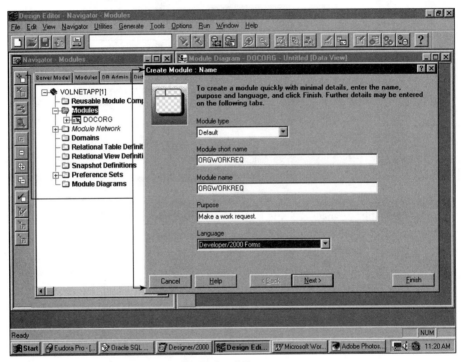

Figure 3-2: Create a new module in the Design Editor.

For the sample system, I have created a variety of module types:

◆ **Menu Forms module.** This is where the user can select which module to run. This is a Developer Forms application. Choose a module type of Menu and module language of Developer Forms.

◆ **Default Forms module.** This uses the module type of Default and the module language type of Developer Forms. The top module in the organization module network, which has several of these default Forms modules, is VIEWORG.

◆ **Default Reports module.** Two reports in the sample system are of this type. When creating modules that will result in reports, use the module type of Default and the module language of Developer Reports.

◆ **Web application module.** The Web modules result in Web pages that run in Oracle WebServer. Then create this kind of module, select the module type of Default and the module language of Oracle WebServer.

Each type of module has different parameters or properties that are set when you create the module. You can also edit the properties by double-clicking on the module's icon in the Navigator to open the module's property palette. Figure 3-3 shows the property palette of a Developer Reports module.

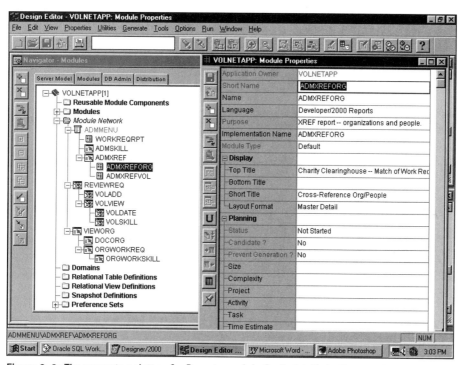

Figure 3-3: The property palette of a Reports module feeds details to the report generator.

CONNECT MODULES

After designing the basic modules, we must connect the modules as shown in Figure 3-1. The steps to connect modules are quite easy:

1. **Open the parent module's property sheet.** Do this by double-clicking the module's icon in the Navigator.

2. **Click the Module Network tab to select children.** This opens the window where you define which modules should be called from the parent module, as shown in Figure 3-4.

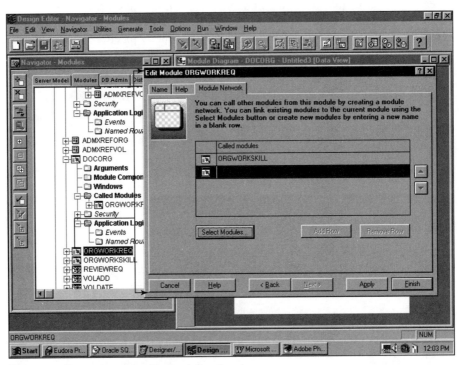

Figure 3-4: Connect modules in a module network.

CREATE MODULE DIAGRAMS

Include all the modules into a module diagram. If you have not already created the module diagram, simply double-click the Module Diagram folder icon in the Design Editor Navigator. Next, choose the top node in one of the module networks as the module for diagramming.

Figure 3-5 shows two module diagrams along with the Module Navigator window in the Design Editor.

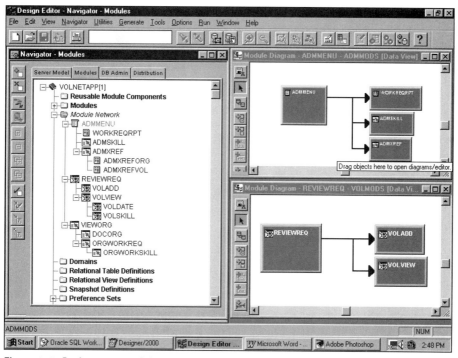

Figure 3-5: Review your module connections in the Module Diagram and the Navigator.

Step 2: Designing the database

You have many choices when it comes to designing the database in Designer:

◆ **Develop Entity Relationship Diagrams (ERD).** These are in turn converted into table structures. Figure 3-6 shows an Entity Relationship Diagram. To reach the ERD tool, click the Entity Relationship icon in the main startup window of Designer.

◆ **Use the Database Capture tool.** This tool (found in the Design Editor) creates database definitions in Designer. Figure 3-7 shows the selection window where you define the objects to capture. To run the Database Capture tool, select Generate from the menu at the top of the Design Editor's main window, and then choose Capture Design of→ Server Model from Database.

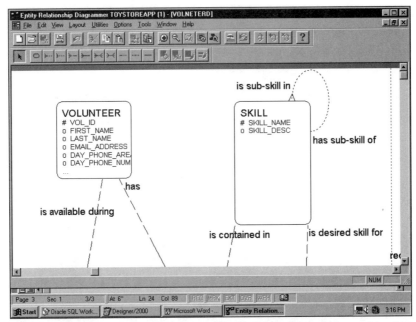

Figure 3-6: An entity relationship diagram shows relationships, entities, and attributes.

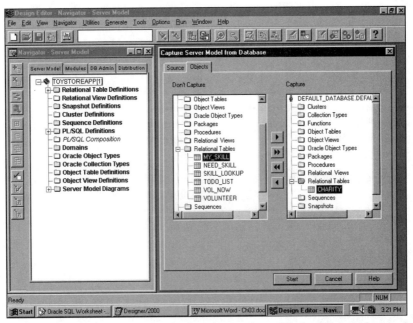

Figure 3-7: Capture your real live database in one piece with the Database Capture tool.

♦ **Design the database in Design Editor.** The Server Model tab of the Design Editor enables you to create tables, relationships, Oracle8 objects, and other structures you need for your database. Figure 3-8 shows the Design Editor with the Server Model Diagram open.

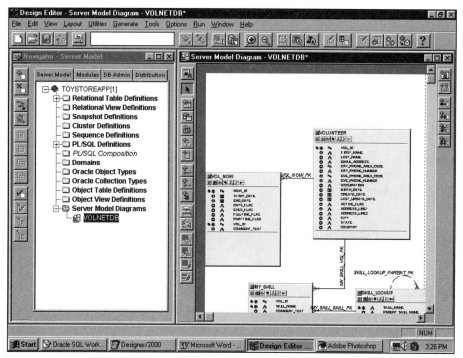

Figure 3-8: The Design Editor can view and create a database.

We will complete the sample system for a charity clearinghouse using the Design Editor to draw tables, columns, and relationships.

To create new objects, start in the Server Model tab of the Design Editor. Then create a new diagram, and save it to the repository. Add tables, columns, primary keys, foreign keys, validation constraints, triggers, and so on in the diagram. Figure 3-9 shows the Server Model Diagram in the Design Editor with some of the object types labeled.

Don't forget to save your diagram! The repository does not automatically save the diagram the way it saves the Navigator tree objects. So remember to click the Save icon inside the Server Model Diagram window.

You can use the Design Editor Navigator to create tables and all the same objects that you can create with the diagram. Simply click the Plus icon after selecting the type of object you wish to create in the Navigator tree.

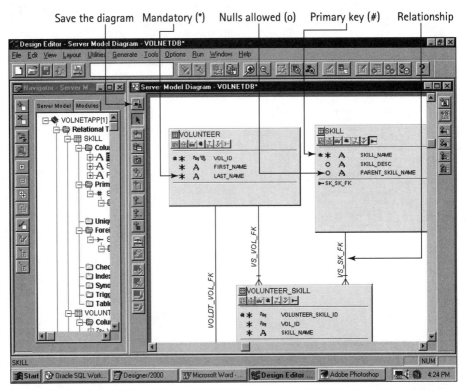

Figure 3-9: The Design Editor's Server Model Diagram can create tables and other objects.

 To make the best of the autolayout feature of the Diagrammer, separate your database into functional area diagrams. This reduces the number of tables displayed (and rearranged) in each diagram. Drag and drop the tables from the Navigator into each diagram. You can have a table on more than one diagram. I have found that if I select the Layout → Autolayout menu selection several times in a row, the Diagrammer revises its layout. By repeating this a few times, I found an autolayout that I liked, and I saved that one.

When creating your objects, the Diagrammer likes to arrange things so the objects never overlap and so that there are more straight lines than angles. Do not be surprised if your diagram morphs before your eyes.

After creating your database structure, it is time to create some reusable data modules.

Step 3: Creating reusable module components

The purpose of creating *reusable module components* is to standardize your use of validation, display, and lookup tables within all your modules. Once created, you can drag and drop the component's icon to attach it to your modules.

For the example system of the charity clearinghouse, we will create a reusable module for viewing a list of charity organizations in a form. To create a reusable module component, follow these steps:

1. **Open the Diagram Editor with the Module tab opened.** This gives you a view of the modules in the Navigator.

2. **Create a new object and save it.** Select the Reusable Module Component folder icon, and then click the plus icon to open the Module Component Properties window. At a minimum, you must name the module component. For the example, I have named the object ORGLIST. If the component is to be used in a form, as in our example, then select Developer Common Library or Developer Forms as the language property. Figure 3-10 shows the Module Component Properties window for the sample object. After you have defined the properties, click the Save icon in the properties window to save the component to the repository. It will automatically be displayed in the Navigator.

3. **Attach a table to the module component.** Do this by clicking on the table in the Navigator and dragging it up to the Table Usages folder under your component.

Step 4: Connecting design objects

Here is where the drag-and-drop capabilities of the Navigator work wonders. You will easily add data tables to modules and module components to modules.

For example, we created a shell of the Work Request Report by defining a module as a default module type with a language of Developer Reports.

To create data on the report, simply click and drag the tables into the report. When you click and drag the table, you are automatically prompted to choose which items in the table you want to display and in what order.

For the sample report, I have dragged the CHARITY and the TODO_LIST tables into the Reports module. In addition, I want to use the foreign key relationship between the two tables to arrange the rows in the report as a master detail layout. To accomplish this, follow these steps:

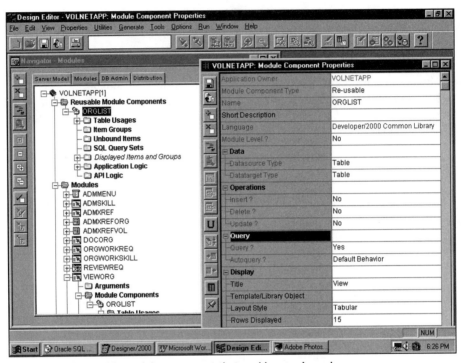

Figure 3-10: A reusable module component that enables queries only.

1. **Click and drag the related tables into the module.**

2. **Display the Module Diagrammer, and create a diagram for this module.** Click the Module Diagrams folder in the Design Editor, and click the plus icon to create a new diagram. Then select the appropriate module to include in the diagram.

3. **Switch to Data View.** Select View → Data View from the top menu of the Design Editor while the Module Diagram window is current. Figure 3-11 shows the module diagram of the report.

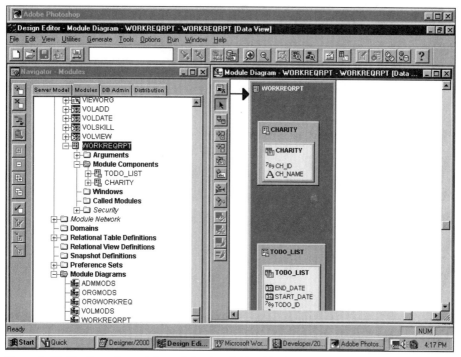

Figure 3-11: The Reports module contains two table objects.

4. **Connect the two tables with a key-based link.** Click the Key Based Link button on the right edge of the Module Diagram window. Then click the Master table (CHARITY), and drag the line to the Detail table (TODO_LIST). Designer knows about the foreign key that connects the two tables and automatically uses it for the link. Figure 3-12 shows the resulting change in the diagram.

Step 5: Creating the database schema

In order to create the schema for your application, you must answer a few questions:

1. Will the schema reside on an already existing database? If so, you do not need to generate the CREATE DATBASE statements. If not, then you will generate an entire database when it is time to write the Data Definition Language (DDL).

2. Do any administration objects, such as roles, tablespaces, users, and rollback segments need to be created? If so, define them in the Database Administration tab of the Design Editor, and then create the DDL and execute it.

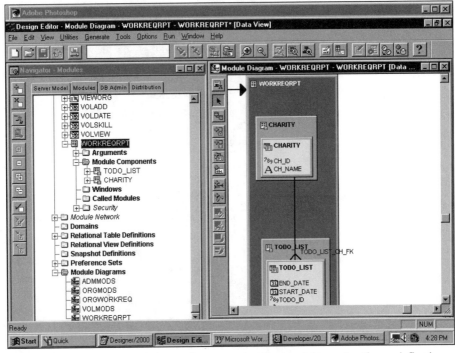

Figure 3-12: The Reports module now has connected the two tables using the predefined foreign key.

In our example, we will use an existing database, and we will generate DDL statements for:

1. New roles for the database.

2. New tables and sequences for the schema.

Follow along in the next sections.

GENERATE AND EXECUTE DDLS FOR NEW DATABASE ROLES

Database roles are used for setting up security. You can define roles in the Database Administration tab of the Design Editor. Figure 3-13 shows the new roles that we define for the sample application system.

To create the DDL script for these new roles, use your mouse to select all the roles. Then click Generate→Generate Database Administration Objects from the menu in Design Editor. You will see a window where you can select various options and objects to generate. Fill in the required fields, click the Objects tab, and verify that the role names that you need to generate are displayed on the right side (labeled "Generate"). Figure 3-14 shows the Objects window after the three roles have been selected.

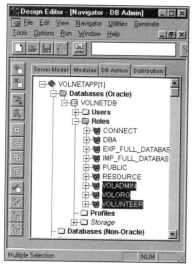

Figure 3-13: Three roles are defined in
the charity clearinghouse example.

A file is created in the directory of your choice that contains the CREATE ROLE commands. Execute the file in the SQL execution stage you like, such as SQL*Plus.

GENERATE AND EXECUTE DDLS FOR NEW DATABASE OBJECTS

This process works for all the database server objects you have defined in the Server Model portion of the Design Editor. Your goal is to generate a file with the DDL commands for all the tables, foreign keys, sequences, indexes, and so on, that you defined. To do this:

1. Click the Server Model tab in the Design Editor.

2. Select Generate → Generate Database from Server Model.

3. Select the DDL Only button, and fill in other details on the main window.

4. Click the Objects tab, and move all the objects that need to be generated into the Generate box on the right.

Figure 3-15 shows the window after you have selected all the tables and sequences defined in the Server Model as objects to generate.

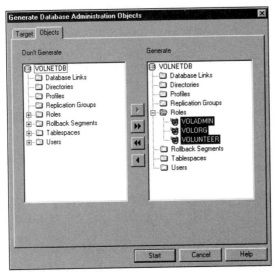

Figure 3-14: DDL commands to create three roles will be generated.

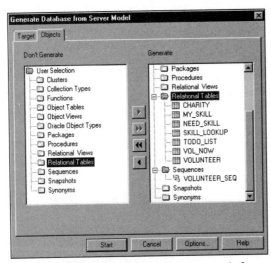

Figure 3-15: Select to generate DDL commands for creating tables and sequences.

Once again, you can use this script to execute the DDL in the database of your choice.

Step 6: Generating the applications

Now that the schema is in place, you can proceed to generate the modules that use this schema.

For our sample application system, there are many modules of different types. We will begin with the Form modules.

GENERATING FORM MODULES

Find the module you wish to generate. Choose Generate → Generate Module from the Design Editor menu. This brings up a window where you place options. Figure 3-16 shows the options in the Generate Form window. I have selected the Include Module Network checkbox.

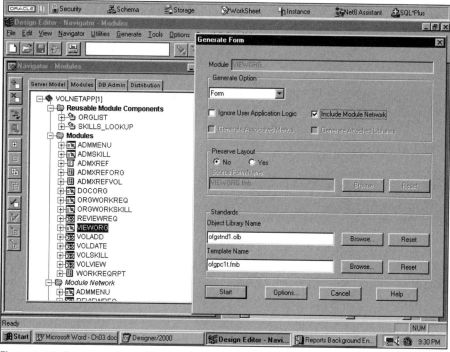

Figure 3-16: Set generator preferences here.

You set more of the detailed generator preferences in another window. To find it, select the module or object that you wish to set preferences for. If you want to set preferences for the entire application, select the top node in the Design Editor. Right-click the object, and then select Generator Preferences from the pop-up menu. This opens the Generator Preference window, as shown in Figure 3-17.

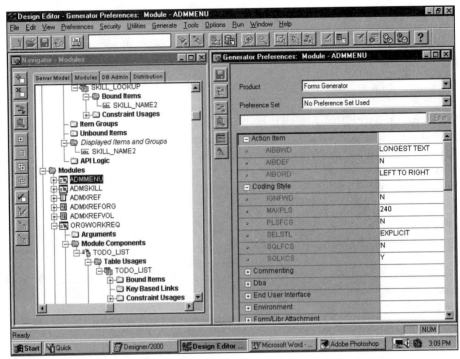

Figure 3-17: Set many generator preferences here.

Once this window is displayed, you can expand or contract the items to see the preference names. You can also toggle between the name and the description of the preference using the toggle button on the right edge of the window.

 The generator preference names are listed in the online help, so it is often easier to find the preference you wish to set by toggling to display the preference name. The default setting displays the preference description.

 When you select the top module of a module network to generate and select the Include Module Network checkbox in the Generate Form window, all the called modules are automatically generated.

Click the Options button to specify the connect string that will generate and (optionally) run the application. Figure 3-18 shows the finished VIEWORG application window. This is generated with minimal modifications to show what you get with Designer's defaults. Of course, you can modify the forms template that you will use to generate your forms to make the application look very different.

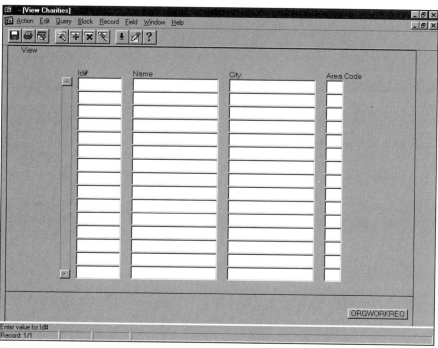

Figure 3-18: The VIEWORG application uses Designer's default template.

After generating the forms, you can run them immediately or later. Next, we look at generating Reports modules.

GENERATING REPORTS MODULES

The generating of Reports modules is simply a matter of clicking a button on the menu, just like generating a form. Select the module you wish to generate, and then choose Generate → Generate Module.

Figure 3-19 shows a generated report that uses the default settings for the template.

GENERATING WEBSERVER MODULES

The generating of WebServer modules is just like generating the other modules: a matter of clicking a button on the menu, selecting the module you wish to generate, and then choosing Generate → Generate Module.

TIP Be sure you have Web Application Server installed and configured correctly.

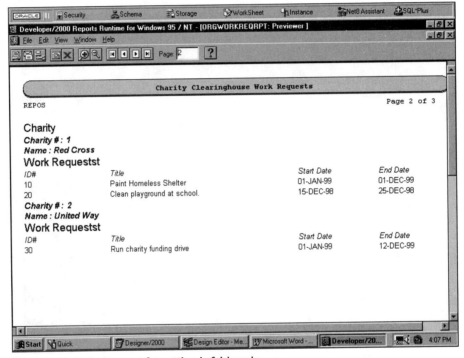

Figure 3-19: Default report formatting is fairly ugly.

NOTE You need to decide what user will hold the WebServer applications after they become database packages. This user must run several utility packages to be compatible with both the Web Application Server and the WebServer Generator of Designer.

XREF For a complete description of setting up your Designer environment to generate and run WebServer applications, see Chapter 6.

Summary

This chapter covers the tools in Designer that enable you to quickly generate your database and application design. These tools promote using Designer as a Rapid Application Development (RAD) tool.

The chapter goes through the steps to create a sample application system for a charity clearinghouse. The design requires the generation of a set of relational tables and a series of several Developer forms, Developer reports, and WebServer applications. All the modules are generated using as many default settings as possible to demonstrate that the tool can be used quickly to create complete applications. (The default formats are somewhat unattractive.)

The first step in our sample design project involves using the Design Editor to create a set of modules and connecting the modules on the Module Diagrammer.

The next step generates the DDL statements needed to create the database tables, primary and foreign keys, and sequences.

The third step shows how to generate reusable modules based on a table. A reusable module helps keep your application design consistent.

The fourth step connects the module shells with the tables and the reusable modules to create complete applications.

The fifth step generates the actual database tables for the system.

The sixth step generates all the applications so they can be run.

Chapter 4

Security

IN THIS CHAPTER

- ◆ Reviewing database roles
- ◆ Deciding what level of security you need
- ◆ Setting security levels in forms, reports, and Web applications
- ◆ Implementing external user validation (ops$ users)

MOST APPLICATIONS REQUIRE SECURITY. Many levels of security exist – for example, module level, table level, row level, field level – and each requires its own method of implementation. No one level of security is appropriate for all your applications. Each application may require a different level of security – sometimes none at all – and often these diverse needs are not a problem.

Note that these levels must be decided and implemented for each of the access types: create, read, update, and delete.

This section will not go into details about all the security issues and different implementation methods in general but it will give some specific hints about methods to implement different security levels when using Designer to generate applications. **The methods discussed here will not require any postgeneration changes.**

Database Roles

A *database role* is a set of privileges on database objects assigned a name (role name). You can assign one user to one or more database roles. The user inherits the privileges of all roles he or she is assigned (granted). Standard database roles provide consistent ways to perform a variety of tasks; for example, the CONNECT role enables the user to log in to the database.

TIP Database roles are important to simplify your security model (although you can claim that they actually add one layer of complexity to your security implementation). Designers can create their own roles and assign privileges to them to enforce security rules for access to tables, views, and other objects in the schema. For example, the VISITORMGR role might enable a user to see and modify (SELECT, INSERT, UPDATE, and DELETE) rows in the VISITOR_LOG table.

Database role strategies

You have to choose between the following two strategies when implementing roles:

◆ **User group roles.** Each user group role is granted all the rights needed for a specific type of user. Typical names for user group roles include MANAGER_ROLE, CLERK_ROLE, SECRETARY_ROLE, ARCHITECT_ROLE etc.

When you use this strategy, grant each person only a single role (maybe two or three roles in some cases).

◆ **Process roles.** Each process role is granted the rights needed to perform a specific process. I use the term *process* instead of *application* because different process roles can invoke the same application with different access levels. Process roles would typically be called MAINTAIN_EMPLOYEES_ROLE, ACCOUNT_MANAGEMENT_ROLE, MAINTAIN_PAYMENTS_ROLE, and so on.

When you use this strategy, grant each person one process role for each process the person is allowed to perform.

Choosing a strategy

Which strategy should one use? It seems that Oracle intended us to use user group roles. On the other hand, here are two good arguments to use the process roles:

1. You'll need the flexibility of process roles if people seldom conform to a single user group, or to only a few. Making a user group role for each user makes roles pointless.

2. Names of process group roles reveal far more information about the grants you've actually given your users than do user group roles.

My experience is that even when using process roles you hardly grant more than 48 roles to any single user. Even so, keep it in mind when you make your decision on role strategy.

The following sections will describe how to implement security on these different levels:

♦ No security

♦ Database security

♦ Module-level security

TIP — You can apply the content of these sections to your environment regardless of the particular role strategy you have chosen.

No Security

Sometimes you will not want any security at all for a certain application. Usually this situation only applies to read-access-only applications; even users with no account should be able to access the application.

Client/server

For client/server applications you would implement this by including a user name, password, and connect string in the command line when calling the application. As this user ID will be readable to everyone, it should be highly restricted; grant it only the minimum necessary access rights it needs to perform the application in question.

Web modules

Web modules offer a better way to handle such "No Security" access to modules. In fact, "No Security" is the default security level for Web modules.

XREF — Chapter 6 explains the Web-related terms used in this section.

By default, each DAD is set up on the Web server with an Oracle account that must be used when connecting to the database.; users are not prompted for username and password.

Again, when you use an Oracle account for the Database Access Descriptors (DADs), be sure to grant only the necessary access rights. Although users cannot see the actual username and password, they can use that DAD to run any other application.

 You can use the Listener process to prevent the use of DADs to run applications — a topic I recommend for further study.

Web Forms

You can handle security on Web Forms as you would for client/server forms. Specify a highly restricted username and password.

 You cannot access the DAD from Web Forms.

Database-Level Security

Although database-level security should be least visible to your users, it is far more important than module-level security — largely because it is the best way to ensure and document consistent security throughout your environment.

On the other hand, database-level security is hardest to control. Many fine-grain security features that are easy to control on the client are hard to control on the server. The usual solution to this problem is to combine the two security levels.

Implementing security on the server is can guarantee that no matter how a user accesses the database, he/she gets the same access rights to the data. What good is a secure form if users can access the database with SQL and get full access to all tables?

The next section proposes a solution that integrates database-level security with your module-level security design.

Creating one role for all database access

To avoid the problems with handling fine grain security on the server, I recommend a simple security model that gives all access to database elements to a single role (the role could be called GLOBAL_ACCESS_ROLE). You can grant this role to all users, but add a password and set DEFAULT to NO. By doing this everybody can access the database if they can provide the password of GLOBAL_ACCESS_ROLE. This role then serves as a handle by all client modules to access the database objects (the next section explains this function in detail.)

The principle is to allow users access to the database only through the client application. Users who enter the database through SQL *will not have access to any database object.*

> **TIP** If you are working in an environment that needs database access through SQL or ODBC, you must define special process roles (or user group roles) that provide access to the necessary database objects. The bottom line is to keep the server side as restricted as possible.

Granting privileges to GLOBAL_ACCESS_ROLE

The following Designer API script grants access to all database objects to the role GLOBAL_ACCESS_ROLE (make sure that the role does exist). It is beyond the scope of this book to explain how to make programs that use the Designer repository API but the following code is pretty easy to follow even without experience in Designer repository API programming.

The code creates a procedure named GRANT_TO_GLOBAL_ACCESS_ROLE. The procedure requires one variable: the application name. The procedure reads in all the objects used by the application – tables, views, and sequences – and then loops through them all. As it does so, the procedure generates a GRANT record for each object – loading the variable, V_ACCESS, along with the table name and TRUE (or 'Y') values. These values correspond to capabilities granted the user to INSERT, UPDATE, DELETE, and SELECT from the table. The command that generates these grants is as follows:

```
ciodatabase_object_grant.ins(NULL, v_access);
```

Listing 4-1: Procedures to grant privileges to GLOBAL_ACCESS_ROLE

```
/* ——- code4-1.sql ————— */
PROCEDURE GRANT_TO_GLOBAL_ACCESS_ROLE
 (P_APPLICATION VARCHAR2
 )
```

```
  IS
  — Program Data
  /* ID of application to update */
  V_APPLICATION NUMBER;
  /* Property list for Module access */
  V_ACCESS CIODATABASE_OBJECT_GRANT.DATA;
  /* Activity status */
  V_ACT_STATUS VARCHAR2(1);
  /* Activity warning flag */
  V_ACT_WARNINGS VARCHAR2(1);
  /* ID of the role GLOBAL_ACCESS_ROLE */
  V_GLOBAL_ACCESS_ROLE NUMBER;

  — PL/SQL Block
  /* Initiate API and get ID of application and GLOBAL_ACCESS_ROLE */
  BEGIN
    BEGIN
    —
    — Fetch application ID
      SELECT id
      INTO v_application
      FROM ci_application_systems
      WHERE
        name =p_application AND
        latest_version_flag='Y';
    EXCEPTION
      WHEN NO_DATA_FOUND THEN
        raise_application_error
        (-20000,'Unable to find application:' ||p_application);
    END;
    —
    — Get ID for GLOBAL_ACCESS_ROLE
    BEGIN
      SELECT id
      INTO v_GLOBAL_ACCESS_ROLE
      FROM ci_roles
      WHERE
        NAME = 'GLOBAL_ACCESS_ROLE';
    EXCEPTION
      WHEN NO_DATA_FOUND THEN
        raise_application_error
          (-20000,'Unable to find GLOBAL_ACCESS_ROLE');
    END;
    —
```

```
— Initialize API activity
BEGIN
  IF cdapi.initialized = FALSE THEN
  — Initialize the API globals
  cdapi.initialize(p_application);
  END IF;
  — Open API-activity
  cdapi.open_activity;
EXCEPTION WHEN OTHERS THEN
  raise_application_error
    (-20000,'Unable to initialize activity');
END;
  —

— Create access for tables ***********************
BEGIN
  FOR tab IN (
    SELECT id, 'T'typ
    FROM ci_table_implementations t
    WHERE
      t.application_system_owned_by = v_application AND
      NOT EXISTS
        (SELECT id FROM ci_database_object_grants g
          WHERE g.ROLE_reference = v_GLOBAL_ACCESS_ROLE
          AND g.table_reference = t.id)
    UNION SELECT id, 'V'
    FROM ci_view_implementations v
    WHERE
      v.application_system_owned_by = v_application AND
      NOT EXISTS
        (SELECT id FROM ci_database_object_grants g
          WHERE g.ROLE_reference = v_GLOBAL_ACCESS_ROLE
          AND g.table_reference = v.id)
    UNION SELECT id, 'S'
    FROM ci_sequence_implementations s
    WHERE
      s.application_system_owned_by = v_application AND
      NOT EXISTS
        (SELECT id FROM ci_database_object_grants g
          WHERE g.ROLE_reference = v_GLOBAL_ACCESS_ROLE
          AND g.table_reference = s.id)
  )
  LOOP
    v_access.v.role_REFERENCE:= v_GLOBAL_ACCESS_ROLE;
    v_access.v.REMARK:=
```

```
      'Created by API-module ACCESS_TO_GLOBAL_ACCESS_ROLE';
    v_access.v.SELECT_FLAG:= 'Y';
    v_access.v.TABLE_REFERENCE:= tab.id;
    v_access.i.role_REFERENCE:= TRUE;
    v_access.i.REMARK:= TRUE;
    v_access.i.SELECT_FLAG:= TRUE;
    v_access.i.TABLE_REFERENCE:= TRUE;
    IF tab.typ IN('T', 'V') THEN
      v_access.v.DELETE_FLAG:= 'Y';
      v_access.v.INSERT_FLAG:= 'Y';
      v_access.v.UPDATE_FLAG:= 'Y';
      v_access.i.DELETE_FLAG:= TRUE;
      v_access.i.INSERT_FLAG:= TRUE;
      v_access.i.UPDATE_FLAG:= TRUE;
    END IF;
    — do the grant *****************************************
    ciodatabase_object_grant.ins(NULL, v_access);
  END LOOP;
EXCEPTION
  WHEN OTHERS THEN
    raise_application_error
    (-20000,'Unable to insert grant');
END;
— **************************************************
—        End API activity
BEGIN
  cdapi.validate_activity(v_act_status, v_act_warnings);
  —
  —        Display all violations and other messages
  —        regardless of the activity warnings flag
  REPORT_VIOLATIONS;
  — Attempt TO CLOSE the activity
  cdapi.close_activity(v_act_status);
  —
  — If the activity did not close successfully,
  — roll back all changes made
  — during the activity*/
  IF v_act_status != 'Y' THEN
    — Could not close the activity
    cdapi.abort_activity;
    dbms_output.put_line
      ('Activity interupted by "constraint validations"');
    — Otherwise, we're done
  ELSE
```

```
                    — Ok
                  dbms_output.put_line
                    ('Activity closed without errors');
               END IF;
           EXCEPTION WHEN OTHERS THEN
             raise_application_error(-20000,'Unable CLOSE activity');
           END;
             —
       EXCEPTION WHEN OTHERS THEN
         raise_application_error
           (-20000,'Unable CREATE grants FOR GLOBAL_ACCESS_ROLE');
       END GRANT_TO_GLOBAL_ACCESS_ROLE;
```

The Listing 4-1 example makes an external call to the REPORT_VIOLATIONS procedure that reads all violations in the CI_VIOLATIONS table and then displays them on standard output. The REPORT_VIOLATIONS procedure looks like this:

```
/* ——- Plsql/Reportviolations.sql —— */
PROCEDURE REPORT_VIOLATIONS
 IS
— Program Data
ARG3 VARCHAR2(64);
M_FACILITY VARCHAR2(3);
ARG4 VARCHAR2(64);
ARG5 VARCHAR2(20);
M_CODE NUMBER(38, 0);
ARG6 VARCHAR2(20);
ARG1 VARCHAR2(240);
ARG7 VARCHAR2(20);
ARG2 VARCHAR2(64);
ARG8 VARCHAR2(20);

— PL/SQL Block
BEGIN
— Report all violations regardless of the activity status
FOR viol IN (SELECT * FROM ci_violations) LOOP
  dbms_output.put_line(cdapi.instantiate_message(
      viol.facility, viol.code,
      viol.p0, viol.p1, viol.p2, viol.p3,
      viol.p4, viol.p5, viol.p6,viol.p7));
END LOOP;
—

— Pop messages off the stack and format them
— into a single text string
```

If You Grant Access Privileges to GLOBAL_ACCESS_ROLE

A user who uses the two procedures shown here to grant access privileges to GLOBAL_ACCESS_ROLE must first have access to the Designer repository views (for example, the Designer repository owner). After the installation is complete, you grant access to all tables, views, and sequences in the TOYSTORE application to the role named GLOBAL_ACCESS_ROLE by issuing the following command:

```
begin
  GRANT_TO_GLOBAL_ACCESS_ROLE('TOYSTORE');
end;
```

```
WHILE cdapi.stacksize > 0 LOOP
  rmmes.pop(m_facility, m_code, arg1, arg2, arg3,
          arg4, arg5, arg6, arg7, arg8);
  dbms_output.put_line
    (cdapi.instantiate_message(m_facility, m_code,
     arg1, arg2, arg3, arg4, arg5, arg6, arg7, arg8));
END LOOP;
END REPORT_VIOLATIONS;
```

 You can only grant this access if you have already defined and implemented the database objects in the repository. In this version of Designer (release 2), you can grant only to an object implementation — not to an object definition (as you could in Designer 1.3.2). You can implement your database objects from the DB Admin tab of the Design Editor Navigator.

Module-Level Security

In the previous section, I argued for making the server as restricted as possible. I even demonstrated how to implement an environment (through Designer) where virtually no one had any access rights. To continue this strategy, this section illustrates how to implement the GLOBAL_ACCESS_ROLE in your modules.

To make this setup work, we need some code that enables a module to perform two tasks:

♦ Decide whether a user should be allowed access to the module.

♦ If access is appropriate, activate the GLOBAL_ACCESS_ROLE for that user.

The following sections demonstrate how to implement such activation of GLOBAL_ACCESS_ROLE on the different client application types.

Deciding whether a user has access to a module

First, you have to decide which process roles (or user-group roles) should give access to which modules. To do so, use the Repository Object Navigator (RON) and follow these steps:

1. Create the necessary roles.

2. Grant the roles to the appropriate modules.

You can create the roles in the DB Admin tab of the Design Editor Navigator under the appropriate Oracle database.

In early versions of Designer 2.1, you may encounter problems if you use the Design Editor to define certain grants (especially if you're granting roles to Web modules). Even so, I have found it easier to use the RON (Repository Object Navigator). Here you can create grants by highlighting Module Design→Modules→ *(selected module)*→ Security→Role Access and clicking the Create Association button on the toolbar.

This information must be accessible at runtime; therefore we need to extract it into a reference table. We could call the table MODULE_ROLES and define it like this:

```
create table MODULE_ROLES (
  MODULE_NAME varchar2(30),
  ROLE_NAME varchar2(30));
grant select on MODULE_ROLES to public;
```

The PL/SQL code in the Listing 4-2 example extracts the module-access information from Designer and inserts it into the MODULE_ROLES table:

Listing 4-2: Building the MODULE_ROLES table

```
/* --------- Plsql/Extract_access.sql ------ */
CREATE OR REPLACE PROCEDURE EXTRACT_ACCESS
 (P_MODULE_SHORT_NAME IN MODULE_ROLES.MODULE_NAME%TYPE
 )
 IS
- PL/SQL Block
-  Delete all access rights to modules being updated.
BEGIN

DELETE module_roles
WHERE
  module_name LIKE p_module_short_name;

IF (SQL%notfound) THEN
```

```
    NULL;
END IF;

- Loop through all modules to be updated.
FOR r_modules IN
 (SELECT id , name, short_name
  FROM ci_modules
  WHERE short_name LIKE p_module_short_name)

LOOP
    - Loop through all roles granted to each module.
    FOR r_role_access IN
    (SELECT cg.name, cm.short_name
     FROM ci_role_module_accesses cma,
          ci_roles cg, ci_modules cm
     WHERE cma.general_module_reference=cm.id
     AND cm.id = r_modules.id
     AND role_reference = cg.id)

    LOOP
       BEGIN
          - insert access row in MODULE_ROLES table.
          INSERT INTO module_roles(MODULE_NAME, ROLE_NAME)
          VALUES
             (r_role_access.short_name, r_role_access.name);
       EXCEPTION
          WHEN DUP_VAL_ON_INDEX
          THEN
          NULL;
       END;
    END LOOP;
END LOOP;
END EXTRACT_ACCESS;
/
```

This procedure works only on a Designer 2.1 repository because some repository views and columns have been renamed (mainly the term GROUP has been changed to ROLE).

As a rule, you won't place your Designer repository in your production database. Therefore you need to distribute the contents of the MODULE_ROLES table to both your test and production database(s). The following SQL code creates a link between two databases and copies the contents of MODULE_ROLES from one database to the other:

```
/* ———- Plsql/Copymod.sql ————- */
accept table_owner    char prompt -
    "Enter username of the table owner: "
accept from_db        char prompt -
    "Enter database connect string to copy from: "
accept pw_from char prompt -
    "Enter password of repository_owner on from database
(&&from_db): "
accept to_db          char prompt -
    "Enter database connect string to copy to: "
accept pw_to   char prompt -
    "Enter password of table_owner on to database (&&to_db): "
connect &&table_owner/&&pw_to@&&to_db
drop database link moduleroles;
create database link moduleroles
  connect to &&table_owner identified by &&pw_from
  using '&&from_db';
prompt deleting old rows in module_roles
delete from &&table_owner.module_roles;
prompt Inserting new rows.
insert into &&table_owner.module_roles
select * from &&table_owner.module_roles@moduleroles;
drop database link moduleroles;
```

Of course, you must secure the MODULE_ROLES table so users cannot edit its contents. On the other hand, all users must have access to look up their module-level privileges. To provide such access, I suggest using a PL/SQL function to return a value that specifies whether the current user has access to a given module. Such a function could look like this:

```
/* ———- Plsql/Modaccess.sql ——— */
  FUNCTION MODULE_ACCESS(
  p_module_name IN varchar2 DEFAULT NULL)
  RETURN VARCHAR2 IS
    —
    — Dummy for selecting from module_roles
    v_dummy VARCHAR2(1);
  BEGIN
    SELECT 'x'
    INTO
      v_dummy
    FROM
      module_roles m, sys.dba_role_privs b
    WHERE
      m.module_name = p_module_name
```

```
      AND m.role_name = b.granted_role
      AND b.grantee = USER
      AND rownum = 1;
   RETURN('Y');
   EXCEPTION WHEN NO_DATA_FOUND THEN
   RETURN('N');
END;
```

The function returns 'Y' if the current user has access to the specified module and 'N' otherwise. In fact, you can grant this function to the public without threatening the security of your database and applications.

 TIP It would be simple to expand this code to handle different types of access like Update, Query, None, and so on.

The method and code described in this section is completely generic; the following sections base their handling of security for forms, reports, Web modules, and packages entirely on the contents of the MODULE_ROLES table.

Activating access on the client

As specified previously, Oracle users should have no (or minimal) access rights on database objects when they first log in. Every module should then meet the following two requirements at startup:

◆ **It must specify whether the current user is granted access to the module.** You can make it do so by looking up the current user's roles in the MODULE_ROLES table. If access is not granted, the module must terminate right away.

◆ **If the current user is granted access to the module, then the module must grant database access.** That means you must allow the user to perform inserts, queries, updates, and deletions after the module has started. The database object grants can be made through the GLOBAL_ACCESS_ROLE role described in the previous section about database-level security.

Access is given by module through Designer and stored in the MODULE_ROLES table in the following way: Each row in MODULE_ROLES specifies that role ROLE_NAME gives access to module MODULE_NAME.

The module should activate access rights to database objects only if the user who is starting up the module already has a process role (or user group role) that gives access to that module.

As the module ends, it should revoke all database-object grants given to the user when it started up.

Maintaining access to forms modules

You can implement module-level security in forms by using a generic (CHECK_FORMS_ACCESS) procedure called by the WHEN-NEW-FORM-INSTANCE trigger of all forms. Figure 4-1 shows a process flow diagram of how database-level security and module-level security interact.

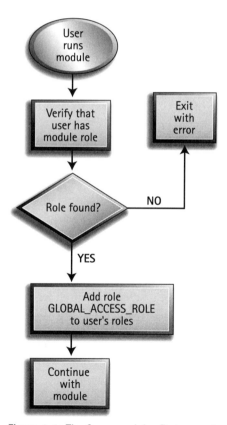

Figure 4-1: The forms modules first request validation and then initiate the user's privileges.

The procedure begins by looking up the current user's roles in the MODULE_ROLES table to see whether the user should be allowed to run the current form:

```
/* —— Plsql/Chkform.sql —— */
Procedure CHECK_FORMS_ACCESS IS
l_module_access vachar2(1);
l_dummy varchar2(1);
begin
  — Find out if the current user is granted a role that
  — gives access to the current form.
  begin
    select 'Y'
    into l_module_access
    from module_roles m, dba_role_privs r
    where
      m.module_name =
      get_application_property(current_form_name) and
      m.role_name = r.granted_role and
      r.grantee = USER and
      rownum = 1;
  exception when no_data_found then
    l_module_access:= 'N';
  end;
```

If the user does not have a role that gives access to the current form the form is terminated:

```
if l_module_access = 'N' then
  message('You do not have access to this screen');
  synchronize;
  exit_form;
end if;
```

At this point, the user is already accepted — but we still need to activate the GLOBAL_ACCESS_ROLE. If the current form has been called from another form, then that previous form has probably activated the GLOBAL_ACCESS_ROLE. To save time, activate the role only if it is not already active. To activate the GLOBAL_ACCESS_ROLE, use the dbms_session package in the following manner:

```
  — activate the GLOBAL_ACCESS_ROLE (if it isn't already)
  begin
    select 'x' into l_dummy
    from session_roles
```

```
    where role = 'GLOBAL_ACCESS_ROLE';
  exception
    when no_data_found then
      dbms_session.set_role(
        get_default_roles||', GLOBAL_ACCESS_ROLE identified by
<password>');
  end;
```

In this example, the GLOBAL_ACCESS_ROLE password is hard-coded into the CHECK_FORMS_ACCESS procedure. You might want to store the password in a table (encoded) instead. This approach would make the password easier to maintain (you don't have to recompile routines every time the password is updated) and harder for unauthorized persons to find.

The GET_DEFAULT_ROLES function called by the previous code returns a comma-separated string containing all the current user's default roles. This string is necessary because dbms_session.set_role undoes the settings for all roles not included in the call. Implement the GET_DEFAULT_ROLES function like this:

```
/* ———- Plsql/Getroles.sql ———- */
FUNCTION get_default_roles RETURN varchar2 IS
  default_roles varchar2(2000);
  — All default roles, comma separated
  cursor get_system_role is
    select granted_role
    from user_role_privs
    where
      default_role = 'YES' and
      granted_role <> 'GLOBAL_ACCESS_ROLE';
BEGIN
  for def_role in get_system_role loop
    default_roles := def_role.granted_role||','||default_roles;
  end loop;
  default_roles := rtrim(default_roles,',');
  return(default_roles);
END;
```

Depending on your Designer template setup, you could add the calling of CHECK_FORMS_ACCESS to the WHEN-NEW-FORMS-INSTANCE trigger of your template form. Alternatively, if you use an event handler (such as those designed by Headstart and DesignAssist), you could add it to the WHEN-NEW-FORM-INSTANCE event in your company-level or application-level library. Doing so ensures that all your Designer-generated forms contain the necessary code for maintaining module-level security without needing any postgeneration changes.

Maintaining access to reports modules

In reports, you can implement module-level security by using a generic (CHECK_REPORT_ACCESS) function; the `before-parameter-form` trigger of all reports calls this function. You could make one generic to use on both forms and reports, but the result would be less elegant.

As the CHECK_FORMS_ACCESS procedure, the function begins by looking up the current users roles in the MODULE_ROLES table to see whether the user should be allowed to run the current form.

In reports, you cannot access the module name directly (as you can in forms if you use the `get_application_property` build-in; you have to pass on the module name as a parameter when you call the report. In this example, the parameter passes on as clear text.

TIP You might want to encode the module name to prevent users from calling a report with nothing more than the name of another report as the parameter (which is possible as soon as they find out what parameter name the report is expecting).

```
/* ———— Plsql/chkrpts.sql ———-- */
Function CHECK_REPORTS_ACCESS (p_report in varchar2)IS
l_module_access vachar2(1);
l_dummy varchar2(1);
begin
  — Find out if the current user is granted a role that
  — gives access to the current report.
  begin
    select 'Y'
    into l_module_access
    from module_roles m, dba_role_privs r
    where
      m.module_name = p_report and
      m.role_name = r.granted_role and
      r.grantee = USER and
      rownum = 1;
  exception when no_data_found then
    l_module_access:= 'N';
  end;
```

If the user does not have a role that gives access to the current report the report is terminated. A report doesn't provide you with an exit command so you can terminate it quietly. Instead, the trigger must return the value FALSE:

```
if l_module_access = 'N' then
  return(FALSE);
end if;
```

Unfortunately, we cannot generate a user-friendly message to explain that the report is terminating because the user does not have access to it. The user will just receive an error and the report will terminate.

If we pass the if-statement just shown, the user has been accepted – but we still need to activate the GLOBAL_ACCESS_ROLE. If the current report has been called from a form, probably the calling form has already activated the GLOBAL_ACCESS_ROLE (see the previous section for a review). To save time, activate the role only if it is not already active. To activate the GLOBAL_ACCESS_ROLE, use the dbms_session package in the same way you would for activating forms (as explained earlier). The code looks like this:

```
 - activate the GLOBAL_ACCESS_ROLE (if it isn't already)
 begin
   select 'x' into l_dummy
   from session_roles
   where role = 'GLOBAL_ACCESS_ROLE';
 exception
   when no_data_found then
     dbms_session.set_role(
       get_default_roles||', GLOBAL_ACCESS_ROLE identified by
<password>');
 end;
```

As with the example in the previous section, the GLOBAL_ACCESS_ROLE password is hard-coded into the CHECK_REPORTS_ACCESS function. You might want to store the password in a table (encoded) instead. This technique can make the password not only easier to maintain (you won't have to recompile routines every time the password is updated), but also harder for unauthorized persons to find.

If this process looks familiar, it should. Compare it to the example given in the earlier section titled "Maintaining Access to Forms Modules," which explains the GET_DEFAULT_ROLES function called by the code.

Because all triggers are implemented as functions, the trigger must end with the following line:

```
return(TRUE);
```

Define this trigger in the `before-parameter-form` trigger of your template report(s). Doing so ensures that all your Designer-generated reports contain the necessary code for maintaining module-level security, without requiring postgeneration changes.

Maintaining access to Web modules

Because Web modules are packages, we can maintain access to such modules more directly by using the following techniques:

◆ Grant the roles listed in the MODULE_ROLES table to the appropriate packages.

◆ Revoke any roles not listed in the MODULE_ROLES table.

◆ Define public synonyms on all packages that the end user can call directly.

◆ Create grants for the process roles as specified in the MODULE_ROLES table.

Web packages called indirectly (through calls to other packages) don't need synonyms nor grants.

In the following sections I will describe the phases needed to apply the correct grants and synonyms automatically between roles and Web modules (package modules). The code that does so makes only the necessary changes to the existing environment. For example, if some needed grant is already granted, this code does not grant it again; if an unnecessary grant is granted, the code does not revoke it. This requirement does make the code a little more complex – but you get a better overview of how many changes (and which ones) actually occur.

 The CD-ROM contains a complete listing of the code that distributes such Web module access.

PARAMETERS
Use the following parameters to perform the grant distribution:

- ◆ **&&DB.** Corresponds to the connect string to the database to be updated.

- ◆ **&&OWNER.** Corresponds to the schema name of the schema that owns the database objects to be updated.

- ◆ **&&OWNER_PWD.** Corresponds to the password of &&OWNER.

CONNECTING TO THE DATABASE
Begin by connecting to the correct database:

```
connect &&owner/&&owner_pw@&&db
```

CREATE OUTPUT TABLE
Create an output table to store all the grants, revokes, and so on needed to apply the access rights of the MODULE_ROLES table to the package modules (in this case, the Web modules).

The following code generates the table OUTPUT_TAB if it does not already exist. The table contains three columns:

- ◆ **SESSION_NO.** This column allows multiple sessions to insert rows into the table simultaneously. Note that in the following code I hard-code the session number to 0. This works because we never commit out inserts to the OUTPUT_TAB table. As long as they remain uncommitted, multiple sessions can insert rows with session number 0 simultaneously without seeing each other's rows.

- ◆ **SEQ.** This column records the order of the command lines of the table.

- ◆ **LINE.** This column records actual command lines to be executed against the database.

```
/* ——- Plsql/genWebtab.sql —— */
spool output.tab
  select decode(count(*),0,
    'Prompt Creating output table OUTPUT_TAB.'||chr(10)||
    'CREATE TABLE output_tab'||chr(10)||
    ' (session_no NUMBER(10,0) NOT NULL, seq NUMBER(10,0)||
    ' NOT NULL, line VARCHAR2(2000) NULL);'||chr(10)||
    'ALTER TABLE OUTPUT_TAB ADD (CONSTRAINT OUT_PK' ||
    ' PRIMARY KEY (SESSION_NO, SEQ));'||chr(10)||
    'insert into output_tab (session_no, seq, line) '||chr(10)||
```

```
        ' values (0,0,''Prompt Table OUTPUT_TAB created.'');',
        'insert into output_tab (session_no, seq, line) '||chr(10)||
        ' values (0,0,''Prompt Output table OUTPUT_TAB' ||
        ' already exists.'');')
    from user_tables
    where table_name = 'OUTPUT_TAB';
spool off

@output.tab
```

DROP OLD PUBLIC SYNONYMS

Now we can begin to implement the access rights of the MODULE_ROLES table.

First we drop unnecessary public synonyms – for example, synonyms to the Web Server Generator packages (including CG$-packages) except those referenced in the MODULE_ROLES table. I also exclude packages whose names begin with DA$ because the DesignAssist tools probably need them.

The cursor that returns the public synonyms to be dropped would look like this:

```
/* ——- Plsql/Dropsyn.sql ——— */
BEGIN
DECLARE
cursor old_synonyms is
    select s.synonym_name
    from all_synonyms s
    where
     s.owner = 'PUBLIC' and
     s.synonym_name in
     (select o.object_name from user_objects o
      where
        o.object_type = 'PACKAGE' and
        o.object_name not like 'DA$%' and
        o.object_name like '%$%' and
        (substr(o.object_name,1,instr(o.object_name,'$'))
        not in
          (select mr.module_name||'$' from module_roles mr)
        or
         o.object_name like 'CG$%'))
    order by 1;
```

As you can see from the cursor code, we have to match the module's short name with packages called <module short name>$<something>. This is how the Web server generator names the packages it uses to generate a Web module.

To drop the unnecessary public synonyms, we must loop through our cursor, adding lines to the output table as follows:

```
BEGIN
for c in old_synonyms loop
    I:= I+3;
    — Prompt
    insert into output_tab (session_no, seq, line)
    values (0,I,'Prompt drop public synonym'
            ||c.synonym_name||';');
    — Command
    insert into output_tab (session_no, seq, line)
    values (0,I+1,'drop public synonym '
            ||c.synonym_name||';');
    — Blank line
    insert into output_tab (session_no, seq, line)
    values (0,I+2,null);
  end loop;
END;
END;
```

Only the second insert is necessary; the other two inserts are included only for cosmetic purposes.

CREATE NEW PUBLIC SYNONYMS

After dropping the unnecessary public synonyms, we can create new public synonyms that include the following:

◆ WSG packages referenced in MODULE_ROLES

◆ HTF, HTP, and OWA packages, excluding API packages (CG$ packages) and packages that already have public synonyms

The cursor that returns the packages in need of public synonyms is as follows:

```
/* —- Plsql/Newsyn.sql ————- */
BEGIN
DECLARE
cursor new_synonyms is
    select distinct o.object_name from user_objects o
    where
      ((o.object_name like '%$%' and
        substr(o.object_name,1,instr(o.object_name,'$')) in
         (select mr.module_name||'$' from module_roles mr))
    or
```

```
          o.object_name in ('HTF','HTP','OWA')) and
          o.object_name not like 'CG$%' and
          o.object_name not in
            (select s.synonym_name from all_synonyms s
            where s.owner = 'PUBLIC')
      and o.object_type = 'PACKAGE'
        order by 1;
```

The loop that actually creates the public synonyms looks like this:

```
BEGIN
for c in new_synonyms loop
    I:= I+3;
    — Prompt
    insert into output_tab (session_no, seq, line)
    values (0,I,'Prompt create public synonym '
            ||c.object_name
            ||' for &&owner..'||c.object_name||';');
    — Command
    insert into output_tab (session_no, seq, line)
    values (0,I+1,'create public synonym '
            ||c.object_name||' for &&owner..'
            ||c.object_name||';');
    — Blank line
    insert into output_tab (session_no, seq, line)
    values (0,I+2,null);
  end loop;
END;
END;
```

GRANT ACCESS TO NECESSARY WSG-PACKAGES

The next step is to grant public access to the WSG packages – but doing so raises a security issue. Ideally, these packages should not need to be granted to public because they should not be called directly. I tried to grant them to the DAD account instead; they would not work unless I granted them to public. If you can find and implement a more restrictive solution, use it instead of this one:

```
/* ———-- Plsql/Acc_wsg.sql ——— */
BEGIN
DECLARE
cursor access_to_wsg is
    select o.object_name
    from user_objects o
```

```
where
   o.object_name in ('HTF','HTP','OWA') and
   o.object_type = 'PACKAGE' and
   o.object_name not in
     (select p.table_name from user_tab_privs p
       where p.grantee = 'PUBLIC')
   order by 1;
```

The corresponding loop to implement the code looks like this:

```
BEGIN
for c in access_to_wsg loop
   I:= I+3;
   — Prompt
   insert into output_tab (session_no, seq, line)
   values (0,I,'Prompt grant execute on '
           ||c.object_name||' to public;');
   — Command
   insert into output_tab (session_no, seq, line)
   values (0,I+1,'grant execute on '
           ||c.object_name||' to public;');
   — Blank line
   insert into output_tab (session_no, seq, line)
   values (0,I+2,null);
   end loop;
END;
END;
```

REVOKE MODULE ACCESS

Next we revoke two types of module access. First, revoke all EXECUTE grants on WSG-packages not referenced from the MODULE_ROLES table. Next, revoke all EXECUTE grants on the API packages (CG$-packages), excluding the DesignAssist packages. The code that does so looks like this:

```
   /* ———— Plsql/Rev_wsg.sql ———— */
BEGIN
DECLARE
 cursor old_module_access is
   select p.table_name, p.grantee
   from user_tab_privs p
   where
    (p.table_name like '%$%' and
     substr(p.table_name,1,instr(p.table_name,'$')) not in
```

```
            (select mr.module_name||'$'
              from module_roles mr
              where mr.role_name = p.grantee) or
        p.table_name like 'CG$%') and
        p.grantor = '&&owner' and
        p.table_name not like 'DA$%' and
        p.privilege = 'EXECUTE'
    order by 1;
```

The corresponding loop looks like this:

```
BEGIN
for c in old_module_access loop
    I:= I+3;
    — Prompt
    insert into output_tab (session_no, seq, line)
    values (0,I,'Prompt revoke execute on
      &&owner..'||c.table_name||' from '||c.grantee||';');
    — Command
    insert into output_tab (session_no, seq, line)
    values (0,I+1,'revoke execute on
      &&owner..'||c.table_name||' from '||c.grantee||';');
    — Blank line
    insert into output_tab (session_no, seq, line)
    values (0,I+2,null);
  end loop;
END;
END;
```

GRANT MODULE ACCESS
Finally, we can grant the necessary access to the Web modules. We can include all packages that match the following syntax: <module name>$<something> where <module name> exists in the MODULE_ROLES table (that is, where EXECUTE is not already granted).

```
    /* ——- Plsql/grt_mod.sql ——- */
BEGIN
DECLARE
 cursor new_module_access is
    select o.object_name, mr.role_name
    from user_objects o, module_roles mr
    where
      substr(o.object_name,1,instr(o.object_name,'$')) =
```

```
mr.module_name||'$' and
    o.object_type = 'PACKAGE' and
    o.object_name not in
      (select p.table_name from user_tab_privs p
        where p.grantee = mr.role_name)
  order by 1;
```

To implement the necessary grants, use a loop that looks like this:

```
  BEGIN
for c in new_module_access loop
    I:= I+3;
    — Prompt
    insert into output_tab (session_no, seq, line)
    values (0,I,'Prompt grant execute on
     &&owner..'||c.object_name||' to '||c.role_name||';');
    — Command
    insert into output_tab (session_no, seq, line)
    values (0,I+1,'grant execute on
     &&owner..'||c.object_name||' to '||c.role_name||';');
    — Blank line
    insert into output_tab (session_no, seq, line)
    values (0,I+2,null);
  end loop;
END;
END;
```

GENERATE GRANT SCRIPT
The last thing to do is to extract the command lines from the OUTPUT_TAB table
and build a script file for applying all the necessary changes.

I have found it useful to add a prompt line indicating the amount of commands
that have been generated (not counting prompts and blank lines). Do so as follows:

```
/* ——- Plsql/add_prmt.sql —— */
insert into output_tab (session_no, seq, line)
  select
   0,
   I+3,
   'Prompt '||to_char(count(*))
     ||' commands have been executed.'
  from output_tab
  where
   session_no = 0 and
```

```
      upper(line) not like 'PROMPT %' and
      line is not null;
end;
```

The actual grant script is easy to make; the code looks like this:

```
spool doWebgrt.SQL

  select line
  from output_tab
  where session_no = 0 order by seq;


spool off
```

As another service, I suggest showing an installation guide to the user before he/she decides to apply all the grants and revokes of the OUTPUT_TAB table. You could generate such an installation guide as follows:

```
/* —————— Plsql/Makegd.sql —————- */
select null from dual;
select
'********************************************************************'
||chr(10)
||          '                          Installation
Guide'||chr(10)
||'********************************************************************'
from dual;
select replace(line,'Prompt ',null)
from output_tab
where session_no = 0 and Seq = 0;
select chr(10)||
'To create grants and synonyms:'||chr(10)||chr(10)||
     '   Start file DOWEBGRT.SQL'||chr(10) from dual;
select '('||to_char(count(*))
||' commands have been generated into the file DOWEBGRT.SQL)'
from output_tab
where
 session_no = 0 and
 upper(line) not like 'PROMPT %' and
 line is not null;
select chr(10)||
'********************************************************************'
from dual;
```

The absolute last thing to do is to remove all the commands from OUTPUT_TAB. As they were never committed, we can do this with a single command:

```
rollback;
```

This completes the tasks needed to apply Web module security as it is defined in the MODULE_ROLE table.

The script just needs to be run every time the MODULE_ROLE table is updated, that is, whenever the security definition for Web modules is changed (usually when new Web modules are made).

Activate role in packages

You can implement security on packages to fit your needs in at least two ways:

◆ Follow the method of the Web module packages by having access granted or revoked based on rows in the MODULE_ROLES table. In this case you can use the scripts shown earlier directly on your own packages.

◆ Use the method described earlier for forms and reports: You would start by making a CHECK_PACKAGE_ACCESS function that resembles the CHECK_REPORT_ACCESS procedure shown earlier. You would use this function in all package bodies to set a package variable (such as ACCESS) if it is not already set. Doing so ensures that no function or procedure is called unless the owning package's ACCESS variable is set to either 'Y' or 'N.' When you have this measure in place, all your public functions and procedures should check the value of ACCESS and then terminate immediately if it is set to 'N.'

You can also choose whether to terminate with the following code:

```
raise_application_error
(-20000, 'Your access violation message goes here');
```

Base your choice on whether the user should be told about his/her access violation.

Ops$ Users (Problem and Workaround)

If you are accessing your database through a secure operating system (such as UNIX or NT), Oracle supports login by *operating-system-authenticated users* (*ops$ users* for short). This approach differs from the traditional Oracle login that requires users to specify a username and a password.

In effect, the secure operating system expects any user designated an ops$ user to have been accepted within it already. Such acceptance means the user can access the Oracle database without having to specify a username nor a password. In practice, you can bypass the Oracle login by using a slash (/) as username and password. For example, an ops$ user could use the following command to invoke the Sqlplus:

```
plus33w /
```

The user would be logged in to the database with an operating-system username prefixed by OPS$ (exceptions are described in the next section).; For example, if a user with the username JOE who uses a slash to connect to an NT network, he would connect to the Oracle database as the user OPS$JOE.

Setting up ops$ users

To be able to use ops$ users on a database you must add the following two lines to your init.ora file:

```
OS_AUTHENT_PREFIX=OPS$
REMOTE_OS_AUTHENT=TRUE
```

To make an operating system Oracle schema (ops$ user), just create the user using the EXTERNALLY keyword:

```
create user <user name> identified externally;
```

If the schema already exists, the command looks like this:

```
alter user <username> identified externally;
```

 No password is specified for ops$ users. Every time you assign that designation, you depend on the operating system to handle security.

As soon as you have set up your database and users, the ops$ users can connect to your database without specifying a password. To avoid the login dialog box all together you will have to specify the user ID as a slash (/) where users previously were confronted with the login dialog box. Exactly where to change your applications would depend on your application setup; normally you would have to change a command line for calling a specific Oracle main menu.

Ops$ users and Web modules

Unfortunately, ops$ users cannot run Web modules, even though they are logged in on a secure operating system.

The problem is that the PL/SQL agent does not know the concept of an ops$ user. One workaround is to define ops$ users as ordinary password users.

To set up your database and Web application server so that ops$ users can call Web modules through a Web browser, follow the instructions in the following subsections.

CREATE DAD

Create a DAD on the Web application server. When you create the DAD, be sure to take these two preliminary steps:

1. Check the box that says: Identified by: Operating System ("externally").

2. Select the box to install the Developer's Toolkit.

DEFINE PASSWORDS FOR YOUR OPS$ USERS

Although adding a password to an ops$ user account might sound like a contradiction, doing so gives you the option of connecting with or without specifying a password.

Add passwords as you would for an ordinary user:

```
alter user <username> identified by <password>;
```

 Even if you have defined passwords for your ops$ users, they can still connect using the slash (/) without the password (!).

 All users must have the same password — and it must be so secret that even they don't know it. If the password became known, anyone could use it to connect to any ops$ account.

SET UP THE PASSWORD IN THE OWA.CFG FILE

Edit the owa.cfg file on the Web application server (manually) and locate the section containing owa_service=<DAD name>. Under owa_user, add the following code:

```
(
owa_password=<password>
)
```

RESTART THE LISTENER

After you restart the Listener, all ops$ users can access the Web modules through a browser.

Summary

Database roles enable you to assign sets of privileges to groups of users based on either the user's affiliation with a job or with a process.

You can implement "no security," provided no user requires a database account. To accomplish this level of security, you place a username and password in the application startup script.

Database-level security can complicate your application's implementation by requiring that you assign multiple roles to many users. As one user acquires more database roles, that user's capabilities within the database become difficult to restrict; especially if he or she can reach the database outside your carefully constructed applications.

One strategy can prevent the possible security problem of too many roles: Create a single database role for all table, view, and sequence privileges, and then assign only that database role to users, keeping it in effect only during their particular sessions on your application.

To implement this strategy, you create a database role called (for example) GLOBAL_ACCESS_ROLE. Then you grant the appropriate privileges to this role. The chapter shows source code for a procedure that uses the Designer repository API to extract all required privileges and grant them to the database role.

After creating the database role with all necessary privileges, you now must create a set of procedures and functions (to be invoked at the beginning of each form, report, or Web application) to determine a user's privileges.

The chapter's source code illustrates the necessary procedures, functions, and triggers; none require additional changes after you generate your applications from Designer.

The chapter demonstrates how to generate the database role and its privileges for Web-based applications. The example grants, only those privileges not already granted to the user, and creates only those synonyms that don't already exist.

Ops$ users are users logged into the database from a secure system (such as an intranet or WAN) and don't require an additional password. This chapter shows how to create such a user account in Oracle.

This chapter also shows how to work around a Web module's nonacceptance of ops$ users.

The next chapter covers the task of generating modules directly from Designer — in particular, forms and reports.

Chapter 5

Application Generator

IN THIS CHAPTER

- ◆ Understanding application logic
- ◆ Designing reusable module components
- ◆ Using advanced form and report generation
- ◆ Reviewing Oracle8 object support

DURING THE ENTIRE PROCESS of analysis and design, you are building the logical representation of how your application will function and storing the definitions in Oracle's CASE tool. Application generation is the transmogrification of the definitions you create into useful and working pieces of the application.

The previous version of Designer under release 1 was version 1.3.2. It contained generators for Oracle Forms 4.5, Oracle Reports 2.5, Oracle SQL*Plus reports, Oracle Graphics 2.5, Oracle WebServer PL/SQL code, Microsoft Visual Basic 4.0, Microsoft help, and C++ data objects.

The application generation feature in the current version of Designer has gone through a major upgrade. Not only have the generators been upgraded to the latest versions of the tools they support, but a much more extensive definition can be made in Designer for generation. Two new generators have been added: Table API and Developer Common Libraries (PLLs). Two generators have also been removed: Oracle SQL*Plus and Oracle Graphics.

Successful generation of simple modules can be achieved easily by most computer professionals who can read the help text. This chapter describes how to generate modules that meet real-world needs. The topics include new features, undocumented features, and changed functionality.

Application Logic

The meat of an application is the logic that is running behind the scenes. In the Oracle world, this logic exists in the form of PL/SQL. This chapter discusses four specific types of application logic that can exist with an application and/or a module. These types are known as:

◆ Action items

◆ Events

◆ API logic

◆ Common libraries

All of these types are new to release 2 of Designer and provide design capabilities that existed only in post-generation modifications, complicated template schemas, or not at all.

Action items

Action items exist in three forms within a module: navigation, generator, and custom. Not all types of action items can be used in each type of module. Table 5-1 shows where each type can be used.

TABLE 5-1 ACTION ITEM TYPES FOR FORMS, REPORTS, AND VISUAL BASIC

FormsType	Form	Report	VB Form
Navigation	Yes	Yes	Yes
Generator	No	No	Yes
Custom	Yes	No	Yes

NAVIGATION ITEMS
A navigation item enables you to identify one of two types of navigation:

◆ Navigation within the same module

◆ Navigation between two modules

The next two sections describe each navigation type.

NAVIGATION WITHIN THE SAME MODULE With this navigation type you can define a method for moving around within your module. For an Oracle form or Visual Basic form, this means you can control movement from one block or zone to another. Oracle Reports enables you to build in a drill-down fashion. By default, this navigation is performed via a button. It is also possible to perform this navigation via a menu command.

The only requirement for navigation is the definition of multiple module components. The significance of this new feature is that it replaces the need for creating place-holder columns with hard-coded navigation. The Display View in the Design Editor will show the navigation as seen in Figure 5-1. Another important part of navigation is the definition of parameters. Once you define the objects that should go between module components, the new navigation definition capabilities of Designer build the parameters for you.

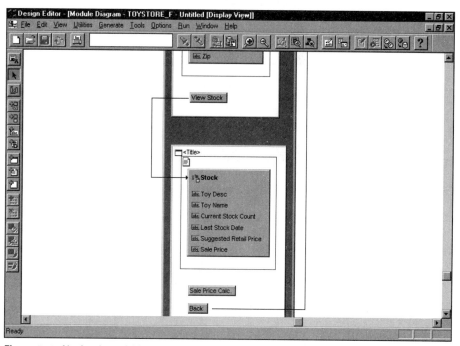

Figure 5-1: Navigation within a module is shown in the Design Editor.

NAVIGATION BETWEEN MODULES   The second form of navigation can be used to define navigation to other Designer modules. This is different from the common module network definition that has been used in the past. The module network definition for nonmenu definitions requires a template item (CG$FF) and cannot pass arguments without post-generation changes. This form of navigation item defines not only the call, but also a button to call the other module. The module network can also be used to define parameters to pass. Thus, if you have fields on a form that you want to pass to another form or to a report, you no longer need to write custom PL/SQL to perform parameter setup. Figure 5-2 shows the Design Editor with navigation between two modules.

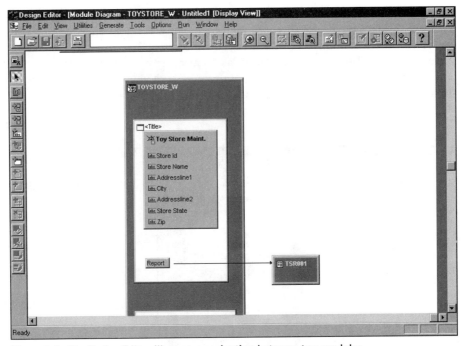

Figure 5-2: The Design Editor illustrates navigation between two modules.

Named values (predefined parameters found in every form or report) such as PARAFORM also exist for a report. Thus, you now have documented parameter usage within Designer, as seen in Figure 5-3.

GENERATOR ITEMS

Generator items are available only with Visual Basic modules. They provide a means to execute generated or template code in the context of a zone and thus may only be used in the context of a module component – for example, a custom Delete record or Query button.

CUSTOM ITEMS

These are available only for forms and Visual Basic modules. A custom action enables you to define your own code to perform. For example, you may want to perform some special calculations when your button is pressed. By creating a custom item, you can define your own logic for the When-Button-Pressed trigger. In Figure 5-4, you can see that a special stored procedure/named routine is called to figure a new_sale_price for a stock item based on last_stock_date and the current_stock_count.

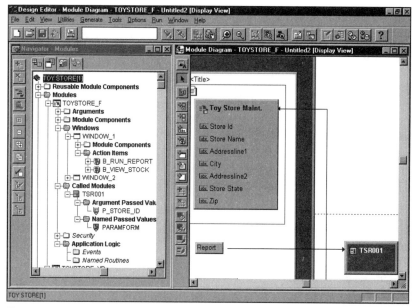

Figure 5-3: The TOYSTORE form calls modules with both argument parameters and named parameters.

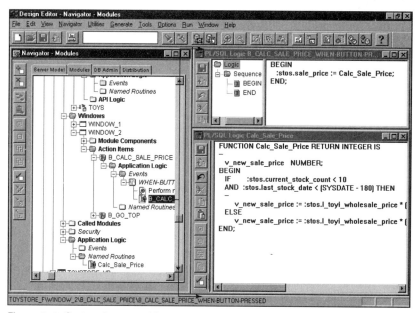

Figure 5-4: Custom items enable you to create any special action you need.

Named routines

A *named routine* is a procedure, function, or package that is stored within the generated module (that is, a form, report, and so on). This translates into a program unit in a form. If you have PL/SQL code that is unique to the module, use a named procedure within the module. If it is even remotely possible that the procedure can be reused, then use either a common library or a stored procedure. Named routines can be referenced or called from events and action items within the module definition.

Events

Action items use certain events to function properly. An *event* is basically something that happens in your form or report or in a Visual Basic, WebServer, or API module. Events relate back to custom code that you write. For example, you may need to write an event to perform code in the pre-form trigger. The event will relate back to the language's triggering events.

Events can be defined in any of the following places (based on the module type and the language capabilities):

- Module application logic

- Window application logic

- Module component application logic

- Arguments

- Action items

- Bound items

- Unbound items

Figure 5-5 is an example of an event code in a form. The event code defines the locations where certain text is added to the form.

Here is an example of event code:

```
BEGIN
  /******************
   EXAMPLE EVENT CODE
   WNFI - Maximize MDI Window
  ******************/
  Set_Window_Property(FORMS_MDI_WINDOW, POSITION, 5,10);
  Set_Window_Property(FORMS_MDI_WINDOW, WINDOW_STATE,
          MAXIMIZE);
  /******************
```

```
  WNFI - Application Startup Code
  *******************/
  app.startup;
END;
```

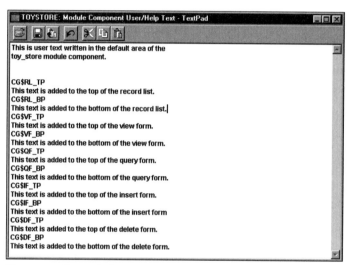

Figure 5-5: Events help customize your application.

API logic

As you may already know, release 2 of Developer enables you to develop interfaces that deal directly with a table (as in the past) or that interface with tables via program units. This provides the capability to code the entire transaction rather than depending on the Developer tools to interface in an efficient manner.

The fact that this new interface exists poses the question, "How do I do this in Designer?" The answer actually consists of two parts. First, you must generate the Table API logic. This can be used by WEB interfaces directly. Second, you must generate the Module Component API logic. This is the code that a form, report, and so forth interface with.

This is all fine and dandy, but we all know that the default functionality is not always enough. Thus, we have API Logic definitions with which we can define code snippets that will be embedded into the Module Component API. Not only that, but we can actually control where the extra code is executed in the transaction (for example, coded prior to "Pre" or after "Post" the transactional code). This also holds true for the Table API logic.

Common libraries

PLLs or *common libraries* enable us to place reusable code outside of our module for use at run time without storing the code in the database. In the past, there were three ways to attach a PLL to an Oracle form or report module. PLL was attached via:

1. Generator preferences

2. Template

3. Post generation

Let's see how to create a common library, attach it to another module, use its functionality, and finally generate it.

TIP Common libraries are one of the more important features you can learn to use because this feature enables you to define within CASE a completely modular application system.

To create a common library and use it in a module, follow these steps:

1. **Create a module.** The module is of type "Library" and language "Developer Common Library." Figure 5-6 shows the edit window for the common module.

2. **Define named routines.** The routines are Procedures, Functions, or Packages.

3. **Link the library module to the module that needs to use it.** The link should be of type "CALL."

4. **Generate.** Generation can be done independently or in conjunction with the module that uses it.

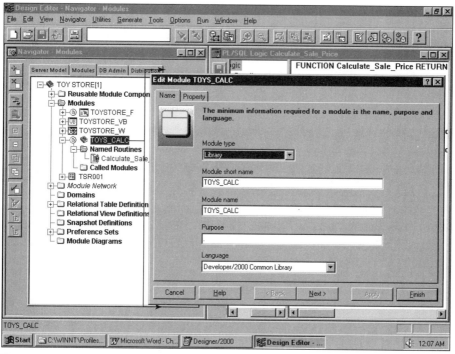

Figure 5-6: Create a common module by using the Library type and Developer Common Library language.

Reusable Module Components

As has been a common theme so far, we are seeking ways to define modular applications. The reason for this is to make it easier to maintain, provide commonality, and enable black-box thinking (encapsulated logic).

Another new feature of release 2 is the *reusable module component*. In a module definition, you define a module component, which normally coincides with a base table usage. The reusable component enables you to define a module component once and reuse it in multiple module definitions. This promotes a common look and feel across your application.

A lack of common look and feel and functionality in your application can be a number one killer. It will be the first complaint that your users make.

An example is to define a reusable module component for the toy store, which would enable you to use the toy store module component in multiple form modules with the same definition used in every instance. Figure 5-7 shows the common module for the toy store. The advantage is that you define the reusable module component once. Not only have you reduced the maintenance effort, but you have also set some standards.

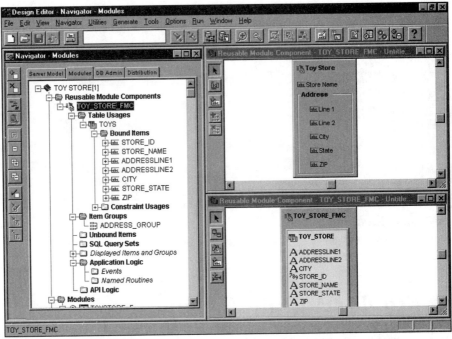

Figure 5-7: Reusable module components save maintenance time and set standards.

Here are a few important things to note and rules to live by:

1. A reusable module component has all of the same characteristics of a specific module component within a module. This includes application logic, bound and unbound items, and so on.

2. Reusable module components are specific to a language type. Thus, you must create a new reusable module component for each language that needs one.

3. Adjustments to a reusable module component affect all modules that use it. You cannot adjust a reusable component within the module. If you require a similar look and feel but may make changes, copy the module.

4. Ensure that a reusable component is the best choice. Do not use this in place of a single screen. For example, you may want to provide a user several different paths to address entry into the database. If the entry is done the same way in every case, it may be better to just call an address maintenance form rather than having the functionality found in many different forms.

Advanced Form and Report Generation

Oracle form and report generation, from Designer, are the most prevalent methods of code generation used today. Release 2 provides many more features to enable nearly 100 percent generation.

Generator preferences

If you remember the old preferences navigator, it was separate and independent in its use. Very little in the true functionality has changed. It is the new usage method within the Design Editor that is worth looking at. We will review the usage first and then look at some of the preferences and how and when to use them to your advantage.

NAVIGATOR USAGE

The navigator for the Design Editor also is used as the navigator for the generator preferences screen. Thus, it is important to remember that wherever your cursor is on the Design Editor's navigator window, the preferences seen are those for that level. The navigator is also smart enough to change the language used based on the module highlighted. If you are not on a module (that is, application level), then you can easily change the language via the listbox provided.

One important strategy is the use of *preference sets*. Preference sets enable you to identify standard, or named, ways to generate a form. In the example shown in Figure 5-8, you see that there is a "General Forms" set that will be used at the application level for default settings. You will also note that two sets can actually be used at the module component level to better define how a component displays and works depending on whether it is multirow or single row in nature. This standard can be very useful in preventing your forms, reports, and so on from looking and acting differently due to preferences not being set the same.

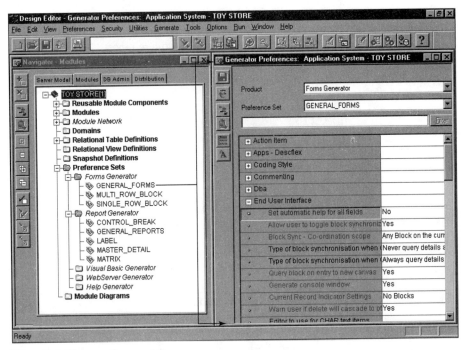

Figure 5-8: Three preference sets.

FORM PREFERENCES

One of the goals of release 2 of Designer is to better achieve 100 percent generation. With this emphasis, many preferences have become obsolete due either to new definitions within the module itself or to new features in the templates. Many of these preferences have been replaced by object library definitions within the template.

TIP If you have migrated from older versions of Designer or do not have time to learn the new methods, you can set the OLBOLD preference to YES to continue to use these preferences. The obsolete and removed preferences are listed in Table 5-2 and Table 5-3.

TABLE 5-2 OBSOLETE FORM PREFERENCES AND THE EQUIVALENT OBJECT LIBRARY

Obsolete Form Preference	New Object Library
AUTOHP	Display hint automatically
BLKVSB	Show vertical scrollbar

Obsolete Form Preference	New Object Library
COLSEC	Enforce column security
IMGBEV	Image item – Bevel
IMGCMP	Image item – Compression quality
IMGDHT	Image item – Height
IMGDWD	Image item – Width
IMGHSB	Image item – Show horizontal scrollbar
IMGQLT	Image item – Display quality
IMGSZS	Image item – Sizing style
IMGVSB	Image item – Show vertical scrollbar
LOVNAV	Push button – Keyboard navigable
TXTBEV	Text item – Bevel
WINCLO	Window – Close enabled
WINDLG	Window – Window style
WINFHT	Window – Height
WINFIX	Window – Resize enabled
WINFWD	Window – Width
WINFXP	Window – X position
WINFYP	Window – Y position
WINHSB	Window – Show horizontal scrollbar
WINICN	Window – Icon filename
WINICO	Window – Minimize enabled
WINICT	Window – Minimized title
WINMOV	Window – Move enabled
WINVSB	Window – Show vertical scrollbar
WINZOO	Window – Maximize enabled

TABLE 5-3 REMOVED FORM PREFERENCES AND THE REASON FOR REMOVAL

Name of Removed Preference	Reason for Removal
ADNTRT	Functionality replaced by the Add Notes checkbox on the Forms Design Capture Options dialog box.
AUTOQY	Preference renamed USEPKR (and default changed to NONE).
BLKNAV	Superseded by new navigation functionality.
BLKNME	In release 2, forms generator uses module component names to name generated blocks.
CCEWN	This preference has been superseded by the "Enforce when Null" property of check constraints.
CCTABL	Superseded by Scope of Code Control Table option on General Generator Options dialog box.
CGTBLS	Superseded by option on General Generator Options dialog box.
DVTABL	Superseded by Scope of Reference Code Table option on General Generator Options dialog box.
DVDSPM	Functionality replaced by the Show Meaning item property.
FLDNAV	Superseded by new navigation functionality.
GRPENB	Functionality replaced by capability to define item groups graphically in the Design Editor.
LAYCLP	Functionality replaced by capability to set the Fill Pattern property of graphic objects and/or text.
MNUCDR	Functionality no longer required because MNUDRN is used to determine whether to assign a default role to menu items.
MNUCMN	Functionality no longer required because Repository module Short Name/Implementation Name properties meet the uniqueness requirements necessary for menu generation.
MNUDBG	Functionality no longer supported by Form Builder.
MNUOSC	Functionality no longer supported by Form Builder.

Name of Removed Preference	Reason for Removal
MNUPFX	Functionality no longer required because the MNUUMN preference has been removed.
MNUSAS	Functionality replaced by new preference MNUSEC.
MNUUMN	Functionality no longer required because Repository module Short Name/Implementation Name properties meet the uniqueness requirements necessary for menu generation.
MODLCK	Functionality replaced by the "Prevent Generation?" module property.
MSGFLP	Functionality replaced by MSGSFT.
NPNAVB	Preference renamed NAVNPB.
PHDMSK	Functionality replaced by capability to set format mask of CG$DT generator item in template form.
REGXXX	Regeneration functionality has been replaced by new forms generator functionality to capture application logic and to generate preserving layout. For more information, see the section "Change Generation" in Chapter 8.
REWHFD	WHERE clauses are always captured and formatted correctly. For more information, see the section "Design Recovery" in Chapter 8.
SPINCR	Superseded by option on General Generator Options dialog box.
SYDUAL	Superseded by Name of Dual Table field on General Generator Options dialog box.
TEMSIZ	Superseded by a new process for obtaining window, content canvas, and stacked canvas size and/or dimensions.
VBXBEV, VBXDHT, VBXDWD	Preferences removed because 16-bit VBX functionality is not supported in 32-bit Developer/2000 Form Builder applications.
WHTIME	Superseded by Record Time on Change History Columns checkbox on General Generator Options dialog box.
WINBOR	Not required in latest release of Developer/2000.

Continued

TABLE 5-3 REMOVED FORM PREFERENCES AND THE REASON FOR REMOVAL
(Continued)

Name of Removed Preference	Reason for Removal
WINUSR	Functionality replaced by capability to create a Repository window definition called ROOT_WINDOW.

Preferences work in levels, which enable you to define defaults for generations that are overridden as the levels become more detailed. The levels are shown in Figure 5-9. The generators look at the preferences from left to right and top to bottom. Thus, if a preference is set at the application level and at the module level, the module level preference will be used.

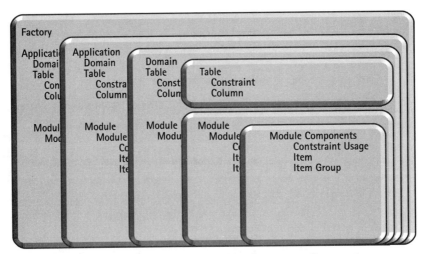

Figure 5-9: An inner level of preference overrides the same preference at an outer level.

Some of the preferences to be aware of are around block and item group layout. Through the use of and adjustment to tabulation tables, you can better control layout. Note that you have to weigh the advantages gained with the time spent. The tabulation table preference is BLKTAB and contains positional numbers. All of this is for naught, though, if the BLKUTT preference is not set. This preference tells the generator how to use the tab stops.

REPORT PREFERENCES

The report preferences have gone through changes, too. Removed preferences are too numerous to list. *Basically, a lot of the preference functionality has moved to the report template.* Table 5-4 lists the preferences that have changed.

TABLE 5-4 REPORT PREFERENCES THAT HAVE CHANGED

Preference	Change Notes
DOJOIN	Combine queries. The value of this preference can no longer be specified at generation time.
FTCRET	Display group titles. This preference can now be set at module component level.
LOVTYP	List of Values type. The default value is now Base Table (BT).
PARNME	Prefixes of generated parameter names. The default value is now CG$P_.
SUPFRM	Hide boilerplate objects when no records are retrieved. The values of this preference are now Yes and No. The default value is now Yes.
TRCPCT	Change the degree of field truncation. The default value is now 20 percent.

HINT FOR CODING REPORTS

One way to make coding reports easier is to adjust the default names used in the data model objects (COLNME, CPNAME, CURNME, FRMNME, GRPNME, JNGNME, PARNME, QRYNME and SUMNME). Here's how:

1. First remove the dollar sign ($) from all names if you plan to connect via ODBC or other non-SQL*Net communications. The dollar sign can cause errors that take a while to track down.

2. Leave the parameter prefix blank. Have your developers name the parameters properly — in the reports themselves. Doing so eliminates confusion about the names of parameters when used on code, where clauses, or called modules.

Template definitions

Templates have been a part of Form Generator in release 1 of Designer. The Form templates in release 2 are more robust and lend themselves to 100 percent generated forms.

New in Designer version 2, Report Builder enables you to create templates.

The next two sections explore the Form templates and the Report templates.

FORM TEMPLATES

Form templates now have two different definitions. You can, of course, use your old templates. And if you do, you should take the time to use referenced items from a standard reference form. In the old style, you can create a CG$ control block that contains generator items. You can also add named visual attributes to control display.

REPLACING OLD TEMPLATE ITEMS WITH OBJECT LIBRARY ITEMS   For those of you who say "Out with the old and in with the new," we now have *object libraries*. The named items are now prefixed by CGSO$ and CGAI$ (which are source objects and action items, respectively). The object library items can also be suffixed as follows:

1. _MR. Multirecord block or an item in a multirecord block

2. _CT. Control block (that is, the module component contains only unbound items)

3. _DO. Display only item

4. _MD. Mandatory item

You can use the preceding suffixes individually or in combination. The forms generator uses the most appropriate standard source item, according to the order it falls in the hierarchy. Thus, if the generator cannot find one of the more detailed hierarchy items, it follows up the hierarchy until an object is found. If nothing is found, form defaults are used.

Here is an example from the hierarchy in a Form template:

```
CGSO$DEFAULT_ITEM
        CGSO$DEFAULT_ITEM_MR
        CGSO$DEFAULT_ITEM_CT
        CGSO$DEFAULT_ITEM_DO
        CGSO$DEFAULT_ITEM_MD
            CGSO$BUTTON
                CGSO$AIBUTTON
                    CGSO$AIBUTTON_CT
                CGSO$BUTTON_MR
                CGSO$BUTTON_CT
            CGSO$CHAR
                CGSO$CHAR_MR
```

```
CGSO$CHAR_CT
CGSO$CHAR_DO
CGSO$CHAR_MD
        CGSO$ALPHA
            CGSO$ALPHA_MR
            CGSO$ALPHA_CT
            CGSO$ALPHA_DO
            CGSO$ALPHA_MD
```

Furthermore, the previous release included CG$ items that provided special functionality within the form. These too have been replaced. The items have really only been renamed and moved to object libraries. Table 5-5 shows the old CG$ item and the corresponding CGAI$ item that replaced it.

TABLE 5-5 OLD FORM TEMPLATE ITEMS AND THE REPLACEMENT OBJECT LIBRARY ITEMS

Old Item	New Object Library Item
CG$CQ	CGAI$CANCEL_QUERY
CG$CB	CGAI$CLEAR_BLOCK
CG$CF	CGAI$CLEAR_ITEM
CG$CR	CGAI$CLEAR_RECORD
CG$CM	CGAI$COMMIT
CG$CP	CGAI$COPY
CG$CH	CGAI$COUNT_HITS
CG$CT	CGAI$CUT
CG$DE	CGAI$DISPLAY_ERROR
CG$DF	CGAI$DUPL_ITEM
CG$DR	CGAI$DUPLICATE_RECORD
CG$ED	CGAI$EDIT
CG$EQ	CGAI$ENTER_QUERY
CG$XQ	CGAI$EXECUTE_QUERY
CG$EX	CGAI$EXIT
CG$FN	CGAI$FETCH_NEXT_SET

Continued

TABLE 5-5 OLD FORM TEMPLATE ITEMS AND THE REPLACEMENT OBJECT LIBRARY ITEMS *(Continued)*

Old Item	New Object Library Item
CG$HP	CGAI$HELP
CG$IR	CGAI$INSERT_RECORD
CG$KY	CGAI$KEYS
CG$LQ	CGAI$LAST_CRITERIA
CG$LR	CGAI$LOCK_RECORD
CG$LV	CGAI$LOV
CG$NB	CGAI$NEXT_BLOCK
CG$NF	CGAI$NEXT_ITEM
CG$NP	CGAI$NEXT_PAGE
CG$NR	CGAI$NEXT_RECORD
CG$PA	CGAI$PASTE
CG$PB	CGAI$PREV_BLOCK
CG$PF	CGAI$PREV_ITEM
CG$PP	CGAI$PREV_PAGE
CG$PR	CGAI$PREV_RECORD
CG$OP	CGAI$PRINT
CG$RF	CGAI$REFRESH
CG$RR	CGAI$REMOVE_RECORD
CG$RB	CGAI$ROLLBACK
CG$SD	CGAI$SCROLL_DOWN
CG$SU	CGAI$SCROLL_UP

Layout is only one thing you can control within a template. *You can also include reusable code.* One advanced technique is to create an application library and optionally create module libraries, as described in the next section.

USING LIBRARY HIERARCHY TO ADD PROCEDURES TO YOUR TEMPLATE   This is an advanced technique involving the use of library hierarchy. You can create an application library and optionally create module libraries to your advantage. Add procedures to the PLL to perform event handling.

Here is an example of how to use the calling hierarchy. Let's use the four procedures defined in previous sections.

The application library contains each of the four procedures.

The module-specific code in the application library actually does no processing and only indicates that the application common code should be run.

Next, you can optionally attach a module specific library *with procedures of the same name*, excluding the application common code. Here is where you can add some module-specific code and also indicate whether the application common code should be run.

The module-specific library should appear before the application library in the list of attached libraries. In release one of Designer, the libraries actually generated in the desired order. It may be necessary to make a post-generation change if you attach the application library in the template. Remember that a form or report looks for a procedure first in internal program units, next in attached libraries (first to last), and finally in the database. Thus, the order of library attachment is important.

In release 2 of Designer, it is not necessary to use the generator preferences to attach libraries any longer. What can be done in this release is to actually attach the libraries within the Design Editor as illustrated in Figure 5-10.

REPORT TEMPLATES

Report templates in the past were actually just report definitions with named items that caused the generator to recognize fonts and sizing. *Now, Oracle Reports version 3 comes with a new file type (TDF), which is a template definition.* The reports generator uses this new template format. The new template is actually more flexible because you can define default layout definitions. Figure 5-11 shows an example of a template in the Reports Builder.

There are also override definition areas for each type of report. An example is to set the default label to ARIAL-10-Bold, but override the label definition for tabular reports and set the label to ARIAL-10-Bold-Underlined.

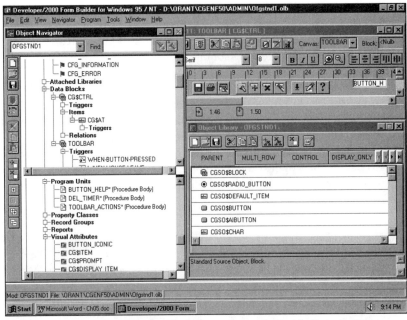

Figure 5-10: Form template and object library can be defined in Form Builder.

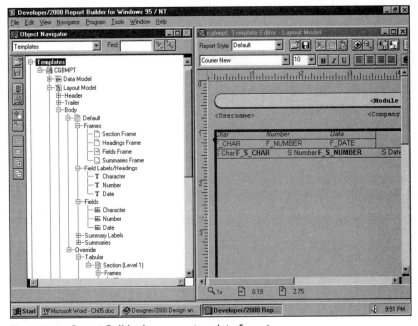

Figure 5-11: Report Builder has a new template format.

Bound and unbound items

If you used release 1 of Designer, you will remember the odd way in which you had to implement fields that were not columns in the database. Of course, it is a reasonable request to have the capability to define derivable fields, buttons, or other items.

With release one, a block and a table usage were synonymous within a form module. With release two, we now have module components to represent a block. There are also two types of items that can be defined within a module component. One is a bound item, which always corresponds to one column in the database. The other is an unbound item. *Unbound* refers to the fact that the item does not necessarily correspond to a single column in the database. An unbound item appears as a part of a module component but outside of the table usage, as shown in Figure 5-12.

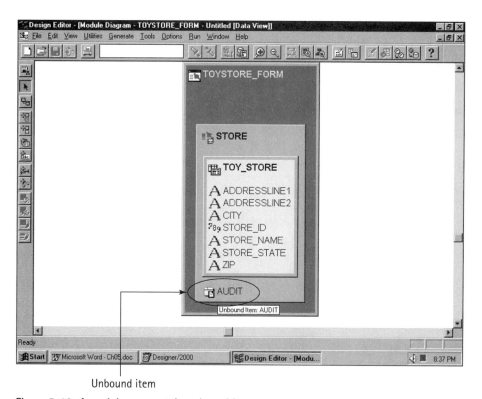

Unbound item

Figure 5–12: A module can contain unbound items.

Several types of unbound items are available, and each module type can use only certain sets of these. Table 5-6 shows where each type of unbound item can be used.

TABLE 5-6 UNBOUND ITEMS THAT CAN BE USED IN FORMS AND REPORTS AND WEB AND VB APPLICATIONS

Unbound Item	Forms	Reports	Web	VB
Computed	√	√		
SQL aggregate		√		
SQL expression	√	√	√	
Client-side function	√	√	√	
Server-side function		√	√	
Target specific		√	√	
Custom	√		√	√

A *computed item* provides the capability to calculate a value based on other items in the module on the client side. The following functions can be used on a computed item:

- AVG
- COUNT
- MAX
- MIN
- SUM
- STDDEV
- VARIANCE
- %TOTAL
- FIRST
- LAST

For example:

```
AVG(stos.sale_price);
```

A *SQL aggregate item* also enables you to compute values, but the calculations are performed on the *server* side. Only the following functions can be used for a SQL aggregate:

- AVG
- COUNT
- MAX
- MIN
- SUM
- STDDEV
- VARIANCE

A *SQL expression item* is really a derived value. It is really a formula type of column in which you as the developer have lots of flexibility. You can use any of the provided Oracle functions such as ABS, CEIL, NVL, TO_DATE, and so on. Even more importantly, you can also call your own functions on the server or client side. For example:

```
calc_overhead (toys.store_id);
```

A *client-side function item* enables you to write your own PL/SQL code to be used on the client side. Note that you must write all of your code within the dialog box. *For all of you Web heads, this is where you can actually include JavaScript to enhance your Web pages.*

A *server-side function item* is similar to a client-side function item, but it enables you to also pick from your predefined server-side PL/SQL modules.

A *target-specific item* is an item in which the text entered tells the generator specific things to do. For instance, if you would like to have a report in which images located in the file system are printed as part of the output, you can create a target-specific item. Within the target-specific information text, you place the complete directory path and filename. Make sure the display type is set to image.

A *custom item* enables you to create and fully control an item generated. These items normally are buttons, checkboxes, radio buttons, and the like, for which you write your own PL/SQL code. For example, if you need to kick off some special auditing or archiving functionality for a record, you can create a button to perform the actions.

Oracle8 Object Support

One of the reasons for the delayed release of release 2 of Designer was the newly released database server Oracle8. As you may know, one of the main features of Oracle8 is the object-oriented enhancements.

Oracle has included a separate tool (which may *optionally* be installed) with release two of Designer. This tool is known as the *Object Database Designer*. Using this tool you can do two types of design and development work:

♦ **Type modeling.** With the type modeling section, you can model your C++ data types and define your methods.

♦ **Sever modeling.** The server modeling section enables you to build object tables and views for use in Oracle8.

The next section takes a closer look at these tools.

Server and type modeling

In the server model, you will see that we have changed our Toy_Stores table a bit, as shown in Figure 5-13. You will see that a store can have multiple addresses. But beyond that, these address records are referenced. Second, you will notice that an address includes a phone number. But phone numbers are actually embedded within the address records.

To access these object tables directly, it is necessary to define UML-based type model definitions that can be used to generate DDL (Data Definition Language) and files that contain C++ definitions that can perform OCI (Oracle Call Interface) calls to access the object tables. When you generate DDL from the type model definitions, the generator actually creates a temporary server model, as illustrated in Figure 5-14. This server model is defined based on the type model definitions. This model is *not* saved in the repository.

The most useful piece is probably the *capability to create object types and object views based on your existing relational tables.* This can be done by running the following two operations under the Utilities menu item:

1. **Create Oracle object types.** You need to run the Create Oracle Object Type operation. You select from the relational table definitions that exist, as shown in Figure 5-15.

   You can stop here or you can continue if you want object views.

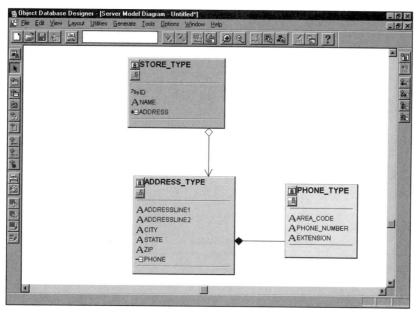

Figure 5-13: The Toy Store model now has an object-oriented twist.

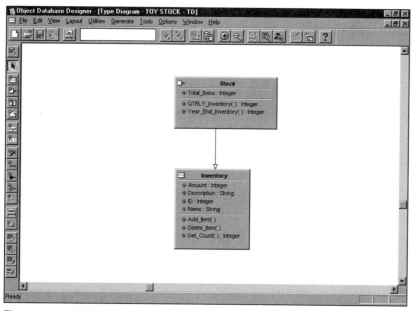

Figure 5-14: UML type model can be used to generate Oracle8 object DDL.

2. **Create object views.** You need to run the Create Object View operation. The selection will contain only object types that are mapped to source tables, as shown in Figure 5-16.

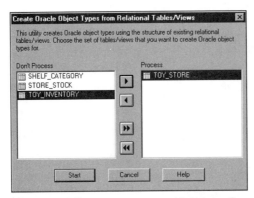

Figure 5-15: Create one or more object types from relational tables.

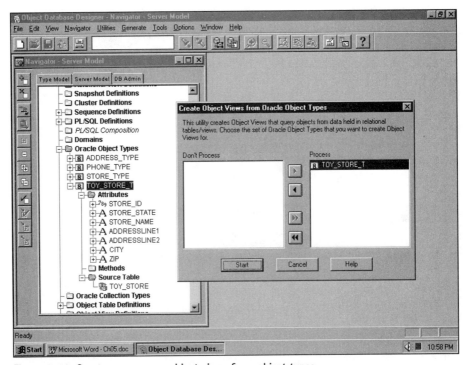

Figure 5-16: Create one or more object views from object types.

The view will also have a row-level trigger created to interface with the relational tables correctly. The following is example code that is generated.

```
DECLARE
  i Number;
BEGIN
INSERT INTO toy_store VALUES (
  :NEW.store_id
, :NEW.store_state
, :NEW.store_name
, :NEW.addressline1
, :NEW.addressline2
, :NEW.city
, :NEW.zip
);
END;
```

For those of you who want to access your object tables with Forms and Reports, you are going to have to do some additional work—especially for those object tables such as our store object with referenced addresses that have embedded phone numbers. You will have to create relational tables or views that reference the object types.

Another way to use object tables inside forms is to use the new procedure-based data blocks. See Chapter 12 for a complete description of how to do this.

Summary

Release 2 of Oracle Designer is much more robust in functionality than its predecessors. Those who used the older version first will have preferences for using that tool. Having used the previous tool, I think that all of the new enhancements and features far outweigh the things that I don't like. And most of the things I don't like are really because they are different.

My advice is to learn to be persistent with the help. There is actually quite a bit of good information available there. But as I have seen in the past with the help provided with Oracle's development tools, it takes a little work to actually find everything that is available. The best help is found in the easy-to-read steps on how to do things.

The more you use the tool, the slower it may get. This is because it is based on the cost-based optimizer. *Use the Repository Administration utility to rebuild statistics frequently as well as updating hash tables and indexes.* With all of the new stuff in there, you cannot afford to be slow when it's avoidable.

Finally, with all of the new features, you will need to add much more planning and thought to your CASE projects. Good luck, friends.

The next chapter covers the new Web Server Generator that is a part of the Web Application Server.

Chapter 6

WebServer Generator and WebForms

IN THIS CHAPTER

◆ Understanding the Web Application Server

◆ Creating WebServer modules in Designer

◆ Running WebServer modules

◆ Considering your options when you convert from the client/server model to the Web

THE WEBSERVER GENERATOR is a Designer generator that can generate Web modules in PL/SQL for the Web Application Server. This is not to be confused with WebForms. The WebServer modules use the PL/SQL cartridge of the Web Application Server and are strictly HTML (and JavaScript) based.

To be able to run WebServer modules, you must install a Web Application Server in your environment. The following section will briefly introduce the main concepts of the Web Application Server.

The next section describes how to make simple and advanced WebServer modules with the Designer WebServer Generator.

The last section of this chapter describes some important considerations when Web-enabling your client/server (forms and reports) applications.

A Look Ahead

As this book is being written, a new release of Oracle — Oracle8i — is on the horizon. This release is expected to include a new Web development kit that Java programmers can use. The development kit will provide a suite of tools that will help you create Web database pages.

Modelers and generators for WebDB (the application tool that is bundled with Oracle8i) will most probably not become a part of Designer until the next major release in 1999.

The Concepts of the Web Application Server

This section provides a brief introduction to the core concepts of the Web Application Server.

Listeners

The *listeners* are the front end of the Web Application Server. Each listener is listening for Web requests from clients (browsers) on a given port.

All Web servers need a listener (not only the Oracle Web Application Server). Listeners determine the nature of incoming requests and dispatch them to the appropriate services. HTML and CGI requests are dispatched by the listeners themselves, while other request types are handed to the Web Request Broker.

The Web Request Broker

The *Web Request Broker* is an Oracle-specific element (but it is not Designer specific). It handles the overall execution of the system. It allocates and invokes cartridges to handle the incoming requests.

Client requests are broken down into the following objects:

```
http://<server name>.<domain name>/<dad name>/<agent name> /<module
name>?<parameters>
```

For example, the following text might be typed into the client browser's location window to call the application named toystore_w.

```
http://nne14.novo.com/des/plsql/toystore_w$.startup
```

Database Access Descriptors

DADs are Oracle-specific elements. They enable you to define a set of environmental values to be used when executing a client request.

One of the important settings of the DAD is the Oracle account and connect string to be used when accessing the database. When setting these values, you also decide if the Oracle account should be predefined or if the client should be prompted for the username and password to be used.

Cartridges/agents

The *cartridges* are the server applications that execute the actual requests made to them. The Web Application Server comes with a number of cartridges but third-party vendors also offer cartridges.

The WebServer Generator generates code specifically for the PL/SQL cartridge, which can execute PL/SQL code contained in functions and procedures within a database.

Other cartridges are:

◆ Java cartridge – For running Java applications

◆ LiveHTML cartridge – Handles SSI (server side include)

◆ ODBC cartridge – For connecting to ODBC databases

The htf, htp, and owa packages

The `htf` package contains functions for basic HTML tagging. For example, here is the function call to apply a bold font to a word:

```
htf.bold('Important')
```

The string returned is:

```
'<b>Important</b>'
```

The `htp` package corresponds to the `htf` package except that all PL/SQL routines are procedures instead of functions. The `htp` procedures generate the same output as the `htf` functions, but they send their output to the client browser instead of returning it as function output.

The `owa` packages are more advanced PL/SQL tools that can perform complex Web-related processes such as handling cookies, security, and data formatting (for example, calendar output).

All of these packages come with the PL/SQL cartridge of the Web Application Server and can be used by your own PL/SQL Web applications without Designer.

The wsgl library

The `wsgl` library is specific to the WebServer Generator of Designer. It contains the skeleton routines for generating the HTML pages of your Designer modules.

The `wsgl` library corresponds to the template and the object library used by the Forms Generator.

Even though it is not recommended by Oracle, making changes to the `wsgl` library is supported. The following example shows the changes you can make to the `wsgl` library to turn the asterisk (*) and underscore (_) characters into wildcards such as the percent sign (%) and question mark (?) characters on all query screens generated by the WebServer Generator.

Locate the `wsgl.pkb` file in the `oracle_home\cgenw20\cvwetc` directory. Find this bit of code within the BuildWhere procedure of the `wsgl` package:

```
    elsif (instr(l_field1, '%') != 0) or
(instr(l_field1,'_') !=0) then
```

and replace it with:

```
    elsif (instr(l_field1, '%') != 0) or
(instr(l_field1, '?') != 0) or (instr(l_field1,'*')
!=0) or (instr(l_field1,'_') !=0) then
        l_field1:= replace(l_field1,'*','%');
        l_field1:= replace(l_field1,'?','_');
```

Because the wsgl library is similar to a template for the WebServer Generator, all Web modules generated on this altered wsgl package handle asterisk (*) and question mark (?) characters as if they were the percent (%) and underscore (_) Oracle wildcards.

TIP Changes made to the wsgl library take effect as soon as you recreate the wsgl package. You do not have to recreate the individual Web modules.

Generating Web Modules

The design of Web modules is very similar to the design of forms modules. You build the module by defining module components containing table usages and column usages.

Web module design

The most interesting differences between the two types of module design will be covered in the following sections.

As can be seen in the following sections, the basic structure of Web modules has not changed much since Designer release 1.3.2. However, the following features make the WebServer Generator a stronger tool in Designer release 2.1:

◆ Templates

◆ More preferences

◆ New module design features

Table API

All table access through Web modules uses the table API. Therefore, you must generate and install a table API for each base table used in your Web modules.

Generation and installation of table APIs is done from the Server Model tab of the Design Editor. Select the tables for which you want to generate the API, and select Generate → Generate Table API from the menu. The table API generator generates a package specification file (.pks), a package body file (.pkb), and a trigger file (.trg) for each of the selected tables. To execute all the generated files, run the table API installation script (the default name is FP_.sql).

A table API does not need to be generated each time the module is generated but only when the underlying table is altered (such as when you add or deleted columns, change constraints, and so on).

After generating the table API, you can install the Web module packages.

Web module packages

The output of the WebServer Generator is not .FMB and .FMX files but PL/SQL packages.

The WebServer Generator generates one package for the module. The package name is formatted like this:

```
modulename$
```

Replace *modulename* with the actual module you are calling.

In addition, the WebServer Generator generates one package for each module component within the module with this naming convention:

```
modulename$componentname
```

Replace *componentname* with the actual module component you are calling.

These packages must be installed in a schema with access to the PL/SQL cartridge packages (htp, htf, owa, wsgl, and so on).

Both generation and installation of the WebServer modules are handled using the Generate WebServer dialog box. Using the Options tab on the Generate WebServer dialog box, you can set the package installation to be done automatically after generation of the Web module packages.

Web module structure

Web modules are built around a predefined structure using the elements described in the following sections. Some of these elements can be skipped depending on module settings and preference settings. Not counting skipped elements, the module structure is fairly fixed. All modules more or less follow the same structure.

The modules can be generated using frames or not using frames, and templates can be defined for each of the elements described in the following sections. Figure 6-1 shows how the elements relate to one another.

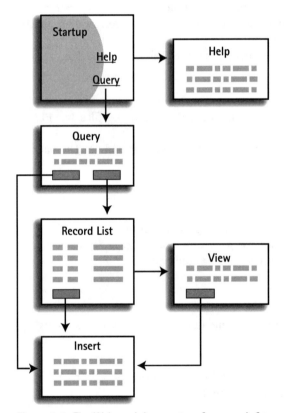

Figure 6-1: The Web modules create a framework for your application.

STARTUP PAGE

Each module contains one startup page. The startup page is the first page of the module. It is used to introduce the module.

To access the startup page of a module, call the procedure named:

```
modulename$.Startup
```

Replace *modulename* with the actual module you are calling. Startup is the standard name that is always used in generated WebServer modules.

ABOUT PAGE

Each module can contain one about page. It is accessed through a hyperlink on the start page.

The about page contains version information about the module and can be used to show module level user and/or help text.

 User help text is discussed in more detail later in this chapter.

The about page is included in the module depending on the MODALR preference. (You can find this preference in the Startup Page group of the WebServer Generator preferences.)

QUERY FORM

Each module component within the module has a query form if at least one of the module component's display items has its query property set to Yes.

This screen enables the user to define a query criteria to restrict the number of rows to work on. The query form is placed below the startup page. The record list is opened when the Find button is clicked. See the following section called "Record List."

If one of the items of the module component has the insert property set to Yes, a hyperlink that accesses the insert form is placed at the bottom of the query form (see the "Insert form" section on the next page).

RECORD LIST

Each module component contains a record list showing a set of records for that module component. Each record is composed of one or more items identifying the record. The first column of the record list is a hyperlink to the "View form" section following this section.

If one of the items of the module component has the insert property set to Yes, a hyperlink is placed at the bottom of the record list to access the insert form (see the "Insert form" section on the next page.

VIEW FORM

The view form shows the entire content of a single record. This form is also used to update and delete records (should these properties have been set).

If one of the items of the module component has the insert property set to Yes, an Insert button is placed at the bottom of the record list to access the insert form (see the next section).

INSERT FORM

The last element that can be included in a Web module structure is the insert form. The insert form lets you insert new records for the module component.

If one of the items of the module component has the insert property set to Yes, an insert form will be accessible from the query form, record list, and the view form.

Menu structure

You can specify menu structures for Web modules in the same way you specify forms modules.

Note that menu security is not implemented on Web modules. This means that all menu items are shown to all users.

The Web browser menu cannot be controlled by HTML. Instead, Web module menus are implemented as lists of text item links. The startup page of each module contains a list of links to all modules that can be called from that module, as shown in Figure 6-2.

When a user clicks on one of the menu item links, the module related to that link is started up.

The text shown on the menu item list is taken from the top title or short title (if the top title is not set) of the underlying modules. If neither are set, the menu item list is made using the module short name.

Generating User Help

This section, which covers user help text, will be rather detailed and will include code examples. It will cover help text generation, PL/SQL coding (including the usage of the `htp`, `htf`, and `wsgl` packages), and HTML coding. The "Including JavaScript" section found later in the chapter covers JavaScript coding of user help for Web modules. We will also cover an alternate way to generate user help text that resembles help generated by the Forms Generator more closely than the user help native to the WebServer Generator.

Menu items

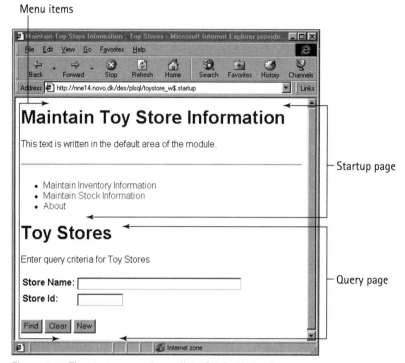

Figure 6-2: The startup page has a list of links that act as a menu.

Native user help in Web modules versus forms help and MS help

As with menu generation, user help generation is different on the Web modules from what we know when generating forms applications. Web browsers cannot show MS help files from a server to a client, and HTML cannot control the F1 key of the client machine.

You can still specify the user help text within your Web modules, but the WebServer Generator will include the text directly on the module screens instead of hiding it until it is called for.

If text is added to the user help text property of the module, the entered text is shown at the top of the related Web module screen, as you see in Figure 6-3.

As a supplement to the forms design type user help text, the Web design user help text property enables different positioning of different segments of the user help text. The easiest way to get access to these positioning features is through the Edit Module Component dialog shown in Figure 6-4. The property dialogs are accessed by selecting Options → Use Property Dialogs on the Design Editor menu.

Figure 6-3: The user help text is displayed near the top of the Web page.

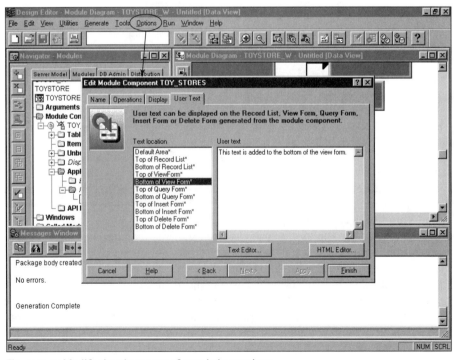

Figure 6-4: Modify the placement of user help text here.

Figure 6-5 shows how user help text can be displayed in various places on your modules. The figure shows the record list module.

Figure 6-5: This module has user help text in three locations.

 TIP Even though the Edit Module Component dialog shows multiple text areas for the different positions, these texts are actually all placed within the user help text property. This is handled by using different headers for the different user help text positions (as shown in Figure 6-6). These headers can be used directly within the user help text property. Thus, you do not have to use the Edit Module Component dialog to do this.

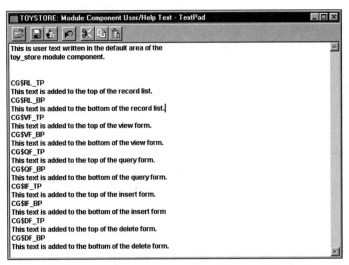

Figure 6-6: For convenience, you can edit all the user help text at one time.

A parallel set of user help text positioning features is implemented on the Edit Module Component dialog.

Alternative user help in Web modules

If your user help text does not fit on the related page, you can choose to implement your user help text on a separate screen. Two methods for doing so are:

◆ **Use the About screen.** For module-level text, this can be done using the About screen.

◆ **Use help button items.** For module component, table, column, or domain-level text help screens must be done through an unbound help button item that calls a procedure that shows the user help text on a new screen.

Another benefit of implementing the help button alternate help system is that doing so makes it possible to make a generator for a paper help document from the same source that is used for generating help screens.

The following sections describe how to implement such a simple user help text procedure generically as well as describing how to implement a Designer repository-driven user help text procedure. The help utility described in the following sections can be expanded to become more inclusive than what is described. Some extension possibilities are mentioned where relevant.

Place user/help text in the repository

The first thing to do is to decide where to place these new user help texts. We cannot use the user help text property because it would result in showing all the text on the Web module screen. I recommend that you use the description property for the following reasons:

- The contents of the description property are never generated into any end-user screen.

- The only multiline properties notes and description are available from any Web module element.

- It seems to me that the user help text is closely related to the description text.

Place the user help text at the bottom of the description property to get it somewhat out of the way.

Define a heading that you can use to specify where the user help text begins within the description property (it could be USER_HELP$TEXT).

TIP You could make up more headers such as USER_HELP$KEYWORDS or USER_HELP$LINKS to be able to implement a more advanced help utility.

Figure 6-7 shows an example of creating the headers in the module description area.

ON THE CD Example code shown in this chapter is available on the CD-ROM at the back of the book.

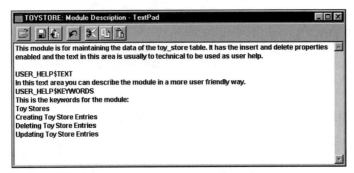

Figure 6-7: Define help headers in the module description area.

The next step is to retrieve this data from the module description, as described in the next section.

Extract user/help text from the repository

Now we got all our user help texts placed within the Designer repository. To be able to access it in a production environment, we need to extract the information into a reference code table such as the ones made by Designer. If you want to make your user help text utility a little advanced, you need at least two reference tables. One version of such a set of reference tables might look like this:

```
/* —-- make/User_help.sql —— */
PROMPT Creating Table 'USER_HELP'
CREATE TABLE USER_HELP
 (HELP_REF NUMBER(38) NOT NULL
 ,MODULE_NAME VARCHAR2(20)
 ,MODULE_COMPONENT_NAME VARCHAR2(50)
 ,TABLE_NAME VARCHAR2(50)
 ,COLUMN_NAME VARCHAR2(50)
 ,KEYWORDS VARCHAR2(2000)
 )
/
PROMPT Creating Table 'USER_HELP_TEXT'
CREATE TABLE USER_HELP_TEXT
 (HELP_REF NUMBER(38) NOT NULL
 ,SEQ NUMBER(10,0) NOT NULL
 ,TEXT_LINE VARCHAR2(2000)
 )
/
PROMPT Creating Primary Key on 'USER_HELP'
ALTER TABLE USER_HELP
```

```
ADD CONSTRAINT USER_HELP_PK PRIMARY KEY
  (HELP_REF)
/
PROMPT Creating Primary Key on 'USER_HELP_TEXT'
ALTER TABLE USER_HELP_TEXT
 ADD CONSTRAINT USER_HELP_TEXT_PK PRIMARY KEY
  (HELP_REF
  ,SEQ)
/
PROMPT Creating Foreign Keys on 'USER_HELP_TEXT'
ALTER TABLE USER_HELP_TEXT ADD CONSTRAINT
 USER_HELP_TEX_USER_HELP_FK FOREIGN KEY
  (HELP_REF) REFERENCES USER_HELP
  (HELP_REF) ON DELETE CASCADE
/
```

The program to extract the user help text from the repository could look like the following. (Be aware that this procedure does not handle user help texts of a single type that wrap over multiple 2,000-character fields in CDI_TEXT.)

```
/* —— plsql/cdsddl.pks ——- */
— cdsddl.pks
—
— Generated for Oracle 8 on Tue Aug 18  04:48:01 1998 by Server
Generator 2.1.19.5.0

PROMPT Creating Package 'HELPPACK'
CREATE OR REPLACE PACKAGE HELPPACK IS
— Sub-Program Unit Declarations
PROCEDURE extract_help
 (P_APPSYS IN VARCHAR2
 );

END HELPPACK;
/
— cdsddl.pkb
—
— Generated for Oracle 8 on Tue Aug 18  04:48:02 1998 by Server
Generator 2.1.19.5.0

PROMPT Creating Package Body 'HELPPACK'
CREATE OR REPLACE PACKAGE BODY HELPPACK IS
cursor modules(v_app in number) is
  select id, application_system_owned_by, short_name from ci_modules
```

```
  where application_system_owned_by = v_app;

cursor module_components(v_app in number) is
  select id, application_system_owned_by, name from
ci_module_components
  where application_system_owned_by = v_app;

cursor texts(ref number) is
  select txt_seq, txt_text
  from cdi_text
  where
    txt_ref = ref and
    txt_type = 'CDIDSC';— Program Data
/* The prefix of user help text headers */
V_TYPE_PREFIX VARCHAR2(240) := 'USER_HELP$';

— Sub-Program Unit Declarations
FUNCTION get_text
 (P_TEXT IN VARCHAR2
 ,P_TYPE IN VARCHAR2
 )
 RETURN VARCHAR2;

— Sub-Program Units
FUNCTION get_text
 (P_TEXT IN VARCHAR2
 ,P_TYPE IN VARCHAR2
 )
 RETURN VARCHAR2
 IS
— Program Data
/* The description text of p_text matching the p_type header */
V_TEXT VARCHAR2(2000);
/* Start position of matching text */
V_START NUMBER(4, 0);
/* End position of matching text */
V_END NUMBER(4, 0);

— PL/SQL Block
BEGIN
v_text:=p_text;
    v_start:= instr(v_text,v_type_prefix||p_type);
    if v_start > 0
    then
```

```
        v_start:= v_start + length(v_type_prefix||p_type)+1;
        v_text:= substr(v_text,v_start,2000);
        v_end:= instr(v_text,v_type_prefix)-2;
        if v_end = -2 then v_end:= 2000; end if;
        v_text:= substr(v_text,1,v_end-1);
        return v_text;
     else
        return null;
     end if;
END get_text;

PROCEDURE extract_help
 (P_APPSYS IN VARCHAR2
 )
 IS
— Program Data
/* Application system to extract */
V_APP NUMBER(38);
/* Text to be stored in help table */
V_TEXT VARCHAR2(2000);

— PL/SQL Block
BEGIN
SELECT id INTO v_app
  FROM ci_application_systems
  WHERE name = p_appsys;

DELETE FROM user_help_text
WHERE
EXISTS (SELECT 1 FROM USER_HELP
WHERE user_help_text.help_ref = user_help.help_ref AND appsys =
v_app);
DELETE FROM user_help
WHERE appsys = v_app;

FOR m IN modules(v_app) LOOP
  INSERT INTO user_help (
    HELP_REF,
    APPSYS,
    MODULE_NAME)
  VALUES (
    m.id,
    m.application_system_owned_by,
    m.short_name);
```

```
FOR t IN texts(m.id) LOOP
  v_text:=get_text(t.txt_text,'TEXT');
  IF v_text IS NOT NULL
  THEN
    INSERT INTO user_help_text (
      HELP_REF,
      SEQ,
      TEXT_LINE)
    VALUES (
      m.id,
      t.txt_seq,
      v_text);
  END IF;
  v_text:=get_text(t.txt_text,'KEYWORDS');
  IF v_text IS NOT NULL
  THEN
    UPDATE user_help
    SET keywords = v_text
    WHERE help_ref = m.id;
  END IF;
END LOOP;

END LOOP;

FOR c IN module_components(v_app) LOOP
  INSERT INTO user_help (
    HELP_REF,
    APPSYS,
    MODULE_COMPONENT_NAME)
  VALUES (
    c.id,
    c.application_system_owned_by,
      c.name);

  FOR t IN texts(c.id) LOOP
    v_text:=get_text(t.txt_text,'TEXT');
    IF v_text IS NOT NULL
    THEN
      INSERT INTO user_help_text (
        HELP_REF,
        SEQ,
        TEXT_LINE)
      VALUES (
```

```
        c.id,
        t.txt_seq,
        v_text);
    END IF;
    v_text:=get_text(t.txt_text,'KEYWORDS');
    IF v_text IS NOT NULL
    THEN
      UPDATE user_help
      SET keywords = v_text
      WHERE help_ref = c.id;
    END IF;
  END LOOP;

END LOOP;
END extract_help;

- PL/SQL Block

END HELPPACK;
/
```

TIP You could easily extend the tables and code to handle user help text on the application-system level, column-usage level, domain level, problems level, and so on.

The next step is a procedure that calls the package from within your Web modules.

Make showhelp procedure

Now we just need to present the user help text in your Web modules. Using the wsgl and htp packages makes this a straightforward operation.

```
PROCEDURE SHOWHELP
 (P_APPSYS IN USER_HELP.APPSYS%TYPE
 ,P_MODULE IN USER_HELP.MODULE_NAME%TYPE default null
 ,P_MODULE_COMPONENT default null
USER_HELP.MODULE_COMPONENT_NAME%TYPE default null
 ,P_COLUMN IN USER_HELP.COLUMN_NAME%TYPE default null
 )
 IS
- PL/SQL Block
```

```
BEGIN
 wsgl.OpenPageHead('Help Screen');
 wsgl.ClosePageHead;
 wsgl.OpenPageBody(NULL);
 wsgl.DefaultPageCaption(NULL);
 FOR texts IN (
  SELECT text_line
  FROM user_help h, user_help_text t
  WHERE
  h.help_ref = t.help_ref AND
  p_appsys = h.appsys AND
  (p_module IS NULL OR p_module = h.module_name) AND
  (p_module_component IS NULL OR p_module_component =
h.module_component_name) AND
  (p_column IS NULL OR p_column = h.column_name)
  ORDER BY t.seq)
 LOOP
  htp.p(texts.text_line);
 END LOOP;
 wsgl.ClosePageBody;
END SHOWHELP;
```

This simple solution can be extended in many ways:

1. You could include the module, module component, column title in the USER_HELP table so that it can be displayed on the help screen.

2. You can do a lot with the layout, using frames, fonts, JavaScript, added HTML tags, graphics, and so on, instead of just using a simple htp.p call.

3. You can add code to display table user help text on module components with no user help text defined. (You can also add code to column text when missing detailed column usage text.)

4. You can add a utility to search the entire user help text table.

We are coming to the final step in our customized help utility.

Call help procedure

The last thing to do is to call the ShowHelp procedure from within your Web applications, which is demonstrated in the next section.

Calling PL/SQL Procedures from the Web

To call a PL/SQL procedure from the Web at run time, you need to translate the PL/SQL call to the HTTP format.

The actual call to your ShowHelp procedure looks something like this:

```
HelpPack.ShowHelp('TOYSTORE','MAINSCREEN','TOY STORES');
```

The corresponding HTTP call method looks like this (except it is one long line, rather than two lines of text):

```
HelpPack.ShowHelp?p_appsys='TOYSTORE'&p_module=
'MAINSCREEN'&p_module_component='TOY STORES'
```

Note the syntax of HTTP calls:

- The parameter list begins with a question mark (?) character.

- The parameters are separated by an ampersand (&) character.

- The parameter names are included in the call.

If you had implemented user help text on the application system level, the call would look like this:

```
HelpPack.ShowHelp('TOYSTORE');
```

HTTP call method:

```
HelpPack.ShowHelp?p_appsys='TOYSTORE'
```

Where do you place this call in Designer to have it included in your applications? You have three choices, only two of which function at this time:

- **Unbound button items.** You cannot generate buttons as unbound items in Web modules (as you can in forms and Visual Basic). It seems, though, that Oracle plans to remove this restriction in a future version of Designer.

- **Hyperlink.** This is the simplest implementation method.

- **Submit button.** This is a more advanced method.

Hyperlink to call help

The hyperlink can be made as an unbound item of URL format or by using the user help text property. In version 1.3.2 of Designer, the hyperlink could also be made as a module network link to a PL/SQL module (however, this method does not seem to work anymore). When using the user help text property, you can place help links at the top and bottom of the different screens. When using the unbound item, you can place help links in between the other items of the view form.

To implement a hyperlink to your help screen using the unbound item method, just create an unbound item with the following properties:

```
        Name = Any_name
        Unbound Type = Server Side Function
        Display Type = Text
        Derivation Text = '<A HREF="http_call_method"
TARGET="_NEW">Show Help</A>'
```

For example, to call the help screen for the Toy Store module, define the unbound item as follows:

```
Name = gotohelp
Unbound Type = Server Side Function
Display Type = Text
Derivation Text =
'<A HREF=" HelpPack.ShowHelp?p_appsys='TOYSTORE'"
TARGET="_NEW">Show Help</A>'
```

Figure 6-8 shows how the hyperlink looks on the main page and what the help window looks like when the link is clicked.

Note that the TARGET="_NEW" property makes the help pop up in a new window.

TIP   If you want to use the user help text property instead of the module definition text, just add the following line to the appropriate user help text position:

```
<a href="<HTTP call method>">Show Help</a>
```

Figure 6-8: A customized help window adds user-friendly help text to your pages.

 To be able to apply HTML through the user help text property, you must set the MODSUB preference to No (choose WebServer Generator → Text Handling → Substitute HTML Reserved Characters).

Button help

The following code can be used to generate a button instead of a hyperlink. Make a very small HTML form (only with a Submit button) that shows the appropriate help text:

```
<form
  name=ShowHelp
  method=post
  onsubmit= document.showhelp.action=
'helppack.showhelp?p_appsys=1&p_module=TOYSTORE_W'
  target="_new"
>
<input
  type=submit
```

```
name=Help
value="Show Help"
>
</form>
```

This code can be placed in the user help text property or sent using `htp.p` from a PL/SQL package.

The button will look like the Show Help button in Figure 6-9.

Figure 6-9: The Show Help button is a small HTML form embedded in your module page.

The next section covers the technique of using JavaScript in Designer.

Including JavaScript

This section is not a complete JavaScript course, but it will show you how to use JavaScript with Designer.

Before you actually start coding in JavaScript, you might need to read some more specific literature on the subject, such as *JavaScript Bible,* 3rd Edition, by Danny Goodman, published by IDG Books Worldwide.

What does JavaScript look like?

JavaScript is a scripting language like C that can perform assignments, function calls, loops, and so on. The following is a simple example of a function definition:

```
<script language="JavaScript">
function MakeHelpURL (p_appsys, p_module, p_module_component)
{
  u ="HELPPACK.Show_Help?p_appsys="+p_appsys;
  if (p_module != "")
  { u = u + "&p_module="+p_module; }
  if (p_module_component != "")
  { u = u + "&p_module_component="+p_module_component; }
  return u;
}
</script>
```

As you can see, you do not need to declare your variables; they attain the type of the value assigned to them.

All JavaScript program units are functions, but they can be invoked as both functions (as expressions) and procedures (as commands). If you invoke a JavaScript function as an expression, you must make sure that it returns a value.

A simple example of how you would call this function as an expression is a function that starts a Web page named TOYSTORE_W:

```
<script language="JavaScript">
document.writeln(MakeHelpURL(1,"TOYSTORE_W",""));
</script>
```

Note that you need the <script> tag, both when making definitions and when invoking them. You can have more than one <script> tag in an HTML page.

The "document.writeln" method used in the preceding example refers to an output method of the HTML page object. Many built-in methods and properties are assigned to HTML objects that can be referenced from JavaScript. You can look them up in a JavaScript manual.

To elaborate, we could change the previous form definition (for making a Submit button) so that it uses the MakeHelpURL function. (Doing so makes it easier to implement the individual help Submit buttons of your applications because you can use the JavaScript syntax when calling MakeHelpURL instead of the much longer HTTP syntax.) Here's the previous form definition changed so that it uses the MakeHelpURL function:

```
<form
  name=ShowHelp
  method=post
  onsubmit=document.ShowHelp.action=MakeHelpURL(1,"TOYSTORE_W","")
  target="_new"
>
<input
  type=submit
  name=Help
  value="Show Help"
>
</form>
```

Note that when invoking JavaScript functions from within a tag, you do not need the <script> tag.

Be aware that the names are case sensitive, which means that "MakeHelpURL" is not the same as "makehelpurl."

You can add JavaScript code to your Web modules the following three ways:

1. Building PL/SQL procedures that output JavaScript code

2. Defining events or named routines in Designer

3. Generating it through the user help text properties or the derivation expression properties

These three methods will be described in the following sections.

Building PL/SQL procedures

This method should be used for complex and/or reusable programs and/or components. When using PL/SQL procedures, the code is usually called as independent routines operating on their own page.

To build PL/SQL procedures, just follow the same method used in the ShowHelp procedure (see the section "Make Help Procedure," earlier in this chapter). It's essential to use the wsgl procedures to open and close the generated HTML page heads and bodies and whatever else you want the modules to do. Use the htp procedures to send data to the browser.

Defining events or named routines

If you need to make module-specific code, you could define your JavaScript code using the event or named routine objects.

The named routine object of the JavaScript language is only applicable to module components. These named routines are placed as definitions in the page head of the specified page (between the <head> and </head> tags).

JavaScript placed in the page head is not executed automatically. It is interpreted as a definition and is not executed before it is invoked by some code within the page body.

Generating JavaScript through the user help text properties or as derivation expressions

Any JavaScript definitions made in the user help text or using the derivation expression property are placed in the page body (between the <body> and </body> tags).

JavaScript placed within the page body is executed when it is encountered by the browser. Function definitions are defined when they are encountered in the page body. They are not executed automatically.

It could be an advantage to implement the code as a PL/SQL function that returned the JavaScript code as a string, and then include it in the user help text or derivation expression. By doing this, you have the advantage of being able to reuse your code within many modules, module components, detailed column usages, unbound items, and so on.

Including Applets

Java applets are small applications (often graphical) that can be placed on the WebServer and executed by the browser. From the Internet, you can download free Java applets that do all sorts of things such as displaying values using graphics, showing scrolling text, and so on.

The method for including Java applets is similar to the one just described to include JavaScript.

Instead of using the <script> tags, you use the <applet> tags like this:

```
<applet>
  codebase="codebasename"
  code="codename"
  width="widthno"
  height="heightno"
>
<param name="param1name" value="param1value">
<param name="param2name" value="param2value">

</applet>
```

The variables in the command are defined as follows:

♦ *codebasename* is the virtual path to where the Java applet is located on the Web server.

♦ *codename* is the name of the Java applet.

♦ *widthno* is the width allocated for the Java applet (which is relevant only for graphical applets).

♦ *heightno* is the height allocated for the Java applet (which is relevant only for graphical applets).

♦ *paramXname* is the name of the Xth parameter.

♦ *paramXvalue* is the value of the Xth parameter.

You can use Java applets to display your database values in graphical ways as colored bars and so forth.

Java applets can be downloaded from the Web (some are free and some must be paid for), or you can code them yourself.

Web-Enabling Client/Server Applications

FMX files generated by Oracle Forms version 5.0 can be executed both as:

♦ Client/server applications using the runform command

♦ WebForms through a Web browser using the Forms Server

Even though the FMX files are executable on both platforms without any recompilation, you must be aware of and handle the following issues before Web enabling your client/server forms.

Problem areas when moving from client/server to WebForms

♦ *ICO to GIF conversion.* Icon files cannot be viewed through a Web browser. You have to convert all your ICO files to GIF files. A number of conversion programs are on the Internet that can do ICO-to-GIF conversion, such as:

www.tucows.com

If your converted icons do not look correct, you probably need to move the graphic to the center of the picture (small icons are placed in the top left corner of the picture).

◆ *No MDI window.* If you have toolbars or console output assigned to the MDI window, these items are not shown when running Forms through a browser. This is because the concept of an MDI window is not implemented in the Web environment. When assigning the toolbar to another window, make sure that the window is big enough to show the toolbar.

If a module contains multiple windows and only the first window shows the toolbar, strange behavior results when accessing the toolbar from other windows. (For example, the window containing the toolbar will be sent to the front, and the window you were working on might disappear from view.) You could try to use a separate window specifically for the toolbar alone.

◆ *No backslash (\).* The backslash character is currently not accessible through the browser. You can copy and paste the backslash character using Ctrl+C and Ctrl+V, but the backslash key does not produce a backslash character. Oracle is currently working on a solution for this problem.

◆ *Problems with parameter forms for reports.* The built-in parameter forms of reports cannot be showed through the Web browser when using run_product, show_document, or run_report_object to invoke a report. Until the bug is fixed, you must use the Web cartridge or CGI to start reports that contain a parameter form.

◆ *No Microsoft objects.* You cannot display objects of some types through the Web browser: MS help, ActiveX, OCX, OLE, and VBX. These objects are shown on the server where they are not visible to the user.

◆ *Missing triggers.* The When-Mouse-Enter/Move/Leave triggers are not fired when the form is executed through the Forms Server.

◆ *Browser plug-in.* Because Web browser vendors do not support all the Java code generated by the Oracle WebServers, you need a Java plug-in called the Initiator. The Initiator plug-in must be installed on all browsers. This can be set up so that the plug-in is downloaded to the user if he or she does not already have it. The Initiator plug-in is still in beta but should soon be available in production.

◆ *System variables.* The system variables (on NT and Windows 95 usually read from the registry) are read by the Forms Server and not from the client machine. This means that the client machines cannot be set up individually. For example, one client machine wants the LOCAL system variable set to something specific. This is possible when running forms with runform but not when running WebForms.

Summary

Web forms perform surprisingly well, but problem areas still are too significant to rely entirely on WebForms and WebReports instead of the client/server versions. Some screens and reports probably work on the Web, but the most interesting aspect of going to the Web is that you no longer have to support local client/server installations. If you have to support both the Web and local client/server installations, you haven't saved much money for your company. (On the contrary, you are spending extra money buying the Forms Server and Reports Server.)

Should you decide to go with the Forms Server and Reports Server, do not underestimate the lengths you have to go to make it work.

If you have based your development on MS help, you'll have to do a lot of work to get similar functionality using forms help instead.

The same goes for any other operating system–specific objects (such as VBX, OCX, ActiveX, and so on). The functionality of these must be recoded.

If you have placed toolbars of your applications in the MDI window (which most of us have), you may have to change all your forms manually to make the toolbars behave in an acceptable way.

And finally, make sure that the problems concerning beta release browser plug-ins, parameter forms, and backslashes have been fixed.

Chapter 7

Making User-Friendly GUIs

IN THIS CHAPTER

- ◆ Setting standards for GUI design
- ◆ Constructing help messages that really help
- ◆ Creating good visual design without postgeneration changes
- ◆ Using the Repository to create help messages in forms
- ◆ Generating documentation using the Repository

THIS CHAPTER WILL DESCRIBE the whys and hows of making user-friendly GUI interfaces using the Designer generators. It will show that even with the restrictions of the Designer generators, it is possible (and important) to make user-friendly interfaces.

Making user-friendly GUI interfaces is not so much about making loads of animated graphics and spacey controls but rather to *assure the best communication between the user and the application.*

Why Should We Be User Friendly?

First of all we need to understand why we should make user-friendly applications. What is in it for us? If the application does the job, why should we bother adding more resources to make it user friendly? Well, there are a number of good reasons.

Because we must

Actually, user-friendly interfaces are increasingly demanded. Users expect applications to be user friendly and are less and less likely to accept the same kinds of applications that they did only five years ago. The increasing exposure of people to the World Wide Web, with its simple, user-friendly navigation, has probably contributed to this expectation.

Because it is cheaper

The easier it is to use your applications, the less support you have to provide. A small company can offer hot-line support on an application sold to a large number of users if the application is easy to use. If your applications are too hard to understand, you will be swamped with support calls.

In addition, the company buying the application saves money if your application has a low learning curve. The more end-users that will use your application, the higher the interest in a low learning curve. The optimal solution is that users can use your application without any training.

 Expending resources on user testing should not be considered an extra expense. Problem areas found during user testing have to be fixed at some point anyway. You might as well get it right before releasing the application than after.

Users become more productive

When users feel confident about the tools they are using, they are more motivated and are able to manage more problems.

 Applications that do not require special training can be used by people from different work areas. It increases the quality of the data entered into the system when people from all work areas understand the applications and work together.

Setting Your GUI Standards

Setting standards helps you to implement consistent applications. It is a great help to end-users when all their applications look and function in similar ways. Users who already have learned to use one application find it easier and faster to learn to use a new application. The same argument goes for the different screens within the same application. If screens look and feel the same, less training is necessary.

Setting standards is one of the strong points of Designer because the generators automatically follow a consistent standard. Through templates, preferences, libraries, domains. and so on, you can define the standard within the tool and generate all your applications under the same standard.

The tool still enables you to change the standards for any item, so you must be conscious about how you use (or misuse) this freedom. Remember that a consistent look and feel still can be of higher value than some fancy (but inconsistent) features.

You can define your own standard or use one of many existing standards (such as ISO, Microsoft, IBM, Apple, OSF, and so on). Whether you choose one standard or the other is not so important. Using any standard is better than having to discuss unimportant aspects of the user interface, such as "Should this item be red or green?"

If standards are well-chosen, they strengthen the general quality of your user interface. Standards also help developers focus on the user interface part of system development.

Creating Helpful Dialogs

A *dialog* is a pop-up window where the user is either receiving new information, asked to take action, or both.

This section will describe guidelines for making effective dialogs using Designer. You may not always choose to apply these guidelines, but you should think about them when you develop your applications.

One key guideline that almost always applies is to *keep your dialogs simple.* This means that you include only essential elements in your dialog. Eliminate any element that you can remove from the dialog without losing functionality.

Create intuitive dialogs

Design the dialogs so that they signal what they are used for. The user should automatically know what to do when seeing the dialog.

The following guidelines will help you to make intuitive dialogs:

♦ **Write clearly what the dialog does in the window title or block title.**

♦ **Be careful when naming buttons.** For example, the button text "Exit" does not indicate whether or not changes will be saved when the button is pressed. Use "OK" or "Cancel" for button text instead (these terms are understood by most users).

◆ **Write helpful prompts and hint text (and user/help text as well).** Use analogies and examples that are familiar to the users. Define the texts on the tables and/or views rather than on the modules. Prompts and hints are automatically copied to your modules while user/help text is looked up on the tables if they are not found on the module.

◆ **Place the fields so that they show how the dialog should be used.** For example, an airline company may want to place the fields of a travel registration dialog so they look like an airline ticket. This would make it easier for the users to find the fields they are looking for.

The last hint is the most difficult to accomplish in Designer because you do not have a way to freely position the items on the screen, but you can do a lot with preferences, field lengths, item groups, overflow styles, stacked canvases, and so on.

If you still cannot get your fields placed where you want, you can use hidden items to prevent fields from being placed too close to each other or to force a field to be placed on a new line instead of to the right of the previous field.

Hidden Items is a utility in the DesignAssist template package but you can implement it yourself by following the these instructions:

1. **Decide on a name for hidden items** (for example, $$HIDDEN_ITEM$$).

2. **Add a routine in the when-new-form-instance trigger.** Place a routine in the when-new-form-instance trigger of your template form that loops through all items and sets the display property to FALSE on items where the hint property = '$$HIDDEN_ITEM$$' (or whatever name you decide to use).

3. **Create all the hidden items needed.** Now you can create hidden items in Designer by defining unbound items and setting their hint text to '$$HIDDEN_ITEM$$'.

The preceding item looping routine could be implemented like this:

```
/* ——— Plsql/Loop_items.sql ———- */
PROCEDURE Loop_Items is
  v_block_name varchar2(30) := get_form_property
              (name_in('SYSTEM.CURRENT_FORM'),first_block);
  v_item_name  varchar2(30);
  v_original_cursor_item  varchar2(70) :=
name_in('SYSTEM.cursor_item');
  v_original_cursor_record  number(10) :=
name_in('SYSTEM.cursor_record');
  v_original_top_record  number(10) := get_block_property
              (name_in('SYSTEM.cursor_block'),TOP_RECORD);
BEGIN
  - loop through all blocks
```

```
   LOOP
        — Loop through all items
        v_item_name := get_block_property (v_block_name,first_item);
        LOOP
              IF
get_item_property(v_block_name||'.'||v_item_name,item_type) =
                      'TEXT ITEM' and

get_item_property(v_block_name||'.'||v_item_name,hint_text) =
                                  '$$HIDDEN_ITEM$$' THEN

set_item_property(v_block_name||'.'||v_item_name,
                                  Visible, property_false);
              END IF;
              — get next item
              v_item_name := get_item_property
                      (v_block_name||'.'||v_item_name, NextItem);
              — exit if no more items
              EXIT WHEN v_item_name is null;
        END LOOP;          — end of item loop
        — get next block
        v_block_name := get_block_property (v_block_name,
NextBlock);
        — exit if no more blocks
        EXIT WHEN v_block_name is null;
  END LOOP;                       — end of block loop
  —
  — return to the original cursor location
  go_item(v_original_cursor_item);              — return to the
original block
  go_record(v_original_top_record);             — return to the
original top record
  go_record(v_original_cursor_record);          — return to the
original record
  go_item(v_original_cursor_item);              — return to the
original item
END;
```

The procedure script is found in the Plsql directory of the CD-ROM accompanying this book. The filename is Loop_items.sql. (The directory and filename are always listed at the top of the code section.)

Support the user's memory

The guideline provided in the previous section was about visualizing what the dialog is used for. The guideline in this section is about helping the user who already knows what the dialog is for but who cannot remember all the codes, keys, and so on to use.

To support the user's memory, you can do the following:

1. Use descriptive prompts, hints, messages, and help text.

2. Use checkboxes, pop-up lists, and radio groups where applicable to make the choices more obvious.

3. The consistency of using a standard minimizes the number of things that the user has to remember.

Each of these techniques is described further in the next sections.

Tell the user what is happening

Users need to get feedback to be assured of what they have done.

Fortunately Designer generates a lot of messages when the state of the applications change (such as when the user inserts, updates, or deletes a row). Remember to provide feedback on buttons that perform some hidden activity when pressed.

Feedback messages such as "OK" and "Ready" do not inform the user what has happened. Users usually do not know how their commands were interpreted by the application.

The messages should be displayed quickly. If a task takes more than a couple of seconds, a message saying that should be displayed. You can use the NO_ACKNOWLEDGE parameter when creating this kind of message so that no response is required of the user. A message such as "Generating questionnaires, please wait." is shown but is overwritten by the following message without requiring the user to acknowledge the first message.

Hour glasses and progress bars are descriptive for long-running transactions. These types of objects can easily be made in forms. The progress bar in Figure 7-1 is composed of a button within a rectangle and an accompanying procedure.

To create a progress procedure, use the following UPDATE_PROGRESS procedure:

```
/* — Plsql/Update_progress.sql —- */
PROCEDURE update_progress
    (p_progress in number, p_max in number default 100) IS
BEGIN
```

Figure 7-1: A progress bar helps the user know a long-running process is taking place.

```
set_item_property('progress_block.progress',width,p_progress*250/p_m
ax);
  set_item_property('progress_block.progress',
                      label,to_char((p_progress/p_max)*100)||'%');
  synchronize;
END;
```

Include the PROGRESS_BLOCK and PROGRESS_WINDOW in your template form. Then you just have to go to the PROGRESS_BLOCK and call UPDATE_ PROGRESS with the appropriate values between each subtransaction.

Construct helpful messages

The four types of messages are described in the following list. Be sure to use them correctly.

◆ **Fatal error messages.** Messages given in situations when a routine will terminate because of an error that cannot be handled – for example, "Database is corrupt. Terminating." The user cannot change anything to save the routine from terminating.

◆ **Error messages.** Messages given in situations when the application cannot proceed until the user has performed a correction of some sort – for example, "Valid values are Y and N." Note that the term "error message" gives the false impression that the user has made an error. The actual condition is that the system cannot understand what the user is trying to do; therefore, if you formulate your messages in a way that implies the user has done something wrong, it can lead to problems.

◆ **Warning messages.** Messages informing the user about some unusual situation that might be unwanted – for example, "The sales price is lower than the cost price."

◆ **Information messages.** Feedback messages indicate that everything is fine – for example, "All accounts have now been balanced."

The forms generator preference MSGSFT (found under the End User Interface section) can be set to the name of a package to be used instead of the built-in MES-SAGE command when issuing user messages. An example package (CG$FORM_ERRORS) that handles these four message types using alert boxes is supplied with Designer. You can use the CG$FORM_ERRORS package directly or change it to suit your message standards. This package can also be used to make language-specific messages based on message codes rather than message texts.

You should follow guidelines when formulating your message texts. Table 7-1 lists suggested techniques and provides examples that can help you create user-friendly messages.

TABLE 7-1 TECHNIQUES FOR CREATING USER-FRIENDLY MESSAGES

Tip	Good Example	Bad Example
Be constructive. Messages should be constructive rather than reject what the user has done.	Valid values are Y (Yes) and N (No).	Invalid value
Be precise. Messages should clearly state the problem.	Could not find contract number 9821201.	No data
Take responsibility. Messages should be defensive rather than aggressive.	The system can only handle amounts less than 100,000.	The amount must be less than 100,000.

TIP If you cannot fit a complete explanation into the message line or alert box, guide the user to the help system or another source where the matter is covered more completely.

Writing a good message takes no longer than writing a bad one, but it makes a great difference to the end-user's perception of the application. If the application is perceived as offensive and unhelpful, users will avoid using it.

Prevent problems

This guideline is harder to apply and sometimes more expensive to implement, so you might want to follow it only when actual problems arise during user tests.

If users misunderstand the usage of specific items in your application, then try to:

1. **Prevent the misuse.** Change the interface. For example, if users tend to confuse two text items for codes (type: A; B, or C and level: 1, 2, or 3), then use pop-up lists instead of text items to prevent users from entering type codes in the level item and vice versa.

2. **Trap the misuse, and provide specific messages that inform the user of the specific misunderstandings.** If users tend to overlook a Title field, for example, and often enter the title in the Name field (such as "Dr. Joe Jackson"), you could add validation code to look for titles in the Name field and return a warning message explaining how to use the Title field.

One well-known Oracle Forms problem is the dreaded *query mode*. Users often begin creating new rows while in query mode and try to enter search criteria in insert mode. The response given by the Designer-generated forms when users are doing this can be very confusing to them.

This problem can be prevented with some PL/SQL code to be executed when switching between insert mode and query mode. *This can be done within a Designer-generated form containing no postgeneration changes in insert mode and in query mode.*

Figure 7-2 shows the form in insert mode. Notice the toolbar has up and down navigation buttons and the white color of fields in which text can be entered.

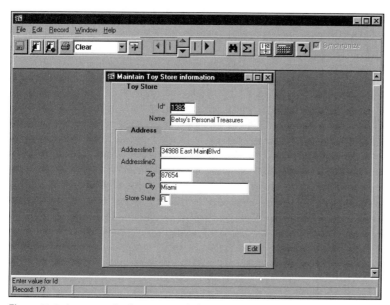

Figure 7-2: Insert mode shows up and down navigation buttons on the toolbar.

Figure 7-3 shows the same form in query mode. In this figure, the queryable fields are highlighted in black, and the toolbar shows only valid query-related buttons.

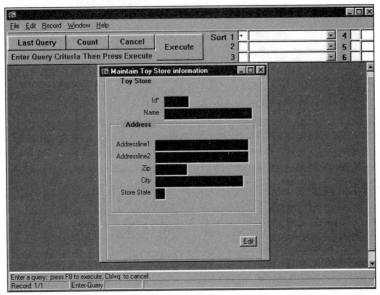

Figure 7-3: Query mode shows no navigation buttons and highlights queryable fields.

All queryable items and the toolbar completely change when going from one mode to the other. With this interface, users are never in doubt what mode they are in.

Visual Design Without Postgeneration Changes

Because many books on the subject of graphical design are available, we will not cover the basics of graphical design in this book. I will only point out the most important graphical design principles that can be implemented by the Designer generators without having to make postgeneration changes. You can implement these design issues using templates, preferences, and PL/SQL code.

Visual design guidelines describe how to consistently handle visual elements such as:

◆ Fonts. Serif for normal text, sans serif for headlines, and so on

- ◆ **Colors.** For example, red for errors, yellow for warnings and/or tests, green for OK

- ◆ **Frames.** Such as those for grouping items

- ◆ **Spaces.** For helping to group items

- ◆ **Icons.** Choice of symbols, placement, and so on

A form generated with the default template and default preference settings of Designer is not very attractive. Many developers try to remedy this situation by changing the FMB file using Form Builder. Much can be done about default modules without having to make postgeneration changes. For example, look at Figures 7-4 and 7-5, which show the same module generated twice.

The first example, in Figure 7-4, shows the module generated using the default settings of Designer.

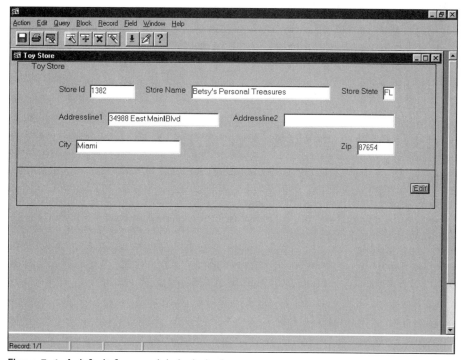

Figure 7–4: A default form module looks boring.

The second example, in Figure 7-5, shows the same module generated by using module settings and the templates, preferences, and PL/SQL code supplied by a template package vendor.

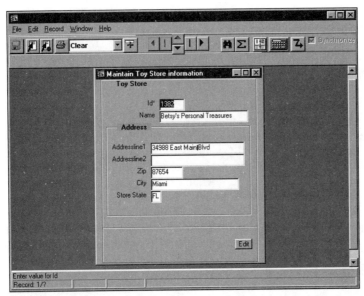

Figure 7-5: A third-party vendor template creates a more attractive form.

No postgeneration changes have been made to any of the forms.

Designing Effective Online User Help

User help is an important issue that is often taken too lightly. When implemented well, it strengthens the user's confidence in the application and in himself or herself and diminishes the need for support.

Poorly made help systems are almost as useless as no help systems because users simply do not use them.

As with the other documentation facilities of Designer, the user help generation features are very good. A quick glance at the default user help generated in Designer does not reveal the full potential of the Designer repository.

Help system options

This section will describe some of the options you have when deciding how to implement your user help using Designer. The options discussed are:

◆ Web modules help

◆ Forms help

WEB MODULES HELP

Chapter 6 describes the default help generation of the Web Server Generator and provides a method for making a more advanced user help utility without having to make postgeneration changes to the generated Web modules.

FORMS HELP CREATED IN DESIGNER

The default help generation for forms is far more advanced than that of Web server modules. The forms generator enables two types of help generation:

◆ **MS help.** The forms generator can connect with MS help files generated by the Designer's MS help generator to display context-sensitive help.

◆ **Forms help.** The forms generator can also extract the user help text and place it in external tables and show context-sensitive help through a help form. (A default help form is supplied with Designer, but a more advanced one can be created to replace it.)

When generating default help, the MS help generator makes the most advanced help system of the two types of help generation. On the other hand, you can do much more to improve the Forms help utility than you can with the MS help utility. You can add all the PL/SQL code that you can dream of into the help form making it far more advanced than an MS Help file.

Important aspects of the two help systems that you should consider when choosing between MS help or Forms help for your applications are:

◆ MS help can be viewed only in a Windows environment. This also excludes running Web forms through a browser (even in Windows).

◆ Forms help can run on any platform that forms can run on, including Web forms running through a browser.

◆ Forms modules and Visual Basic modules can share MS help files. Visual Basic modules cannot show Forms help.

◆ Users familiar with one or more Microsoft applications immediately know how to use the MS help files.

◆ Special features enhance Forms help but not MS help features such as looking up information in the database, opening external documents (PDF, Word, Excel, HTML files, and so forth), and recognizing the current user. These can be made only with Forms help.

Creating Printed Help Documentation

Old-fashioned paper help documents are important. This section describes how to combine help text in your Designer repository with MS Word to create your own help documents.

Users generally need two types of help documents:

◆ **Introduction.** An introduction to the application tells what the application does and guides new users by giving them some basic instructions on how to use the application.

◆ **Reference.** A reference manual describes the entire application in detail. This manual is not usually read from cover to cover. It should be constructed in a way that users can easily find the information they need.

The Designer does not have a generator for making these type of documents, but you can extract your help text from the Designer repository.

You can create beautiful help documents in MS Word by using its built-in macro language to reformat what you extract from the Designer repository. The next section describes how to do this.

Creating documentation with the repository and MS Word

Creating your own MS Word generator takes time, but once you have completed it, you can generate advanced documentation for all parts of your applications (not just the user help).

The two basic steps for creating an MS Word generator using the built-in macro language are:

1. Extract data to a text file.

2. Reformat the text into a Word document.

The next two sections describe these steps.

EXTRACT INFORMATION TO A TEXT FILE

First you must make a PL/SQL procedure for each document type that you wish to generate that can extract the appropriate user help text into a text file. This task is not trivial. You have to decide how to organize the document in parts, chapters, sections, and so on.

To be able to generate headlines, tables of contents, indexes, and so on, you must mark the relevant text items so they can be recognized by the MS Word macro. An obvious choice would be to use HTML tags or maybe even XML tags. You can also choose to mark the text items by using your own keywords such as:

```
MSWORD$HEADLINE_1_BEGIN
MSWORD$HEADLINE_1_END,
MSWORD$INDEX_REF_BEGIN
MSWORD$INDEX_REF_END
```

Make small generic functions that add these keywords so that you do not risk misspelling them. This function adds the keyword WORD$HEADLINE_x_ BEGIN to the beginning of a headline and the keyword MSWORD $HEADLINE_x_END to the end. (The "x" is replaced with the appropriate heading level number.)

```
/* —- Plsql/Headline_tag.sql —- */
function HeadlineTag (
    p_headline in varchar2,
    p_level in number default 1,
    p_product in varchar2 default 'MSWORD') is
begin
    return(
        p_product||'$HEADLINE_'||to_char(p_level)||'_BEGIN'||
        p_headline||
        p_product||'$HEADLINE_'||to_char(p_level)||'_END');
end;
```

If you want to generate HTML tags, you can just use the HTF package that comes with the Web Application Server.

REFORMAT THE TEXT FILE TO MS WORD

The next step is to convert the extracted file to MS Word.

This can be done by loading the extracted file into MS Word as a raw text file and then converting all the tags to MS Word elements. You can do all this using the MS Word macro language.

Again, this task is not trivial. You must go through the document several times to create the necessary MS Word elements. The basic steps of a simple MS Word generator macro are:

1. Load the extracted text into MS Word.

2. Define the page numbering style of your choice.

3. Apply the default MS Word gallery style to the entire text.

4. Use the search command to find all headline tags, and apply the corresponding MS Word gallery style to them (and remove the tags).

5. Use the search command to find all the index tags, and add MS Word cross-references instead.

6. Go to the end of the document, and add an index for all the cross-references.

7. Go back to the beginning of the document, and add a table of contents.

8. Save the text as an MS Word document.

Many more elements can be created including:

◆ **Front page features.** You could have a simple PL/SQL function including tags for author, title, version, date, and so on into the extract file and have the MS Word macro set up these texts as your cover page.

◆ **Graphics.** You could place tags in the user/help text in the repository indicating which graphics to use (for example, <IMG SRC="create_emp.gif">) and include the graphics, both in the document and through the Forms help.

◆ **Bullets and numbered lists.**

◆ **Special styles.** You might create a style for examples, quotes, names, and so on.

Guidelines for writing user documentation

Even though presentation is significant, the actual content of the user help text is still the most important part of the user help systems and documents.

User help has a bad reputation. Oftentimes, user help is written by people with no training and no interest in writing user help text (or any other documentation). This results in user help text that is boring to read and does not solve the problems that the users encounter.

The same situation applies to generating user help from Designer. The individuals who fill out the user/help text properties in Designer are developers who are more interested in developing than in documenting.

It is important to revise the documentation continuously to ensure that problems that have resulted in calls to the support staff are included in the help text. Doing so avoids receiving the same type of support calls in the future. If users are calling support about a problem whose solution is already in the help text, then you should check to see whether the solution is too difficult to find.

When you store your help text in the Designer repository, it is significantly easier to keep your help texts up to date than when you write the help text in a traditional word processor. The structure of the Designer repository helps you synchronize the application and its documentation.

We can split the help text usage into the following four phases that the user goes through every time a problem is encountered:

◆ Find a solution.

◆ Understand the solution.

◆ Apply the information.

◆ Verify that the problem is solved.

The simple guidelines described in the next sections describe how to write good, usable user help. The guidelines focus on how the user help will be used.

HELP THE USER FIND A SOLUTION

When the user experiences a problem, he or she first tries to find a solution. To help the user locate the relevant information, you can do the following:

◆ Make sure that the index is sufficiently detailed and that it contains plenty of synonyms.

◆ Make sure that the headlines contain the important keywords of the section's content.

◆ Write easy-to-read headlines.

◆ Make sure that the most important information is placed in the beginning of a section.

HELP THE USER UNDERSTAND THE SOLUTION

After finding the information in the help system or document, the user tries to understand what the text is saying. To help the user understand the information he or she finds, you can do the following:

◆ Use simple sentences and a simple language.

◆ Include plenty of examples to explain the terms and concepts used in the text.

HELP THE USER APPLY THE INFORMATION

When the user has understood the help text he or she tries to apply the information in order to continue the current task. To help the user apply the information he or she finds, you can do the following:

◆ Make sure that the examples are relevant so that the users can copy them to solve their problems.

◆ Explain the consequences of applying the solution. Explain what will happen behind the scenes when the user applies the information?

HELP THE USER VERIFY RESOLUTION OF THE PROBLEM

Finally, the user must be reassured that the information was applied correctly and, hence, that the problem is solved. To reassure the user that everything has gone as expected, you can do the following:

◆ Explain how the application is expected to react to the applied information so that the user can recognize the application's feedback.

◆ Explain the error situations that could occur and how to solve them.

Using these tips can help you create user documentation that is readable and usable and solves problems.

Summary

User-friendly applications have become more common due to user demand. Two benefits of user-friendly application design are that it costs less to support and the users are more productive.

When setting your GUI standards, choose standards that are appropriate for your work. The most important aspect is consistent use of the standard you choose.

An important aspect of GUI design is the design of messages that users encounter in dialogs. Messages should be intuitive, remind the user what he or she should do, and inform the user of the current status.

You can apply templates, preferences, and PL/SQL code to create visually appealing forms that are generated in Designer.

Web modules help for Designer-generated modules is described in Chapter 6.

Online help for Forms can be developed several different ways, including Forms help and MS help. Each style of help has advantages and disadvantages.

Printed documentation is still an important aspect of design. Too often, this documentation is boring and ineffective.

One interesting method of creating hard copy documentation is to extract the documentation placed in the Designer repository and then apply MS Word macros to the text.

Guidelines for user documentation are outlined to help you create detailed, easy-to-use manuals.

The next chapter describes how to effectively manage changes in Designer systems that have multiple modules and numerous application designers.

Chapter 8

Managing Changes

IN THIS CHAPTER

♦ Retrieving database structures

♦ Managing forms that are not 100 percent generated

♦ Managing the repository

THERE ARE MANY ISSUES that you face when managing an application system. You may need to load an old database or application into Designer. You may need to regenerate an application to restore it after invalid changes were made. Your form might include customized changes that must be preserved, even if you regenerate the form from Designer. You may need to save a complete version of the application system design so that you can restore that version if needed. All these issues are addressed in this chapter, beginning with the issues surrounding recovering an application design.

Handling Application Changes

Wouldn't it be nice if you could develop an application once and be done with it? Now back to reality! No matter how much analysis, design, planning, and testing you do, those darn users come up with something else. And for those of us that actually have to work with others, there are always those rogue developers who seek the quick fix and bypass using Designer. Luckily, Oracle has provided a solution for both of these issues. For the never-ending maintenance cycle, you can actually manage these changes in lots of ways. And for that rogue developer, you can recover the designs back into Designer.

Design recovery

Design recovery is the process of reading existing application definitions and putting them into the Designer repository. Design recovery can *only* be performed within the Design Editor. The process begins by choosing Generate→Capture Design of on the Design Editor menu, as shown in Figure 8-1. The two sides to design recovery are server and module.

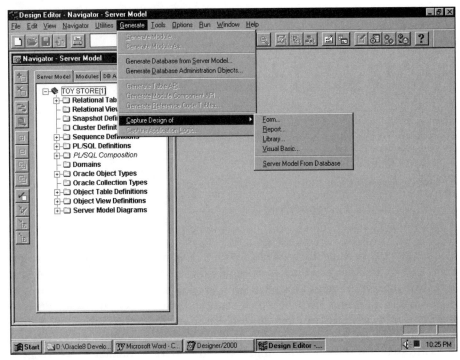

Figure 8-1: Start the process of recovery in Design Editor.

Server-side recovery can be used to recover the database definitions that have been added outside of the application design or to recover designs of existing applications that exist in Oracle databases, other databases (via ODBC), or DDL scripts. Figure 8-2 shows the window you see when you choose to recover a database.

The second type of recovery is client-side, or *module recovery*. With Designer you can actually recover Oracle Forms, Oracle Reports, Oracle Libraries, and Microsoft Visual Basic. The previous version of Designer basically captured only table and column usages. With release 2, you can capture nondatabase-related blocks and items, custom code segments, and some minor layout properties such as optionality, prompts, and usage order. The how-to is straightforward, too. Run the appropriate utility, point to the file, and press the Start button.

You need to be aware of a few things that will not be captured:

◆ Blocks and items that are named CG$ . . .

◆ Data blocks not based on a table or view

◆ Anything marked CG$IGNORE. . . . You can actually prevent design
   capture of any object by putting CG$IGNORE_ON_DESIGN_CAPTURE in
   the comment property of the object.

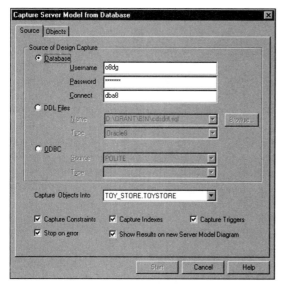

Figure 8-2: Capturing a database design is a server-side function.

Change generation

Because we cannot go back to Neverland, the reality is that changes occur. And to make matters worse for the CASE bigots, most applications are not 100 percent generated. That is, most applications contain code added after the application was generated in Designer. So you must have the capability to make changes to an application within Designer without losing customizations.

To be able to make changes in Designer without losing custom code, there are two rules:

1. You must be working on an Oracle Forms module.

2. You must tell the forms generator to save the layout, as shown in Figure 8-3.

Having said this, I have to say that change generation is still not one of Designer's strong points. You can do some things to help improve your regeneration:

◆ Keep custom code in libraries or stored procedures where possible and keep it up to date in the repository definitions.

◆ Keep form layout simple. Do not even try to regenerate complex screens. Just keep the module definitions up to date.

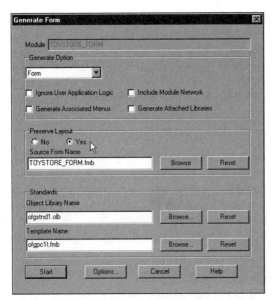

Figure 8-3: Choose the Yes radio button under Preserve
Layout to save customization.

Keep in perspective what Designer is for and what Developer is for. Designer
enables you to design and document your entire application. When you focus on
these goals first, regeneration then becomes icing on the cake.

Repository Management

The Repository Object Navigator (RON) is the portion of Designer that enables you
to view all objects related to your project. The RON has been improved in several
ways:

- It has eliminated redundant functionality for generating.

- Navigator is laid out clearly and is customizable.

- A new and powerful search tool has been added.

The RON in Designer release 2 has become a leaner and stronger tool than it was
in previous versions of Designer. It is now used solely for object creation, deletion,
modification, and querying. You can no longer generate from the RON. However, it
has become a much stronger tool from the navigation standpoint. It is easier to find
objects and to do audits of your data from within the RON without having to use
other tools or run reports.

The Navigator is no longer an exhaustive list of items that are in a somewhat illogical order. Nodes are now set at area levels, as shown in Figure 8-4. You can find within an area all the items related to that area. You may even customize what nodes you see by choosing Options from the main RON menu. You can select what nodes you want to see and what objects are within each node.

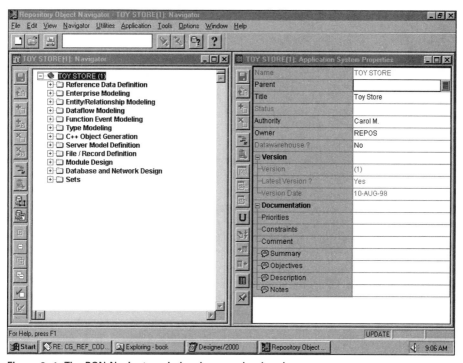

Figure 8-4: The RON Navigator window has area level nodes.

To customize your RON, you can select Options → Customize Navigator Groups from the menu. You can also customize the property palette and the search capabilities from this menu item. Under the Customize Navigator Groups selection, all of the current nodes are displayed. You may chose to remove those you never use to make your screen less cluttered. You may also create your own from scratch or copy a node to edit it. Figure 8-5 shows how you might begin customizing a new node.

The RON now has a powerful search tool. The typical search flashlight that is available on many of Oracle Developer and Designer tools is also available in the RON. But a more advanced tool is also available to enable searches for specific items with queries in the search. This item is the Search Repository tool, which is accessible from the second icon on the right on the icon toolbar in the RON. Selecting this icon brings up a specific window where you can enter search criteria for any object in the repository. This logic can be especially helpful in quality-checking a model.

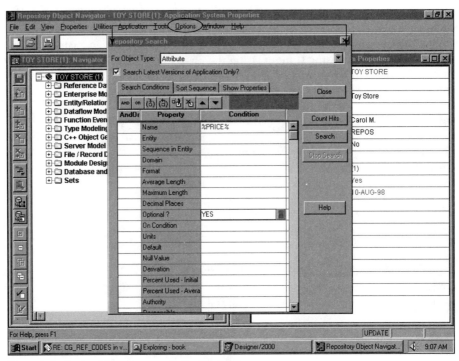

Figure 8-5: Customizing a new node for the RON.

The Toy Store example shown in Figure 8-6 contains a number of cost- and price-related fields. If you want to insure that these fields are always set to Not Null, you can set up the Search Repository to do so. After selecting the icon, you fill in the window under name with "%PRICE%" and under optional, you select YES.

Multiple developers

From the RON, multiple developers may be enabled to change or query a specific application. First, the users must be added to the Oracle database, and the repository administrator must add them to the CASE tool as users through the RAU (Repository Administration Utility). In the RON, the owner of the application can grant users query or update capabilities. The owner can even transfer ownership to another user.

By choosing Application from the main menu of the RON, you can choose "Grant access by Application" or "Grant access by User." From these choices you can set the specific roles for a Designer user. Figure 8-7 shows the submenu that enables you to transfer ownership and handle other functions in the RON.

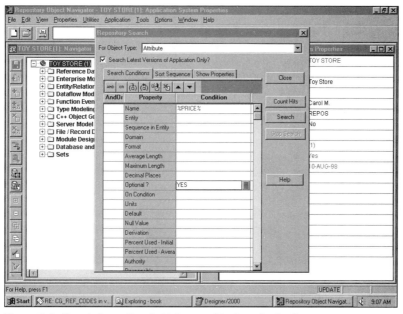

Figure 8-6: Search for optional attributes with the price in them.

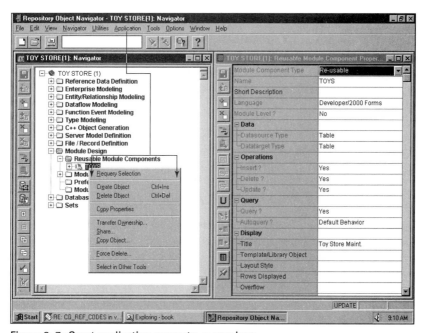

Figure 8-7: Grant application access to a user here.

Sharing reusable module components

Similar to sharing objects such as entities or tables, reusable module components can be shared. The reusable module component can be extremely useful, as long as any application using the reusable module also shares modules that are needed by the reusable module itself. For example, to share a module that calls PL/SQL and reports, the PL/SQL and reports must also be shared.

To share an object with another application, select the object you wish to share from the RON. Then right-click the object. A menu is displayed that includes a Share option.

After you select the Share option, the Share Objects window is displayed, as shown in Figure 8-8.

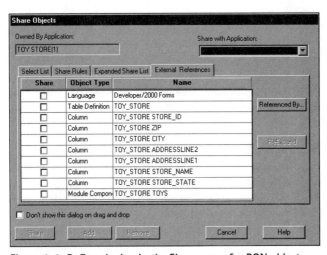

Figure 8-8: Define sharing in the Share menu for RON objects.

The Share Objects window contains the following tabs:

◆ **Select list.** This tab lists all the items you have selected.

◆ **Share Rules.** This tab shows all the object types (such as item groups, SQL query sets, and so on) affiliated with the items you selected.

◆ **Expanded Share List.** This tab lists all items selected plus any affiliated object types.

◆ **External Reference.** This tab shows all the specific objects that must be shared to share this item. At this point, you could share an item and all its associated items. All the module component's affiliated objects are listed here.

Source management techniques

An application owner may be concerned with the following two types of source management:

◆ Controlling changes made outside the repository

◆ Controlling versions of the source

The following sections describe these two types.

CONTROLLING CHANGES OUTSIDE THE REPOSITORY

It is important to manage the constant changes to a module that may occur within the repository as well as outside the repository. With the advent of round-trip engineering, many of the changes that kept forms and reports from being 100 percent generated can now be incorporated into the Designer tool. But you still may come across a form or a report that cannot be 100 percent generated.

 Keep notes within the repository to ensure that future designers understand that the module was not 100 percent generated and that they do not wipe out some manual changes you have made. Each object level contains notes and description fields in which you can add text to explain your changes.

HANDLING VERSION CONTROL

Version control is also important. Once an application has been delivered to the users, you should lock the application in time. From that point forward, any work on the application will be for a new version, and the old application will be stored exactly as it was when you delivered it.

To lock an entire application or version, you choose Application from the main menu in the RON. The menu contains the Freeze and New Version options.

◆ **Freeze locks the application so that others may not change it.** Only those with application privileges to the application can freeze it.

◆ **New Version actually creates a new version of an application.** The prior version is locked, and it cannot be changed. Figure 8-6 shows the New Version window in the RON.

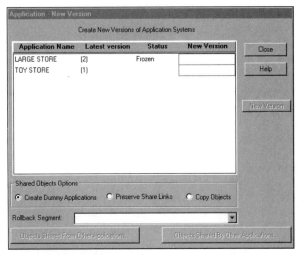

Figure 8-9: Create a new version of the application in the RON.

   If an application is first frozen and then a new version is created, the new version will be frozen as well. The application owner (or person with privileges) must choose the Freeze/Unfreeze option to unfreeze a frozen application.

Summary

When developing applications and database systems, changes are inevitably required. You can use Design Editor to recover or restore designs from databases and from application modules.

Even if the Form application has been modified after generating, you can preserve the customized code with several new techniques.

The Repository Object Navigator (RON) has become leaner and stronger with release 2 of Designer. You can even customize the nodes and the arrangement of objects in the Navigator. The RON also contains a powerful search tool.

You can add multiple developers to a project so that they can edit or view the repository by using the Repository Administration Utility (RAU).

Reusable module components can save time and become easily reusable if designed carefully.

The Designer has added many capabilities that make the creation of 100 percent generated applications easier than ever. Even so, you may find applications that require manual changes. Keep notes and document these changes to avoid confusion.

After delivering your application to the users, you can use the RON to freeze the application so that no changes can be made. In addition, you can choose to create a new version so that the previous version remains intact.

This concludes Part I of the book. Part II follows, with lots of great information about Developer. Stay tuned!

Part II

Oracle Developer

Chapter 9

Concepts of Developer

IN THIS CHAPTER

- ◆ Looking at Developer features
- ◆ Reviewing the new features in Versions 2.0 and 2.1
- ◆ Exploring Forms 5.0
- ◆ Checking out Reports 3.0
- ◆ Using graphics
- ◆ Examining Procedure Builder

THE DEVELOPER PACKAGE has been on the market for several years. This latest version, 2.1, contains new features as well as the best of the previous versions.

This chapter reviews the features, especially the newer features, of the tools contained in Developer. You get a fly-by view of each tool and a quick look at what the tool's primary windows look like.

Surveying Developer Features

This chapter is not intended to be a sales manual for Oracle. Judging from billion-dollar sales figures, Oracle salespeople are doing just fine. What you will find here instead is a quick description of all the tools and features in the Developer package. Mingled with the descriptions are definitions of key terms that you will find useful in later chapters. Figure 9-1 shows that Developer has four primary builders, several different ways to deploy applications, and open architecture so it can access diverse databases.

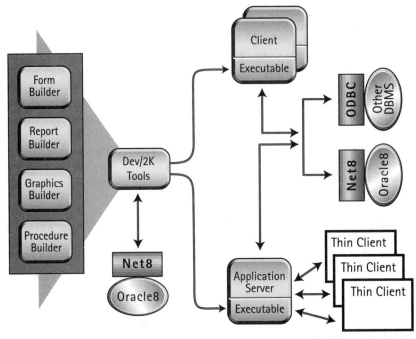

Figure 9-1: The main packages of Developer interface with the database and with the end user.

Figure 9-1 shows a development Oracle 8 database and a production database for deploying executable objects. Some clients use traditional client/server architecture where the executable resides on the clients. Other end-users have thin-client interfaces such as a Web browser. These users interact with Oracle application server, your Web server, and the compiled versions of forms, reports, and so on.

The combination of thin client, application server, and database server is called *triple-tier* (or *three-tier*) *architecture*. This combination has gained popularity over the last few years. Oracle's Developer Versions 2.0 and 2.1 debut new features that support triple-tier architecture. Of course, the varieties and combinations of databases, clients, servers, hardware, and software are endless. It is difficult to describe a "typical" Developer platform.

The next section describes some common features of Developer, focusing on newer features that make the product easier to use and deploy.

Favorite features of Developer

As a set of tools, the Developer package gives the developer a handy way to create a user interface for the Oracle database server. Such a user interface may include data entry forms, reports, charts and other graphics, and portable program units that work directly with the database or directly with the user interface. Some primary advantages of working with Developer are:

- Designer can generate Developer applications

- Generated applications can be built upon

- Customized applications can be created without Designer

- Many platforms run Developer applications

- The Application Server provides fairly smooth transition from client/server to the World Wide Web.

You can generate Developer applications using Designer. The two packages are fully compatible. Most designers find, however, that a 100-percent-generated system is difficult to implement. Some custom coding often adds the unique touch needed for your business applications.

Taking full advantage of the features within Developer, you can customize generated applications, or create your own applications from scratch. You can even base a form on a procedure instead of a data block, making it capable of handling all kinds of unusual functionality.

Another advantage of using Developer is that, unlike most Oracle products, it leaves your applications fully portable across many platforms and uses native Oracle drivers to connect to your database.

As the World Wide Web becomes more deeply ingrained in our business applications, Oracle has worked hard to integrate its applications and tools with the Web. When you add the Oracle applications server, your forms become Web forms. (When porting forms to the Web, design considerations may encourage you to maximize response time.)

The next section describes some more interesting Developer features introduced or improved in Version 2.0 and 2.1.

Introducing Developer's new features of Versions 2.0 and 2.1

For this section, I have chosen four important features that have effects throughout the Developer package. These are:

- More flexible data sources for data blocks

- ODBC compliance

- Oracle 7.3 support

- Report server for Web

A data block in forms, reports, and program units can now be based on procedures in addition to the traditional tables and views. This allows great flexibility and intelligence to be built into the I/O functions for your database. Data blocks can also be based on a query that uses the new FROM clause structure. In effect, instead of naming a table in the FROM clause, you embed a complete sub-query. This enables you to use complex object-relational constructions in your query.

Oracle has made all of the components of Developer ODBC compliant. You can, for example, build a Forms front-end for an MS-SQL database. Another possibility might be to integrate your legacy databases with your new Oracle database system while using the same applications for reporting, data entry, and charts.

Developer uses Oracle 7.3 as its primary platform; you can take advantage of the newer features of Oracle 7.3 and of PL/SQL 2.3. It's about time, I'd say.

Finally, the middle report server is bundled with Developer and serves reports over the Web without running Oracle application server. This is a first step toward full triple-tier architecture supports for Developer.

The following sections look at each of the four major tools within Developer and describe some additional features added for Versions 2.0 and 2.1.

Perusing Each Developer Tool

Every tool that makes the primary package for Developer has new features to review. Five sections in this next part of the chapter – one for each of the four tools and one final review section – present the new and interesting tools in the current version of Developer.

Looking at Forms 5.0

The migration from Forms 4.5 to Forms 5.0 is the most striking change you'll see in Developer. The new version offers enough new features to make a starting point hard to choose. I will focus on features that enhance form building by saving time, adding functionality, and improving convenience.

DATA BLOCK WIZARD

The Data Block Wizard has enough intelligence to make it useful even for experienced designers. It is re-entrant so you can make changes quickly. Figure 9-2 shows the Data Block Wizard as it appears when you use it with an existing form.

ARRAY PROCESSING

Before Version 5.0, you could only define array processing for queries. Now you can specify array processing for inserts, updates, and deletes. Although array processing does not affect your design speed, it does affect your forms' runtime favorably by reducing the number of database calls each form requires for doing its work. This advantage is especially important in thin clients and triple-tier applications.

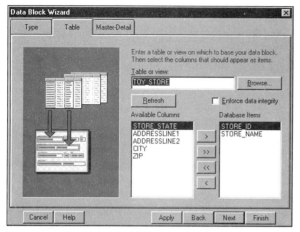

Figure 9-2: The Data Block Wizard provides tabs for convenient and fast adjustments to your form.

TAB CANVASES

The Tab canvas feature enables you to design forms by using layered canvases to produce sequential tabs. Clicking the tab at the top of the window brings a new canvas to the front.

POP-UP MENUS

This new feature enables you to design menus that pop up when you right-click items in a form. You can put useful functions to in the menus so they work in Windows in much the same way as other familiar applications. Right-clicking a text box, for example, might pop up a menu of edit commands such as cut, paste, copy, clear, and so on.

TOOL TIP HINTS

Tool tips pop up when your mouse pointer navigates over an item and pauses for a second. The text in the tool tip shows up in a small box right next to the item. This is great for hints and for quick definitions of items in the form.

Chapter 12 describes how to use database values to serve as tool-tip text in a form.

If you need to display information and a tool tip is not the appropriate method for doing so, you can choose to display another hint automatically in the status bar at the bottom of a screen.

SOUND

The sound-editing feature in Forms 5.0 enables you to retrieve sound files stored in long raw datatype columns in the database. Developer displays a set of controls that enable you to play, edit, stop, start, and save sound files without leaving your form. All you have to do is define the item as "sound" in the item type property.

IMAGE PROCESSING

The Forms feature now has excellent built-in handling of many types of imagery. If you simply define an item as an image type, Forms knows it must interpret the data as an image. Even if you don't specify an image format, Forms analyzes the data and determines what format to use when it displays the image. This process adds overhead, however, so I recommend that you provide the format type (TIF, JPEG, and so on) when you define the image item in Form Builder. Forms has built-in features to read imagery from a file or from the database. It even can use an HTML link as the source of imagery.

You can write a file to your operating system from Forms. You can paste an image from your clipboard into your form and save it in the database.

TEXT LABEL

This may seem like a small thing, but I find it to be a great timesaver. Forms finally has made a label that is attached to an item. This means you no longer have to define a separate static text item to act as the label for your input field. Now you can use the built-in label, tell Forms in what position (relative to the item) you want that label to display, and the text, and formatting of the label. Figure 9-3 shows the property window with the selections highlighted for labels.

TEMPLATE FORMS

Most of us who have been designing forms for a while have simulated template forms all along. A consistent look and feel to your application helps end-users understand and navigate easily and quickly through your form. With Version 5.0, Forms implements a protocol that enables you to make template forms; several built-in templates may encourage you to build your own. You could apply a template form – complete with logos, standard heading text, styles for items of each data type, and common menus – throughout your development.

SMART TRIGGERS

The Smart Trigger feature interprets the context in which you're building a trigger and then displays a list of triggers most commonly used in that context. Considering the many triggers you could use, this bit of help can save you some time during design. Although the trigger you create may not become any smarter as a result, it will be easier to create.

Text label attibutes

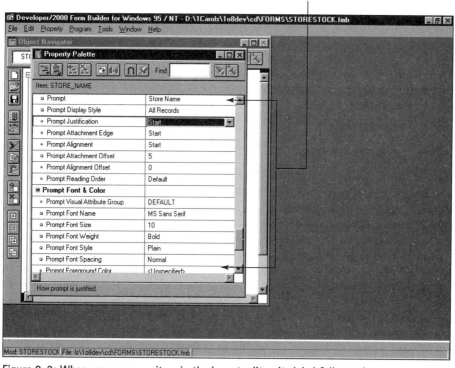

Figure 9-3: When you move an item in the layout editor, its label follows along.

TIP

I've found the Smart trigger feature to be useful as a reminder of what triggers typically appear in certain levels of my form.

SUBCLASSING

Subclassing is the latest version of inheritance to help you reuse code, styles, and menus. Build object libraries to store common objects and then click and drag them to a new form. Form Builder asks you at this point whether you want to copy or subclass the object. If you select subclassing, your new form references the object stored in the object library. Any changes to the source code of that object will be passed along to your form. All you need to do is recompile the form.

Subclassing is a powerful tool for standardizing your application work;
Chapter 13 covers it in detail.

GET FILE FROM OPERATING SYSTEM

A new, built-in function enables you to retrieve or save a file in your operating system. The function opens a graphical display of your directory system, through which you can navigate to a file that you can then load into your form. (For example, you might want to load images into database columns.)

You can use the same function to save a file to your operating system. For example, you could build a form that prompts your user to enter a query, executes the query, and then tells Forms to save the query to a file. The function is named:

```
GET_FILE_NAME (dir_name, file_name, file_filter,
message, doalog_type, select_file);
```

For example, if you want to open a dialog box to save a file (user specifies the file name later) in the D:\newquery directory, you would write the command:

```
GET_FILE_NAME('D:\newquery',null,null,null,SAVE_FILE,TRUE);
```

Reviewing Report Builder 3.0

The latest changes in Developer's report tool (now called Report Builder) have made this product so much easier to use that developers who have shunned Report Writer in the past may want to reconsider.

REPORT WIZARD

The biggest improvement comes in the form of a Report Wizard that helps you format your report and add a style from a template. Dozens of built-in templates are available. In addition, as with in the Forms Builder, you can always build your own report template.

The Report Wizard enables you to revisit your selections and make changes at any time. For example, you can add a new column to your report query and place the column on your reports – almost effortlessly.

Chapter 14 goes over the Report Builder in more detail.

WEB WIZARD

If you have static reports that you wish to display on the Web, the Web Wizard helps you perform this task. An interesting feature of Report Builder is the capability to prepare for porting a report to the Web by defining the HTML tag for each object. For example, you could adjust the display color of fields, or turn a drill-down button into a link to another HTML page by specifying the appropriate tags on the Report item's property window.

Chapter 14 shows you a demonstration of how to use the Web Wizard to create several interconnected reports.

You have your choice of two formats when you converge the report for the Web: PDF or HTML. If you choose PDF, yet another attribute in the properties window of each report object that enables you to specify PDF tags so your report is optimized for PDF display.

TEMPLATES AND THE TEMPLATE EDITOR

The Report Builder takes advantage of templates. Many standard templates are available, though you may want to build your own. Use the template editor to create your own template. Figure 9-4 shows the template editor in action.

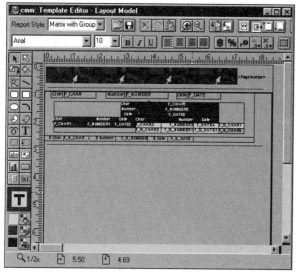

Figure 9-4: The Template Editor helps you create reports with a consistent look and feel.

LIVE PREVIEWER

This new feature helps you get a better idea of what your report will look like when it is completed. It gives you an advance look at your report with actual data display. At the same time you are viewing your data, you can modify the width of fields, the font, the background color, and many other features of your report. I found this feature extremely useful in designing an attractive report.

DIRECT COLUMN REFERENCE

You can now display data from your columns without creating a hidden field on your report. This saves time during design. To reference the column, use the following format:

```
&<columnname>
```

Replace columnname with the actual column from your query. In addition, several system variables that are new in this version of Report Builder. You can reference these using the above format as well. The new system variables are:

- ◆ SYSTEM.CUSTOM_ITEM_EVENT. This stores the name of the event fired by a VBX control.

- ◆ SYSTEM.CUSTOM_ITEM_ EVENT_PARAMETERS. This is for VBX controls, and shows parameters for the VBX event.

- ◆ SYSTEM.LAST_FORM. This shows you the previous form if you have multiple forms opened. Use it when you open forms using the OPEN_FORM command. It is not valid when you use CALL_FORM.

- ◆ SYSTEM.MOUSE_FORM, the form that the operator's mouse is in.

- ◆ SYSTEM.TAB_NEW_PAGE. You can use this variable in When-Tab-Page-Changed. It stores the name of the tab page that the operator is navigating into.

- ◆ SYSTEM.TAB_PREVIOUS_PAGE. Like TAB_NEW_PAGE, this variable exists especially for navigation between tab pages; it contains the page out of which the operator moved.

STRETCH THE WIDTH AND HEIGHT OF ITEMS

Finally! The Report Builder offers an alternative to providing lots of empty space so you can accommodate a few rows of data (that nearly always take up more room). Now you can define a reasonable size for your item and then tell it to stretch either width or height to accommodate larger values. Figure 9-5 shows where to specify stretching function in an item.

Horizontal or vertical stretch

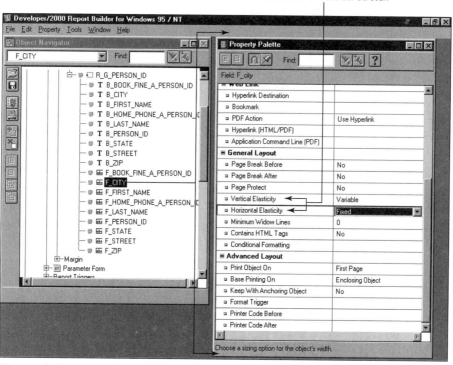

Figure 9-5: When you stretch the height of an item, your report grows and the next row is aligned properly below it.

 When you use this feature, be careful not to specify more than one "stretchable" item in any frame.

DATA WIZARD

You can use the Data Wizard to integrate additional queries into your report.

To reach the Data Wizard, open a report and click Tools → Report Editor. This brings you to the graphical representation of your report query. Next, click the icon on the tool bar that starts the Data Wizard, as shown in Figure 9-6.

Not only can the Data Wizard help you build more complex reports smoothly, you can also use it to design a matrix report.

Although similar to the Report Wizard, the Data Wizard is not re-entrant.

The Report Builder can contain graphics such as charts built using the Chart Wizard. The next section tells about the Graphics Builder that runs the Chart Wizard.

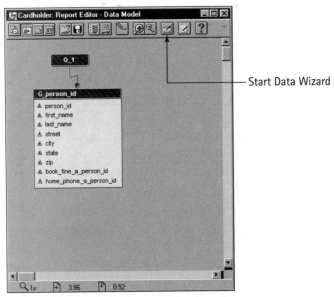

- Start Data Wizard

Figure 9-6: Start the Data Wizard from inside
the Report Editor.

Flying over Graphics 3.0

I have seen some interesting applications created using the Report Builder and
Graphics. One application drew a scaled street map by using functions to calculate
the length of lines to draw – and that capability is by no means the only one available. Among the improvements available in Graphics 3.0, two features stand out as
the most intriguing developments for chart designers:

◆ Chart Wizard

◆ The capability of exporting graphic images

The Chart Wizard – like the Report Wizard and Data Wizard – is a re-entrant
wizard. You can create a chart within a form or a report by activating the Chart
Wizard. Figure 9-7 shows a form with an embedded chart. The chart was created
using the Chart Wizard inside the Layout Editor.

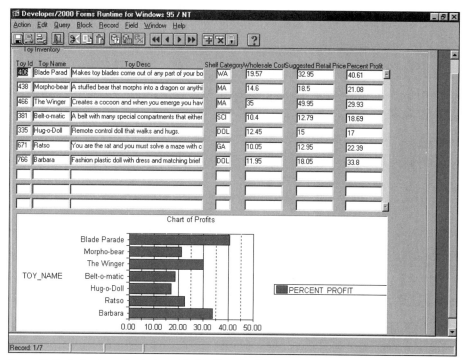

Figure 9–7: A chart can be designed inside Form Builder using the Chart Wizard.

To start the Chart Wizard in Form Builder, go to the Layout Editor, click the Chart icon on the left toolbar, and then click-and-drag the area in which you wish to display the chart. If you base your chart on a multirow block (such as the one shown in Figure 9-7), you must create a separate control block in which to place the chart. Figure 9-8 shows the Chart Wizard after you have already created your chart and now want to revise the specifications. To reach the Chart Wizard, go to the Layout Editor, select the chart, and then choose Tools → Chart Wizard from the menu.

EXPORT IMAGE

You can now save your chart as an image in any of these formats: TIF, GIF, JPEG, BMP, PICT. To save a chart, go to the Graphics Editor, select the full chart, and then click on File → Export → Image.

This action brings up the dialog box shown in Figure 9-9. Next you define the image format, the save location, and so on.

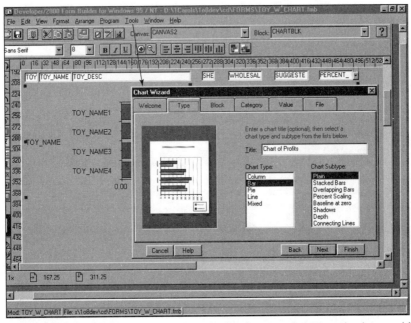

Figure 9-8: Re-enter the Chart Wizard to change the type of chart or the data used in the chart.

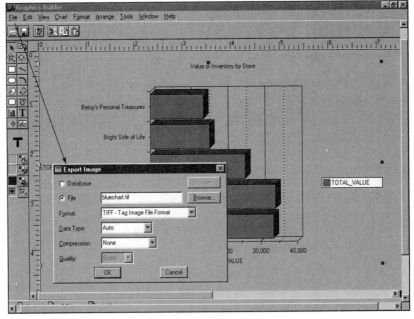

Figure 9-9: Specify how to save an image of your chart.

This procedure can be useful for creating documentation and historical records of the chart.

Debugging with Procedure Builder 2.0

The Procedure Builder gives you an environment in which to create PL/SQL code, after which you can save it into a library and share among your forms, reports, and charts. Procedure Builder features an Object Navigator (useful if you have created libraries of procedures in `.pll` format) and it highlights any line of code in which it finds a syntax error.

 Chapter 12 goes into detail on how to use the Procedure Builder.

The debugger, although a good tool, is the same one available when you run a form in Debug mode. Generally, though its documentation looks impressive, in practice Procedure Builder lacks the usability found in the best tools.

Other Tools Bundled with Developer

The remaining chapters in this part of the book focus on the "big four" tools just introduced. I have added a quick review of four other tools here; although they are not as well known, they may be helpful to you.

Project Builder

The Project Builder offers a way to review, open, or run any application in your entire project. Although Project Builder is not a source-code controller, it can help you keep track of where your applications are – and help ensure that you open the appropriate tool when you click an application. (For example, when you click TOYS.RDF, the Project Builder starts the Report Builder.)

You can combine the Project Builder with your own third party source controller if you wish. You can also distribute copies of your entire project to other developers using the Export function.

Another capability of the Project Builder is creating a project installation script. Using the Delivery Wizard, you can send all the applications associated with the project to a special staging directory. Then you can have the Delivery Wizard guide you through creating a script so you can use Oracle Installer to install your project.

The Enterprise Manager (bundled with Oracle8 Enterprise Edition) also has the capability to create an install script for your application.

Query Builder

Query Builder can be invoked from most of the tools where you must define a query, such as a Forms data block, a chart, or a report. You can also invoke it by itself from your operating system.

Figure 9-10 shows a tiled set of windows in the Query Builder. You can see the SQL, the graphical representation of the query, and the result set in the three windows.

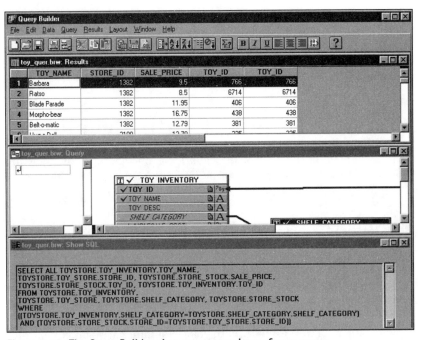

Figure 9-10: The Query Builder gives you many views of your query.

Translation Builder

The translation Builder facilitates translations between your current language and another language. You can specify the phrases that are used in standard messages for all the applications (forms, reports, and so on). You can use the default translations if you wish. However, using the Translation Builder is an extra step that will make your applications more readable and understandable.

The translation builder supports more than fifty languages. To view the translated version of your applications, you must reset the NLS_LANGUAGE environment variable to the appropriate language. If you wish to develop in one language and run in another language, you can set these two environment variables:

- ◆ DEVELOPER_NLS_LANG

- ◆ USER_NLS_LANG

In Forms, you can use the ALTER SESSION command to modify the default language, date format, sort order, and other language-specific parameters. For example, you can modify the currency symbol to the ISO international currency symbol of Hong Kong with this command:

```
ALTER SESSION(NLS_ISO_CURRENCY=HONGKONG);
```

With Report Builder and Graphics Builder, you are limited to setting only the NLS_SORT parameter.

Find documentation on the National Language Support features and system variables in the *Oracle8 Server Reference*, Chapter 1: Initialization Parameters.

Schema Builder

The Schema Builder is a graphical database design tool. If you do not have Designer, this might be a useful tool. However, I found that the Schema Manager in the Enterprise Manager (standard with Oracle8 Enterprise Edition Server) was much easier and more robust. Figure 9-11 shows the Table Diagrammer in Schema Builder.

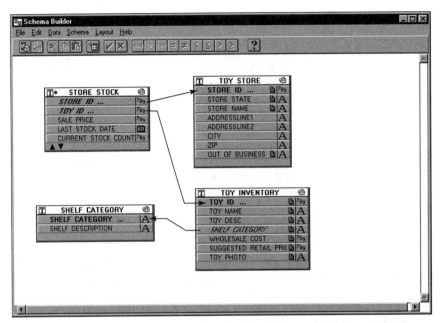

Figure 9-11: Schema Builder resembles Query Builder in its graphical layout of tables.

Summary

This chapter looks over the components of Developer with a special emphasis on the new additions to the product that come with Version 2.0 and 2.1. The most intriguing features are described along with good reasons to use Developer.

The four primary tools that make up Developer are:

◆ Forms Builder

◆ Report Builder

◆ Graphics Builder

◆ Procedure Builder

Each of these four tools has new features that are introduced in this chapter.

Form Builder has to most dramatic changes because it went from Version 4.5 to Version 5.0. Among the new features are:

◆ Data Block Wizard

◆ Tab canvases

◆ Support for sound and image processing

Report Builder has a new Web Wizard that translates any report into either PDF or HTML format. You can specify HTML and PDF tags for specific elements in the report that do not interfere with the report's format when you aren't running the Web version of the report.

Report Builder and Form Builder both support design templates.

Graphics Builder has a new feature called the Chart Wizard, which you can invoke from inside Form Builder or Report Builder. Like most new Wizards in this release of Developer, the Chart Wizard is re-entrant for convenience in modifying chart details.

You can use Procedure Builder to create shared libraries of PL/SQL code, but its debugger seems unable to run except from within other products (such as Form Builder).

This chapter also reviews the following tools, which – although not primary components of Developer – are highly useful:

♦ Project Builder

♦ Translation Builder

♦ Query Builder

♦ Schema Builder

In the next chapter, we will look at how to increase your productivity by taking advantage of the best timesaving and work-saving techniques for Developer tools.

Chapter 10

Quick Start – Using Developer

IN THIS CHAPTER

- ◆ Using forms
- ◆ Events and triggers
- ◆ Referencing forms items
- ◆ Basic trigger structure
- ◆ Advanced trigger techniques
- ◆ Types of blocks
- ◆ Introduction to control blocks
- ◆ Creating control blocks
- ◆ Control block example – a GUI calendar
- ◆ Control block tips
- ◆ Migrating forms to the Web
- ◆ Using reports with graphics

DEVELOPER HAS A LOT of new features in its Version 2.1 release. And a new release of Developer (Version 6) will soon be released in beta. The current direction of Developer is clearly toward Web and network computers. The so-called "universal server" is on its way.

 Yes, the version numbers are correct. Who knows why, but Oracle has gone from Version 2.1 to Version 6 with Developer.

What can you, as a developer, do to prepare for the future? Plan your new development so that you are prepared if (and when) your management says, "You have one month to migrate our entire sales order and inventory tracking system to the Internet."

This chapter discusses how to get a quick start using forms, reports, and graphics with an eye toward two important themes: integration into the World Wide Web and faster delivery of applications.

Get ahead of the game now, and you will be positioned to lead your clients or your company with confidence.

Using Forms

You can use appropriately designed triggers and control blocks to customize your forms and make them easier to maintain. This section describes the basics of trigger functionality, some advanced techniques for triggers, and how to use control blocks to your best advantage.

Using triggers in forms

Event-driven programs, such as Forms, execute program logic in response to something that has happened. When the response is complete, the program waits for the next thing to happen. The thing that happens is an *event*. The program logic that responds to an event is a *trigger*. A trigger is said to have "fired" when it is executed in response to an event.

Forms has a predefined set of events, triggers, and default behavior. If you create a simple form without any triggers, its default behavior enables the user to perform basic operations such as insert, update, and deletion of data. To add to the default functionality of the form, you must create additional triggers.

When you create a trigger to fire for an event, you must also consider the *scope* of the trigger. Triggers can be scoped to fire for an event at the item, block, or form level.

BASIC STRUCTURE OF TRIGGERS

To create a trigger, select the trigger node in the Form Builder Objects Navigator for the appropriate scope (form, data block, or item). If no triggers exist for the scope you have selected, you may create a trigger by double-clicking the trigger node, or you may click the create icon. Figure 10-1 shows the location of the form-level, block-level, and item-level trigger nodes.

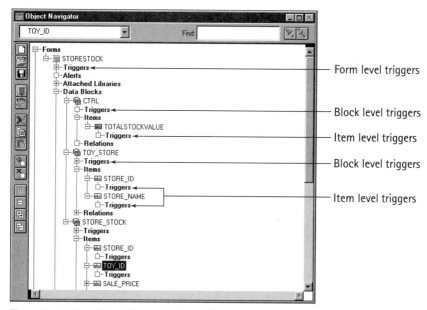

Figure 10-1: The Object Navigator view of the three levels of trigger definition.

When you create a trigger, you are presented with the list of predefined triggers as shown in Figure 10-2. The name of the trigger is similar to the name of the event it fires for. The first part of the trigger name indicates when the body of the trigger executes relative to the event. The predefined trigger names begin:

- ♦ **PRE.** These triggers fire just before the event occurs. A PRE-BLOCK trigger may be used for initializations that have to be performed before a block is entered.

- ♦ **POST.** Immediately following an event, the corresponding POST trigger fires. A POST-BLOCK trigger can be used to hide a canvas that is visible only while the user is in the block.

- ♦ **WHEN.** These triggers fire as an event occurs. The often-used WHEN-VALIDATE trigger fires during validation processing. Typical uses of WHEN-VALIDATE triggers are validation of user input or populating another item based on user input.

- ♦ **KEY.** The KEY triggers respond to pressing a key or the DO_KEY build-in. The KEY-COMMIT trigger at the form level could be used for special commit processing.

- ♦ **ON.** The ON triggers replace forms default behavior. The ON-INSERT trigger replaces forms default behavior of inserting a record into the database.

Figure 10-2: Select a trigger name
from the predefined
trigger list.

 The list of triggers autoreduces as you type the trigger name.

The body of a trigger can be composed of:

◆ **Restricted built-ins such as NEXT_BLOCK.** Restricted built-ins can be used only in certain events and cause either compile errors or run-time errors if defined outside the defined restrictions.

◆ **Unrestricted built-ins such as GET_ITEM_PROPERTY.** Unrestricted built-ins have no restrictions and therefore can be used in any trigger, regardless of when it is fired.

◆ **Assignments of data block items and global variables.** Use the := sign to assign values.

◆ **SQL and PL/SQL statements.** End statements with a semicolon.

Figure 10-3 shows an example of a trigger body in the Form Builder.

Local program units, local variables, and exception handling are implemented in triggers by creating anonymous PL/SQL blocks. The example shown in Figure 10-4 illustrates a typical "prevent duplicated records" check.

Figure 10-3: An example of the body of a trigger.

Figure 10-4: PL/SQL constructs in triggers can have local variables.

ADVANCED TRIGGER TECHNIQUES

The number and complexity of triggers required in a form is typically proportionate to amount and complexity of the required functionality. Implementing a large amount of nonstandard forms behavior greatly increases the number and complexity of triggers. This section discusses advanced trigger techniques.

EXECUTION HIERARCHY   The execution hierarchy trigger property determines how triggers with overlapping scope interact. The default behavior for triggers with overlapping scope is that the trigger defined at the lowest scope overrides all triggers of enclosing scope. For instance, consider the KEY-COMMIT trigger defined at the form- and data-block-levels in Figure 10-5. By default, the trigger defined for the block overrides the form-level trigger when the event occurs while the focus of the form is in the TOY_STORE block. When the focus occurs in any other block, the form-level trigger will fire.

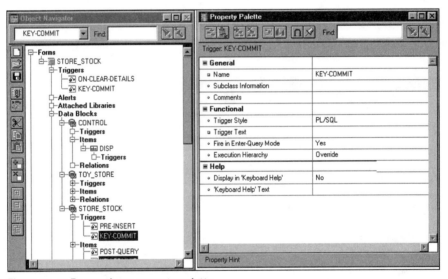

Figure 10-5: Forms trigger property palette.

 TIP   When you change the execution hierarchy to either "Before" or "After," Forms fires both triggers. By setting the execution hierarchy on the block trigger to "Before," the block-level trigger fires first and is followed by the firing of the form-level trigger. If you set the execution hierarchy on the block trigger to "After," the form-level trigger fires first.

FIRE IN QUERY MODE   All forms triggers fire in response to their related event when the form is in "normal" mode. Some triggers may also fire when the form is in "query" mode. To enable a trigger to fire in query mode, you must set the Fire in Enter-Query Mode trigger property to Yes. The default value for this property is Yes for triggers that are enabled to fire in query mode. The list of triggers that may fire in query mode is available in Forms online help.

USER-NAMED TRIGGERS   You may create a trigger with a name that is not on the list of predefined triggers. When you specify a name other than one of the predefined triggers, your trigger is said to be *user-named*. Forms does not recognize events that would cause a user-named trigger to fire. The EXECUTE_TRIGGER built-in must be used to cause user-named triggers to fire.

User-named triggers are most useful when your application uses menu modules. You must use user-named triggers when a menu item has to execute a stored program unit of the form that is using the menu.

TRIGGER DESIGN SUGGESTIONS

Designing efficient, effective, and maintainable triggers can be challenging. When designing trigger logic, consider the following:

- Keep the body of the trigger simple. When possible, create the trigger body to be a call to a program unit in the form, an attached library, or a stored procedure.

- Implement redundant code as a procedure or function that is called from the trigger.

- Limit the possibility of triggers causing side effects – for example, a WHEN-VALIDATE trigger that assigns a value to another item that has a WHEN-VALIDATE trigger.

- Define the scope of the trigger to the lowest possible level.

- Avoid splitting program logic between the same trigger at different scope levels.

- Fewer is better.

Another important design factor is the use of control blocks. The following section examines control blocks.

Quick start for control blocks

A block is said to be a *control block* when it is not associated with the database. Blocks that are based on a table, view, procedure, or on transactional triggers are called *data blocks*. When a block and one or more items within the block are associated with the database, Forms provides default functionality for query, insert, update, and delete operations. Forms can't provide this default functionality for control blocks because the data source for queries and the target for insert, update, and delete is undefined. In fact, if your application does not prevent the operator from initiating one of these DML statements in a control block, a run-time error will occur.

INTRODUCTION TO CONTROL BLOCKS

After reading the description of control blocks in the previous section, you may be wondering what are they good for. Control blocks are often defined in terms of what they are not. When you think about all the restrictions imposed on data blocks to support the default functionality, the value of control blocks becomes clear:

◆ Each record in a data block is associated to one record in the data source. Presenting data in an aggregate or decomposed form is difficult.

◆ Because the data associations are specified when designing the form, dynamic queries are difficult to implement.

◆ Preventing unnecessary updates can be involved. When an operator types the same value in a database item for a queried record, the form changes the record status. This can be confusing to the operator.

Control blocks are good for:

◆ Presenting data that is not a direct query from a data source.

◆ Creating a meta-block that contains objects that don't belong to any block but are used throughout the form. For example, a checkbox that the user can check to enable auto-query for all blocks in the form.

◆ Items that are used for variables. The scope and life of item used as variables is greater than variables declared in PL/SQL blocks.

◆ Grouping several related nondatabase items such as a toolbar.

To create a control block, follow these steps:

1. Click on the data blocks node in the Object Navigator.

2. Click the create button in the toolbar.

3. Select Build New Data Block Manually from the New Data Block dialog. The Data Block Wizard assumes that the block will be a data block.

4. Set the Database Data Block property for the block to No.

5. Rename the block if desired.

CONTROL BLOCK EXAMPLE — A GUI CALENDAR

Viewing a graphical calendar is often helpful for an operator to maintain date information. The following example describes the control block items used to implement this calendar.

Depending on your implementation of a calendar, approximately 50 items will be required. The control block items used to implement the calendar in Figure 10-6 are:

- ◆ A control block

- ◆ To represent Sunday through Saturday for six weeks, 42 individual display items are required.

- ◆ The arrow buttons at the top of the calendar enable the user to move from month to month and year to year. One button item is required for each arrow.

- ◆ One display item is needed to display the month and year.

- ◆ One display item is needed to display the current selection toward the bottom of the calendar.

- ◆ Two button items are needed for the Cancel and OK buttons at the bottom of the calendar.

- ◆ A variety of triggers to respond to the user clicking and double-clicking a date and six buttons.

Figure 10-6: A GUI calendar
stored in a control block
aids data entry.

As you can see, implementing this calendar requires many items, none of which are related to a database data source in any way. Grouping these items into a control block dedicated to the calendar makes it possible to have block-level triggers.

CONTROL BLOCK TIPS

The following tips can help you implement control blocks:

◆ **Most forms have to manage items that are not directly associated with a database data source.** Establish a standard that requires at least one control block to manage these items.

◆ **Consider using control block items instead of global variables.**

◆ **Control blocks are cleared when the form is cleared.** Consider creating a control block initialization routine that is executed when the form is started and after the form is cleared.

◆ **Control block buttons require careful planning.** Usually, we recommend that you avoid navigable buttons in control blocks. Navigable buttons in control blocks cannot be pressed if the user is in a different block and the focus cannot leave the current block (such as when the form is in query mode). In addition, if the control block button can be pressed when the user is in another block, the user's action causes navigation triggers, such as POST-BLOCK, to fire.

◆ **Create specialized control blocks to group related control items.**

◆ **Prevent the operator from initiating query, insert, update, or delete operations on control blocks.** Attempting any of these operations in a control block will result in a run-time error.

Chapters 11, 12, and 13 provide details on how to best use Forms and Form Builder.

Next, we take a brief look at fast report building.

Fast Reports

Oracle Reports has been around since the late 1980s. Thank goodness it has improved since then.

Use the Report Wizard for the quickest results. Once you are familiar with the various styles of reports and get used to the layout editor, you will find Report Builder to be convenient and fairly fast for designing.

Figure 10-7 shows the selections available with the Report Wizard's standard templates.

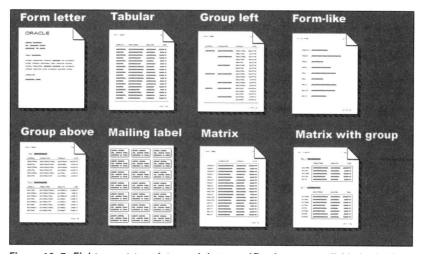

Figure 10-7: Eight report templates and data specifications are available in the Report Wizard.

Oracle magazine contains articles on how to use Report Builder. Look for back issues online.

Chapter 14 contains details on how to create reports that can be deployed on the Web as standalone reports (no special servers needed).

Graphics for reports

Graphics can enhance a report by adding visual appeal. A picture often is worth a thousand words, as the old saying goes. Add one bar chart to your next sales report, and find out for yourself how powerful an image can be in conveying your data.

Chapter 15 shows you how to create graphics with intelligence and use them inside forms, and even how to call reports from inside a graphic.

The Graphics Builder online help contains many great examples. Figure 10-8 shows a sample of the instructions available for your use when you click on the Help menu item in Graphics Builder.

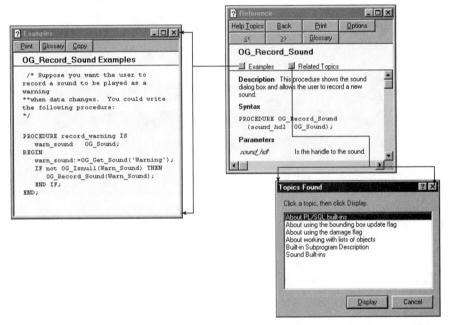

Figure 10-8: Many how-to instructions in Oracle Graphics Builder are simple and useful.

Graphics Builder's Chart Wizard

The clever Chart Wizard can be invoked from within Graphics Builder, Form Builder, or Report Builder. The most daunting part of the Chart Wizard is determining which of the chart types and subtypes will give you the best results, and what kind of data you need to use these chart types. Figures 10-9, 10-10, and 10-11 show the chart types and subtypes that have predefined templates.

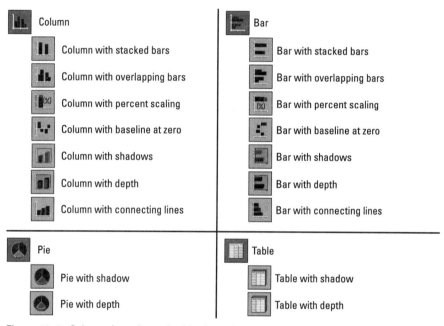

Figure 10-9: Column, bar, pie, and table charts have many standard templates.

Building Simple Procedures

When creating procedures for forms, reports, modules, or graphics, you can use the same tool: Procedure Builder. This tool is invoked from the other Developer tools whenever you double-click on a PL/SQL object, such as a Forms trigger.

Chapter 16 shows how to use the Procedure Builder tool in detail. You learn how to invoke the tool alone or within other tools and how to create reusable libraries.

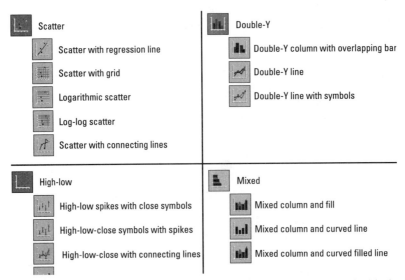

Figure 10-10: Scatter, double-Y, high–low, and mixed charts can be used with the Chart Wizard.

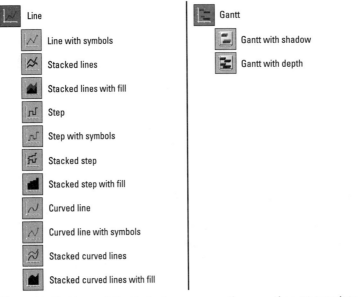

Figure 10-11: Line and Gantt charts are among the more than 50 templates in the Chart Wizard.

Figure 10-12 displays a typical edit session in the Procedure Builder.

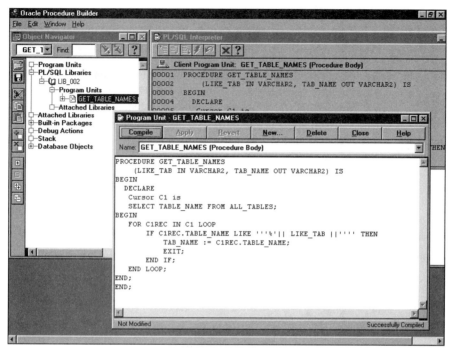

Figure 10-12: PL/SQL can be edited from any Developer tool using this common editor.

Running Forms on the Web

Deploying forms on the Web involves some planning and testing but is easier than you might think. The instructions in the Oracle documentation are complete and easy to read. Use the following URL (replace *<oraclehome>* with your actual Oracle home path) in your Web browser to go straight to the section that describes how to configure your Web server and deploy existing forms without making any code changes.

```
file://<oraclehome>/TOOLS/DOC20/guide21/d2k_web.htm
```

Here are the basic steps you need to run a form on the Web:

1. Start the Forms Server Listener.

2. Configure the Web server with a set of virtual files.

3. Create `fmx` files for your forms.

4. Define a path to the `fmx` files.

5. Create a startup Web page for the form.

The following sections briefly cover each step.

Starting the Forms Server Listener

The Forms Server sits between the Web server and the database server, as a middle tier in the three-tier architecture shown in Figure 10-13. The Forms Server runs the fmx version of the form. From the database server side, it behaves just like the executable that runs when you start up the Forms run-time application. From the Web server side, it behaves just like a CGI script as it interacts with the user's Web browser.

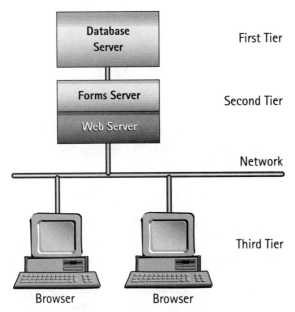

Figure 10-13: Three-tier architecture contains layers or levels of software that interact with each other.

To start the Forms Server Listener on NT, execute this command in the Start → Run window on the toolbar:

```
oraclehome\bin\f50srv32 port=nnnn
```

Replace oraclehome with the full path of your Oracle home directory, and replace nnnn with the actual port number.

To start the Forms Server Listener on UNIX, execute these two commands on the command line:

```
cd $ORACLE_HOME
f50srvm port=nnnn &
```

Replace *nnnn* with the port number that the Forms Server will use. This is an optional parameter. The port is assigned to 9000 by default.

A Forms Server Listener process starts running in the background and waits for a call to come in from the Web server when a form is initiated on the Web.

Configuring the Web server

The Web server must be able to find these items:

♦ JAR files

♦ Applet code

♦ HTML pages that interact with the form

Each of these should be defined as a virtual directory on the Web server. Figure 10-14 shows the administration page for assigning virtual directories using the Xitami NT Web server.

The virtual directory names you assign are arbitrary. These names are used later when you define the HTML page that starts up the form.

Preparing the form for the Web

At a minimum, you must generate an executable version of your form: the FMX file. The FMX file must be located in either of these two directories:

♦ ORACLE_HOME/bin

♦ Path defined by the FORMS50_PATH

Running the Forms applet

The Forms applet can be invoked using either a *static Web page* or a *Forms Cartridge Handler.*

The static Web page can be used with any Web server and requires you to create a new Web page to call each new form. This section describes the components of the static Web page method.

The Forms Cartridge Handler can be run only using the Oracle Web Application Server. The Forms Cartridge Handler dynamically generates a startup Web page for each form, based on parameters in the URL.

Virtual path   Actual path

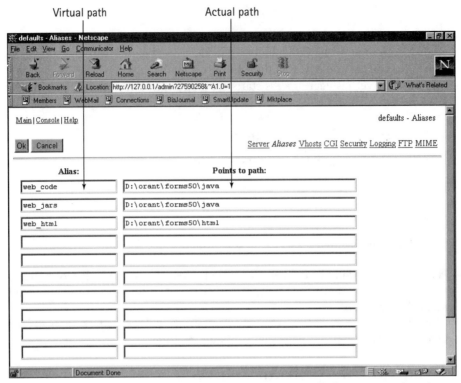

Figure 10-14: Define virtual directories to aid the Web server in finding source code and executables.

Here is the syntax required on the static Web page:

```
<APPLET CODEBASE="/yourwebcode/"
        CODE="oracle.forms.uiClient.v1_4.engine.Main"
        ARCHIVE="/yourwebjars/f50web.jar"
        HEIGHT=20
        WIDTH=20>
<PARAM NAME="serverPort"
        VALUE="yourport">
<PARAM NAME="serverArgs"
        VALUE="module=yourform
userid=youruser/yourpassword@yourdblink">
<PARAM NAME="serverApp"
        VALUE="default">
</APPLET>
```

Replace the following variables in the syntax:

- ◆ yourwebcode. This is the virtual directory defined for the applet code.

- ◆ yourwebjars. This is the virtual directory for the JARS you have created, if any.

- ◆ yourport. This is the port number you specified when you started the Forms Server Listener. The default value is 9000.

- ◆ yourform. This contains the form's filename (with or without the FMX suffix). This variable can optionally contain path information. If not specified, the path is assumed to be the ORACLE_HOME/bin directory or the path named in the FORMS50_PATH variable.

- ◆ youruser, yourpassword, yourdblink. Place a valid username, password, and database link here. This variable is optional. If you leave out the "userid=" parameter, the applet displays a login window where the user enters his or her own ID.

Here is an example of the complete HTML. This Web page calls the Storestock form using the schema username and password.

The Storestock form can be found in the Forms directory of the CD-ROM accompanying this book. The Web page described here can be found in the Web directory in the STARTUP.HTM file.

First, the Web page is initialized:

```
<HTML>
<!———————— starter.htm ————-- >
<HEAD><TITLE>Start the STORESTOCK Form on the Web</TITLE></HEAD>

<BODY BGCOLOR="FFFFFF">
<H1>Store Stock for the Busy Bee Store Chain</H1>
<H3>Initiating now.... please wait a moment....</H3>
```

Next, the applet definition begins. Here, you name the virtual directory for the applet code and the JARS:

```
<!- applet definition (start) —>
<APPLET CODEBASE="/web_code/"
        CODE="oracle.forms.uiClient.v1_4.engine.Main"
        ARCHIVE="/web_jars/f50web.jar"
        HEIGHT=20
        WIDTH=20>
```

Several parameters are defined for the applet. The first one is the port where the applet can find the Forms Server Listener. In this example, it is port 5555.

```
<PARAM NAME="serverPort"
       VALUE="5555">
```

The next parameter defines the form to start and the user ID to use:

```
<PARAM NAME="serverArgs"
       VALUE="module=STORESTOCK userid=toystore/toystore@tcpnow">
```

Chapter 4 shows how to implement default login (the OPS$ login) via the Web.

The final parameter defines the server application. When using a static Web page, the value of "default" is used.

```
<PARAM NAME="serverApp"
       VALUE="default">
```

The applet definition ends:

```
</APPLET>
<!- applet definition (end) ->
```

The Web page definition is completed by adding tags to end the body and the HTML page:

```
</BODY>
</HTML>
```

Now you are ready to run the application by calling the Web page just defined. Figure 10-15 shows the initial Web page.

After the applet loads, the window that runs the form looks much like the form when it is running in client/server mode. Figure 10-16 shows the applet window.

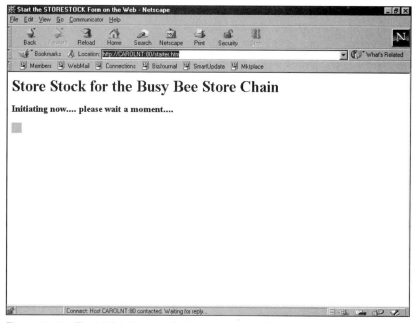

Figure 10-15: The initial display tells the user to wait for the applet to load.

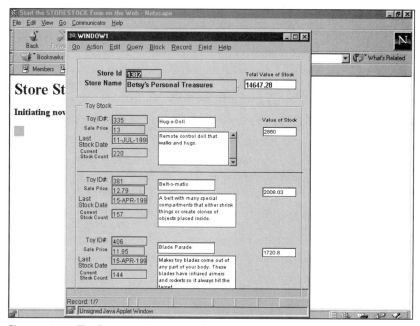

Figure 10-16: The Forms applet runs on the user's browser.

The initial testing of your forms may prove that they can be run without any changes to their structure. However, you should look into many considerations that can make your forms more efficient when running on the Web.

These are the Forms features that are not supported on the Web:

◆ ActiveX

◆ OCX

◆ OLE

◆ VBX

◆ When-Mouse-Enter trigger

◆ When-Mouse-Leave trigger

◆ When-Mouse-Move trigger

◆ MDI (window and toolbars)

Table 10-1 shows features that require some conversion to function in forms on the Web.

TABLE 10-1 FORMS FEATURES THAT REQUIRE
CHANGES TO FUNCTION ON THE WEB

Feature Name	Comment
HOST_COMMAND,ORA_FFI, USER_EXITOCX	Be aware that if these host calls display data, the user will not see it; the data is displayed on the server.
Iconic buttons	You must convert these to GIF format and store the GIF files in the same directory as your HTML pages.
Combo boxes	These will be supported in Version 2.1 "pending Java implementation of combination box widget," according to the documentation. The feature shows the combo box, but treats it like a pick list. The user cannot type in the field except as a method to locate a selection on the pick list. (As of this writing, Version 2.1.1 does not support the combo box.)

Keep in mind also that any trigger with a query or other SQL call to the database requires a call from the browser to the server, to the database, and back again.

Minimize these by using packaged procedures stored in the database and by taking advantage of array processing whenever possible.

Summary

Using Forms for quick startup can be best achieved by using the wizards and by careful planning of the design and of how best to use shared libraries, modules, and templates.

Triggers are an important part of forms and often are misused or misunderstood. Use the guidelines in this chapter to make efficient use of triggers.

Control blocks serve as storage containers for static data that can be referenced throughout the form. Other uses of control blocks are discussed in this chapter.

Reports can contain drill-down reports, charts, and many other intelligent features. This chapter lists the standard templates available for your use when you invoke the Report Wizard.

The Chart Wizard is another tool that will serve you well. This chapter includes a handy reference chart of all the different types and subtypes of chart layouts that are available with standard templates.

Procedure building is briefly described in this chapter. The Procedure Builder tool is covered in detail in Chapter 16.

One of the burning questions on the mind of developers is "Can the design I create today run on the Web tomorrow?" The answer is yes — and no. For the most part, you will be able to port your forms to the Web without changing them. However, some triggers and other features are not supported, or they function slightly differently on the Web. This chapter guides you through configuring your Web server, starting your Forms Server, and creating a startup page for your form. In addition, this chapter lists the features that are not supported and features that require extra work to deploy on the Web.

The remaining chapters in this part of the book contain great examples of how to get started using Developer. Chapter 11 includes basic examples of how to work with all the formats of forms items, including images and sound.

Chapter 11

Working with Fields

IN THIS CHAPTER

◆ Using different item types

◆ Calling other applications in your form

◆ Running a spreadsheet with ActiveX

WHEN CREATING A FORM, your entire user's input is received in *items*. Items are usually mapped to one column in a table. Items can also be placeholders for non-table data, such as the current date, or a calculated value. Items can also be functions in the form of buttons and charts.

This chapter describes each of the item types available to you and the best way to use each type. The last section in the chapter shows how to set up a default template for each item type so you can standardize the look and behavior of that item type in all your forms.

Understanding Item Types

Form Builder has many item types from which to choose. Table 11-1 outlines all item types and their usage.

TABLE 11-1 **FORM BUILDER ITEM TYPES**

Item Type	Description	Common Use
text item	A single- or multi-line text box.	Free text data entry fields, such a Name, Address, or Product description.
display item	A read-only text box. The user cannot type in this item.	Text containing a calculated value, or data retrieved from a related table.

Continued

TABLE 11-1 FORM BUILDER ITEM TYPES *(Continued)*

Item Type	Description	Common Use
check box	A text label with a graphic state indicator that displays the current value as either checked or unchecked	Selecting a checkbox toggles it to the opposite state.
list item	A selection list of values. Also called a combo box	A list of valid choices for a foreign key field. The list can be based on a query (record group) or a static list.
radio group	A set of at least two mutually exclusive choices	A set of static choices, such as Salary Range or Marital Status.
image item	A placeholder for an image	An image stored in the database, such as an ID Photo. Also can display an image retrieved from outside the database using a file name stored in the database, or a static file name, such as a file containing the company logo.
sound item	Audio clips	Music samples, or voice instructions. Users can record, play, edit, and save sounds.
button	An icon or text label that can be pressed with the mouse	The button can be programmed to execute various functions, such as "Exit" or "Commit."
chart item	A placeholder for a chart or graphic	Used for displaying charts created with Developer's Graphics Builder
OLE container	A display space for an embedded object	A spreadsheet, text document. The object is handled by the OLE server application within the OLE container space.
ActiveX control	A custom control button	Used for applications that need an ActiveX look and feel.

Each type has many built-in features. This chapter explains how to create all these types of items.

Text box

The text box is by far the most commonly used item type. This enables users to type in data that is stored in a column and row of a database table. Figure 11-1 shows a typical form with text box.

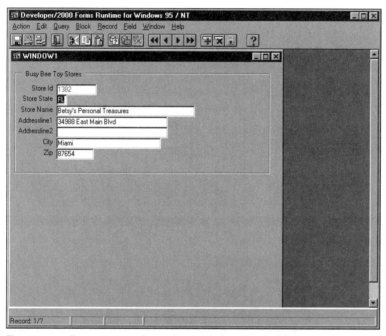

Figure 11–1: Forms use text boxes for quick data entry fields.

Creating a default form results in many text box fields. Figure 11-2 shows typical properties and window for a default text box.

Display item

The display item is similar to the text box, except the user cannot enter any data. The data in a display item is filled in by the Form (usually in a trigger) and cannot be modified by the user. However, the contents of the display item can be changed programmatically during run time.

Figure 11-3 points out a display item in our default form. All the field labels are display items.

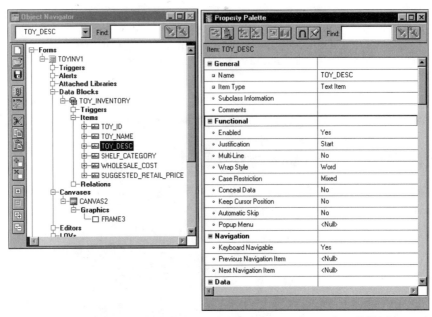

Figure 11-2: The properties of a default text box include mapping to data fields, font, and more.

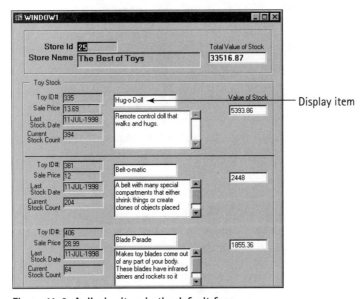

Figure 11-3: A display item in the default form.

The properties window for a display item enables you to design the look of the text. Figure 11-4 shows the properties window for a display item.

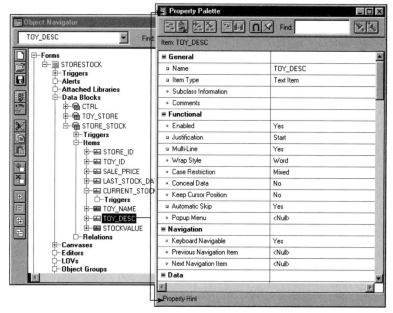

Figure 11-4: The properties window for a display item.

Display items often contain data retrieved from a table that is related to the block's base table. For example, the display item in Figure 11-3 above contains data retrieved from the TOY_NAME column in the TOY_INVENTORY table. Here is the PL/SQL for loading a person's name into a display item in the POST-QUERY trigger on the AQUATIC_ANIMAL block:

```
SELECT TOY_NAME
INTO :TOY_DESC
FROM TOY_INVENTORY
WHERE TOY_INVENTORY.TOY_ID - :TOY_ID;
```

Another typical use for display items is that of holding calculated summary data.

TIP   Developer has a new feature that enables you to define calculated fields without any programming.

As an example, let's create a form that shows revenue for the TOYSTORE schema and keeps track of a stock value for each item and the total stock value for the store on the form. Whenever the user changes a value in the stock form, the totals get recalculated. If the user adds a new record, or removes a record, the totals again recalculate. The form's base table is the STORE_STOCK table of the TOYSTORE schema. Follow these steps to create the form and add the calculated display items.

1. **In Form Builder, create a new form named STORESTOCK.** This is a master-detail form where the master table is TOY_STORE and the detail table is STORE_STOCK.

2. **Add a new item to the block for holding the value of the toy stock.** Name the item STOCKVALUE and make it a display item type.

3. **Let Form Builder generate the appropriate triggers by defining the Formula that creates the STOCKVALUE.** Do this by opening the Properties Window for STOCKVALUE and choosing the FORMULA box.

   Type in the following formula:

   ```
   :STORE_STOCK.CURRENT_STOCK_COUNT *
    :STORE_STOCK.SALE_PRICE
   ```

   Figure 11-5 shows what the formula window looks like after filling in the formula.

4. **Click OK to save your formula.**

5. **Create another display item named TOTALSTOCKVALUE in the master block.** This field will have a summary of the other calculated field in the detail block. Choose SUMMARY in the Calculation Mode property. Choose SUM as the Summary Function, STORE_STOCK as the summarized block, and TOTALSTOCKVALUE as the summarized item. Figure 11-6 shows the property values for the TOTALSTOCKVALUE item.

6. **Save and execute the form.**

Checkbox

A checkbox is a familiar sight to anyone who uses HTML forms on the Web. The checkbox is intuitive and easy to use. All you need do is supply the actual value stored in the database table to represent the On and the Off state of the checkbox.

Figure 11-7 shows where in the Properties Window to supply Form Builder with the values for On and Off.

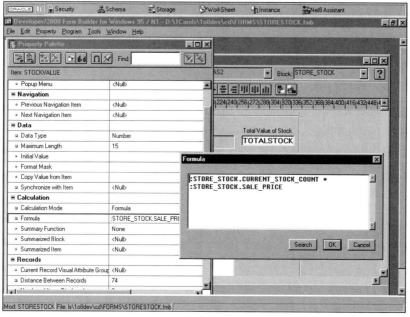

Figure 11-5: The formula window of a display item enables you to enter any calculation you need.

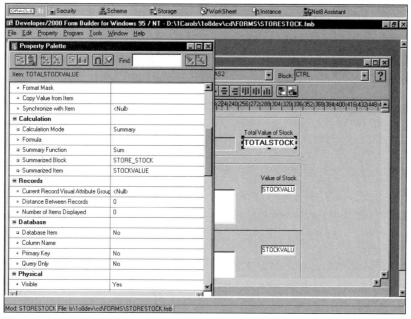

Figure 11-6: TOTALSTOCKVALUE is a summary field that Forms calculates for you.

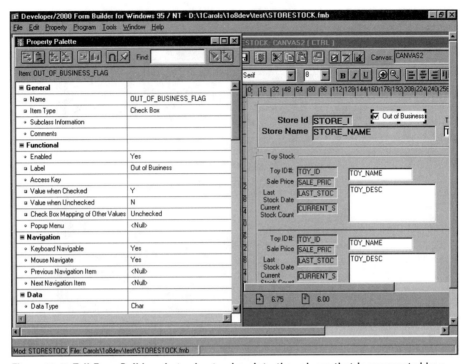

Figure 11-7: Tell Form Builder what value to place into the column that is represented by a checkbox.

You can also choose the default position of the checkbox (On or Off) by listing the default value in the Properties Window. As an example of using the checkbox, take the sample form created above for the Toy Store table. Use the Form Designer to change the item type of the OUT_OF_BUSINESS_FLAG from text box to checkbox. Figure 11-8 shows the checkbox type on the form.

TIP

If you have a standard for your Boolean-style columns, create a class that supports this. For example, if you use the letters Y and N to indicate "true" and "false," then you might set up a class for the checkbox item that uses these values as default settings. After creating this class, place it into your Object Library and click and drag it into any form you create that needs a checkbox.

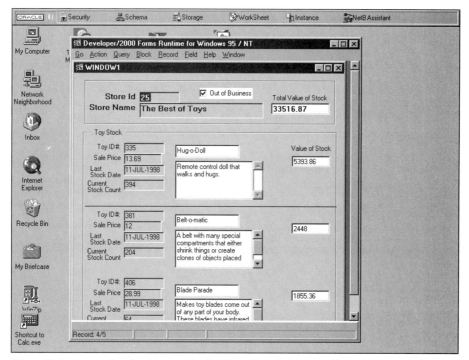

Figure 11-8: Toggle the checkbox on to signify a store that is out of business.

List item

You can choose any of several ways to populate a list item with selections:

◆ A **pre-defined List of Values (LOV)**. The list may be shared among several blocks in your form.

◆ A **custom list of values**. Define this list as you create the list item.

◆ A **static list defined either during the creation of the list item or defined earlier as a list of values (LOV)**.

After deciding how you will create the list of values, you also need to decide which of these three presentation styles you want to use for the list item:

1. **Pop-list.** This list appears only when you click the Display List menu selection. (You can create a button with the same menu function if you wish.)

2. **T-list.** This list displays a set of selections that are always visible in a rectangle. If there are too many selections to fit within the rectangle, a scroll bar appears on the right side. You specify the size of the rectangle in the Properties window.

3. **Combo box.** This list is embedded in the list item itself. The default selection appears in the box (or the current value for queried rows). The user clicks the arrow on the left side of the item to view and choose other selections.

Figure 11-9 shows a form with all three presentation styles.

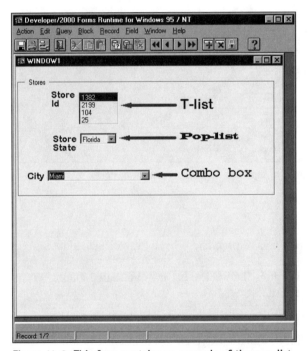

Figure 11-9: This form contains an example of the pop-list, the t-list, and the combo box.

The trickiest part of list items is creating the List of Values. The LOV is a form object all its own. The LOV is usually based on yet another form object: the Record Group. Figure 11-10 shows the typical mapping of a list item, a List of Values, and a Record Group.

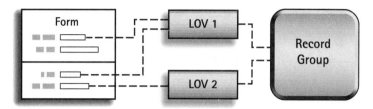

Figure 11-10: A list item is the top of the hierarchy that includes a List of Values and a Record Group.

Record Groups are great for creating lists of values for a foreign key. A Record Group can be re-used for more than one LOV item.

You can also create a List of Values by typing in the allowable values. This might be good for times when you have a finite list that is not stored in a table anywhere. For example, you need a field that stores the suffix of a file name. You create a LOV item and type in the three valid suffixes: gif, jpg, and htm.

Create a default form using Form Builder. Create a Data Block for the STORE_STOCK table. Now, change the STORE_ID item to a List Item.

The STORE_ID is a foreign key to the TOY_STORE table. Therefore, create a record group named STORELIST that lists all the stores. Use this query to populate the Record Group:

```
SELECT STORE_ID, STORE_NAME
FROM TOY_STORE
ORDER BY STORE_NAME
```

Now connect the LOV item (STORE_ID) with the Record Group (STORELIST) using the Record Group attribute in the Property Window. Figure 11-11 shows the property window and points out where you choose the Record Group.

Radio group

A radio group enables you to create two or more choices for the value stored in the column.

You can use either the Check Box or the Radio Group for columns that have only two choices for values.

Figure 11-12 shows the Property window for a radio group.

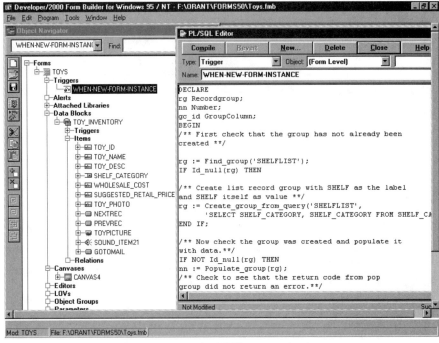

Figure 11-11: Connect a record group and a LOV item together here.

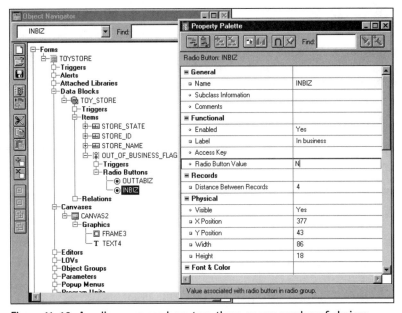

Figure 11-12: A radio group can have two, three, or any number of choices.

Image item

As you would expect, an image item holds an image. Forms enable you to display a variety of image formats without any special coding. These image formats are:

- GIF
- JFIF
- TIFF
- BMP
- JPG
- PICT
- RAS
- CALS
- PCX (read only)
- PCD (read only)

The image item provides you with a way to map your image onto the form canvas. You decide the dimensions of the display for the image. You also name the source of the image. The image might be stored directly in the database. The image might be stored in a file outside the database with a file name stored in the database. Either type of image storage is acceptable.

For example, create a default form with a data block that uses the TOY_INVEN-TORY table as its base table. Now, convert the TOY_PHOTO column into an image type item. Figure 11-13 shows the Properties window with the various details, such as Height and Width, defined for the TOY_PHOTO item.

Now generate and run the form. You will see the correct photo of each toy appear in the form as you have specified. Figure 11-14 shows the form with the image of one toy.

Sound item

Similar to Image items, a sound item can be embedded into the form and needs no outside applications to make sounds.

When you have defined these, you can use Forms built-in functionality to handle playing the sound, and even editing the sound. To edit the sound, it must be in one of these formats:

- WAV
- AIFF
- AIFF_C AU

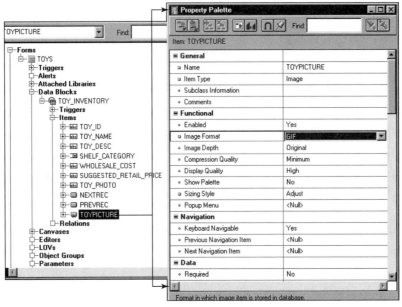

Figure 11-13: The image item has different attributes than the text item.

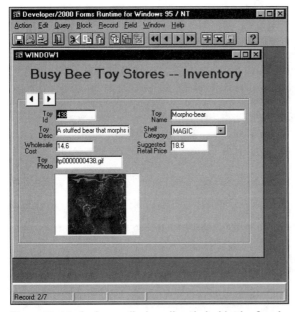

Figure 11-14: An image displays directly inside the form's canvas.

The sound file can be stored in the database as a BLOB or you can opt to store only the location of the sound file in the database. In either case, Forms will play the sound for you.

When you run a form that has a sound item embedded in it, Forms pops up a control window for the sound file as soon as you enter the field. Figure 11-15 shows the sound effects audio control window you see.

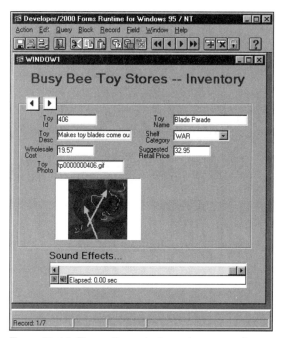

Figure 11-15: The audio control panel pops up when you enter the audio item field.

You can define exactly where this audio control window appears using the Properties window of the audio item. You can also enable or disable the editing controls (record, edit, erase, and so on) using the Properties window for the audio item.

Button

Buttons are used generally as control points within the form. You can define the exact function of a button to suit your needs. For example, you could create a "refresh" button that goes to the database and re-runs a query for you that summarizes current activity on the database.

You want to create a button that contains the image of a mailbox and starts up a new form called "domail." The mailbox image is in a file called `mailbox.gif`.

To create the button, follow these steps on an existing form:

1. Run Form Builder and open the form called `button.fmb`.

2. Open the canvas editor.

3. Click the button icon on the left side of your screen.

4. Draw a rectangle on the canvas that is the size you wish to use for your button. This creates the button item.

5. Double-click the button item to open the Properties window.

6. Modify the Image attribute to contain the file name `mailbox.gif`.

7. Rename the button item to "domail."

8. Go to the Form Navigator and right click the "domail" button. This opens a pop-up menu.

9. Choose Smart Triggers; and then choose on-mouse-click trigger. This opens a window for typing the PL/SQL commands for the trigger.

10. Type in the following PL/SQL commands:

```
IF FORM_STATE = QUERY then
    NEWFORM('domail');
ELSE
    COMMIT('ask');
    IF FORM_STATE = QUERY then
        NEWFORM('domail');
    ELSE
        HANDLE_ERROR;
    END IF;
END IF;
```

11. Compile and run the form.

12. The form now has a functioning button embedded into it. Figure 11-16 shows what the form looks like to the end-user.

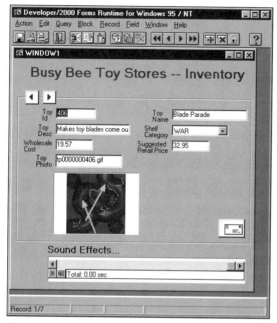

Figure 11–16: A simple mail button within a form.

 TIP

Your template form can contain standard buttons for functions you need. Usually, buttons that are standardized can be located in a standard control block. This enables you to add data blocks to a form without disturbing the buttons layout.

Chart item

A chart item is similar in its attributes to an image item. The chart item contains a non-editable image of a chart that is created with Graphics Builder. To embed a chart item into a form, you must first create the chart using Graphics Builder and then create a chart item and name the chart you just created in the Properties window of the chart item.

The great thing about a chart item is that it is dynamic. If data changes, the chart changes when you requery.

Figure 11-17 shows an example of a form with a chart item in the lower left corner.

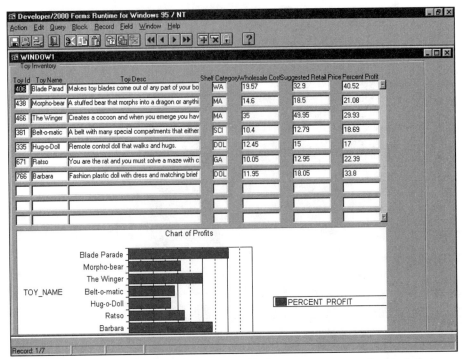

Figure 11-17: An embedded chart regenerates itself whenever you requery the block that contains it.

This sample form is included on the CD-ROM and is named `chartsample.fmb`. The chart that it references is also on the CD-ROM and is named `chart11.gpx`.

OLE container

OLE stands for Object Linking and Embedding. That means you can add the following two functions to your forms:

♦ **Linking.** Add a button in your form that starts up another application and loads a file. For example, your button might start an Excel spreadsheet and read a worksheet into Excel and display it for editing.

♦ **Embedding.** This enables you to open a space inside your form in which another application is executed. For example, you might open up a window where you can read and edit a Word document.

Forms supports the any OLE application you install on your client's platform. For example, these are some typical OLE applications:

◆ Microsoft Word

◆ Microsoft Excel

◆ Adobe Acrobat Reader

One advantage of using OLE is your ability to use database security to define access to various applications or documents. OLE container items also give your end users a central or a single method of accessing information, which can simplify training.

Figure 11-18 shows a form with an embedded drawing tool. A window fills about half the screen and displays a Word document.

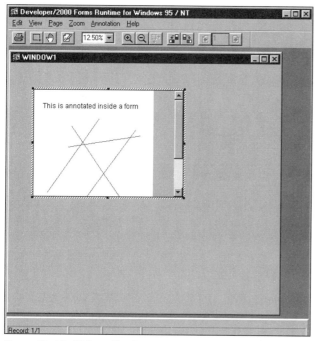

Figure 11-18: OLE applications are supported on Windows and Mac platforms.

ActiveX container and controls

The ActiveX item type defines an area called an *ActiveX container* within your form where certain ActiveX controls can be activated and manipulated. ActiveX controls are similar to OLE applications because they must be installed on the client machine. Unlike OLE applications, however, the ActiveX controls are not full blown applications, but simply ways of manipulating data that is then passed on to your form for complete processing.

For example, you can create a window that has rows and columns for a mini spreadsheet within your form. The data within the spreadsheet can be retrieved using special functions. For example, to retrieve the value found in Row 1, Column 3 of the spreadtable and place it into the field called UNIT_AMT, use the following code:

```
OLE_OBJ := ORACLESPREADTABLE_DMMTX.GetCellByColIndexRowIndex
(:ITEM('SPREADTBL_BLK.SPRDTBL').interface,3,1);
  :SPREADTBL_BLK.UNIT_AMT :=
ORACLESPREADTABLE_ICELL.Text(OLE_OBJ);
```

Figure 11-19 shows a spreadtable in a form.

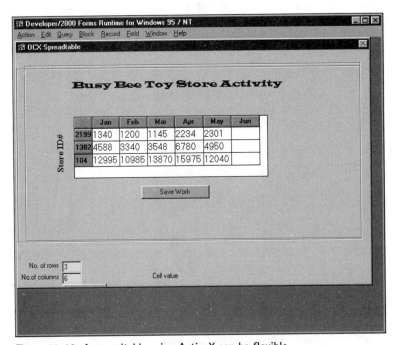

Figure 11-19: A spreadtable using ActiveX can be flexible.

 ActiveX controls are available only on the Windows platform and are supported within Forms Builder, but no other Developer components.

Chapter 17 contains many examples of how to implement ActiveX smoothly within your forms.

Summary

You can use eleven different item types in all your forms to store data, display graphics and titles, and perform many other functions.

New item types enable you to handle multimedia and OLE functions inside your forms such as the following:

♦ Recording and editing sound

♦ Displaying video

♦ Viewing and modifying Word documents

♦ Displaying and storing graphics in the database

The next chapter shows how to write efficient queries to use within your applications (forms, reports, procedures, and so on).

Chapter 12

Using Oracle8 Objects in Forms

IN THIS CHAPTER

♦ Creating procedures that manipulate Oracle8 objects

♦ Using Procedures as base tables

♦ Manipulating Oracle8 objects in forms

THIS CHAPTER COMBINES two different concepts: using procedures in place of tables in forms, and using Oracle8 objects in forms. By using procedures you can support object data of types that are not available by default in the Forms Builder.

Using a Procedure As the Base Table in a Form

A procedure can be used in place of a base table for the data block in a form. The procedure must pass a table as one of its parameters. When designing a procedure-based data block, you must specify the name of a procedure for querying, inserting, updating, deleting, and locking the table. These procedures are called when your user runs the form.

Introducing the sample form

The sample form that is developed in this chapter illustrates all five types of procedures and does so by using procedures that work with Oracle8 objects. Figure 12-1 shows what the final form looks like to the user.

This form enables a user to specify one person by ID number, view the books this person has checked out, and then either add more books or remove books from this person's list. The person's book list is stored in a nested table within an object table.

Figure 12-2 shows the Object Navigator display for our sample form.

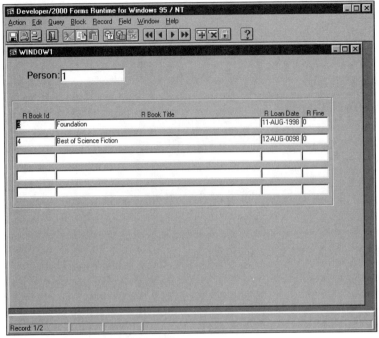

Figure 12-1: A form based on procedures looks the same as a form based on a table.

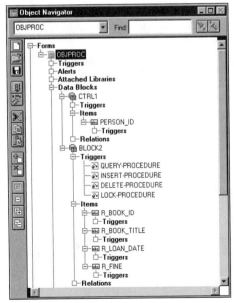

Figure 12-2: The structure of the sample form developed in this chapter.

The form contains two blocks:

♦ **CTRL1.** This control block serves to specify which person is borrowing or returning library books.

♦ **BLOCK2.** This data block is based on a set of procedures that work with the object table (PERSON_TABLE_T) and the object column (PERSON_BK_LOANED) in that table, which contains a nested table of borrowed books.

How procedures work as base tables

Whether you use relational tables or object tables, the concept behind data blocks based on a procedure remains the same. Five basic functions are performed in place of standard form behavior in a procedure-based data block:

1. **Queries.** The query procedure receives query criteria from the form through one or more IN parameters. It retrieves data from the database and constructs rows in which to place the data. When all the rows are constructed, they are placed into an IN OUT parameter that is defined to match that table structure. The form accepts the parameter and loads each row into a data block row.

2. **Inserting rows.** The form sends a table to the insert procedure. The table is an IN OUT parameter and contains rows of data to insert into the database. The procedure processes each row by inserting data into the database.

   In our example, new rows are inserted into a nested table within an object table. The two parameters sent to the insert procedure include the object table primary key and the table of rows ready for inserting into the nested table.

3. **Updating rows.** The update procedure is similar to the insert procedure. The procedure receives a table containing rows that are to be updated. The procedure updates the appropriate data in the database.

4. **Deleting rows.** The delete procedure again receives a table from the form. The form sends all of the rows that must be deleted. The procedure deletes the appropriate rows in the database.

5. **Locks.** The lock procedure is required as a companion to an update or delete procedure. The form calls this procedure prior to calling either the update or the delete procedures. The form also calls this procedure if the user explicitly clicks the lock button.

When creating a data block based on procedures, use the Data Block Wizard. A section later in this chapter illustrates how.

TIP

The Data Block Wizard asks you to specify procedures for all five functions listed previously. However, if you don't need all five, you can skip the functions you don't need. Remember: If you define a procedure for update or delete, you must also define a lock procedure.

The next section describes the objects in the sample database that are used in the sample form.

Reviewing Oracle8 Objects

Oracle8 enables the definition of business objects in a way that helps create logical centers of data and processing. Oracle8 implements objects as *user-defined datatypes*. User-defined datatypes are structures that are used in place of built-in datatypes. You can create your own user-defined datatypes by using the CREATE TYPE command. A user-defined datatype can combine the built-in datatypes (DATE, VARCHAR, NUMBER, and so on) and other user-defined datatypes as building blocks. When created, the user-defined datatypes are used in place of built-in datatypes when defining object tables.

How Oracle8 Objects Fit into System Design

Oracle8 objects work in the following ways:

♦ Oracle8 models the complexity of today's businesses naturally by embracing object technology without compromising the performance of the relational database system. Oracle8 has now become an object-relational database, enabling data architects to model the client-side business objects as object types in the database and keeping the data within a relational framework. Oracle8 takes advantage of both the object and relational worlds.

♦ Oracle8 implements object technology using the Objects option. The Objects option enables Oracle8 to store the business objects in their most natural form, enabling the efficient manipulation and retrieval of related business data. Thus business objects in the client-side applications can be directly mapped to their respective Oracle8 relational tables.

◆ Oracle8 implements objects as user-defined datatypes. User-defined datatypes use the built-in datatypes and other user-defined datatypes as building blocks for objects that model the data structure in the client business objects. Object tables use the created objects as a storage schema for the data, just like any other datatype. In addition to creating a natural structure to store business object data, Oracle8 also enables you to encapsulate the behavior of business objects into the objects in the form of member methods.

My book *Oracle8 Bible* (IDG Books Worldwide) completely covers Oracle8 objects and user-defined datatypes, including many sample SQL commands that create and manipulate Oracle8 object tables, object views, and object types.

For the sample form created in this chapter, use an object table. The table contains information about a person who borrows books from a library. The books that are borrowed are tracked in a nested table within the object table. Figure 12-3 shows the object schema for the object table on which the form is based.

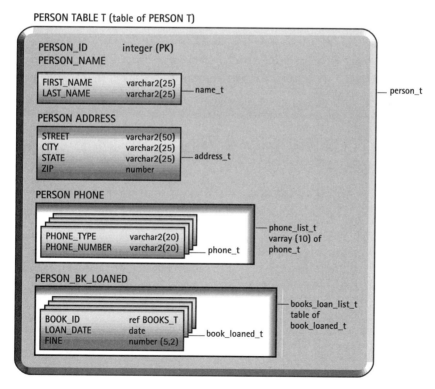

Figure 12-3: The Oracle8 object name PERSON_TABLE_T contains a nested table.

PERSON_TABLE_T is an object table containing a combination of traditional data types and user-defined datatypes.

For the example form, we use procedures that query, insert, update, and delete elements from the nested table in the column named PERSON_BK_LOANED. This nested table contains three columns:

- ◆ BOOK_ID. This column contains a pointer to another object table called BOOK_TABLE_T. BOOK_TABLE_T is an object table tracking library books (titles, authors, and so on).

- ◆ LOAN_DATE. This contains the date the book was checked out by this person.

- ◆ FINE. This column has a value that can be calculated and updated by another procedure in the database. The sample form contains a button that executes this procedure and refreshes the list of books displayed.

Creating a Package of Procedures

The first step in assembling the sample form is to create a package that contains all the procedures necessary for the form to function.

It is not required to create a package for your procedures. Rather, it is conve-nient because variables and datatypes are defined and then shared among the procedures.

The package is named BOOK_HANDLING. All the procedures in the package use the same two parameters:

- ◆ I_PERSON_ID. This is the primary key to the PERSON_TABLE_T object table. This is an IN parameter that tells the procedure which person's book lists to access.

- ◆ O_BOOK_LIST. This parameter is defined as IN and OUT. It contains a table of data reflecting the nested to table PERSON_BK_LOANED. The O_BOOK_LIST table has four columns:

◆ R_BOOK_ID. This is the primary key to the BOOK_TABLE_T object table.

◆ R_BOOK_TITLE. This column contains the book title from the BOOK_TABLE_T object table.

◆ R_LOAN_DATE. This contains the loan date from the corresponding row in the PERSON_BK_LOANED nested table.

◆ R_FINE. This contains the current fine for this book.

Table 12-1 describes each procedure included in the BOOK_HANDLING package.

TABLE 12-1 PROCEDURES INCLUDED IN THE BOOK_HANDLING PACKAGE

Procedure Name	Description
GET_BORROWED_BOOKS	This procedure loads the table parameter, O_BOOK_LIST, with rows. One row is loaded for each row in the nested table, PERSON_BK_LOANED.
LOAN_A_BOOK	This procedure receives a person ID and a table with rows to be inserted. This is how the library loans books.
DELETE_BOOK	This procedure removes a book when a person returns it to the library. The procedure receives a person ID and a table of all books returned. (In the form, the user simply removes rows.)
UPDATE_BOOK	This procedure changes to LOAN_DATE of a book. If a person renews her loan, the librarian can modify the loan date to reflect that change. The procedure receives a person ID and a table of all books updated. (In the form, the user simply updates the date in the appropriate rows.)
LOCK_TABLE	This procedure issues a LOCK command on the object table PERSON_TABLE_T.

Figure 12-4 shows a data flow diagram of how the form interacts with the procedures and the database.

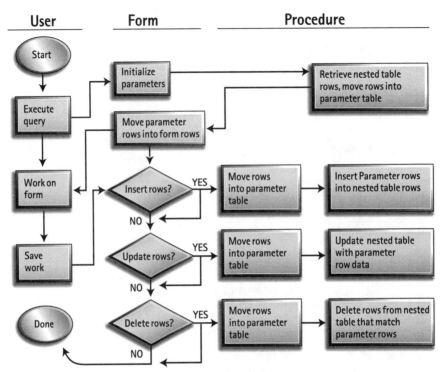

Figure 12-4: The sample form uses parameters to communicate with procedures.

The following code creates the sample package.

```
/* ———————- PACKAGE BOOK_HANDLING ———————- */
CREATE OR REPLACE PACKAGE BOOK_HANDLING IS
    TYPE V_BOOK_REC IS RECORD
      (R_BOOK_ID NUMBER(10),
       R_BOOK_TITLE VARCHAR2(100),
       R_LOAN_DATE DATE,
       R_FINE NUMBER(5,2));
    TYPE BOOK_TBL IS TABLE OF V_BOOK_REC INDEX BY BINARY_INTEGER;
PROCEDURE GET_BORROWED_BOOKS
(
I_PERSON_ID         IN NUMBER,
O_BOOK_LIST         IN OUT BOOK_TBL
);
PROCEDURE LOAN_A_BOOK
(
I_PERSON_ID         IN NUMBER,
O_BOOK_LIST         IN OUT BOOK_TBL
```

```
);
PROCEDURE UPDATE_BOOK
(
I_PERSON_ID          IN NUMBER,
O_BOOK_LIST          IN OUT BOOK_TBL
);
PROCEDURE DELETE_BOOK
(
I_PERSON_ID          IN NUMBER,
O_BOOK_LIST          IN OUT BOOK_TBL
);

PROCEDURE LOCK_TABLE
(
I_PERSON_ID          IN NUMBER,
O_BOOK_LIST          IN OUT BOOK_TBL
);

END BOOK_HANDLING;
```

After creating the package, all the procedures are created within the package body. The general (somewhat simplified) syntax for creating the package body is:

```
CREATE [OR REPLACE] PACKAGE BODY package_name { IS | AS}
[variable_declarations ]
[procedurebody ] ;
[procedure body ] ;
[procedure body ]; ...
END [package_name];
```

Replace *package_name* with the actual name of the package.

Replace *variable_declarations* with one or more declarations for variables, cursors, exceptions, record types, user-defined datatypes, or table types.

Replace *procedure_body* with the procedure execution code. You can have as many procedures as you need defined sequentially. You can also define functions here.

For the sample package, book handling, the syntax looks like this:

```
/* ————————— PACKAGE BODY————————-- */
CREATE OR REPLACE PACKAGE BODY BOOK_HANDLING  AS
    V_BOOK_LIST BOOK_TBL;
    V_PERSON_BK_LOANED BOOKS_LOAN_LIST_T;
    V_BOOK_LOANED BOOK_LOANED_T;
    V_BOOK BOOKS_T;
    V_REF_BOOK REF BOOKS_T;
```

```
PROCEDURE GET_BORROWED_BOOKS
(
I_PERSON_ID         IN NUMBER,
O_BOOK_LIST         IN OUT BOOK_TBL
) IS
BEGIN
... procedure code here
END GET_BORROWED_BOOKS;
PROCEDURE LOAN_A_BOOK
.... procedure parameters here
... procedure code here
END LOAN_A_BOOK;
... repeat for all procedures
END;
END;
```

The next sections show each procedure in detail.

Procedure for querying the nested table

The first few lines of code for this procedure within the package body define the two parameters needed. The code shows how:

```
PROCEDURE GET_BORROWED_BOOKS
(
I_PERSON_ID         IN NUMBER,
O_BOOK_LIST         IN OUT BOOK_TBL
) IS
```

The procedure starts off by deleting all rows coming in with the O_BOOK_LIST table parameter.

```
BEGIN
    /* — REMOVE INCOMING (OLD) BOOK LIST — */
    FOR V_CNT IN 1..O_BOOK_LIST.COUNT LOOP
        O_BOOK_LIST.DELETE(V_CNT);
    END LOOP;
```

Next, the procedure uses the incoming parameter, I_PERSON_ID, to query the object table, PERSON_TABLE_T, retrieving this person's list of loaned books. The book list is placed in a local variable, V_PERSON_BK_LOANED. The code continues:

```
    /* —- GET CURRENT BOOK LIST — */
```

```
BEGIN
   SELECT P.PERSON_BK_LOANED
      INTO V_PERSON_BK_LOANED
   FROM PERSON_TABLE_T P
   WHERE P.PERSON_ID = I_PERSON_ID;
   EXCEPTION
      WHEN NO_DATA_FOUND THEN
            V_PERSON_BK_LOANED := BOOKS_LOAN_LIST_T(NULL);
END;
```

Now, a loop begins. Each row in the book list is read. For each row, the procedure defines the reference to BOOK_ID and the associated book title. Both these variables are loaded, along with the LOAN_DATE and FINE, into a row in the local variable named V_BOOK_LIST. V_BOOK_LIST is a table that matches the definition of the IN OUT parameter O_BOOK_LIST. Here is the code for this loop.

```
FOR V_COUNTER IN 1..V_PERSON_BK_LOANED.COUNT LOOP
         /* —- LOOP THROUGH EACH ROW IN THE NESTED TABLE. —- */
         V_BOOK_LOANED := V_PERSON_BK_LOANED(V_COUNTER);
         V_REF_BOOK := V_BOOK_LOANED.BOOK_ID;
      /* —- USE DEREF TO RETRIEVE THE BOOK_TABLE_T
                           ROW THAT IS REFERENCED ———- */
         SELECT DEREF(V_REF_BOOK) INTO V_BOOK
         FROM DUAL;
      /* —- ADDS THE BOOK ID INTO THE OUTPUT TABLE. —- */
         V_BOOK_LIST(V_COUNTER).R_BOOK_ID := V_BOOK.BOOK_ID;
         V_BOOK_LIST(V_COUNTER).R_BOOK_TITLE := V_BOOK.BOOK_TITLE;
         V_BOOK_LIST(V_COUNTER).R_LOAN_DATE :=
V_BOOK_LOANED.LOAN_DATE;
         V_BOOK_LIST(V_COUNTER).R_FINE := V_BOOK_LOANED.FINE;
END LOOP;
```

The final step of the procedure copies the local variable containing the book list into the outgoing parameter:

```
   O_BOOK_LIST := V_BOOK_LIST;
   RETURN;
END GET_BORROWED_BOOKS;
```

When the form calls this procedure, it specifies the PERSON_ID whose books are to be listed. When the procedure completes, the form reads the book list found in the returned parameter and writes each row into a corresponding row in the data block.

Procedure for inserting into nested table

When the user adds new rows into the data block, the form keeps track of the rows in its own internal table. Then, when the user saves his or her work, the form calls the insert procedure and sends this procedure a table of all rows to be inserted.

The procedure begins by defining the same two parameters: PERSON_ID and O_BOOK_LIST:

```
PROCEDURE LOAN_A_BOOK
(
I_PERSON_ID          IN NUMBER,
O_BOOK_LIST          IN OUT BOOK_TBL
)
AS
BEGIN
```

Next, the procedure loops through each row in the O_BOOK_LIST parameter. For each row, a new row becomes inserted into the nested table called PERSON_BK_LOANED. For inserting into nested tables, you use a new feature of SQL created for objects called "THE." This feature enables you to use a straightforward SQL command to insert into Oracle8 objects. Another new feature of SQL used here is the REF function. The REF function returns the primary key of an object table in the new format needed for foreign keys (called *references*) within objects. Here are the LOOP and the INSERT commands for the sample procedure:

```
/* ———-- INSERT ROWS INTO BOOK LOANED NESTED TABLE — */
FOR V_COUNTER IN 1..O_BOOK_LIST.COUNT LOOP
     INSERT INTO THE(
     SELECT A.PERSON_BK_LOANED
     FROM PERSON_TABLE_T A
     WHERE A.PERSON_ID = I_PERSON_ID
     )
     SELECT REF(C),
     O_BOOK_LIST(V_COUNTER).R_LOAN_DATE,
     O_BOOK_LIST(V_COUNTER).R_FINE
     FROM BOOK_TABLE_T C
     WHERE C.BOOK_ID = O_BOOK_LIST(V_COUNTER).R_BOOK_ID;
END LOOP;
```

The final step in this procedure erases all the rows in the book list table parameter and ends the procedure:

```
/* ———-- RETURN NULL TABLE ——— */
   FOR V_CNT IN 1..O_BOOK_LIST.COUNT LOOP
```

```
      O_BOOK_LIST.DELETE(V_CNT);
   END LOOP;
END LOAN_A_BOOK;
```

Procedure for deleting from nested table

As the user removes rows on her data entry screen, the form prepares a table of deleted rows. When the user saves her work, the form calls the procedure for deleting rows. In the sample form, this procedure is named DELETE_BOOK.

As with the other procedures, the first part of the code defines incoming and outgoing parameters:

```
/* ——————- PROCEDURE DELETE_BOOK ———— */
PROCEDURE DELETE_BOOK
(
I_PERSON_ID          IN NUMBER,
O_BOOK_LIST          IN OUT BOOK_TBL
)
IS
BEGIN
```

Next the procedure declares local variables. Most of these variables define special object datatypes.

```
DECLARE
V_REF_BOOK REF BOOKS_T;
V_BOOK_RESERVED BOOK_LOANED_T;
V_PERSON_BK_LOANED BOOKS_LOAN_LIST_T;
V_ID NUMBER;
V_BOOK_ID NUMBER(10);
V_BOOK BOOKS_T;
V_DELETE_BOOK_SUBSCRIPT NUMBER;
CURSOR C1 IS
SELECT A.PERSON_ID, A.PERSON_BK_LOANED
     FROM PERSON_TABLE_T A
     WHERE PERSON_ID = I_PERSON_ID
     FOR UPDATE;
BEGIN
```

This procedure contains three nested loops. Figure 12-5 shows how these loops fit together. The first loop works with the incoming list of rows to be deleted. It also initializes a subscript variable, V_DELETE_BOOK_SUBSCRIPT. Later, this variable is checked to see which row to delete.

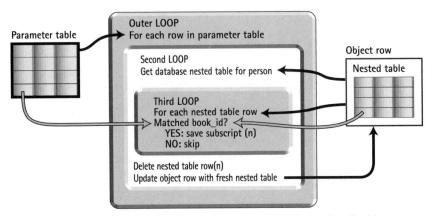

Figure 12-5: The loops for deleting a row from a nested table are described here.

The code for the first loop is:

```
/* —- OUTER LOOP IS INCOMING TABLE OF DELETED BOOKS — */
FOR V_DELCOUNTER IN 1..O_BOOK_LIST.COUNT LOOP
    V_BOOK_ID := O_BOOK_LIST(V_DELCOUNTER).R_BOOK_ID;
    V_DELETE_BOOK_SUBSCRIPT := -1;
```

The second loop always executes one time because it is based on the incoming PERSON_ID. One person's book list is retrieved using this loop. A loop offers programming convenience; combining a loop with a cursor tells PL/SQL to handle the open, fetch, and close functions implicitly. This loop reads one book list (in a nested table) and copies the entire nested table into a local variable.

```
FOR C1REC IN C1 LOOP
V_PERSON_BK_LOANED := C1REC.PERSON_BK_LOANED;
```

The third and final loop steps through each row in the nested table (local variable) and finds the subscript for the row that matches the BOOK_ID set in the first loop. It is not as simple as looking at the BOOK ID in the nested table. This book ID is a REF datatype; it contains a pointer to an object table record. Unlike relational tables, a nested table's foreign keys must be deciphered using the DEREF function. When this is accomplished, the loop can compare the two values of BOOK_ID. If they match, the row is deleted from the nested table. The code for the third loop looks like this:

```
/* ————-THIRD LOOP IS LIST OF BORROWED BOOKS —- */
FOR V_COUNTER IN 1..V_PERSON_BK_LOANED.COUNT LOOP
V_BOOK_RESERVED := V_PERSON_BK_LOANED(V_COUNTER);
V_REF_BOOK := V_BOOK_RESERVED.BOOK_ID;
```

```
SELECT DEREF(V_REF_BOOK) INTO V_BOOK
FROM DUAL;
IF V_BOOK.BOOK_ID = V_BOOK_ID   THEN
/* —— SAVE THE SUBSCRIPT FOR THIS BOOK ——- */
V_DELETE_BOOK_SUBSCRIPT := V_COUNTER;
END IF;
END LOOP;
```

The next step occurs inside the second loop. Here the subscript variable is checked. If it is > 0, that means a matching BOOK_ID was found to delete. The row is deleted like this:

```
IF V_DELETE_BOOK_SUBSCRIPT > 0 THEN
V_PERSON_BK_LOANED.DELETE(V_DELETE_BOOK_SUBSCRIPT);
```

The table, PERSON_TABLE_T, is updated with a new version of the nested table using this code:

```
UPDATE PERSON_TABLE_T
SET PERSON_BK_LOANED = V_PERSON_BK_LOANED
WHERE CURRENT OF C1;
```

Next, the if statement is closed, and the two open loops are closed.

```
        END IF;
    END LOOP;
END LOOP;
```

The last step clears the book list parameter of all rows and ends the procedure:

```
/* ———- RETURN NULL TABLE ——— */
   FOR V_CNT IN 1..O_BOOK_LIST.COUNT LOOP
       O_BOOK_LIST.DELETE(V_CNT);
   END LOOP;
END DELETE_BOOKS;
```

Procedure for locking Oracle8 object table

This procedure simply issues a LOCK command on the object table called PERSON_TABLE_T. The complete procedure code follows:

```
PROCEDURE LOCK_TABLE
(
I_PERSON_ID            IN NUMBER,
```

```
O_BOOK_LIST              IN OUT BOOK_TBL
)
IS
BEGIN
/* ———— LOCK TABLE. ——— */
LOCK TABLE PERSON_TABLE_T IN SHARE UPDATE MODE;
END LOCK_TABLE;
```

This procedure is called by the form at the time when the form usually issues a LOCK TABLE command.

Creating a Form Using the Procedures

Now that we have created all the procedures needed to maintain the nested table in the Oracle8 object table, PERSON_TABLE_T, it is time to create the data block.

 If you wish to follow along, open the form on the CD-ROM named OBJPROC. This form contains the control block, but not the data block that uses procedures.

Starting at the Object Navigator in Forms Builder, create the data block by following these steps:

1. Click the Data Blocks icon in the Object Navigator.

2. Click the Create icon on the tool palette, which opens a dialog box.

3. Select the Create button from the Data Block Wizard. This pops up the first screen of the Data Block Wizard.

4. Select the Stored Procedure button as shown in Figure 12-6. Click Next.

5. Fill in the details for the query procedure. Type in the package and procedure name for the procedure that queries the nested table. In our sample form, type in this name:

   BOOK_HANDLING.GET_BORROWED_BOOKS

   Click the Refresh button. This will bring the columns into the box. Log into the database if the login window appears. Now you see a list of available columns in a box on the screen. These columns are the ones defined in the table parameter, O_BOOK_LIST.

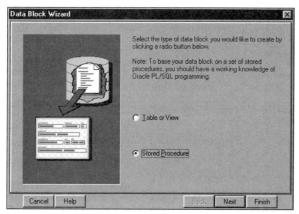

Figure 12-6: Begin defining the data block that uses a stored procedure by selecting the appropriate button.

Click the double greater-than sign button (>) to copy all the columns into the Database Items box. Now type the following data block and column name in the Arguments box for the I_PERSON_ID parameter:

```
:CTRL1.PERSON_ID
```

Figure 12-7 shows the final look of this page. Click Next to see the window for defining the insert procedure appear.

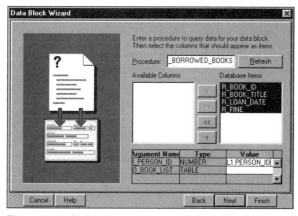

Figure 12-7: Define the query procedure and the argument for the PERSON_ID.

6. Define the insert procedure now. Type in:

```
BOOK_HANDLING.LOAN_A_BOOK
```

Click Refresh. The display now shows the four columns in the parameter table and lists the two parameters. Here you only need to add the argument for I_PERSON_ID:

`:CTRL1.PERSON_ID`

Figure 12-8 shows the final look of this page. Click Next to continue.

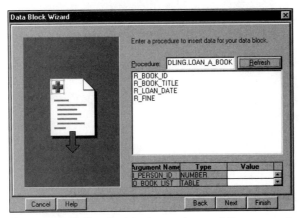

Figure 12-8: Define the insert procedure and the argument for the PERSON_ID.

7. This step is nearly the same as the previous step. Type in the update procedure name:

   `BOOK_HANDLING.UPDATE_BOOK`

   Click Refresh. Type in the same argument for I_PERSON_ID. Then click Next to proceed to the delete procedure window.

8. Again, follow the same format for the delete procedure window. The delete procedure name for the sample form is:

   `BOOK_HANDLING.DELETE_BOOK`

   Click Refresh. Type in the same argument for I_PERSON_ID. Then click Next to proceed to the next window.

9. Repeat the same format for the lock procedure window. The lock procedure name for the sample form is:

   `BOOK_HANDLING.LOCK_BOOK`

   Click Refresh. Type in the same argument for I_PERSON_ID. Click Finish.

10. Complete the process by following the prompts in the Layout Wizard. For the sample form, choose Tabular layout and specify that 5 records should be displayed.

Figure 12-9 shows the final results in the Layout Editor. Of course, you are free to modify the layout to your own standards.

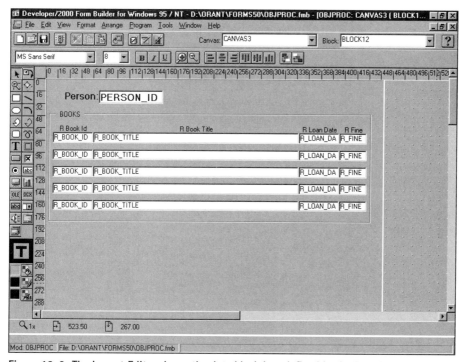

Figure 12–9: The Layout Editor shows the data block just defined in the Data Block Wizard and Layout Wizard.

Now you have a form to run that uses the procedures to insert, update, delete, and query the nested table contained in the PERSON_TABLE_T object table.

Summary

This chapter discusses the concept of using a procedure as the base table of a form data block. In reality, a set of procedures are used: one for each function the form handles, such as query, insert, update, lock, and delete.

In addition, the sample form and procedures here use Oracle8 objects. Oracle8 objects use user-defined datatypes that are not supported by Form Builder. However, by creating appropriate PL/SQL procedures, you can create a form that transparently works with Oracle8 objects.

The first and most demanding step involves creating the PL/SQL procedures for each of the five functions (query, insert, and so on). Next, these are all built in the framework of a single package called BOOK_HANDLING.

Now, the basic form with a single control block is created. The last step employs the Data Block Wizard to create a data block based on the package's procedures. The end result gives you a form where you specify a PERSON_ID and then you can query, add, remove, or update the library books that are in that person's possession, The form enables you to use the usual operator functions, such as Execute Query, Remove Record, and so on.

The next chapter discusses the control block and its many uses.

Chapter 13

Duplicating Forms Objects

IN THIS CHAPTER

- ◆ Reusable object libraries
- ◆ Creating object groups
- ◆ Object groups within object libraries
- ◆ Inheriting objects and subclasses
- ◆ Using template forms

THE DEVELOPMENT EFFORT for any project should be concerned with project standardization, efficiency of development, and ease of future maintenance. Implementing common functionalities and standard look-and-feel attributes as reusable objects reduces redundant code and standardizes the development and behavior of the application.

This chapter shows you how to create and use object libraries, object groups, classes, and template forms for duplicating and reusing forms objects.

If an application is going to use one form, it is more than likely that the application will use more than one form. The screens should have a consistent look and feel. Object libraries and classes enable the designer to create a template from which all forms can collect their attributes. As an object is changed, the changes can be redistributed through the forms without having to go in and change the forms accessing the library. The form you create in this chapter will use examples from the toy store application.

 This chapter assumes you are already familiar with creating a form using Forms 5.0.

Reusable Object Libraries

 The tables of the TOYSTORE schema used in this chapter are found on the CD-ROM.

Initially, you may create a simple form containing objects that you may want to see in other forms. Examples include:

◆ Title visual attributes

◆ Buttons

◆ Window size and border

◆ Triggers

Figure 13-1 shows a simple example of a form for the TOY_STORE table.

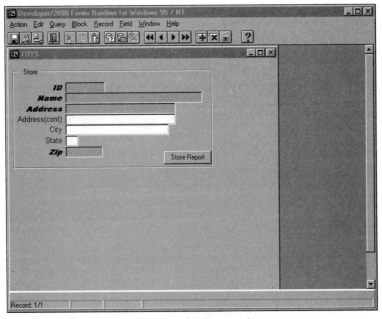

Figure 13-1: The Toy Store form is a simple example.

A number of visual attributes and objects on this form can be carried throughout the application.

- ◆ **Visual Attribute examples.** All the mandatory fields on this form have specific prompt visual attributes as well as specific field visual attributes. The same specific set of visual attributes is set for the optional fields.

- ◆ **Object examples.** The button on this form can be used on other forms to call reports. The When-Button-Pressed trigger can be passed as well. The window size and style can also be used on other forms.

Creating object libraries

Initially, you can add the visual attributes to the object library. To create the library, you simply select Object Libraries from the Object Library node in the Object Navigator. Then either double-click the node or use the plus button on the left side of the window. A default name is given to the object library. All you can store at this point is a name and a comment. An object library is divided into library tabs. You can use the tabs to logically divide the information within the library. When you double-click the Library Tabs node (or use the plus button), you create a new tab with a default name. In addition to storing the name and comments, you can also store a meaningful label for the tab. You will see the tab on your screen, as shown in Figure 13-2.

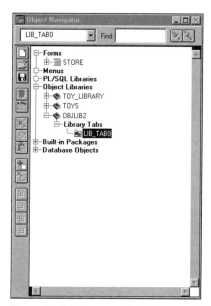

Figure 13-2: The new object library contains one object library tab.

Adding objects to an object library enables you to transport them from form to form.

> If the end-user wants to change certain objects later, a change to the object library can change all the forms in the application.

Once the library tab is open, just drag items from the form to the library. Multiple tabs can be placed in an object library. You can quickly differentiate the different types of items in your library by using different tabs: for example, a tab for visual attributes, a tab for triggers, and one for window attributes. Figure 13-3 shows the single library tab UNIFORMITY.

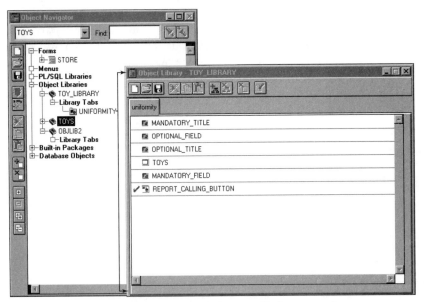

Figure 13-3: A library has one or more tabs for reusable items on a form.

> You cannot add objects directly to an object library. They must be brought in from a source form.

Reusing the items in the object library

When you create a new form, you can use all the objects in the object library we just created. While you have the object library open, create a new form. Now, you can drag items from the object library into the new form. For example, drag the visual attributes – by selecting all of them (individually or together) and dragging them under the Visual Attributes node on the new form. Figure 13-4 shows the Forms dialog box that is displayed.

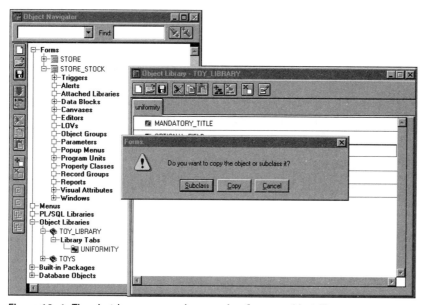

Figure 13-4: The alert box you see when copying from an object library.

If you copy the items from the library, they become a part of the form. If you subclass them, they are still owned by the library. Subclassing will be discussed later in this chapter.

Creating Object Groups

An object group is very similar to a PL/SQL package. While a PL/SQL package is a set of PL/SQL functions and procedures that work together, an *object group* is a set of objects that work together. For example, the button that calls the store report may look very specific for the store screen. It is actually fairly dynamic and is made up of a number of items:

◆ A button for the end user to push

◆ A forms parameter that is passed in with the name of the report

◆ A forms parameter that is passed in with the label for the button

◆ A When-New-Form-Instance trigger that places the label on the button

◆ A When-Button-Pressed trigger that does a run_product routine to call the report

If a report is going to be available from every form, you can package these pieces together in an object group so that the object group can be used in every form. When built dynamically, you can use the same set of objects to call different reports in different forms. Figure 13-5 shows the REPORT_BUTTON object group with three components.

To create an object group, you select the Object Group node in the Navigator. When you double-click the node (or use the plus button), you create an object group with a default name. Just dragging items from the form into the object group loads the object group with information. Figure 13-5 shows the REPORT_BUTTON object group with three components.

Figure 13-5: An object group for the button has several object children.

The items in the object group use the same icons as they would within the form. For example, in the object group in Figure 13-5, the parameters have the same icon they would have in a form.

You can build an object group as a summary of other object groups. Summary levels are helpful when you want to pass large groups of information to some forms, while passing only parts of the whole to other forms. For example, suppose you have two buttons. One button is used for calling a form, and the other is used for calling a report. If some forms only call a report, you would use object group "report." If some forms only call a form, you would use object group "form." If some forms called both, you would use object group "all."

Object Groups in Object Libraries

Once an object group and an object library are created, then the object group can be passed into the object library (see Figure 13-6). Once the object group is within the library, the library has a powerful set of object packages much like the PL/SQL packages that a PLL file has. By putting the object group and the form item (such as the report button) on one tab, all of the pieces to create a report button are encased in the tab for quick replication.

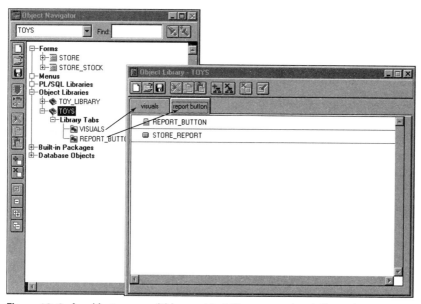

Figure 13–6: An object group within an object library organizes information.

Form block items cannot be stored in an object group.

Inheriting Objects and Subclasses

Now that you have an object library, you can inherit the objects that are in the first form into all of the forms you create in the future. If your user decides they want you to change any characteristics of all the forms, you can change the object library, and the existing forms are changed just by regenerating them. If your user wants one form to operate slightly differently from the others, you can change one inherited characteristic on that form without losing the other inherited characteristics.

When creating a new form, it is initially easiest to just copy the library objects to the empty form. Using the example created previously in this chapter, we open the TOYS object library. The first tab includes all of the visual attributes that will be shared among all the forms. By selecting all of the items on this tab at once (select the first item and hold down the Shift key while selecting the last item), you can drag them to the Visual Attributes node in the Object Navigator. Select Subclass from the alert box, and the visual attributes are added to the form. Figure 13-7 shows the results of these actions.

Notice in Figure 13-7 that the inherited objects have a visual attribute icon with an arrow pointing into the icon. The arrow implies that these items have been inherited.

Subclassing is an improvement over the Forms 4.5 activity of referencing. Referencing enabled you to make changes to the source form or PLL and regenerate the changes in other forms. However, you could not change anything in a subsequent form that had been brought in as a referenced object. In Forms 5.0, you can make a change in the property sheet for any of these visual attribute items you subclassed. The item still has an inherited arrow on it because the item shares any changes from the library source of the inherited object.

The second tab in our example object library holds all the items for the report button. You can choose the object group from the report tab and drag it to the Object Group node in the Object Navigator. If you just choose Copy from the alert box, the objects are copied to the form, and no reference is kept of the source of the information. Figure 13-8 shows that the icons look the same as if the items were created on the new form.

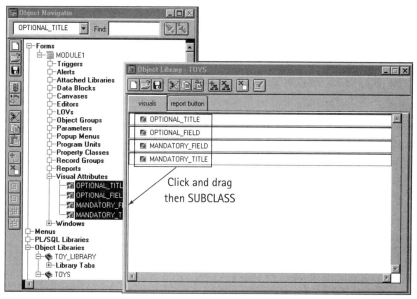

Figure 13-7: Visual attributes have been inherited (subclassed) from an object library.

Figure 13-8: Objects copied into a form appear the same as newly created objects.

TIP Subclassing does not have to been done from an object library. Forms can subclass information from other forms. So a forms template can be used to subclass information from one form to another (much like referencing in Forms 4.5).

Some caveats about subclassing

You need to follow certain rules when using subclassing to insure that subclassing works.

♦ **Do not have a subclassed form open when working on changes to a library or source form.**

If you have opened a form that is sharing information from a library and you try to make changes to the library, you will lose all links to the library. The next time you try to open the subclassed form, you will see the message, "Failed to load the following objects." A list of the objects is displayed.

♦ **Make sure your object libraries are stored in the same place as your executable forms.**

If you are storing forms executables in a common directory for the user, make sure that the object library is in the same directory. Otherwise, the form will not use the library objects (which is similar to the use of PLLs).

♦ **If you change a subclassed object, the change can be lost.**

You change the text color on a subclassed visual attribute to another color. The visual attribute is still subclassed. So if you change the color of visual attribute in the library, the change you made after subclassing is lost, and the new color is inherited by the visual attribute when you regenerate the subclassed form.

Template Forms

The starting point for developers can be template forms that are based on the foundation object and PL/SQL libraries. Template forms are typically developed to the point where a developer can produce a simple form based on the template with minimal effort. Template forms are also generic so that they may be used as the starting point for many other forms. For large systems, a template form for each business area may be necessary to establish a standard for the subsystem.

To create a new form based on a template, select the template option in the Form Builder initial dialog, which is shown in Figure 13-9.

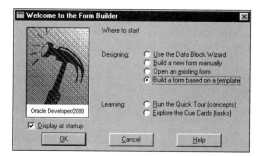

Figure 13-9: Selecting the template option

After you have checked the "Build a form based on a template" checkbox, you have to select the form you will use as a template. Care must be taken when selecting the template form because Form Builder enables you to select any valid form's source file. Keeping the template forms in a separate location, as shown in Figure 13-10, can help avoid confusion.

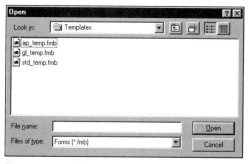

Figure 13-10: When you keep template forms in a separate location, it is easier to choose one.

The default name of the new module is different from the template to help avoid an overwrite of the template. When designing template forms, you should consider future maintenance of forms based on the template. As much as possible, template forms should use object libraries and PL/SQL libraries so that changes to the standard look and feel may easily be incorporated into forms based on those templates.

Summary

Duplication of items between forms is critical for creating an application that carries the same look and feel throughout the entire form set.

Object libraries enable the developer to create a single repository for all of the reusable items they want to share among the forms in their application. Object libraries can be split into tabs, which enables the developer to sort the library into specific development areas.

Object groups enable the developer to store a certain package of information that works together in a form into one "package." An object group can then be stored within an object library.

The subclassing capabilities in Forms 5.0 are very powerful. They enable the developer to create a form that inherits the characteristics of another form or library. The developer can edit these characteristics without losing the inheritance relationship.

With these tools the developer can create a robust application system that can be changed easily and quickly by altering the objects that subclassing originates from.

Chapter 14

Report Builder and Web Reports

IN THIS CHAPTER

- ◆ Creating reports using the Report Wizard
- ◆ Creating a parameter form using the Parameter Form Builder
- ◆ Reviewing reports with the Live Previewer
- ◆ Converting reports into Web-enabled reports
- ◆ Using report templates

THE REPORT BUILDER, like so many other features of Developer, has so many features to look at it is hard to decide where to begin. This chapter focuses on several new features and combines them with advanced features of Oracle8 objects. You will create two linked reports using the Report Wizard, the Parameter Form Builder, and the Live Previewer. Then you will use the Web Report Wizard to convert them to Web pages that are correctly linked together.

Using the Report Wizard

The first report is a simple listing of people who hold library cards. This list must extract data from an object table. The sample object table used for the report is called PERSON_TABLE_T. This object table keeps track of people who borrow books from a library.

A nested table within the table contains all the books a person currently has borrowed – and provides several user-defined datatypes for other attributes within the table. Figure 14-1 shows a diagram of this table.

PERSON TABLE T (table of PERSON T)

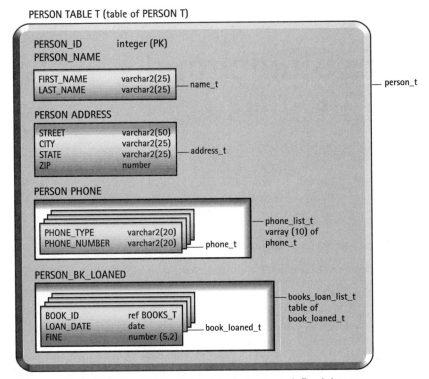

Figure 14-1: The PERSON_TABLE_T object table has user-defined datatypes and a nested table.

The Report Wizard enables you to create a report quickly. Some of the best features of the Report Wizard are:

◆ **Reentrant.** In addition to the first generation of the report layout, the Report Wizard is *reentrant*. This means you can return to the same wizard format to make changes to your report layout.

◆ **Templates.** The wizard takes advantage of the new feature: report templates.

A sample report using the PERSON_TABLE_T table illustrates the wizard. The following query is the basis for this report and was entered into the report Wizard query box:

```
SELECT A.PERSON_ID,
    A.PERSON_NAME.FIRST_NAME first_name,
    A.PERSON_NAME.LAST_NAME last_name
FROM PERSON_TABLE_T A
```

The query takes advantage of Oracle8 object extensions for SQL. To retrieve data from a user-defined datatype, you can specify the object column name followed by a period delimiter, followed by the column named define within the user-defined type. For example, the following code retrieves the VARCHAR2 column named STREET from the PERSON_ADDRESS object column:

```
A.PERSON_ADDRESS.STREET
```

Use a table *alias* whenever you reference object tables. Although a table alias is not required every time, PL/SQL often requires one — so using table aliases may be a good habit to cultivate.

I also used the template that is provided with the Report Builder to simplify the layout. Figure 14-2 shows the final report.

Figure 14–2: A simple report can be generated in minutes using the Report Wizard.

After generating the initial report layout, reenter the Report Wizard by selecting Tools → Report Wizard from the menu. Figure 14-3 shows the query portion of the wizard. Notice the tabs across the top of the Report Wizard window. These tabs can be used to specify field size, headings, calculated fields, and so on.

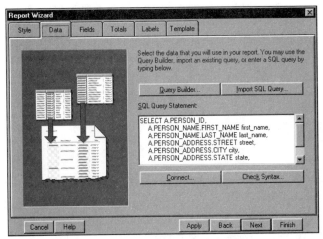

Figure 14-3: The Report Wizard can be used after initially generating a report.

Building a Report with Parameters

The second report illustrated in this chapter contains a user-defined parameter and two stored functions. Figure 14-4 shows the layout of this report when it is run.

The report has these features:

◆ A single person's name and address are displayed. The PERSON_ID that determines which person to display is passed to the report through a user-defined parameter.

◆ The user-defined parameter can be passed two ways. It can come from another report using a report trigger, or it can come from this report's parameter form.

◆ The Home Phone field displayed on the report comes from a varray object. It is retrieved using a stored function.

◆ The Total Fines field also is retrieved using a function that adds up elements within a nested table.

Before creating the report, we must create the two functions within the database.

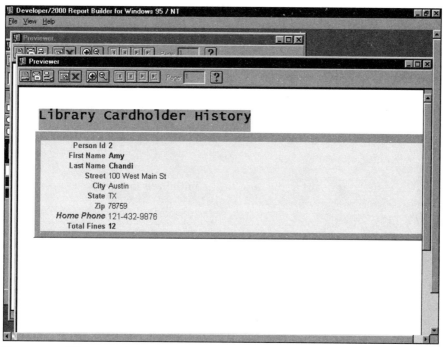

Figure 14-4: This report shows details for one library user.

Creating the BOOK_FINE function

Referring back to Figure 14-1, notice that the PERSON_BK_LOANED column contains a nested table of loaned books. Each book is assessed a fine of 25 cents per day if the book is kept longer than two weeks. The sample report requires a sum of all the fines for one person. The function has one incoming parameter: I_PERSON_ID. The BOOK_FINE function first reads the PERSON_BK_LOANED column into a local variable of the same type:

```
/* ——- BOOK_FINE.SQL ——- */
CREATE OR REPLACE FUNCTION BOOK_FINE
(I_PERSON_ID IN NUMBER)
RETURN NUMBER
IS
BEGIN
DECLARE
V_PERSON_BK_LOANED BOOKS_LOAN_LIST_T;
V_TOTAL_FINE NUMBER;
BEGIN
/* ———— READ IN LOANED LIST ——— */
```

```
BEGIN
    SELECT P.PERSON_BK_LOANED
    INTO V_PERSON_BK_LOANED
    FROM PERSON_TABLE_T P
    WHERE P.PERSON_ID = I_PERSON_ID;
  EXCEPTION
    WHEN NO_DATA_FOUND THEN
        V_TOTAL_FINE := 0;
        RETURN V_TOTAL_FINE;
END;
```

Next, a variable for storing the total fine is initialized to zero:

```
V_TOTAL_FINE := 0;
```

Now, a loop repeats one time for each row contained in the nested table. The loop adds each fine to the total dollar amount.

```
FOR V_COUNTER IN 1..V_PERSON_BK_LOANED.COUNT LOOP
    /* — Add each new fine to the current total. —- */
    V_TOTAL_FINE  := NVL(V_PERSON_BK_LOANED(V_COUNTER).FINE,0) +
V_TOTAL_FINE;
END LOOP;
```

Finally, the grand total is returned, and the function is completed:

```
RETURN V_TOTAL_FINE;
END;
END;
/
show errors
```

The complete code listing for this function can be found in the PLSQL directory on the CD-ROM included with this book.

Creating the PHONE_INFO function

This function returns the home phone number of a library cardholder. The incoming parameter, I_PERSON_ID, identifies which row in the PERSON_TABLE_T object table to look into. The function must retrieve the appropriate phone number from the varray called PERSON_PHONE.

First, the function reads the varray of phone numbers into a local variable, V_PHONE_LIST:

```
/* ——- HOME_PHONE.SQL ——- */
CREATE OR REPLACE FUNCTION HOME_PHONE
(I_PERSON_ID IN NUMBER)
RETURN VARCHAR2
IS
begin
declare
V_PHONE VARCHAR2(20) := 'No home phone';
V_PHONE_LIST PHONE_LIST_T;
begin
SELECT PERSON_PHONE INTO V_PHONE_LIST
FROM PERSON_TABLE_T
WHERE PERSON_ID = I_PERSON_ID;
```

Next, each row of the varray is inspected. If its PHONE_TYPE is "HOME," this is the correct phone number. The function saves the phone number and exits from the loop.

```
FOR V_COUNTER IN 1..V_PHONE_LIST.COUNT LOOP
   IF V_PHONE_LIST(V_COUNTER).PHONE_TYPE = 'HOME' THEN
      V_PHONE := V_PHONE_LIST(V_COUNTER).PHONE_NUMBER;
      EXIT;
   END IF;
END LOOP;
```

If the correct phone number is never found, the initial value of the V_PHONE variable is returned ("No home phone").

```
RETURN V_PHONE;
END;
END;
/
```

Now that the two functions are ready, we can create the parameter-driven report.

Beginning the parameter report

We can use the Report Wizard again to generate the report. At the point in the wizard where a query is required, the following code is entered:

```
SELECT A.PERSON_ID,
```

```
A.PERSON_NAME.FIRST_NAME,
A.PERSON_NAME.LAST_NAME,
A.PERSON_ADDRESS.STREET,
A.PERSON_ADDRESS.CITY,
A.PERSON_ADDRESS.STATE,
A.PERSON_ADDRESS.ZIP,
HOME_PHONE(A.PERSON_ID),
BOOK_FINE(A.PERSON_ID)
FROM PERSON_TABLE_T A
WHERE A.PERSON_ID = :P_PERSON_ID
```

The last line in this query contains the *variable* that is replaced by data from an incoming parameter.

The parameter is named P_PERSON_ID. Now that we have the basic report built, we add the parameter.

Creating a user-defined parameter

To create this parameter, use the Object Navigator, and open the User Parameters area beneath the Data Model label. Figure 14-5 points out the location and displays the property palette for the new user-defined parameter.

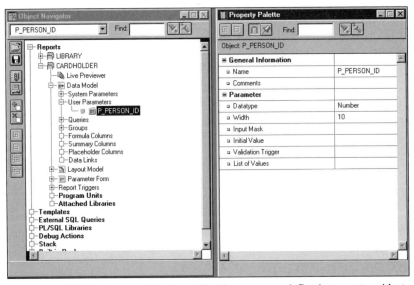

Figure 14-5: Set your own parameters using the new user-defined parameter object.

Building the parameter form

How can you test the form? You need to define the parameter somehow. In addition, if you choose to run this report independently, rather than having it called from within another report, you must allow users to input the parameter. To accomplish these tasks, build a simple parameter form.

Because you define the parameter form within the report, you can choose dynamic settings for all parameters your report requires.

The new Parameter Form Builder feature of Report Builder enables you to create a form with your own user-defined parameters and with standard report parameters. Figure 14-6 shows the main window of the Parameter Form Builder. In this window, build the parameters that appear in the parameter form by highlighting all those parameters you wish to display for user input.

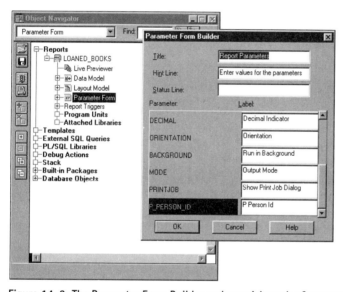

Figure 14-6: The Parameter Form Builder makes quick work of parameter forms.

USING THE PARAMETER LAYOUT EDITOR

After creating the parameter form, another new feature, the Parameter Layout Editor, enables you to handle the form as easily as one created with Form Builder. In addition, because the Parameter Layout Editor is contained inside Report Builder, you can apply the same report templates you use for your report. Figure 14-7 shows the Parameter Layout Editor for our sample report. This parameter form includes the user-defined parameter named PF_P_PERSON_ID (defined in the previous section of this chapter).

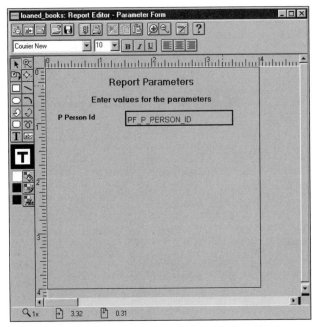

Figure 14-7: The Parameter Layout Editor acts just like the Report Layout Editor.

USING THE LIVE PREVIEWER

Another new feature that quickly becomes essential to report builders is the Live Previewer. Double-click the Live Previewer icon in the Object Navigator to view a WYSIWYG version of your report. You see actual data in your report. At the same time, you can highlight fields and modify their parameters. Figure 14-8 shows the Live Previewer for the Cardholder detail report we are creating.

Notice when you run the Live Previewer with this report, you see the parameter form first. After entering data, you next see the completed report.

Now that both reports are ready to use, it is time to connect the two.

Connecting Reports

In this chapter, you have created two sample reports based on the PERSON _TABLE_T object table:

◆ **Library.** This report lists all library cardholders.

◆ **Cardholder.** This report shows one person's name, address, home phone, and total book fines.

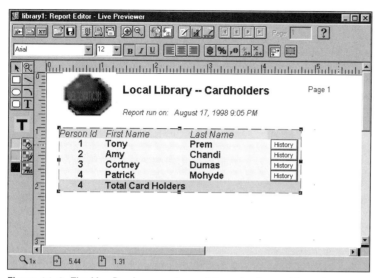

Figure 14-8: The Live Previewer makes quick work of report layouts.

This section of the chapter shows how to connect these two reports and pass the PERSON_ID from the Library report to the Cardholder report. A button will be created on the Library report that calls the Cardholder report when it is pressed. It will pass the corresponding PERSON_ID to the report.

Creating the link

Add a PL/SQL button to the Library report. The button is an automatically assigned PL/SQL trigger that fires when the button is pressed. We will add code to the trigger so this button performs the following two functions prior to calling the second report:

- Builds the parameter with the appropriate value.
- Calls the second report, passing the parameter.

The following code handles these tasks:

```
procedure U_1ButtonAction is
begin
 srw.run_report('D:\1Carols\1o8dev\test\LOANED_BOOKS.rdf
paramform=no
     P_PERSON_ID="'||:person_id||'"');
end;
```

The trigger makes the report run properly in the client/server environment but not in the Web environment. The Cardholder report is called using the parameter sent in the srw.run_report command. However, when running on the Web, the srw command is not translated properly.

To make the button work correctly in the Web version of the report, we add a hyperlink specification to the button. The link calls the Web version of the Cardholder report. See the next section to learn how to add this hyperlink information.

Now here is a twist: when moving the Cardholder report to the Web, *it becomes a static report.* It no longer has the power to retrieve and display information about different people according to its parameter. The following section suggests how we can compensate for this obstacle.

You can choose any of several solutions to the problem:

♦ Create a different report that displays all the Cardholders. Add a bookmark (NAME tag) in front of each person's block of data, and then have the Library report point to the appropriate bookmark.

This concept is illustrated using the Enterprise Manager Web Publishing Assistant in Chapter 21.

♦ Run the Application Server, and execute the report as a dynamic report. This requires no changes to the reports.

♦ Do this by repeatedly running the Web Tool and naming each report so that it contains the PERSON_ID in the name. Even though this requires more work initially, this solution works well in cases where your data set is fairly small and stable.

Consider a third option — creating separate Web reports. A description of how to do it follows.

Open the Properties window for the button in the Library report. Add the following code to the Hyperlink attribute as shown in Figure 14-9:

```
Cardholder&<PERSON_ID>.htm
```

Hyperlink code here

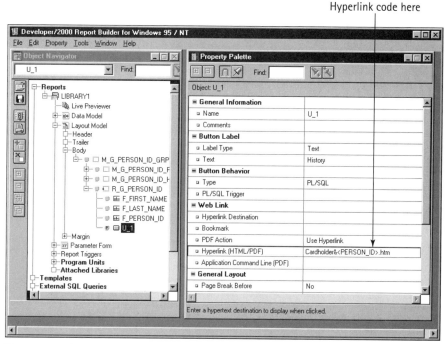

Figure 14-9: Add the Hyperlink attribute in preparation for converting the report to a Web report.

The actual value of the PERSON_ID replaces the variable &<PERSON_ID> in each button on each row of the report.

The Hyperlink code is ignored when the report runs in client/server mode.

Converting the Library report into a static Web page

The Library report was prepared for the Web in the previous section. Next, convert the report to a Web report. The steps for converting the report into a static Web page are quite simple:

1. Open the report in Report Builder.

2. Choose Tools Web Wizard. Follow the prompts, and click the Finish button when you are done. All boxes in the Web Wizard are optional except choosing a filename.

3. Select a directory and filename for the final report page.

You can try out the new Web report by starting up a Web browser such as Netscape (shown in Figure 14-10) and opening the file in the browser. Figure 14-10 shows what the Library report looks like on the Web.

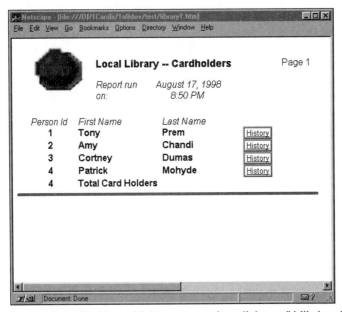

Figure 14-10: The Library Web report contains a link to a "drill-down" report.

Looking at the source code of the Web report page, you can see how the Hyperlink attribute was translated into a normal hyperlink that looks like this:

```
<a href="Cardholder1.htm" target=_parent>
<font size=2 face="Arial">History</font></a>
```

The button has been converted into a link, and the link now calls another Web page named "Cardholder1.htm" for the first row of data (where PERSON_ID = 1).

Now that the Library report has been converted, it is time to convert the Cardholder report.

Converting the Cardholder report into four static Web pages

Following the same steps as before, convert the report into a Web page using the Web Wizard in Report Builder. When you finish the specifications, Web Wizard runs the report. You will be prompted to enter a PERSON_ID in the parameter form. The first time you run the Web Wizard, use the filename Cardholder1, and then specify PERSON_ID = 1 on the parameter form. The second time, use the filename Cardholder2, and use PERSON_ID = 2. Repeat this for Cardholder3 and 4 also.

When completed, you have four distinct Web pages: one for each cardholder. Figure 14-11 shows the first page of the resulting Web page report.

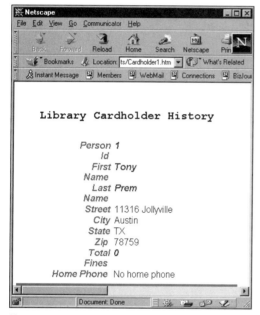

Figure 14-11: The Cardholder report has been converted into four separate reports for the Web.

This report has no hyperlinks and no parameters. Yet, it appears at the right time because the hyperlink specified in the Library report is unique for each Cardholder record displayed. This approach is useful for smaller systems because it requires the manual generation of the Cardholder report for every distinct person record.

Summary

The new Report Wizard feature in Developer Report Builder makes it simple to create your reports. You can modify the columns, layout, or template of a previously created report by using the Report Wizard in its reentrant format.

This chapter creates two reports that access data in an Oracle8 object table. The first report (the Library report) uses SQL that queries several user-defined datatype columns in the object table.

The second report (the Cardholder report) is a detail report intended to be used as a drill-down report inside the report.

When creating the Library report, we build the report using Report Wizard and then add a PL/SQL button. This button passes the value of the needed parameter to the second report.

The Cardholder report is created using two stored functions within its primary query. These two functions operate on a nested table and a varray within the Oracle8 object table and return a number (Total Fines) and a string (Home Phone).

In addition, we define a user parameter that accepts the incoming parameter from the initial report, and then use the parameterin the query.

The new feature, Parameter Form Builder, creates a simple form you can use to define the user parameter. This way, the report can stand alone or be used for the drill-down of the Library report.

The Live Previewer utility is demonstrated. This new feature of Report Builder is a useful layout tool that displays your report exactly as it appears in its final form.

Finally, both reports are converted to static Web page reports using the Web Wizard. The Cardholder report is actually converted into four separate Web pages: one for each cardholder. The Library report has been modified so that it can link to the Cardholder Web report using a predefined hyperlink.

The next chapter focuses on graphics, showing how quickly you can add graphics to forms and reports.

Chapter 15

Fast Graphics

IN THIS CHAPTER

◆ Creating graphics for forms

◆ Using graphics in reports

◆ Using graphics to map locations

AN APPLICATION CREATED in Oracle Graphics is called a *display*. You can create displays that are used as standalone applications. Or you can add displays to forms and reports. You can also combine existing displays with your forms or reports.

This chapter shows you how to create a display that receives a query from a form and uses it to build its display. Next, you will see how to call a report by clicking on a part of your chart. You can call a report in this manner using Form Builder, Graphics Builder, and Report Builder.

You can accomplish many other tasks with Oracle Graphics. The last section of this chapter describes how to create a graphics display that mimics a geographical interface to your data.

Synchronizing a Form and a Display

You can create a chart that is build into your form using the Chart Wizard. Follow the instructions in the online help.

TIP When you create a chart item in the Layout Editor, you are asked if you want to create the chart with the Chart Wizard. If you choose Chart Wizard, you are guided through the creation of the chart. You then are asked to save the chart, and the chart is automatically tied to your form.

Chapter 9 discusses the Chart Wizard. The CD-ROM also contains a sample form, TOY_W_CHART, that contains a chart generated with Chart Wizard.

In addition to using the Chart Wizard, you can create a chart inside the Graphics Builder and call it from a form. You can pass the data that your user has queried on a form to a chart, which can be useful in customizing a chart. You can even show the chart using data that has been updated by the user but has not yet been committed to the database.

For example, say you want to display a pie chart that compares the value of the total inventory of one store to another. You want to compare the stores you have queried on. So sometimes you see a pie chart with two stores, and sometimes you see a pie chart with four or five stores. Each time, the pie chart shows the relative values of each store's inventory.

To accomplish this feat, follow these steps:

1. Create a form using Form Builder. For example, we will create a master-detail form.

2. Add an item in a control block to hold the chart. The item must be a chart item.

3. Create a display using Graphics Builder.

4. Attach the `OG.pll` library to your form. This package is used in to open, run, and close the chart.

5. Add PL/SQL code to your form that builds a record group and passes it to the chart as a parameter.

The following goes over each step in more detail.

The Oracle documentation contains errors in its sample PL/SQL code in several of the critical steps for successfully creating this kind of functionality.

Creating a form that passes query data to the chart

Any form can be used to pass query data. To illustrate the concept and how to implement it, you use the Toy Store schema included on the CD-ROM. The form we build has a master-detail layout. Create the following blocks, as shown in Figure 15-1.

- ◆ CTRL. A control table containing the button to start the chart and a field displaying a total summary of inventory for the displayed store.

- ◆ TOY_STORE. The master block contains the TOY_STORE table and displays the STORE_ID and STORE_NAME.

- ◆ STORE_STOCK. The detail block contains the STORE_STOCK table. It displays information from the STORE_STOCK table and from TOY_INVENTORY.

- ◆ CHARTBLK. This block contains the chart item that displays the chart on a separate page and a button that returns the user to the first page.

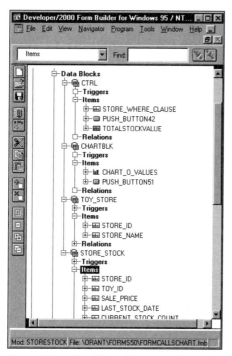

Figure 15-1: The Object Navigator view of the new FORMCALLSCHART form.

Adding an item to hold the chart

Figure 15-2 shows the second page of the sample form in Layout Editor. This is not a requirement for displaying a chart, by the way. It is simply another way to do it. You can easily embed the chart within your main page, in a tab page, or in a separate form.

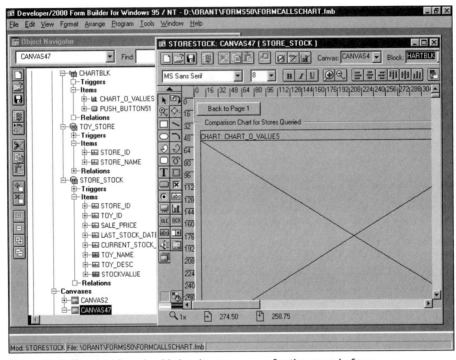

Figure 15-2: The chart item is added to its own canvas for the example form.

The chart item has an item type of "Chart Item."

Creating a display using Graphics Builder

Use Graphics Builder to create a pie chart. The following query summarizes a calculated total value of a store's current stock:

```
select ts.store_id, ts.store_name,
sum(nvl(sale_price,0)*nvl(current_stock_count,0)) TOTAL_VALUE
from toy_store ts,
    store_stock ss
where
```

```
        ts.store_id = ss.store_id
group by ts.store_id, ts.store_name
order by ts.store_id, ts.store_name
```

The query has no WHERE clause. When the query is run using the test data for the Toy Store schema, the pie chart in Figure 15-3 shows the results.

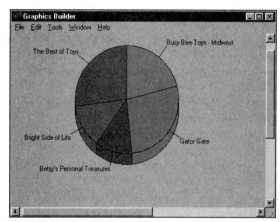

Figure 15-3: The pie chart (`valuechart.ogr`) for all stores in the Toy Store schema.

Three important considerations to keep in mind when creating your display are:

1. The query name is referenced in the form when it passes its parameter list to the display. Remember this name.

2. The column names used in the query must exactly match the column names of the query built in the form trigger. If you use aliases, be sure to use the same ones in the form's query.

3. The chart must be generated. Use the File → Administration → Generate selection on the main menu of Graphics Builder to generate the chart. The form will search for the .ogr file created by the generate function.

A parameter list that contains a smaller set of records will be used when this chart is called from the form.

Attaching the OG.pll library to the form

When you want to pass a parameter list to the graphic display, use procedures and functions that are built into the OG.pll library. To attach this library to your form, select Attached Libraries in the Object Navigator, and then click the plus sign to create an attached library. This opens a window where you can navigate to the directory where the OG.pll file is stored. Select the file, and click Open.

Once you have attached the library, you can reference any of the functions or procedures by name. You must always prefix the name with the library name (OG). For example, to use the OPEN command, write:

```
OG.OPEN...
```

Now it's time to combine the form and the display in a dynamic environment, where the chart changes as the user's queries change the records retrieved from the database.

Writing PL/SQL code to run the chart

A number of triggers and one program unit are required to make the whole scenario run smoothly:

- ◆ KEY-EXEQRY. This trigger is placed on the TOY_STORE block level. It is used to retrieve the WHERE clause after the user executes a query on the TOY_STORE block. This WHERE clause will be used later in the LOAD_QUERY program item.

- ◆ WHEN-BUTTON-PRESSED. This trigger is placed on the button that calls the display. The trigger calls the LOAD_QUERY program item and then navigates to the second page, where the display is viewed. In the example, the trigger is on the PUSH_BUTTON42 field in the CTRL control block.

- ◆ WHEN_BUTTON_PRESSED. This trigger returns the user to the first page. In our example, the trigger is on the PUSH_BUTTON51 item in the CHARTBLK block.

- ◆ LOAD_QUERY. This program unit handles preparing a record group, executing a query, loading a parameter list, and opening the graphic display while passing the parameter list.

The next sections describe the code used in these items.

Coding the triggers

The first trigger is the block-level trigger, KEY-EXEQRY, on the TOY_STORE block. This trigger finds the WHERE clause for the TOY_STORE query and then stores it in a control field. The PL/SQL looks like this:

```
/* ——— Forms/save_where_clause.sql —- */
/* placed in the KEY-EXEQRY trigger in the TOYCALLSFORM form. — */
begin
```

```
execute_query;
/* Save the WHERE clause to build the chart */
IF instr(:system.last_query,'WHERE')= 0 then
    :CTRL.STORE_WHERE_CLAUSE := NULL;
ELSE
    :CTRL.STORE_WHERE_CLAUSE :=
    substr(:system.last_query,instr(:system.last_query,'WHERE'));
END IF;
end;
```

When the WHERE clause does not exist (that is, when the user executes a query with no constraints), the trigger sets the control item to null values.

The second trigger is the WHEN-BUTTON-PRESSED trigger on the main page of the form. Figure 15-4 shows the main form and points out the button. When this button is pressed, the user can view the display item.

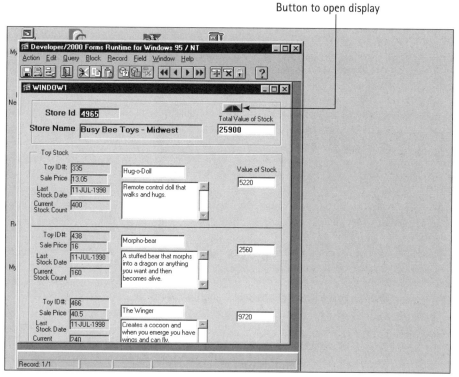

Figure 15-4: The main page of the FORMCALLSCHART form contains a button to invoke the chart.

The PL/SQL in the trigger is:

```
load_query;
go_field('CHARTBLK.PUSH_BUTTON51');
```

The first line invokes the process to open the display. The second line moves the focus to the button next to the display on the second page.

The third trigger is the WHEN_BUTTON_PRESSED trigger on the second page. Figure 15-5 shows this page of the form and points out the button that has this trigger.

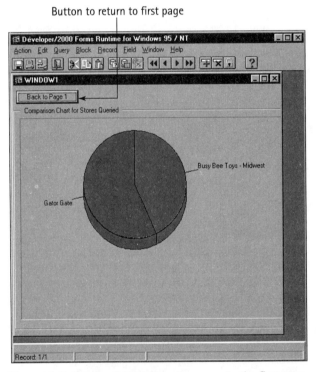

Figure 15-5: Pressing this button returns you to the first page.

The PL/SQL for this trigger is simply:

```
go_field('TOY_STORE.STORE_ID');
```

Finally, we come to the main attraction: the LOAD_QUERY program item.

Creating the LOAD_QUERY program unit

The LOAD_QUERY program unit consists of several steps that prepare and send a parameter list to the graphics display. First, the procedure is initialized, and variables are declared:

```
/* — Forms/Load_query.sql —- */
PROCEDURE LOAD_QUERY IS
BEGIN
DECLARE
parmlist   PARAMLIST;
recgroup   RECORDGROUP;
chartqry      VARCHAR(2000);
returncode    NUMBER;
grp_name VARCHAR(40) := 'CHARTQRY';
```

The first step is to close the chart if it was left open. This ensures that the chart will be refreshed when you call it later.

```
BEGIN
OG.CLOSE('valuechart','chartblk.chart_o_values');
```

Next, the query is built. This query matches the query found in the display, except it adds the WHERE clause from the form. Recall that the WHERE clause was captured when the user performed the execute query on the TOY_STORE block.

```
/*Prepare a query in a string based on the last
 **WHERE clause issued.*/
chartqry := 'select ts.store_id, ts.store_name, '
       || ' sum(nvl(sale_price,0)*nvl(current_stock_count,0))
TOTAL_VALUE '
       || ' from toy_store ts, '
       || ' store_stock ss '
       || ' where ts.store_id = ss.store_id '
       || ' and ts.store_id in (select store_id from toy_store '
       || :CTRL.STORE_WHERE_CLAUSE || ')'
       || ' group by ts.store_id, ts.store_name '
       || ' order by ts.store_id, ts.store_name';
```

Now that the query is stored in a procedure variable, the procedure begins to prepare a record group.

This command returns the current ID of the record group, or a null value if the record group does not exist.

```
recgroup := Find_Group( 'chart_group' );
```

If the record group was already created, it will be deleted and rebuilt.

```
IF Id_Null(recgroup) THEN
        recgroup := CREATE_GROUP_FROM_QUERY('chart_group',
chartqry);
        returncode := POPULATE_GROUP_WITH_QUERY(recgroup, chartqry);
ELSE
    /* clear out and repopulate it based on the new query*/
    DELETE_GROUP('chart_group');
    recgroup := CREATE_GROUP_FROM_QUERY('chart_group', chartqry);
    returncode := POPULATE_GROUP_WITH_QUERY(recgroup, chartqry);
END IF;
```

The command POPULATE_GROUP_WITH_QUERY returns a zero if it successfully loads rows into the record group. Otherwise, it returns an error number.

The following line adds a debugging break so you can inspect the variables if you have debugging turned on.

```
break;
```

The records are now stored in a record group named chart_group. Now the record group must be loaded into a parameter list.

First, the parameter list is created.

```
/*Now create a parameter list*/
parmlist := CREATE_PARAMETER_LIST('pl_chart_data');
```

Next, the parameter list is loaded with the record group. The parameter list must be named the same as the query in the graphics display. In this example, the graphics display's query is toystorecompare, and so the parameter list uses that name in the second variable of the ADD_PARAMETER command.

```
/*Add a data parameter with the same name as the query in the
display*/
Add_Parameter(parmlist,'toystorecompare',DATA_PARAMETER,'chart_group
');
```

Now it is time to start the display and load it into the current form. The OPEN command (found in the OG.pll library) handles this task. The general syntax of the OG.OPEN command is:

```
OG.OPEN(chartname,chartitemname,clip, refresh, plist);
```

The five parameters are:

- chartname. The name of the display. The form starts a process that runs the .ogr file of this name.

- chartitemname. The block and item name where the display is shown in the form.

- clip. Boolean telling the form to either clip (TRUE) or not clip (FALSE) the display if it does not fit into the display item.

- refresh. Boolean telling the form to refresh the display automatically (TRUE) or not to refresh the display (FALSE).

- qplist. Parameter list. If the parameter list contains a parameter of the record group type and the parameter is named the same as the name of the display's query, then the entire query is replaced with the record group in the parameter.

In the sample form, the OG.OPEN command looks like this:

```
/* Open display with the new data*/
OG.OPEN('valuechart', 'CHARTBLK.CHART_O_VALUES', TRUE, TRUE,
parmlist);
```

Finally, the parameter list is deleted, and the procedure ends.

```
/* Destroy the parameter list*/
DESTROY_PARAMETER_LIST('pl_chart_data');
END;
END;
```

All these pieces fit together to create a dynamic record set that is used to build a chart within your form. This same concept can be used for many other tasks. Let this example be a springboard for your own creativity.

The next section discusses how to combine a chart and a report, so that the report is built based on the area in the chart that is clicked with your mouse.

Adding a Report as the Drill-Down Part of a Chart

In this section, you make a copy of the graphic created in the previous section in order to add two interesting features to it. When the user clicks on a pie slice:

♦ The chart calls a detail report of the corresponding store's inventory.

♦ The clicked slice moves (explodes) out from the pie to highlight the store that was selected.

To accomplish these two tasks, complete the following steps:

1. Create a report using Report Builder that uses a parameter for the STORE_ID.

2. Create a button in the chart that activates when the mouse clicks a pie slice.

3. Add a parameter to the chart for STORE_ID that is created when you click a pie slice.

4. Add PL/SQL code to the button in the chart to explode the correct pie slice and then call the report with the appropriate parameters.

The next sections describe how to complete each step.

Creating the detail report

This is the easy part. Use the Report Wizard in the Report Builder to help create the report. When you do so, the wizard creates the parameter for you.

Here is the query that generates the report. The variable P_STORE_ID becomes a parameter named P_STORE_ID.

```
select ts.store_id, ts.store_name, toy_name,
nvl(sale_price,0)*nvl(current_stock_count,0) TOTAL_VALUE
from toy_store ts,
     store_stock ss,
     toy_inventory ti
where ts.store_id = :P_STORE_ID
and     ts.store_id = ss.store_id
and ss.toy_id = ti.toy_id
order by toy_name
```

We have added a summary on the STORE_NAME column, so that it can be displayed one time at the top of the report. We have also added a summary of the TOTAL_VALUE column. Figure 15-6 shows the report as it appears in the Live Previewer.

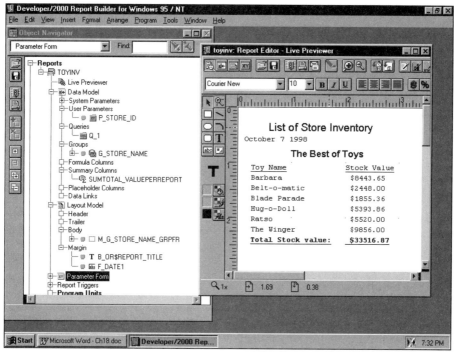

Figure 15-6: A detail report for toy inventory shows one store at a time.

 Be sure to compile the report so that it can be run from the chart with the batch report server.

With the report created, you can modify the chart.

Modifying the chart to explode a slice of pie

Exploding pie sounds messy. In fact, the PL/SQL code to create the explosion is fairly messy! Starting with the chart created earlier in the chapter (shown earlier in Figure 15-5), add some brains in the form of a mouse event.

Work in the Object Navigator of the Graphics Builder to find the pie slices object. Right-click the object, and select Properties from the pop-up menu. Check the Mouse Button Down event, and a procedure name will be created for you. Figure 15-7 shows the Object Properties window.

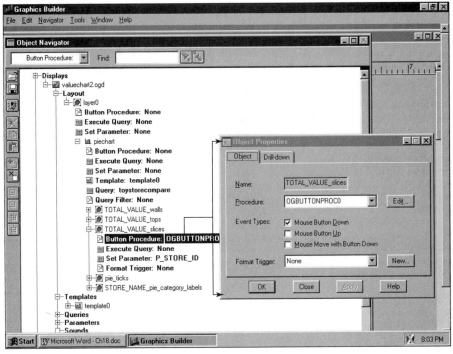

Figure 15-7: Define a mouse event for the pie slices in the Object Properties window.

In addition to creating the mouse event and the procedure that is run, create a parameter that contains the STORE_ID value of the pie slice clicked. Do this by filling in the boxes in the drill-down tab in the Properties window.

Now it is time to create the procedure where all the action occurs: it's the OGBUTTONPROC0 procedure in this example.

The chart (valuechart2) and report (toyinv) are both found on the CD-ROM in the back of this book.

Here is the PL/SQL code for the button procedure. This procedure fires when the user clicks in a pie slice on the chart.

First, begin with the predefined procedure skeleton:

```
/* —— Graphics/Button_in_chart.sql —— */
PROCEDURE OGBUTTONPROC0 (buttonobj IN og_object,
```

```
                        hitobj IN og_object,
                        win IN og_window,
                        eventinfo IN og_event) IS
BEGIN
```

Add declarations for variables needed in the procedure:

```
declare
piechart_in og_object;    — the chart
piequery    OG_QUERY; — the query for the chart
rows_count number;         — use to save total number of rows in the
qeury
row_num number;            — use to store the current row number
V_STORE_ID NUMBER;  — variable for STORE_ID
rep_list  tool_int.paramlist;  — parameter list sent to the report
```

The first section explodes the pie. The commands for manipulating objects in a chart all begin with OG_. Some are functions, and some are procedures. We use only a few of the dozens of commands that are available. First, get the chart and its query into the procedure:

```
begin
/* ———- explode current pie slice —— */
   piechart_in := OG_GET_OBJECT ('piechart');
   piequery := OG_GET_QUERY ('toystorecompare');
   OG_EXECUTE_QUERY(piequery);
```

Now, count the number of rows in the query, and reset the query to begin with the first row:

```
rows_count := OG_NUMROWS(piequery, OG_NEWDATA);
   OG_START_FROM(piequery, OG_NEWDATA, 0);
```

Run a loop until you find the row that contains the STORE_ID that was assigned to the parameter variable, P_STORE_ID:

```
FOR I IN 0 .. rows_count -1 LOOP
V_STORE_ID := OG_GET_NUMCELL
(piequery, OG_NEWDATA, 'STORE_ID');
IF V_STORE_ID = :P_STORE_ID THEN
ROW_NUM := i;
exit;
END IF;
OG_NEXT_ROW(piequery, OG_NEWDATA);
```

```
      END LOOP;
```

Explode the pie slice (specified by the variable ROW_NUM). The slice moves 25 pixels:

```
OG_Set_Explosion(piechart_in, row_num, 'TOTAL_VALUE', 25);
```

Redisplay the chart:

```
OG_UPDATE_CHART(piechart_in, OG_ALL_CHUPDA);
```

The next part of the PL/SQL procedure runs the report. This requires the use of the built-in TOOL_INT that is available to any chart without attaching a library. First, a new parameter list is created:

```
/* ——- call a report now —— */
/*call Report Builder to display the report*/
/*add the USERID executable option to the list  */
  rep_list:=TOOL_INT.CREATE_PARAMETER_LIST('list2');
```

To avoid the log-in prompt, create a userid parameter that holds the user ID and password. userid is loaded into the parameter list:

```
TOOL_INT.ADD_PARAMETER (rep_list, 'userid',
      TOOL_INT.TEXT_PARAMETER, 'TOYSTORE/TOYSTORE');
```

The next parameter passes the STORE_ID from the current pie slice, sending it with the parameter name P_STORE_ID (the same name used in the report parameter):

```
/*add the STORE_ID parameter to the list */
  TOOL_INT.ADD_PARAMETER (rep_list, 'P_STORE_ID',
      TOOL_INT.TEXT_PARAMETER, :P_STORE_ID);
```

The report is run using the RUN_PRODUCT procedure. The general syntax of the RUN_PRODUCT procedure is:

```
TOOL_INT.RUN_PRODUCT (product_to_run, application_name,
synch_or_asynch, run_mode, app_source, parameter_list_name);
```

The parameters are:

◆ `product_to_run`. Here you can name TOOL_INT.REPORT, TOOL_INT.FORM, or TOOL_INT.BOOK (for Oracle book object).

◆ `application_name`. The name of the application to run.

◆ `synch_or_asynch`. The communication mode, which can be TOOL_INT.SYNCHRONOUS or TOOL_INT.ASYNCHRONOUS.

◆ `run_mode`. This is either TOOL_INT.BATCH or TOOL_INT.RUNTIME.

◆ `app_source`. This tells the package where to find the application. It can be either TOOL_INT.DB (for applications stored in the database) or TOOL_INT.FILESYSTEM.

◆ `parameter_list_name`. This contains the variable name of the parameter list that is passed to the application. The variable must be of the type: TOOL_INT.PARAMLIST.

Here is the PL/SQL code for the example. In the code, call the toyinv.rep report, which is found in the file system and is run in RUNTIME mode. The parameters found in the `rep_list` parameter list are sent to the application.

```
/*call Report Builder batch mode to print the report*/
  TOOL_INT.RUN_PRODUCT(TOOL_INT.REPORTS, 'toyinv.rdf',
      TOOL_INT.SYNCHRONOUS, TOOL_INT.RUNTIME,
      TOOL_INT.FILESYSTEM,rep_list);
```

The final step in the procedure is to remove the parameter list so that the whole procedure can be run again if needed:

```
TOOL_INT.DESTROY_PARAMETER_LIST('list2');
END;
END;
```

Figure 15-8 shows the chart after the Bright Side of Life pie slice has been clicked.

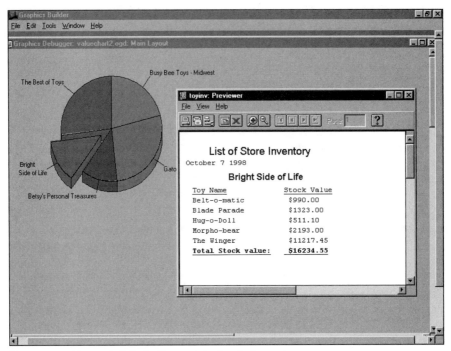

Figure 15-8: The exploded pie slice and the invoked report.

The next section describes how to create a chart that looks like a geographic map of your data.

Creating an Imitation Geographic Map Display

This section describes how you can use Oracle Graphics to create a display that looks like a map with drill-down locations. (You can use this until you implement your full Geo-spatial Information System – or GIS, for short – to interface with your Oracle database.) Figure 15-9 shows the completed chart.

Each dot on the map indicates a store in the Busy Bee store chain. When you click the dot, the lower part of the display changes to show that store's logo, store name, city, and state. The following components make up this chart:

◆ **A scatter chart.** This is how the grid of the latitude and longitude are added and how the locations are plotted on the grid.

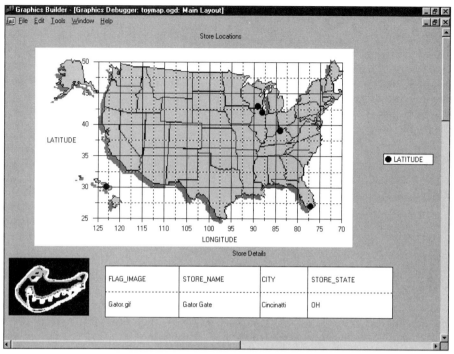

Figure 15-9: Click any dot to see the store name, logo, and location.

◆ **A drill-down function.** This enables the user to click any of the locations and see the store details below the map.

◆ **A table chart.** This is the drill-down chart that is run when you click any dot on the grid.

◆ **An image.** This is fetched from the file system, using the filename retrieved from the database when the drill-down chart is run.

Each of these features will be discussed in the next sections.

Creating the scatter chart to mimic a map

The chart that looks like a map is actually two objects stacked on top of each other:

◆ An image of a map

◆ A scatter chart

The map image is a GIF format file that was imported using the File Import Image selection from the main menu of the Graphics Builder. The file used (USMAP.GIF) is on the CD-ROM in the Pictures directory. The map is adjusted to fit the canvas of the display.

Next, create a chart by clicking the Chart icon in the Layout Editor and clicking and dragging the mouse to the size you need for the chart. The Chart Wizard is displayed and asks you to choose the type of chart. Choose the "Scatter chart with grid" as the template for this chart.

The next step in the Chart Wizard is to define the query that is to be displayed. For this example, the TOY_STORE table was used. It contains a latitude column and a longitude column that can be used to plot the location of each store on the chart. The query for our sample chart is:

```
select store_id, latitude, longitude
from toy_store
```

After defining the query, execute it, and define the X axis as the longitude and the Y axis as the latitude.

Your initial chart will not correctly map the coordinates on the background image because, by default, it automatically scales the chart based on the data found. To fix this, make two changes in the default behavior of the scatter chart:

♦ **Freeze the scale.** Always use a certain range of latitude and longitude on the X and Y axes so the grid is always the same size and scale relative to the map image.

♦ **Reverse the order.** Display the longitude grid (X axis) in descending (not ascending) order to match the numbering order of the longitude on a map of the U.S.

Both of these changes are adjustments to the Axes settings of the chart. To make the changes, right-click the chart in the Object Navigator window. Then select Axes from the pop-up menu. Figure 15-10 shows the Axes Properties window that is displayed. Change the axis direction to descending. Click the Continuous Axis tab, adjust the settings of the range displayed on the X axis to a maximum of 125 and a minimum of 70, and turn off the auto features.

Choose the Y axis in the same property window, change the Continuous Axis settings to maximum of 50 and a minimum of 25, and turn off the auto features. These coordinates are the boundaries of the latitude and longitude for the continental U.S.

Click Apply to make the changes go into effect. Return to the Layout Editor.

Back in the Layout Editor, with some careful nudging of the background image and the chart itself, you can see the store locations in their correct locations (approximately) on the map.

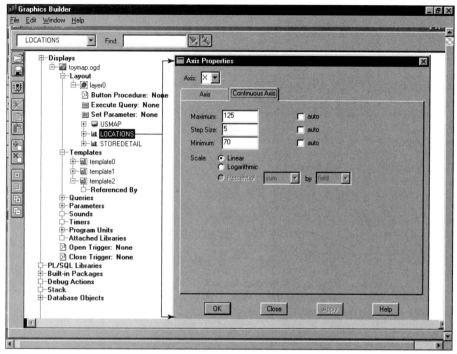

Figure 15-10: Right-click the chart item, and select Axes to view the Axis Property window.

The next step is to add the drill-down feature on the store locations.

Adding a drill-down feature

Add a drill-down feature by simply double-clicking any dot on the chart. Doing so displays the Object Properties window as shown in Figure 15-11. Click the Drill-down tab, and define a parameter that is passed to the drill-down query.

The query that the drill-down executes in the example is:

```
select flag_image, store_name, city, store_state
from toy_store
where store_id = :P_STORE_ID
```

Now that the drill-down feature is in place, create a simple chart below the map display to show details of the store clicked.

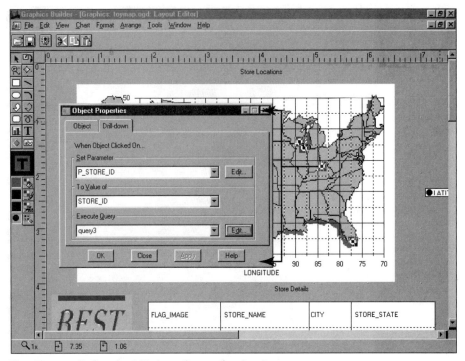

Figure 15-11: Define the drill-down feature for the chart.

Creating another chart for details

The chart created in this section will display the results of the query that is run when the user clicks the drill-down points on the main chart. In the example, the drill-down points are dots on a map symbolizing stores in the Toy Store chain.

Create another chart by clicking the Chart icon and drawing a rectangle below the map image on the Layout Editor. The Chart Wizard will guide you through the steps for creating the chart. This chart uses the query created in the previous section and is a tabular-type chart. There's nothing fancy here, except that the query uses a parameter that was defined in the drill-down item.

This example uses a simple query, just to illustrate how these features can be used. Your applications will probably use multitable joins or summaries in this area instead.

Figure 15-12 shows the new chart in the Layout Editor.

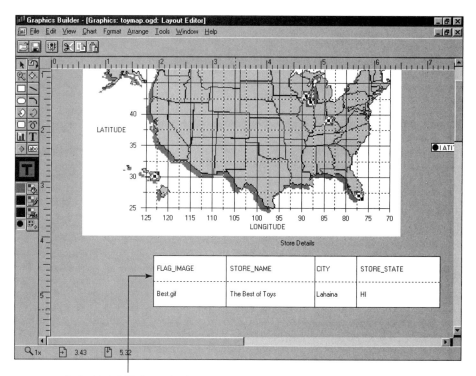

Embedded drill-down chart

Figure 15-12: A second chart displays on the same layer as our original chart.

Now, the final bit of magic will be added to the chart.

Displaying the store logo (image)

The store logo is stored in the file system. The filename is stored in the database. To get the image onto the chart, use the OG_IMPORT_IMAGE command in a chart trigger.

For this example, display the filename as well as the image itself, which is mostly for testing. After designing the report, the filename need not be displayed.

The column containing the store logo filename is called FLAG_IMAGE. It is found in the drill-down chart shown previously in Figure 15-12. It is necessary to add a trigger to get the image from the file system and display it on the chart.

Open the drill-down chart in the Object Navigator, and find the FLAG_
IMAGE_LABELS object. Define a format trigger under this object by double-clicking the Format Trigger icon. This brings up the PL/SQL editor with a predefined
trigger that you can use to complete the trigger definition. Figure 15-13 shows the
PL/SQL trigger shell that is built for you.

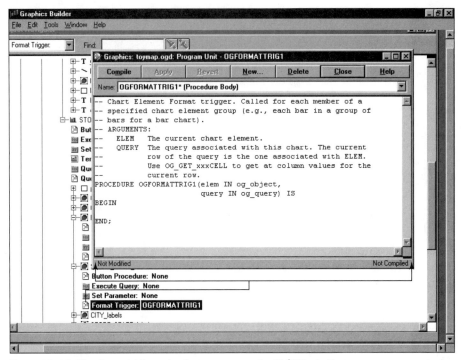

Figure 15-13: The format trigger is given a name and a PL/SQL shell.

The format trigger fires whenever the chart is displayed, which, in this case, is
every time you click a dot on the map. The trigger starts out with the standard text:

```
— Chart Element Format trigger. Called for each member of a
— specified chart element group (e.g., each bar in a group of
— bars for a bar chart).
— ARGUMENTS:
—    ELEM    The current chart element.
—    QUERY   The query associated with this chart. The current
—            row of the query is the one associated with ELEM.
—            Use OG_GET_xxxCELL to get at column values for the
```

```
—          current row.
PROCEDURE OGFORMATTRIGO(elem IN og_object,
                            query IN og_query) IS
BEGIN
```

Next, declare a few variables:

```
DECLARE
image_name VARCHAR2(30);     — file name of the image
image_pic OG_OBJECT;         — image itself as an object
Location_point OG_POINT;     — x,y coordinates
```

The first command gets the value of the filename from the query:

```
BEGIN
IMAGE_NAME := OG_GET_CHARCELL(query,'FLAG_IMAGE');
```

The next command brings the image from the file system into the procedure and loads it into an object:

```
IMAGE_PIC := OG_Import_Image(IMAGE_NAME,OG_Filesystem,
     OG_Gif_Iformat);
```

If you stop here, the image is displayed in the upper-left corner of the chart. To move it down where you want it, define the X and Y coordinates on the layer in inches:

```
LOCATION_POINT.X := (.1*OG_INCH);
LOCATION_POINT.Y := (4.2*OG_INCH);
```

And finally, the image is moved to the specified location:

```
OG_MOVE(IMAGE_PIC,LOCATION_POINT);
END;
END;
```

Voilà! There's an image floating on the layout. Look back at Figure 15-9 to review the final appearance of the map with drill-down details and logos.

Summary

Graphics have myriad uses within applications. This chapter illustrates some of the interesting features available when you use graphics.

One new feature with Developer release 2.1 is the capability to pass an entire query as an array from a form to a chart. An example form and chart are built to show how this is done using parameter lists and the OG.pll library.

Many designers use charts embedded within reports. However, it is also possible to call a report from a chart. This enables you to design an intuitive graphical view of your data and then display more traditional-looking reports that correspond to areas of the display. This chapter develops a sample summary pie chart that starts a detail report.

Getting creative with graphics opens the doors for new uses for applications. In the final section of the chapter, a scatter chart imitates a geographical map interface by plotting store locations onto a backdrop of a map of the U.S. In addition, each location symbol is programmed to display a drill-down chart showing a logo (retrieved from an image file), a store name, and other details.

You may find Oracle Graphics useful in your reports and forms, and even as a lead-in to forms or reports. Use your own ideas, and give it a try.

The next chapter explores the Procedure Builder and more new features of Developer release 2 such as reusable libraries.

Chapter 16

Procedure Builder

IN THIS CHAPTER

- ◆ Working with the Procedure Builder
- ◆ Creating libraries
- ◆ Reusing libraries

THE PROCEDURE BUILDER lends some special tools to developers who create customized PL/SQL libraries, triggers, functions, and procedures. This tool enables you to write code and compile, test, debug, and even migrate program modules to independent platforms via executable libraries.

This chapter looks at how to use the Procedure Builder tool to create a PL/SQL library that is shared between multiple forms.

The examples used in this chapter are based on the Toy Store schema, which you can install by running the TOYSTORE.sql file found in the MAKE directory on the CD-ROM.

Using the Developer's Environment

The Procedure Builder has been part of Developer for several versions. It is the only tool you can use to create standalone procedure libraries based on functions, procedures, or packages. One particularly useful feature is the compiler. You can highlight error messages, and the cursor automatically moves to the line with the error.

In addition to creating procedure libraries, you can use the Procedure Builder anywhere you might use SQL Worksheet or SQL*Plus. However, most developers prefer other products for working with PL/SQL. I use SQL Worksheet more often than any other tool for SQL programming. The debugger in Procedure Builder does not work on Developer Version 2.0. Nor does the debugger work with Version 2.1 if you use Oracle 8.0.3.

Figure 16-1 shows the main window of Procedure Builder. The Procedure Builder contains an Object Navigator, the SQL interpreter, and a compile/code writing window.

Object Navigator   Source code display

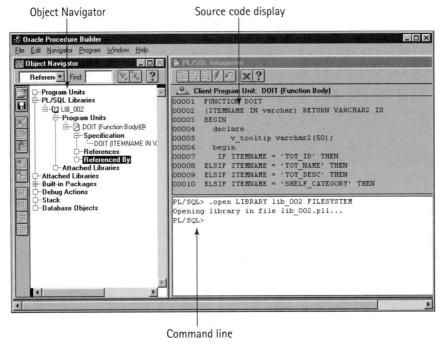

Command line

Figure 16-1: The Procedure Builder has an Object Navigator similar to the Forms Builder.

This chapter focuses on the procedure library function of Procedure Builder. You will build a sample library containing a PL/SQL function. You'll code the function in the Procedure Builder. However, you'll use a SQL query to write part of the body of the procedure. After creating the library, you will attach it to two different forms. Next you'll create triggers in each of those forms that call the function in the library.

The purpose of this function will be to display a tooltip for each column in a block without coding the tooltips individually in the form. The tooltip text will be derived from the column comment stored in the database schema.

Creating a new library

Start a new library using the Object Navigator. Select PL/SQL Libraries, and click the Create icon. When you create a new library, the library can be stored in either the database or the file system. To make the library a standalone unit that is portable among forms and portable between the client and the server, use the file system rather than the database.

The Toy Store Library created in this chapter is named LIB_002. To save a new library in the file system, simply click the Save icon, choose the File System radio button, and name the library. The library file is saved in PLL format. This is similar to the FMB format for forms; it is interpreted at run time.

Libraries can contain procedures, functions, packages, and package bodies. The example will contain one function named DOIT.

 Create a new procedure by selecting Program Units under the current library (LIB_002) and clicking the Create icon. You are prompted with a window where you select the type of program unit (choose Function for the example), and you type the name of the unit (for our example, type DOIT). Now you see the PL/SQL compiler window, where you enter the PL/SQL code.

Editing and compiling PL/SQL

Figure 16-2 shows the compiler window of the Procedure Builder. You can enter the window at any time by clicking the document icon of any program unit in the Object Navigator window.

Asterisk=compile errors   Cursor located at highlighted error

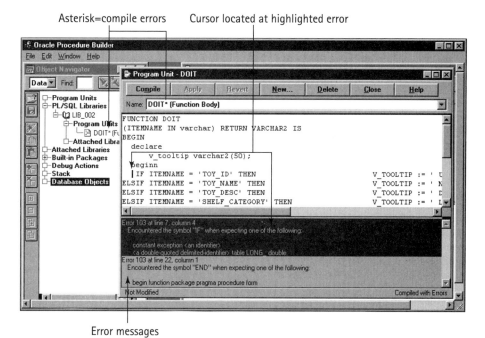

Error messages

Figure 16-2: The compiler window enables you to edit and compile PL/SQL.

If you see an asterisk next to the program unit name, the compile failed.

Editing and compiling are simply a matter of typing in this window and clicking the Compile button. You can close the window even if compiling errors have occurred.

Creating the DOIT function

The function you create in the sample library accepts one incoming parameter: the column name. The function looks through its list of column names and finds the corresponding comments text for the column. The text is placed in a local variable. If the column name is not found, the function returns the default text: "Where am I?" If the column name is found, the function returns the corresponding text.

The function uses a long IF . . . ELSIF . . . ELSE structure. To make it easier to create a long list of columns, the query that writes the IF statement has been created for you. The query looks in the data dictionary views and extracts the comment text for each column in the schema. The appropriate code looks like this:

```
/* -- create_comments_if_stmt.sql — */
SELECT 'ELSIF ITEMNAME = ''' || COLUMN_NAME || ''' THEN ',
    'V_TOOLTIP := '' '
      || SUBSTR(COMMENTS,1,LEAST(100,LENGTH(COMMENTS)))
      || ' '';'
FROM USER_COL_COMMENTS
WHERE COMMENTS IS NOT NULL;
```

Figure 16-3 shows the results of the query as it is run in SQL Worksheet.

Incidentally, you could write PL/SQL code to generate not just these statements but the entire function if you chose to do so. For now, just cut from SQL Worksheet and paste into Procedure Builder. Inside Procedure Builder, change the first ELSIF to IF and complete the code.

First, the initial declarations show what parameters are needed and what format of data is returned:

```
FUNCTION DOIT
(ITEMNAME IN varchar) RETURN VARCHAR2 IS
BEGIN
 declare
   v_tooltip varchar2(50);
 begin
```

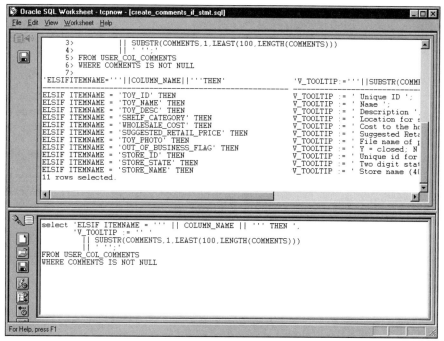

Figure 16-3: Run a query to extract the comment text for each column in the Toy Store schema.

Next, the long set of ELSIF..THEN statements are added to the code (change the initial ELSIF to IF):

```
  IF ITEMNAME = 'TOY_ID' THEN              V_TOOLTIP := ' Unique ID
';
ELSIF ITEMNAME = 'TOY_NAME' THEN            V_TOOLTIP := ' Name ';
ELSIF ITEMNAME = 'TOY_DESC' THEN            V_TOOLTIP := '
Description ';
ELSIF ITEMNAME = 'SHELF_CATEGORY' THEN         V_TOOLTIP := '
Location for shelving this item in the store ';
ELSIF ITEMNAME = 'WHOLESALE_COST' THEN          V_TOOLTIP := ' Cost
to the home office (per unit) ';
ELSIF ITEMNAME = 'SUGGESTED_RETAIL_PRICE' THEN     V_TOOLTIP := '
Suggested Retail Price — usually too high ';
ELSIF ITEMNAME = 'TOY_PHOTO' THEN              V_TOOLTIP := ' File
name of photograph of toy ';
ELSIF ITEMNAME = 'OUT_OF_BUSINESS_FLAG' THEN       V_TOOLTIP := ' Y =
closed; N = in business ';
ELSIF ITEMNAME = 'STORE_ID' THEN             V_TOOLTIP := ' Unique id
```

```
for each store ';
ELSIF ITEMNAME = 'STORE_STATE' THEN          V_TOOLTIP := ' Two
digit state, such as NY ';
ELSIF ITEMNAME = 'STORE_NAME' THEN          V_TOOLTIP := ' Store
name (40 chars max) ';
```

Next, add the ELSE phrase that loads the default value to be displayed on all columns that do not have comment text defined. The code looks like this:

```
ELSE V_TOOLTIP := 'Where am I?';
END IF;
```

Finally, return the tooltip text to the calling unit, and end the function:

```
return V_TOOLTIP;
 end;
END;
```

Compile your code. Now save the library in the file system as a file named LIB_002.pll for our example library. Place the file in the $ORACLE_HOME\BIN directory.

By saving the library to the file system, you have created a reusable, standalone program module. The next step attaches this program module, or library, to other modules. The following section describes how to add libraries to forms.

Implementing Forms with PL/SQL Libraries

A form can access the procedures, functions, or packages found in a library by attaching the library to the form When attached, the form's triggers can reference program units within the attached library.

This section illustrates how to attach a library and create form triggers that reference the library. Two forms have been created using the Toy Store schema. Figure 16-4 shows the Toy Store form. This form queries the TOY_STORE table. When the user moves the mouse into the fields, the tooltip text is displayed. The text found here was retrieved from the library function created in the previous section.

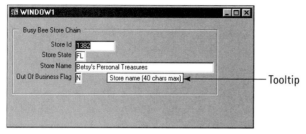

Figure 16-4: The Toy Store form has tooltips created from an attached library.

In a similar way, the second form – called the Toys form – takes advantage of this same attached library to display tooltips for all its columns. Figure 16-5 shows the Toys form.

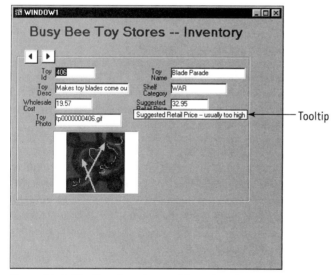

Figure 16-5: The Toys form has tooltips using the same attached library.

Attaching a library to a form

Here is how to attach a library to a form:

1. Open the form in Form Builder.

2. Click the Attached Library object in the Object Navigator.

3. Click the create icon. You'll see a prompt asking you to choose a library from either the database or the file system and attach it. For the sample application, open the Toy Store form and attach the library LIB_002 from the file system. Figure 16-6 shows where the library is attached to the form.

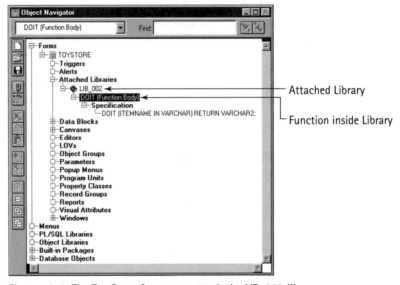

Figure 16-6: The Toy Store form must attach the LIB_002 library.

As you can see, the attached library can be opened in the Object Navigator to reveal the underlying function, what the function's parameter is, and the function's return value.

Now that the library has been attached, the form is ready for a trigger.

Creating a trigger to use the library

A trigger can reference a function in an attached library by using it like any other built-in function. For example, if the library contains the function CALCULATE _AVERAGE, the trigger code might look like this:

```
:AVG_SALES := CALCULATE_AVERAGE(:QTR1_SALES, :QTR2_SALES,
                :QTR3_SALES, :QTR4_SALES);
```

In the sample form, Toy Store, you must find a way to modify the TOOL TIP attribute of each item on the screen. Use a WHEN_NEW_BLOCK_INSTANCE trigger to handle this. Figure 16-7 shows the Toy Store form with the newly created trigger text expanded.

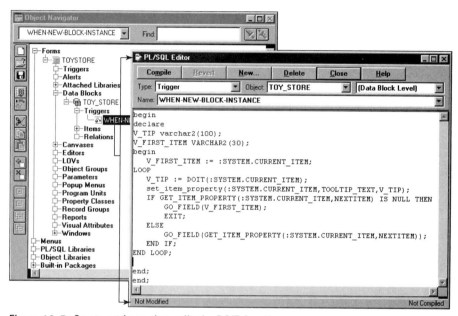

Figure 16-7: Create a trigger that calls the DOIT function.

Here is the trigger code, along with a step-by-step description of how it works:

1. First, declare local variables for the tooltip text (V_TIP) and for the first item that is in the block (V_FIRST_ITEM):

```
begin
declare
V_TIP varchar2(100);
V_FIRST_ITEM VARCHAR2(30);
```

2. Initialize the V_FIRST_ITEM variable with the SYSTEM variable that contains the name of the current item. When this trigger fires, the area of focus is on the first item in the data block:

```
begin
  V_FIRST_ITEM := :SYSTEM.CURRENT_ITEM;
```

3. Begin a loop. This loop executes infinitely, or until an EXIT command is issued. The loop calls the DOIT function, passing the name of the current item. The returned value is placed into the V_TIP local variable, which is then placed into the current item's TOOLTIP_TEXT attribute using the SET_ITEM_PROPERTY function:

```
LOOP
  V_TIP := DOIT(:SYSTEM.CURRENT_ITEM);
  set_item_property(:SYSTEM.CURRENT_ITEM,TOOLTIP_TEXT,V_TIP);
```

4. Now the GET_ITEM_PROPERTY built-in function retrieves the name of the next item in the block. This function returns NULL when you have reached the last item in the block. The IF statement tests the value of the next item. If it is NULL, the loop ends. Otherwise the loop moves to the next item (GO_ITEM) and returns to the beginning of the loop:

```
 IF GET_ITEM_PROPERTY(:SYSTEM.CURRENT_ITEM,NEXTITEM) IS NULL
THEN
    GO_FIELD(V_FIRST_ITEM);
    EXIT;
  ELSE

GO_FIELD(GET_ITEM_PROPERTY(:SYSTEM.CURRENT_ITEM,NEXTITEM));
  END IF;
END LOOP;
```

5. Finally, the trigger ends:

```
end;
end;
```

The same trigger text can be used in the TOY_INVENTORY block in the Toys form.

Tips and ideas for libraries

This chapter contains just one illustration of what you can achieve with attached libraries built in the Procedure Builder. Here are some useful tips on using libraries:

◆ **Use parameters instead of referencing bind variables.** Use IN and IN OUT parameters or function RETURN values as much as possible. You cannot directly reference forms bind variables within an attached library.

◆ **Create toolbars.** Toolbars stored in attached libraries save space because they are stored separately and loaded only when your application needs them.

◆ **Use NAME_IN when you must get data from the form.** Inside a library, the NAME_IN function is a way to get data out of the form. For example, to retrieve the value in the item called STORE_ID, use this code:

```
NAME_IN('TOY_STORE.STORE_ID')
```

Use the NAME_IN function to retrieve GLOBAL and SYSTEM variables as well.

◆ **Use the COPY built-in procedure to place data into the form.** For example:

```
COPY('Carol McCullough', 'CTRL.CREATED_BY_NAME');
```

When the COPY procedure is complete, the block is marked CHANGED. So the block behaves the same way it would if the operator entered the data.

Summary

According to its documentation, the Procedure Builder has every conceivable capability when it comes to PL/SQL coding and debugging. In reality, other tools can work just as well or better for most of your PL/SQL requirements. The Procedure Builder seems to have a niche in the creation and saving of standalone PL/SQL libraries for use in forms.

To illustrate how to create a PL/SQL library, this chapter develops a PL/SQL library containing a single function. The function is called by two different forms. The function has one incoming parameter, an item name, and returns one value, the item's description. The description is retrieved by the form and placed in the tooltip text of the corresponding item.

Part of the code within the function is generated using a SQL query against the data dictionary views. The results of the query are cut and pasted into the Procedure Builder editor.

After this library is built, compiled, and saved in the file system, it is ready for use in multiple forms.

Each form must attach the library before it can reference the function. Then each form references the function inside a trigger. For the sample, the WHEN_NEW _BLOCK_ INSTANCE trigger contains a call to the library function. The end result is a form that has dynamically built tooltip text added to each item in the data block.

Other ways to use libraries include creating toolbars and modifying form data.

The next chapter shows how you can use ActiveX controls to add a special look and feel to your forms.

Chapter 17

ActiveX and Forms

IN THIS CHAPTER

◆ Defining OLE, OCX, and ActiveX

◆ Adding an OLE tree structure to a form

◆ Looking at COM interfaces

◆ Exploring COM variable types

◆ Adding your own OCX to a form

◆ Using PL/SQL to communicate with ActiveX objects

THIS CHAPTER EXPLORES how to change ActiveX objects into forms. In addition, you will see how an OLE control (OCX) functions and how to create your own controls using the standard Component Object Model (COM) interface.

Finally, you learn how to install a new OCX type library into your Windows registry and then write the PL/SQL to call that new control.

 You learn how to install an ActiveX tree navigation tool that is provided in the CD-ROM in the back of this book.

Creating a Tree Navigator for Forms

This section shows you how to install the tree control provided on the CD-ROM.

How it all started

One of my clients chose to build a user interface to a specialized financial system using Developer (with Oracle Forms release 5.0). The client was satisfied with the performance and smooth interaction between the front- and back-ends. However, a couple of months later, the client was prototyping the set of screens that represented the organization hierarchy when he realized there were some limitations to the Forms user interface. The tree control (similar to the left pane of Windows Explorer) could have been the perfect user interface for the organization structure, but it had not been integrated into the Forms environment.

Now, most of us have seen our companies' organization charts. Looking at this chart can be rather unpleasant because many boxes are probably placed higher than the one that carries your name. But if your attitude is "This is business – nothing personal," then you will see nothing more than a graphical representation of a *tree data structure.*

To make this long story short, I designed a three-day workshop for Oracle Forms developers. After that the client was able to integrate the tree data structure as an OCX control and several other advanced features into the screens, and I accumulated enough material to write this chapter.

Clicking your way into OLE

Oracle Forms has been capable of using Object Linking and Embedding (OLE) since release 4. It wasn't until OLE Importer was included in the Forms development environment (in release 5) that it became possible for the Oracle developer to use controls without becoming an OLE expert.

Let's take a look at how to add an OCX object to your form. First, use the Layout Editor in Form Builder, and insert OCX into the form canvas, making it the size you want. Then right-click the OCX container space, and choose Insert Object from the pop-up menu. The Form Builder displays the Insert Object dialog box, similar to the one in Figure 17-1.

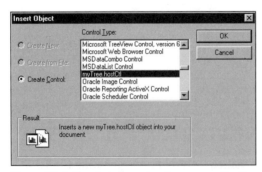

Figure 17-1: Events help customize your application.

Choose the control you want to include in the form. If the control you want is simple enough, then you can select it right away and click OK. Unfortunately Microsoft Tree View Control uses custom datatypes that Forms does not know how to pass. If you are working along with this example, install the MyTree control from the CD. Select it in the "Insert Object," dialog box and click OK.

MyTree is a control that I wrote in Visual Basic 6.0 to simplify the interface to Microsoft Tree View Control. It accepts simple data (CHAR2, INTEGER, and so forth), combines it into the structures that are expected by Microsoft Tree View Control methods, and calls these methods. Now the control is part of your user interface.

If you compile and run the form now, the control will not display anything. You must populate the control with data, which you can do by writing some code.

The most straightforward (but most excruciating) way to handle data is to use the OLE2 Standard package. This requires a fair amount of knowledge about automation technology and requires you to write more PL/SQL code.

We will take a shortcut approach and use the OLE Importer. To use the OLE Importer, highlight the form in the Object Navigator, and choose Program → OLE Importer from the menu. A dialog box similar to the Insert Objects dialog shown in Figure 17-2 is displayed.

Select the myTree.hostCtl entry, and then select the _hostCtl entry in Method Package(s) and __hostCtl entry in EventPackages LOV. The checkboxes at the bottom of the dialog box should be checked.

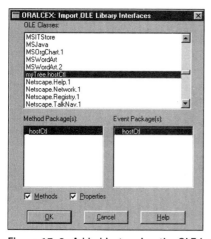

Figure 17-2: Add objects using the OLE Importer.

Observe that the Program Units section has changed. We will be particularly interested in the specification of MYTREE_HOSTCTL and in the body of the MYTREE_HOSTCTL_EVENTS.

Before you go any further, make sure that the names of the block, form, and OCX are the same as shown in Figure 17-3. You can certainly use any names you like, but it will save time if you use the same exact names so that no reprogramming is required.

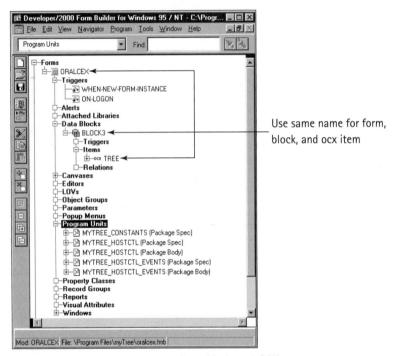

Figure 17-3: Use the names of the form, block, and OCX items to speed the use of the example code.

To display the simple tree of one root node and two leaves, create the WHEN-NEW-FORM-INSTANCE trigger. Insert the following code into the newly created trigger:

```
MYTREE_HOSTCTL.AddNode( :item('BLOCK3.TREE').interface,
   ' ', 'rt' , 'Root');
MYTREE_HOSTCTL.AddNode( :item('BLOCK3.TREE').interface,
   'rt ', 'lf1' , 'Leaf1');
MYTREE_HOSTCTL.AddNode( :item('BLOCK3.TREE').interface,
   'rt ', 'lf2' , 'Leaf2');
```

Fight the temptation to use PRE-FORM trigger because when it is called, the tree control is not initialized yet and is not ready to accept data.

All You Need to Know About OLE (But Were Afraid to Ask)

OLE – which stands for *Object Linking and Embedding* – was originally developed as a standard for how software components should talk to each other under Windows operating systems. Later, the OLE controls, also called *OCX*, were included in the OLE specifications. My attempts to decipher the OCX abbreviation were futile, and I gave up. It turned out that X was here to stay, because when the Internet caught the wave and everything became "live," "killer app," or "active," Microsoft started to use the term "ActiveX" instead of OLE, so "OCX" became "ActiveX control." A little later, we survived another terminology revolution when what was originally "OLE" became "Component Object Model" (COM). So OLE = COM = ActiveX. (Technically speaking, ActiveX is a subset of COM, but for our discussion, you can think of them as the same.

COM defines and categorizes quite a few standard programming interfaces (at least 200 and the number is growing). An interface is a contract between two programs to use certain code structures to communicate.

Imagine two people speaking two different languages, and one wants to greet the other. To do so, they need a contract, which states that the word "hello" will be used as a friendly greeting. In COM terminology, the second person (a person is equivalent to a program) promises to implement the interface (accept "hello" with a smile). Needless to say, that interface and implementation are not coupled in any way. For example, a third person, in response to "hello," can pull out a gun (which would be another implementation).

Usually an interface has several methods, just as a contract contains several paragraphs.

Our example of the contract may specify the interface Greetings, which may have items "hello," "hi," "yo," and so on. Somebody can implement this interface by smiling in response to "hello," grinning in response to "hi," and keeping a straight face in response to "yo."

The paradigm "use and implement" is a cornerstone of COM, so for two software components to be engaged in a meaningful conversation, one should implement a set of interfaces, and the other should use them.

Well, this is hard for software developers, because they have to agree every time on what to use on one end and implement on the other. The solution is interface grouping. If you have an ActiveX control, then this control (and any other control) have to implement a group of interfaces. Otherwise, the control is neither a control nor ActiveX. The same is true about the ActiveX control container, which is how the control can be placed into a container: The container allocates the space and tells the control how big it is via one of the control's interfaces.

Plenty of controls are around, but there are very few containers (for example, Microsoft Internet Explorer, Visual Basic). The most important fact for now is that an Oracle Form is a control container, so it implements all required container interfaces.

If you want to understand more about COM and ActiveX, read the following two sections. Otherwise, skip to the section "Automation Datatypes for OLE in a Form," later in this chapter.

Introducing COM interfaces

As with many basic concepts, it is virtually impossible to define what an interface is. Instead, we can provide an exclusive list of the properties of the subject. The simplest interface is called *IUnknown.*

 All interfaces start with capital *I.*

IUnknown has three methods. Two of them are insignificant to the user of the component and are used to tell the operating system when the component can be deleted from memory. The third one is called *QueryInterface,* and it enables you to get the reference to any interface. This is supported by the object as long as you can get at least one interface, which is a radical proposition. You have to know one interface to get another one, and you have to know that object implements that other interface.

The rule of thumb is: every COM object should support IUnknown.

Now it is obvious that as soon as you get the first interface, you can get any other. The question is how do you get the first one?

COM uses Globally Unique Identifiers (GUIDs) to identify components and interfaces and the system registry to store them. A GUID is a 128-bit, or 8-byte, number, which is generated automatically by the GUIDGEN tool. Every COM object must have a GUID, and that GUID is called a *CLSID,* or class ID. In many cases, an operating system entity (a DLL or EXE) may implement several interfaces. Each implementation is called "class," and every class should be uniquely identified. That is why we cannot assign GUID to the COM component, but we must always have one-to-one correspondence between GUIDs and classes. Each COM class has an entry created in the registry under the HKEY_CLASSES\CLSID where the CLSID is registered. Each COM class also has a pointer to the DLL/EXE file that implements that CLASSID. An *IID* is a GUID for an interface to a COM class. It is used to ask an object if it supports a particular interface. It also gets registered with the system in the registry, under HKEY_CLASSES\Interfaces.

Now we are ready to understand how a COM client uses API to get the first interface of the COM object:

```
CoCreateInstance( rclsid, iid, pUnk ...
```

The three parameters in the command are:

- rclsid. A reference to the CLSID.

- iid. The ID of the first interface we want (usually IID_IUnknown for IUnknown).

- pUnk. An output parameter through which the API returns this first interface.

You will notice, when I included ActiveX in the form, I did not mention GUIDs. It would be extremely awkward if software developers had to remember a bunch of eight-byte numbers. (I already have a hard time remembering the ten-digit phone numbers of my friends.) To help component users, COM enables you to associate CLSID with a *programmatic identifier* – or ProgID. This effectively (but less precisely) identifies the same class. A ProgID (which is considered something that an end-user should not see) is a text string *without spaces* that can be used in programming contexts when referring to the ugly CLSID string isn't appropriate. For example, you can use ProgID to identify an object class in Developer instead of the raw CLSID because Developer doesn't have a way to refer to the GUID structure. The ProgID is thus an alternative language-independent symbolic name, which should be mapped to CLSID. Because we are going to use components, not to develop them, we do not have to worry about that mapping, but if you are curious, you can find it in the registry in the form of:

```
CLSID
{42754580-16b7-11ce-80eb-00aa003d7352} = My.Component
```

My.Component is a ProgID associated with CLSID of 42754580-16b7-11ce-80eb-00aa003d7352.

COM details on custom, standard, and automation interfaces

So far we have discussed only the simplest interface: the IUnknown. In this section we are going to explore COM a little further, but first let's concentrate on issues that are important to the user of ActiveX controls. Because ActiveX is a COM object, it certainly supports IUnknown, but it also should implement many other interfaces. A partial list would be:

◆ IoleObject

◆ IoleInPLaceObject

◆ IoleInPlaceActiveObj

◆ IoleCOntrol

◆ Idispatch

All these interfaces are standard interfaces, and they are described somewhat adequately in the Standard Developer's Kit documentation included with the Windows platform.

A form, which plays the role of the control container, uses those interfaces to host and display the control. *The bottom line is if the control you are using is well written, then the Form knows how to talk to it via the set of standard interfaces.* The only thing that is different for every control is the interface that handles the transfer of custom data to and from the Form. This interface is called a *custom interface* because it is different for every control. In the rest of this chapter, we will be dealing with custom interfaces only, and we'll let Microsoft and Oracle worry about standard interfaces.

COM has two broad types of interfaces, categorized according to how the methods in the interfaces are accessed:

◆ **Static invocation.** This is the mechanism used by custom interfaces.

◆ **Dynamic invocation.** This is the means by which automation interfaces go about their business.

Static invocation is a contract between the client and a server object. The client knows exactly the number of methods in an interface and the signatures of those methods. The object, for its side of the contract, must implement the methods described by the interface. If it does not, the two won't be able to communicate.

Dynamic invocation is how the client objects access automation interfaces. Basically, automation enables the client to ask an object to return information about the interfaces that it supports. Through type information, the object can list all the interfaces it supports. In addition, when queried, it can return information about the methods on a specified interface. Using this information, the client can invoke a method dynamically. In other words, the client can package the parameters in a generic way and then tell the object to call a particular method with those parameters. This invocation is done on the fly and can be performed with no prior knowledge of the object.

Server objects implement automation by enabling clients to use a method on the IDispatch interface to call other methods. The collection of methods it makes available in this way is called a *dispinterface* (short for "dispatch interface"). IDispatch enables an object to indicate what dispinterface methods it supports in two different ways. It can be done at run-time (through other IDispatch methods), or else the object can be a little more expressive and maintain information about its dispinterfaces that a client can use at compile time. The client can still ask the object for information about its dispinterfaces and can call those interface methods dynamically.

As you can imagine, the information that object provides must include details of all the dispinterfaces it supports, all the methods on those dispinterfaces, and all the parameters of those methods. This information is called *type information*. For an object to be an automation object, it means that a client should be able to get access to its type information. The object can supply this directly, or more typically it can be supplied by the type library files.

If the object does not support a particular method, then the call fails. If, however, the data passed from the client is of the wrong type, the object is free to coerce the data to the required type.

How would the object know that the data is of the wrong type? All data passed through automation interfaces uses a special datatype called a *VARIANT*.

Let's summarize how automation works. Once a client obtains this interface on an object, it can use the interface's methods to do three things:

- **Query for type information.** The client asks the object about the automation interfaces it supports, and the methods and properties implemented in those interfaces.

- **Ask the object to translate.** The client asks the object to translate from locale-dependent method and property names to locale-independent dispatch IDs (also called *DISPIDs*).

- **Invoke a method, or access a property via a dispatch ID.**

As you probably have noticed, I have used the term "type library" several times already. Now it's time to describe what that is.

Type library

Why does anybody need a type library? Because it solves a problem. Several tools on the market—Visual C++, Visual Basic, Delphi, and so forth—enable you to create COM objects. From the client's point of view, it shouldn't matter which tool was used to implement the COM object. The simplest solution is to introduce a tool-independent language to be used to describe whatever functionality the COM object exposes. This language is called the Object Definition Language (ODL), which is similar in concept to the Interface Definition Language (IDL) of CORBA. The developer creates an ODL file and then uses the Microsoft Interface Definition Language Compiler (MIDL) to convert the ODL file into a type library. The COM client can read the type library and see what interfaces the object has.

To summarize: A *type library* is a binary file that describes the ActiveX object model. Type libraries are typically embedded as a resource inside an ActiveX EXE or DLL. Type libraries do not store objects; they store type information. By accessing a type library, applications and browsers can determine the characteristics of the object. The kinds of information stored in the type library are:

◆ A list of interfaces supported by the object

◆ The names and addresses of the members of each of those interfaces

Here is a very simple example of the ODL file:

```
[
  uuid(2F6CA420-C641-101A-B826-00DD01103DE1),
  helpstring("Hello 1.0 Type Library"),
  version(1.0)
]
 library Hello
{
    importlib("stdole32.tlb");

    [
      uuid(2F6CA422-C641-101A-B826-00DD01103DE1),
      helpstring("Hello DispInterface")
    ]
    dispinterface  IHello
    {
properties:
methods:
        [id(1)] void SayHello([in] BSTR Message );
    }

    [
      uuid(2F6CA421-C641-101A-B826-00DD01103DE1),
      helpstring("Hello Class")
    ]
    coclass Hello
    {
```

```
        dispinterface IHello;
    }
}
```

The ODL syntax is cryptic, and worst of all, it undergoes significant changes too often. Fortunately, you do not have to write in ODL, but it is helpful to understand what is going on. Let's look over the code piece by piece.

First, look at the construction uuid(2F6CA420-C641-101A-B826-00DD01103DE1):

```
[
  uuid(2F6CA420-C641-101A-B826-00DD01103DE1),
  helpstring("Hello 1.0 Type Library"),
  version(1.0)
]
```

This is the way to tell that 2F6CA420-C641-101A-B826-00DD01103DE1 is a GUID. The type library does have a GUID. You should not be surprised, because in the COM world almost everything does.

The phrase "dispinterface IHello" indicates that IHello will be a dispinterface, and because we rely on the existing definition of IDispatch, we had to include a line importlib("stdole32.tlb"):

```
library Hello
{
    importlib("stdole32.tlb");

    [
      uuid(2F6CA422-C641-101A-B826-00DD01103DE1),
      helpstring("Hello DispInterface")
    ]
    dispinterface  IHello
```

stdole32.tlb is a type library in which all standard interfaces are defined, and it comes with Windows.

The important stuff is in these lines:

```
{
properties:
methods:
        [id(1)] void SayHello([in] BSTR Message );
    }
```

The preceding indicates that the interface does not support any properties, and it has only one method "SayHello." This method has a dispid of 1, and it accepts one parameter of type BSTR.

Installing the Sample OLE Object into a New Form

Enough theory! Let's have some fun. Now you can follow along and implement a real OLE object.

 First of all, copy the tlb file from the CD to any directory, together with the reg file.

Adjust the reg file to point to this directory. You have to change the bold text to point to the directory in which you just copied those files.

Save the changes, open Windows Explorer, and double-click the icon that represents hello.reg. Doing so merges the contents of hello.reg into your registry.

The registry script has three parts. The first four entries describe the type library, and they include the TypeLib token right after HKEY_CLASSES_ROOT:

```
REGEDIT4

[HKEY_CLASSES_ROOT\TypeLib\{2F6CA420-C641-101A-B826-00DD01103DE1}]

[HKEY_CLASSES_ROOT\TypeLib\{2F6CA420-C641-101A-
B826-00DD01103DE1}\1.0]
@="HelloTypeLib"

[HKEY_CLASSES_ROOT\TypeLib\{2F6CA420-C641-101A-
B826-00DD01103DE1}\1.0\0]

[HKEY_CLASSES_ROOT\TypeLib\{2F6CA420-C641-101A-B826-00DD01103DE1}
\1.0\0\win32]
@="c:\\classes\\typelib\\hello.tlb"
```

The second and third parts are needed to make the Form Builder think that it is dealing with an ActiveX control, while in reality, we supply the interface declaration only.

The second part includes all entries with the CLSID token, and for many clients (such as Internet Explorer) the first two parts of the registration are sufficient.

```
[HKEY_CLASSES_ROOT\CLSID\{2F6CA420-C641-101A-B826-00DD01103DE9}]
@="A Hello Control"

[HKEY_CLASSES_ROOT\CLSID\{2F6CA420-C641-101A-
B826-00DD01103DE9}\Control]

[HKEY_CLASSES_ROOT\CLSID\{2F6CA420-C641-101A-B826-00DD01103DE9}
\Insertable]

[HKEY_CLASSES_ROOT\CLSID\{2F6CA420-C641-101A-
B826-00DD01103DE9}\TypeLib]
@="{2F6CA420-C641-101A-B826-00DD01103DE1}"
```

The third part includes the two last entries. Those entries create in the registry a fakeControl.Hello key and a subkey that point to the CLSID via GUID.

```
[HKEY_CLASSES_ROOT\fakeControl.hello]
@="Hello Class"

[HKEY_CLASSES_ROOT\fakeControl.hello\CLSID]
@="{2F6CA420-C641-101A-B826-00DD01103DE9}"
```

In some versions of Windows 95, a bug in Regedit runs the script incorrectly. If this is the case, start Regedit, search for 2F6CA420-C641-101A-B826-00DD01103DE1, open this key, and manually add c:\\classes\\typelib\\hello.tlb for the Win32 subkey.

Now let's start Form Builder, open Layout Manager, and place OCX on the canvas. Right-click on the inserted OCX, and choose Insert Object from the pop-up menu. You will get the Insert Object dialog box. Scroll down the listbox until you see the entry "Hello Control," and highlight it. You should see the menu shown in Figure 17-4.

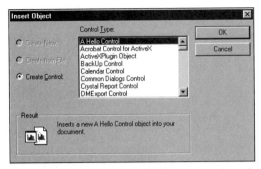

Figure 17-4: Right-click the OCX item, and then choose Insert Object to see this menu.

Look again at the registry script. You should be able to spot where the "Hello Control" string is coming from. Click OK, and Form Builder accepts the fake without complaint.

Close Layout Editor, and click the OLE Importer subitem under the Program menu. In the Import OLE Library Interfaces dialog, look for the "fakeControl .hello" string, and highlight it. You should again get something similar to Figure 17-4.

Be sure to highlight the Ihello in the bottom part before you click OK; otherwise, nothing will be imported.

After you click OK, the OLE Importer creates entries in the Program Units section of the Object Navigator.

Take a close look at the FAKECONTROL_IHELLO (Package Spec), by opening it with PL/SQL Editor.

Here is what you will see:

```
PACKAGE fakeControl_IHello IS
- The Functions:
PROCEDURE SayHello(interface OleObj, Message VARCHAR2);
END;
```

If you want to ask this control to say hello, use the following PL/SQL code:

```
FAKECONTROL_IHELLO.SayHello(:item(  'BLOCK3.ACTIVEX_CTL').interface,
'Hei, Hei, Hei');
```

Now you can see where the pieces are coming from.

◆ FAKECONTROL came straight from the registry.

◆ IHELLO, on the other hand, had a longer way to go. When you selected
the ProgID FAKECONTROL.hello, this is what happened:

1. OLE Importer read the CLSID subkey and got the GUID.

2. OLE Importer then looked inside the CLSID registry key for that GUID.

3. After the GUID was found, the Importer read the GUID from the
TypeLib subkey.

4. The Importer searched inside the TypeLib key for this GUID, which is
how the tlb file was found.

5. The Importer read this tlb file and discovered that there is only one
dispinterface: IHello.

   If the interface IHello was not of the IDispatch type, the Importer would
   not have been able to discover it, and the Method/Packages listbox
   would have been empty. Figure 17-5 shows the correct look of the
   Importer window.

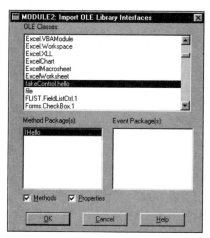

Figure 17-5: Choose IHello to insert the OLE control.

Recall how we define the interface in the hello.odl file:

```
methods:
        [id(1)] void SayHello([in] BSTR Message );
```

There was only one parameter, so why do the package specifications dictate having two, and what is that extra interface parameter?

 TIP You just hit one of the limitations of PL/SQL. When Oracle adopted PL/SQL, object-oriented programming (OOP) was not that big of a deal, so not being object oriented was not a felony. But if worst comes to worst, PL/SQL will share the cell with C (not bad company!). If what you just read does not make sense to you, just remember that the first parameter of any method called for any ActiveX is always a reference to the interface itself. To get this reference, we use the following PL/SQL construction:

```
BL code alone
```

`Block_Name` and `ActiveX_Name` are the names you gave to the block and ActiveX, respectively.

The real parameter, which represented the message we wanted to display originally, had a strange type: BSTR. Importer replaced it with VARCHAR2. That was a very intelligent decision, but to understand what really happened, you need to read the next section.

Automation Datatypes for OLE in a Form

Several datatypes are used within the OLE object in a form. This section describes these datatypes and how to program them.

Using DISPPARAMS types

As you may remember, the Invoke method of IDispatch takes a parameter of DISPPARAMS type.

The definition of this type is as follows:

```
typedef struct tagDISPPARAMS
{
VARIANT* rgvarg;
DISPID* rgdispidNamedArgs;
UINT cArgs;
UINT cNamedArgs;
} DISPPARAMS;
```

The `cArgs` member specifies the number of arguments passed and is the size of the (user-allocated) `rgvarg` array.

Using OLE VARIANT types

The client must be able to pass many different datatypes in the rgvarg array. To do this, the datatype of the array is a discriminated union called a *VARIANT* type. The discriminator is called *vt* and must be set so that the client knows how to access the data. The union itself contains one of the types listed in Table 17-1. (More types actually exist, but we list only those supported by the Forms environment.)

TABLE 17-1 OLE VARIANT TYPES SUPPORTED IN FORMS

OLE-Defined VARIANT Type	Interpretation in Developer
VT_BLOB	VT_UNKNOWN
VT_BLOB_OBJECT	VT_UNKNOWN
VT_BOOL	Boolean
VT_BSTR	String
VT_BYREF 16384	May be added to any of the following types to indicate "pointer-to"
VT_DATE	Date
VT_DISPATCH	OLE object pointer capable of OLE automation calls
VT_INT	Integer
VT_I1	Signed one-byte integer
VT_I2	Signed two-byte integer
VT_I4	Signed four-byte integer
VT_LPSTR	VT_BSTR
VT_NULL	Null
VT_R4 number	Four-byte floating point number
VT_R8	Eight-byte floating point number
VT_UINT	Unsigned four-byte integer
VT_USERDEFINED	Typed data
VT_VARIANT	Any type

Reviewing other types

The types BSTR and SAFEARRAY will be described later, and you may not be familiar with the following other types:

- ◆ CY is a currency type and is held in 64 bits. Forms does not support VT_CY.

- ◆ DATE holds a date and time.

- ◆ DECIMAL holds a large decimal type. It has 64 bits for the mantissa and 8 bits for the exponent. This is truly a large decimal! Unfortunately, Forms does not support VT_I8.

The next two sections cover BSTR and SAFEARRAY and are relatively advanced. If you do not want to mess with C++, go directly to the section "Handling VARIANTS in PL/SQL," later in this chapter.

BSTR

Passing strings between processes is a problem because unlike most other datatypes, there is no predetermined size for strings. This means the client and the component need to know how much data to send or receive. Further, once a process has determined how much data to transmit and then has sent it, the COM at the other end has to create a buffer for the data and pass that buffer to the server. The COM rules state that [out] parameters are released by the caller, so such a caller process must have access to the same allocator that created the buffer.

Automation takes the approach of treating a string as some kind of structure that always knows its own length, which has the side effect of enabling BSTRs to contain embedded NULL characters and hence to be used to pass binary data if required.

As to the second issue, a process receiving a BSTR from another process as an [out] parameter must release that data when it is finished with it. COM cannot use new because it is language neutral, and so instead it uses its own memory allocator.

BSTRs are created with the function SysAllocString() and released with the SysFreeString() function. Both those functions are Windows System APIs and are accessible through any language, but certainly you wouldn't use them in PL/SQL directly. The SysAllocString() function also keeps the size of the buffer alongside the buffer itself. The pointer that you get back from SysAllocString() is a BSTR.

Finally, BSTR must be freed with the SysFreeString() function. This function frees the string, returning the memory back to the BSTR cache.

SAFEARRAY

Passing arrays of data between processes requires special handling because while languages such as C and C++ get access through pointers, other languages such as PL/SQL and Java, which do not have pointers, must still be able to access the same COM arrays.

Here is the SAFEARRAY structure:

```
typedef struct tagSAFEARRAY
{
    USHORT cDims;
    USHORT fFeatures;
    ULONG  cbElements;
    ULONG  cLocks;
    PVOID  pvData;
    SAFEARRAYBOUND rgsabound[ 1 ];
} SAFEARRAY;
```

The first, third, and last members describe the structure of the array. They tell how many dimensions it has and the size of a single element in the array, and they provide information about the number of elements in each dimension. The actual data is pointed to by the pvData member.

The SAFEARRAYBOUND structure is declared as:

```
typedef struct tagSAFEARRAYBOUND

{

    ULONG cElements;

    LONG  lLbound;
} SAFEARRAYBOUND;
```

When using VARIANTS in Forms, you must write PL/SQL to communicate with the OLE objects. The next section shows how to convert PL/SQL variables to OLE VARIANTS.

Handling VARIANTS in PL/SQL

PL/SQL, when used inside a form, has several built-in functions that handle the conversion from and to VARIANTS. More precisely, there are four versions of the function TO_VARIANT that handle the conversion to VARIANT. Several other functions, shown later in the chapter, handle conversion from VARIANT to the PL/SQL datatypes.

Let's look at the four ways to use TO_VARIANT first.

◆ Convert a number to a VARIANT:

```
TO_VARIANT
  ( newval NUMBER, vtype VT_TYPE, persistence BOOLEAN)
```

◆ Convert a character field to a VARIANT:

```
TO_VARIANT
  (newval VARCHAR2,vtype VT_TYPE, persistence BOOLEAN)
```

◆ Convert a table to an array VARIANT:

```
TO_VARIANT
  ( source_table, vtype VT_TYPE, arrspec VARCHAR2,
    persistence BOOLEAN)
```

◆ Convert an OLE variable to a VARIANT:

```
TO_VARIANT
  (var OLEVAR,  vtype VT_TYPE   arrspec VARCHAR2,
   persistence BOOLEAN)
```

The following list describes the parameters:

newval	The value to be placed into a new OLE VARIANT
vtype	This is an optional parameter that specifies the OLE VT_TYPE to be assigned to the new VARIANT. If not specified, the default value for the NUMBER version of the function is VT_R8. For the VARCHAR2 version, the default is VT_BSTR. For the table version, the default is determined from the PL/SQL types of the table. For the OLEVAR version, the default is the type of the source VARIANT.
Persistence	This optional parameter controls the persistence of the VARIANT after its creation. A Boolean value of TRUE establishes the VARIANT as persistent; a value of FALSE establishes the VARIANT as nonpersistent. If this parameter is not specified, the default value is nonpersistent.
source_table	An existing PL/SQL table that is used to establish the bounds and values of the newly created VARIANT table. The source table can be of any type.
arrspec	This parameter indicates which selected element or elements of a source table are to be used in the creation of the new VARIANT. The lower bound always starts at 1. (If you read the two previous sections, then you should see the similarity

between "table VARIANT" and SAFEARRAY. The truth is that "table VARIANT" in reality is a SAFEARRAY.) `arrspec` is an optional parameter. If not specified, the entire source table or source VARIANT is used.

Var   `Var` is an existing OLE VARIANT whose value is to be given to the new VARIANT. (This source VARIANT may be a table.)

A PL/SQL example using a table VARIANT

The following example shows how to send data as a SAFEARRAY, using a table VARIANT:

```
DECLARE

  control    OleObj;
  record number;

    /* Table */
  type    sample_table_type is
      table of  database_tbl%type index by binary_integer;
  sample_table    sample_table_type;
  cursor    sample_cursor  is
  select * from  database_tbl;

BEGIN

  control := :item('ActiveX').interface;

  /* Load Table */
  record := 0;
  open  sample_cursor;
      loop
          record := record + 1;
          fetch  sample_cursor into sample_table(record);
          exit when sample_cursor%NOTFOUND;
      end loop;
  close  sample_cursor;

ATLMYCONTROL..SetTable(control, o_variant(sample_table));

END;
```

The first line declares the variable control as OleObj type; then we define the PL/SQL type sample_table_type and bind it to the database table database_tbl.

In the body we set the control to refer to the ActiveX interface and use it in the last line to pass the table as a parameter of the SetTable method. We coerce the sample_table into the SAFEARRAY (recall that to_variant has a special form that handles a PL/SQL table).

Before calling SetTable, we had to initialize sample_table, and we did this by fetching records into it.

Getting data from the VARIANT

In some cases, the method or property can pass VARIANT data back to the Form. PL/SQL cannot do much with VARIANTS.

If x is a VARIANT, you cannot even do simple addition. The statement x:=x+1; produces an error, even if the VARIANT has a numeric type.

Fortunately, PL/SQL provides a set of built-in functions that help you extract data from a VARIANT and convert it to that certain PL/SQL type. There are three functions:

- VAR_TO_CHAR. The syntax is:

  ```
  VAR_TO_CHAR   (var OLEVAR, arrspec VARCHAR2)
  ```

  This function converts a VARIANT into a VARCHAR2.

- VAR_TO_NUM. The syntax is:

  ```
  VAR_TO_NUM    (var OLEVAR, arrspec VARCHAR2)
  ```

  This function converts a VARIANT into a NUMBER.

- VAR_TO_OBJ. The syntax looks like this:

  ```
  VAR_TO_OBJ    (var OLEVAR, arrspec VARCHAR2)
  ```

  The function converts a VARIANT into an OLEOBJ. The VAR_TO_OBJ function is advanced, and a description of it is beyond the scope of this book. You can use this function to obtain another interface to the COM object.

The first two functions enable you to convert a VARIANT to the character or to the number. They use the same set of parameters:

var	The OLE VARIANT that we want to convert
arrspec	This parameter is used only if the first parameter is an array. It indicates which element of the array is to be converted.

The preceding functions enable you to convert only one element of the array at a time. If you want to pass the array at once, use the procedure VAR_TO_TABLE, which has the following syntax:

```
VAR_TO_TABLE
(var OLEVAR, target_table, arrspec VARCHAR2)
```

The parameters are:

var	The OLE VARIANT that is the source array
target_table	The PL/SQL table to be populated
arrspec	This optional parameter indicates which rows, columns, or elements of the source array are to be used. If not specified, all elements in the source array are used.

Pointers and VARIANTS in PL/SQL

PL/SQL was designed to work with data sets, while the designers of other languages had different goals in mind. As a result, different languages have different capabilities and can require you to deal with objects completely foreign to the PL/SQL programmer. For example, C++ supports pointers and references to the data. You can think about a pointer as if it is an address of a data object. Because the developer of ActiveX was free to use C++, nothing prevents his using pointers as input or output parameters of the methods. We, as Forms developers, have to be prepared to handle that situation. PL/SQL helps us by providing these two functions:

- ◆ VAR_TO_VARPTR. The syntax of this function is:

  ```
  VAR_TO_VARPTR (var OLEVAR, vtype VT_TYPE)
  ```

  This function returns the VARIANT that contains a pointer to the OLEVAR var (first parameter).

  vtype is the type to be assigned to the created OLE VARIANT. Permissible types are VT_BYREF, VT_PTR, and VT_NULL. If this optional parameter is not specified, the default value is VT_BYREF.

◆ VARPTR_TO_VAR. The syntax is:

```
VARPTR_TO_VAR  (pvar OLEVAR, vtype VT_TYPE)
```

This second function enables the PL/SQL user to get the data from the pointer, returned by the method.

`pvar` is an OLE VARIANT that contains the pointer or reference.

`vtype` is the OLE VT_TYPE to be given to the transformed VARIANT. If this optional parameter is not specified, the default value is VT_VARIANT.

This function extracts the pointer from `pvar`, then creates a new VARIANT, in which it places data, referenced by this pointer.

Events

So far we've discussed only one side of the communications between forms and ActiveX, that being communications initiated by the form. When a form wants something from the control, it calls one of the methods. Suppose ActiveX wants to attract the attention of the form. For example, when the user clicks on the ActiveX button, the parent form is to be notified. In the COM world, everything goes through the interfaces. Forms can find out about the interfaces inside ActiveX by reading the type library and then calling the appropriate method of ActiveX.

When ActiveX wants to signal something back to the form, it has to get one of the form interfaces and use one of the methods. The only way to make it work for any container is to standardize on the "Notification" interface.

The standard interfaces are ISink, IConnectionPoint, and IConnectionPoint-COntainer.

The client (the form) implements ISink, and ActiveX should implement IConnectionPoint and ISonnectionPointCOntainer.

When the form starts, it first asks ActiveX for IconnectionPointCOntainer. It then uses methods of this interface to find a connection point for the ISink interface. Finally, it passes the ISink to the connection point.

Later, when ActiveX wants to notify the form, it uses methods of the ISink interface.

Connection points are custom interfaces, and they can be found in the type library of the control.

When OLE Importer reads the type library, it customizes the ISink interface of the form to satisfy the ActiveX connection point. This is what is happening under the hood.

Examining the Ising interface

Let's look closely at what the Importer does. Besides generating packages for methods and properties, Importer also generates a separate package for the event. You can easily distinguish this package by the suffix "_EVENTS." Each event is associated with a PL/SQL procedure defined in the events package. The procedures are named according to an internal numeric representation as defined by the control. Importer, however, places a comment before the procedure name to help you identify the procedure. When the control fires an event, the code in the procedure is automatically executed. You need to modify the body of the procedure if you want to handle the event.

Modifying the Importer event procedure

The event procedure is called to increase the value of a field when a mouse click event is detected.

```
Package Body  myOCX_EVENTS IS

PROCEDURE /*Click*/ event2()
BEGIN
     :block.value := :block.value + 1;
END;

END;
```

The OLE Importer constructed the framework for handling the event. All I had to do was to type the following line:

```
:block.value := :block.value + 1;
```

Summary

There is no built-in support for a tree navigator similar to the one used in the Windows navigator. The CD-ROM contains an OCX control that accomplishes this task. This chapter includes instructions on how to install the control into a form.

OLE is equivalent to OCX, and OCX is the same as ActiveX. ActiveX is a form of COM interface and uses the COM interface standards to communicate with the application.

This chapter reviews the internal commands that are integral to all COM interfaces and how they work. It also discusses the type library and how to use it.

A sample COM interface is included on the CD-ROM, and this chapter contains instructions on how to install it into the Windows registry and then call it in a form.

All the automation datatypes that are supported in Oracle Forms are described in detail.

Sample PL/SQL code demonstrates how to use several different datatypes.

The final section of the chapter describes how to use special PL/SQL functions to convert OLE VARIANT types into PL/SQL datatypes such as number, varchar, and table.

The next chapter describes how to combine forms, reports, and graphics.

Chapter 18

Practical Applications: Libraries, Menus, and Tab Canvases

IN THIS CHAPTER

◆ Writing external libraries for reusable code

◆ Using menus

◆ Designing intuitive tab canvases

USER INTERFACES USED to be nothing more than characters and boxes to fill in. Oracle Forms started this way, but the current version, 5.0, bears no resemblance to its past. Although Version 4.0 started the GUI transformation of Forms, including the use of menus and other graphic tools, version 5.0 brings in the power of packaged procedures and the flexibility of tabbed canvases. This section will show you how to use external libraries, menus, and tabbed canvases with your forms. You will be able to create a powerful user interface with reusable, low maintenance procedures and form templates.

Designing Menus for Forms

There are two very different reasons for using menus in your forms. You may want to use Oracle's standard menu with a smart bar, called *default&smartbar*. The standard menu gives you easy mouse access to standard database functions – for example, Clear Record, Execute Query, and Exit. The second reason to use a menu or toolbar is to give the user access to special functions or custom applications you have written for them.

You don't have to choose between these two options when designing your menus. Most likely you'll take the best from each type of menu to give to the user. You can find out from your users what Oracle functions they use the most or need most on a menu or toolbar. Then you will include the functions and applications you know they will need on a menu or toolbar.

Once you have designed and created your menu, you can use it in a form by adding it at the form level to the property sheet under the item Menu Module. If you saved your menu in the database and not to a file, then you need to specify the menu source just above the Menu Module property. Figure 18-1 shows where to find the menu properties in the Property Palette.

Figure 18-1: The menu properties for a form in the Property Palette.

Once you have entered the name of your menu in the property sheet, you can generate and run the form to see the menu at the top. Be sure that your menu file (if not in the database) is in the FORMS50_PATH.

Table 18-1 lists the properties that can be set to affect how menus are displayed in forms.

TABLE 18-1 PROPERTIES FOR CUSTOMIZING MENUS IN FORMS

Level	Property	Description
Form level	Menu source	Specifies whether to locate the menu module in the database or in the file system.

Level	Property	Description
	Menu module	Names the menu module to be used for this form.
	Initial menu	Specifies a menu within the menu module (named in the previously mentioned Menu Module property) to be used as the top-level menu for this form.
	Menu Style	Pull-down and full-screen menus are available. The latter will not be available in the next major release of Oracle Forms.
	Menu Role	Causes the form to run the menu as though the user were a member of the security role named in this property.
Canvas level	Popup Menu	Specifies a pop-up menu to show for the canvas.
Window level	Horiz. Toolbar Canvas	Names a canvas of type horizontal toolbar to show in window.
	Vert. Toolbar Canvas	Names a canvas of type vertical toolbar to show in window.
	Inherit Menu	Lets window use the current menu for the active form; not valid for MS Windows.

TIP The most useful properties of those in the preceding list are the Initial Menu property, and the toolbar properties. The Initial Menu property lets you choose just one menu in a menu module as the menu the user will see.

For example, let's say you have a large menu called STOREMNU that enables access to forms and reports for all departments, and you want a user to see only the forms for a particular department, DEPTAMNU. You would set the Menu Module property to be STOREMNU and the Initial Menu property to be DEPTAMNU, as illustrated in Figure 18-2.

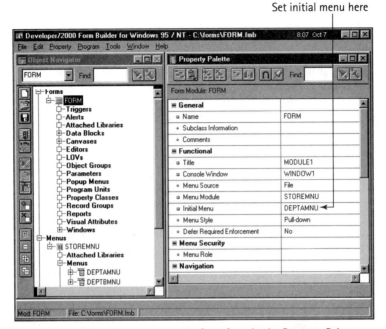

Figure 18-2: Initial Menu property set for a form in the Property Palette.

The toolbar properties enable you to put buttons on your forms that users can press for special functions. Toolbars make life easier than menus do. Instead of a user having to navigate one or two menus down to find a function to execute, a toolbar puts the most frequently used commands right there on the screen for the user to click just once. Whether to have a vertical toolbar down the left side of the screen, or the more common horizontal toolbar across the top of the screen, or even both at once, is up to you. Figure 18-3 shows a customized toolbar on its own canvas in the Layout Editor.

Implementing advanced menu control

Menus are excellent for mapping out all of the forms available in a particular application system. However, not every user should have access to every form. You can prevent users from using menu items they don't have any reason or privilege to use. Oracle Forms provides a built-in way to accomplish this by using *roles*. If you have each system user defined as an Oracle user, you can assign roles to them that define what they can do in the applications and menus. When building your menus, you can use the Menu Security properties for the menu module to take advantage of the roles assigned to the Oracle users, as you see in Figure 18-4. Adding database roles to the menu module determines which Oracle users have access to it.

The Time-Saving Value of Cut and Paste

Many developers overlook one of the most powerful tools available to them: cut and paste. Whether you are creating a form, menu, or toolbar, you will find it much easier to copy a similar object and paste it as many times as you need one like it. The toolbar is a perfect example. Make one of the push buttons look exactly like you want. Then copy it and paste it as many times as you need for more buttons. You can then make the changes you need to the new icons. You can also use drag and drop in the Object Navigator to copy objects between forms.

Let's say that you have created all of your push buttons quickly through cut and paste. They are all scattered on the canvas haphazardly. Select them all, and choose Arrange → Align Objects from the menu. There you can line up your push buttons and space them out neatly. Never do this manually unless you're scared to death you will beat the deadline. (Each Align Objects option is available in the Layout Editor window as a toolbar button. The six align options are just right of the zoom toolbar buttons.)

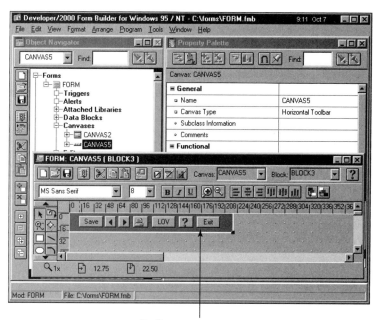

Toolbar menu on a canvas

Figure 18-3: A custom toolbar canvas in the Layout Editor.

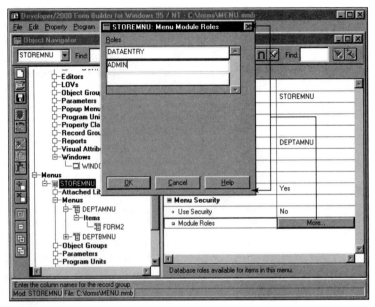

Figure 18-4: Naming roles that can access a menu in the Form Builder.

Roles determine access only at the menu level, so if you want menu-item-level control, you have to build it yourself. Keep reading for how to do this.

In some environments, not every user has an Oracle user ID. The users are most likely defined in the database, and they have a custom designed login screen. In this situation, applications are able to use Oracle's role permissions feature. Fortunately, Oracle still provides many ways to dynamically change the appearance of your menus.

Using the built-in command set for menus, you can change a number of attributes for a menu item within a menu. The four attributes that can be changed are:

- ◆ **Checked.** The Checked attribute is valid only in the context of a radio button or checkbox menu item.

- ◆ **Enabled.** The Enabled attribute simply causes a menu item to grey out. It is still visible and a lighter gray, but the user cannot get the menu item to do anything.

- ◆ **Label.** The Label attribute determines what label the user sees.

- ◆ **Visible.** If you don't want the user to see the menu item at all, then set the Visible attribute property to FALSE.

For example, set the VISIBLE attribute for the menu item named SAVERECORD to FALSE. The menu item is found in the DEPTAMNU menu of the STOREMNU menu module. Here is the SQL command:

```
SET_MENU_ITEM_PROPERTY('DEPTAMNU.SAVERECORD',
VISIBLE, PROPERTY_FALSE);
```

TIP Don't confuse the name of a menu item with its label. A menu item may be named in the Form Builder as SAVERECORD, but in the label property it is Save Record. Sometimes the similarities between names and labels can cause coding mistakes.

Now that you know how to change a single menu item, how are you going to make sure all of the menu items are set appropriately for each user? Setting each user's privilege to each menu item is a little more complicated because you have to specify the menu name and the menu item in order to change each menu item. There is no way to know which menu the user is using once the form is at run time. If you store the menus in the database, you can find those names, loop through all the menus, and make the necessary changes to the menus that are currently active. However, it would be preferable to store the menus and menu items the user has permissions to use in the database as part of the custom security system already in place. After all, the users are logging in through a custom front end, so storing the menus and menu items they will be allowed to use is not difficult. *Along with your tables storing the application names and user names, you can add a table storing the name of your menus and menu IDs.* You should add another table to cross-reference the user table to the menu table so you can define what menus each user has access to.

Once the user's permissions for menus are stored in a table, you can access that table to activate the menu items the users have access to each time they enter a form. The process of checking the menu permissions is a procedure stored in an *external library* available to all forms. External libraries will be discussed in a section later in this chapter. Notice that with the user permissions stored in a table, you can easily find out what users have access to, but it would be more difficult to know what they don't have access to. This situation changes how you build your menus in the Form Builder.

Following this approach, you only want to make Visible or Enable the menu items the user can access. This means that all of the other menu items already are invisible or disabled. Can you do that? Sure. You can set all of your menu items to be invisible or disabled at design time. Without a special procedure to enable your menus at run time, no one will see any menu items at all! Think of it as an added security measure.

You must add one more thing to your menus and your security procedure. You need one placeholding menu item on each menu. *You should name this placeholding menu item with the same name in every menu of a menu module* and be sure to set the Visible and Enabled properties to TRUE. The label property value is irrelevant as you will soon see. Now add to your security procedure a routine that goes through all the menus (not menu items) and turns off the one placeholding menu item for each of them. Why do you have to do this? If your menus do not have any visible menu items at design time, the menu itself will not be visible at run time. Even after making one of the menu items visible, the menu does not become visible. To prevent this, you use a visible placeholding menu item in each menu with one common name that can easily be turned off at run time. Figure 18-5 shows two menus that have the visible menu item named PLACEHOLDER.

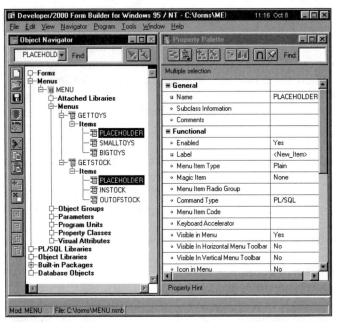

Figure 18-5: Notice that there is a menu item named PLACEHOLDER in each menu of this menu module.

You now have the ability to easily control your menus at run time. Dynamically controlling your menus with tables lets you move control of their appearance from the design-time interface to the database. Now when your user security needs changing, you can make those changes in a table, which is easier than altering roles or changing the menus in the Form Builder.

TIP When attempting to retrieve information from a form or change information for a menu in a form (for example, GET_MENU_ITEM_PROPERTY, SET_MENU_ITEM_PROPERTY) be sure to use ID_NULL in your code. This prevents your procedure from failing should the menu or its menu item not be there for any reason. ID_NULL can and should be used for any object in a form, whether it is a menu item, text item, canvas, or window. Using the set menu item property command, we can check to see if the menu item exists before setting it. With the addition of ID_NULL, no program errors occur when the menu item does not exist in the form.

Here is the PL/SQL code to set a menu item to invisible. The ID_NULL function enables you to verify the existence of the menu item before attempting to modify its attribute.

```
/* — Forms/Idnull.sql —- */
DECLARE
V_MENU_ITEM_ID MENUITEM;
BEGIN
V_MENU_ITEM_ID := FIND_MENU_ITEM('DEPTAMNU.SAVERECORD');
/* —- check for item: does it exist. —- */
IF NOT(ID_NULL(V_MENU_ITEM_ID)) THEN
        /* —- set VISIBLE to FALSE —- */
        SET_MENU_ITEM_PROPERTY
          (V_MENU_ITEM_ID, VISIBLE, PROPERTY_FALSE);
END IF;
END;
```

Now, let's examine another new feature of Forms 5.0: the tab canvas.

Designing Intuitive Tab Canvases

Oracle Forms has an invaluable new tool in Version 5.0 with the addition of tabbed canvases. The tabbed canvas uses the file folder metaphor. The tabs make it possible for one canvas to have multiple tab pages stacked on it with little tabs at the top of the pages that the user can click on see that particular tab page. The tab canvas contains tab pages.

Figures 18-6 and 18-7 show two tab pages on a tabbed canvas. The tab page in Figure 18-6 is the Toys page where you can choose a toy to check inventory for. The tab page in Figure 18-7 shows the detail relationship of the Stockroom page from the toy you selected on the Toys page. The TOY_ID item shows only once on the Stockroom tab page. The multirecord display is for all the stores that carry this toy and lists how many of that toy are currently in stock.

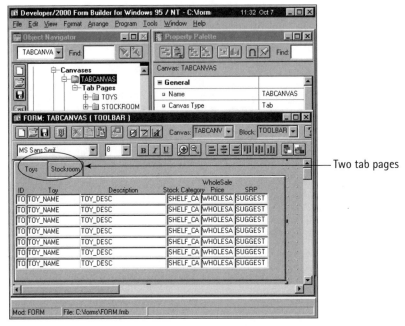

Figure 18-6: The tab page labeled Toys for the tabbed canvas

TIP   If you want to quickly create a block based on a tab canvas, you can use the Data Block Wizard. This tool guides you through choosing a table, the columns you want to use, and what type of canvas to view your block data on. Using this tool is the fastest way to get your basic elements in the Form Builder. From there you can modify them to meet your design standards. Simply click on the Block section of the Object Navigator, and then click on the green plus sign to the left on the toolbar. The dialog that's displayed enables you to use the Data Block Wizard.

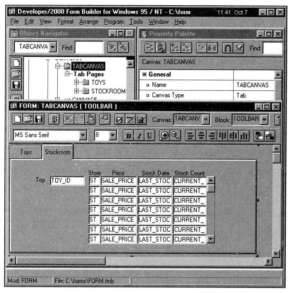

Figure 18-7: The tab page labeled Stockroom for the tabbed canvas.

Building tab canvases and tab pages

To use this new interface element on an already existing block, create a new canvas, and change the Canvas Type property to Tab. In the Object Navigator, your canvas now has a tab pages element under it with two tab pages that are created by default. To place items on the tab pages, you have to have already created blocks in your form. You can go to any item in a block, and under the Physical section of the Property Palette, you can set the Canvas property to your new tab canvas, and the Tab Page property to the name of your new tab canvas. You can only choose tabbed canvases and tab pages that already exist from the drop-down list, so be sure you have made your tab canvas and pages before you attempt this. After you have changed the canvas properties of the items you want on the tab page, they are displayed on the tab page when you open the Layout Editor. You have just created your first tabbed canvas!

TIP

You may notice that your tab page with the longest label name tends to have the label almost hanging off the edge of tab. To fix this, add an equal number of spaces on each side of the label name in the Property Palette for that tab page until you have extended the tab width to your satisfaction. Be fore-warned that adding spaces increases the width of *all* the tabs, not just that one. Normally one or two spaces on each side of the label name is enough.

Implementing advanced tab canvas control

There is one end-user consideration when using tab canvases. You may notice that when you click on a tab page in a tabbed canvas at run time, even after the focus has moved to that tab page, the focus remains on the tab of that page. Your users will appreciate it if you move the focus down to the first item in the block on that tab page.

To move the focus to the first item in the tab page, you need to know what that first item is. You can store the information about your tab pages and their data block items in your code, and when this tab page is clicked on, you will know to go to that particular item. Storing the layout data is certainly the easiest approach and, if you are not going to be making many tabbed canvases, works just fine. Here are the basic steps:

1. Check the :SYSTEM.TAB_NEW_PAGE variable in the WHEN-TAB-PAGE-CHANGED trigger.

2. For each specific tab page that is clicked on, use the GO_ITEM command to move to the appropriate item.

Here is a code example that should be placed in the WHEN-TAB-PAGE-CHANGED trigger:

```
/* — Forms/Tabfocus.sql —- */
IF :SYSTEM.TAB_NEW_PAGE = 'TOYS' THEN
      GO_ITEM('TOY_BLK.TOY_ID');
ELSIF :SYSTEM.TAB_NEW_PAGE = 'STOCKROOM' THEN
      GO_ITEM('STOCKROOM_BLK.STORE_ID');
….<more tab pages can be added as needed>
END IF;
```

We will discuss another method that uses a generic routine for moving to the first item of a tab page in the next section of this chapter.

Writing External Libraries for Reusable Code

If you are interested in getting the most out of your code, then you will find external libraries to be an indispensable tool. External libraries are collections of PL/SQL that can be shared by forms, menus, and reports. These libraries can be stored in a file or in the database. We will focus on libraries stored in a file, usually with a file extension of PLL.

In the Form Builder, you can attach libraries to forms, menus, or reports, and you can edit the external libraries. Note in the split screen Object Navigator of Figure 18-8 that the form in the top half of the screen has the EXTERNALLIB library attached to it. This form can now use any procedure, function, or package that is contained in that library. However, you cannot edit the external library when viewing it inside a form. To edit the external library, you must scroll down (or open a second window, as shown in Figure 18-8) to view the Program Units folder. From here, the library can be opened directly in the Object Navigator for editing.

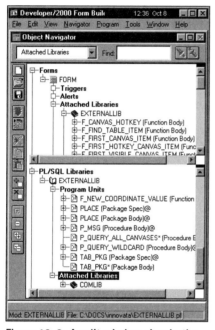

Figure 18–8: A split window view in the Object Navigator showing two different views of the external library EXTERNALLIB.

In the lower half of the Object Navigator, you can see the code units contained in the EXTERNALLIB library. You can actually see what code units are contained in the library in both windows, but you can edit the library only from the PL/SQL Library section of the Object Navigator. You can view the specification for a program in a library only from within a form. The specification of a program unit is the parameters that can be passed in or out of the procedure or function. Also note that the library even has a library attached to it. So libraries can reference other libraries to further expand the reach of reusable code.

The code in a library can be used by a form only when the library is attached and the library file remains in the path or paths specified for FORMS50_PATH. If the library is removed from the path, it is no longer available to the form, and the form may not function properly.

When you edit the programs stored in your external library, you use the same PL/SQL Editor that you use for editing triggers and routines in your forms. There are a few differences in the way the code is treated, however. You cannot directly reference any object stored in a form, nor should you be able to, because the library is external and it has no idea what form will be using it. You also cannot directly refer to system variables or to global variables. Again, the library does not know about the environment that will be calling it. So how can you ever be able to affect an object in your form? How can you get system variables to know what is going on? You have use generic references.

Your most valuable programming commands in an external library are going to be COPY and NAME_IN. These two commands and ID_NULL are the only commands available for indirect referencing. Using these three commands together, you can construct very powerful generic routines to manipulate your forms, menus, and reports from your external libraries. See Figure 18-9 for an example of the PL/SQL Editor and a tiny but useful debugging tool.

In Figure 18-9 you see the PL/SQL Editor has been opened to edit P_MSG. This tiny procedure is in the EXTERNALLIB library. The sole purpose of the procedure is to take a text string and use the two sequential MESSAGE commands to force the text to pop up in a box to be acknowledged. The periods around the text ensure that the pop-up box appears even if the CAPTION parameter is null. This is a quick way to show variables at run time to verify what is going on in a program.

Table 18-2 describes each of the three critical commands for referencing variables found in your form within an external library. You can reference any form, global, or system variables with these commands.

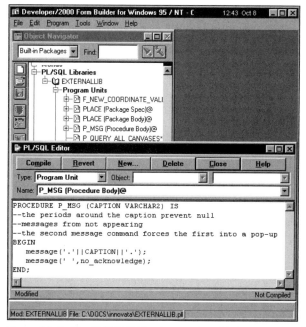

Figure 18-9: The PL/SQL Editor is open to edit the procedure P_MSG.

TABLE **18-2** COMMANDS FOR EXTERNAL LIBRARIES TO REFERENCE FORM,
GLOBAL, AND SYSTEM VARIABLES

Command	Description
COPY(varchar2, varchar2);	Takes the value in the first string and puts it in the variable whose name is in the second string; for example, COPY('Y', 'GLOBAL.GB_HAVING_FUN'); copies "Y" into the global variable, :GLOBAL.GB_HAVING_FUN.
NAME_IN(varchar2);	Returns the value in the variable whose name is in the string; for example, NAME_IN('GLOBAL.GB_HAVING_FUN') returns the value stored in the global variable, :GLOBAL.GB_HAVING_FUN.

Continued

TABLE 18-2 COMMANDS FOR EXTERNAL LIBRARIES TO REFERENCE FORM, GLOBAL, AND SYSTEM VARIABLES *(Continued)*

Command	Description
ID_NULL(id);	Returns a Boolean value TRUE or FALSE as to whether or not the ID supplied is valid, and an object exists by that ID. ID_NULL is an overloaded function that works with all of the IDs available in forms (that is, alert, block, canvas, editor, item, menu_item, LOV, window, and more).

Before you can really get the most use out of an external library, you need to know how to write your PL/SQL routines generically. A generically written procedure can work for other forms without being changed. The previous tabbed canvas section provides a good example of code that can be written generically.

Creating a generic routine to set the focus of tab pages

When the end user clicks on a tab and the tab page appears, the focus remains on the tab. The goal was to move the focus from the tab to the first item on the tab page. The first draft (shown in the previous section) was a simple routine that checked to see which tab page currently had the focus and moved to the particular item known to be on that tab page. This was easy enough, but it doesn't work for any other form. The routine was not generic. That's okay for that example because it served its purpose.

Now the goal is to create a routine that works for any form, for any tab canvas (at least within reason). There are always exceptions and sometimes it is not worth the effort to account for them. This section provides examples of situations not worth writing additional code to account for.

Generically speaking, each tab page has a block on it. Some tab pages may have more than one block. Are multiple blocks on a tab page common enough to account for? Depending on the approach, it may not matter. Looking at the tab page in Figure 18-6 again, we see that the TOY_ID item is the first item on the tab page. On Figure 18-7 the first item is also the TOY_ID item. Remember that on the Stockroom tab, we want to move to the STORE_ID item, not the TOY_ID item. So we really do not want the first visible item, we want the first *enterable* item. Now we have some criteria for choosing the item to go to. How do we find the right block so we can get the correct item?

Unfortunately, we can't use GET_TAB_PAGE_PROPERTY to determine what blocks are on that canvas, and we can't use GET_BLOCK_PROPERTY to find which canvas each block is on. However, we can use GET_ITEM_PROPERTY to see which items are on a particular canvas which may seem circumspect, but remember how objects are arranged in a form. If we use GET_FORM_PROPERTY to find the first block and then use GET_BLOCK_PROPERTY to get the next block, we can eventually go through all of the blocks in the form *in order*.

Going through the blocks in order is crucial because the master blocks are usually first in the Object Navigator, and the items in the master block are usually first on a tab page that has multiple blocks. We can use this knowledge to our advantage. Although this knowledge is an assumption, it is true *most* of the time, and we can easily fix the exceptions to follow this rule.

Once we have the loop in place to go through the blocks, we then get the first item of the block with the GET_BLOCK_PROPERTY command. Now we use GET_ITEM_PROPERTY to get the next item in the block *in order*. Notice again how we are using the common idea that *most* items appear in the Object Navigator in the order that they appear on a form. With this double loop in place, going through the blocks and the items, we can now use GET_ITEM_PROPERTY to determine the first item in a block that appears on the tab page we are interested in. Have we missed anything? Yes! We want only the first item that is visible and navigable. This is part of the conditional logic inside our loops. Now we have the model for finding the first item that is visible and navigable for any canvas. (The code is much simpler than this discussion – but by following the process you can see more easily how writing generic code works.)

TIP Looping through all of the block and items in your form may sound like a lot of overhead. However, these objects are all stored in memory, and there is no noticeable performance degradation.

Here is the code to set the focus on the first visible and navigable item in the specified tab page:

```
/* — Forms tabfocus_generic.sql —- */
FUNCTION f_first_item (tab_page_name varchar2) RETURN varchar2 IS
next_block varchar2(60);
next_item varchar2(60);
first_visible_item varchar2(60);
item_tabpage varchar2(60);
item_tabpage_visible varchar2(10);
BEGIN
first_visible_item := null;
next_block :=
```

```
get_form_property(name_in('system.current_form'),first_block);
—THE FIRST LOOP GOES THROUGH ALL OF THE BLOCKS
while next_block is not null and first_visible_item is null
loop
    next_item := get_block_property(next_block, first_item);
    —THE SECOND LOOP GOES THROUGH ALL OF THE ITEMS
    —  IN THE BLOCKS
    while next_item is not null and first_visible_item is null
    loop
        item_tabpage := null;
        item_tabpage_visible := null;
        item_tabpage :=
get_item_property(next_block||'.'||next_item,item_tab_page);
        if item_tabpage is not null then
            item_tabpage_visible :=
get_tab_page_property(item_tabpage, visible);
        end if;
/***THIS IS THE DECISIVE CONDITION,
        WHERE WE CHOOSE THE FIRST ITEM******/
        if get_item_property(next_block||'.'||next_item, visible) =
'TRUE' and
            nvl(item_tabpage_visible,'FALSE') = 'TRUE' AND
            nvl(item_tabpage,'#$#$#') = tab_page_name
        then
/***THIS ITEM IS RETURN FROM THIS FUNCTION.
        THE CALLING PROCEDURE WILL USE GO_ITEM***/
            first_visible_item := next_block||'.'||next_item;
        end if;
    next_item := get_item_property(next_block||'.'||next_item,
nextitem);
    end loop;
    next_block := get_block_property(next_block, nextblock);
end loop;
return first_visible_item;
end;
```

No doubt you may need to check other conditions before this routine does exactly what you want it to do. However, under the most common conditions, this function returns the first item on a tab page. Notice that the item is returned with the block name prefixed with a period, which enables the calling routine to simply use GO_ITEM. The following example placed in the WHEN-TAB-PAGE-CHANGED trigger does the trick:

```
GO_ITEM(F_FIRST_ITEM(:SYSTEM.TAB_NEW_PAGE));
```

You can create generic routines in many, many other ways that make programming in Forms a joy. Other possibilities include a routine to center LOVs (list of values) on the screen. Or you could write a routine to control LOV buttons so that you can put the WHEN-BUTTON-PRESSED trigger at the form level, and any button without that trigger defaults to the generic code in the form level trigger.

Summary

Combining your new knowledge of menus, toolbars, libraries, and generic coding will make your forms more user and developer friendly. No doubt the greater flexibility and easier maintenance will make you friendlier too! Continue to look for patterns in the way your forms work, and turn those patterns into reusable code. Oracle Forms is a powerful interface designer that can do much of the work for you.

This ends the Developer part of the book. The next part introduces additional tools that are worth exploring, especially if you want to implement applications on the World Wide Web.

Part III

Other Fast-Track Tools

Chapter 19

PL/SQL and HTML Extensions

IN THIS CHAPTER

◆ Using PL/SQL to create HTML

◆ Handling errors

◆ Creating cursors

◆ Writing Web pages that update, insert, or delete

PL/SQL IS A BROAD SUBJECT. Many of the chapters in this book show examples of PL/SQL code. This chapter covers the special capabilities added to PL/SQL to create customized, dynamic Web pages directly from the database.

PL/SQL means Procedural Language for SQL and has been a part of the Oracle database engine for many years. As its name implies, PL/SQL gives you a procedural backdrop in which to develop and execute your SQL commands.

When you install the Oracle WebServer, your database's PL/SQL language set becomes enhanced with specialized functions that work in cooperation with the WebServer to deliver HTML-formatted pages, line by line, to the WebServer.

To run the examples in this chapter, you must first install and configure Oracle WebServer. See Chapter 6 for concepts and tips about Oracle WebServer. My book, *Oracle8 Bible* (IDG Books Worldwide, 1998), has a complete reference guide and instruction manual on how to program using PL/SQL.

Each section in this chapter has sample code that runs using the sample tables included on the CD-ROM. Follow the instructions in Appendix A to install the tables in your database.

Writing a Web Page to Query a Table

If you are comfortable with PL/SQL, you will be pleasantly surprised at how simple it is to write a Web page that delivers the results of a query to the Web.

The tables used in this chapter are found on the CD-ROM. Figure 19-1 shows the database diagram of the tables that are used in this chapter to query, insert, update, and delete data using Web pages generated from PL/SQL procedures.

Figure 19-1: Toy Store tables are used to develop the sample Web pages in this chapter.

In addition to the actual data, the tables used in this chapter enable you to reuse your code and structure your security. Figure 19-2 shows these additional tables.

This chapter will design several Web pages:

◆ **List Stores Page** (STORES). This page displays a list of all the toy stores in our chain. A link on each toy store record enables you to drill down to a store inventory page.

◆ **Store Inventory Page** (STOCK). This page lists all the toys stocked in the selected store. Using the menu selections on this page, you can call up another page so you can insert, update, or delete toy stock.

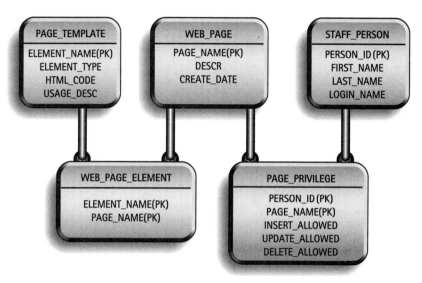

Figure 19-2: Tables for creating reusable PL/SQL Web pages.

- ◆ **Update or Delete Toy Stock Page** (UPDTOY). Use this page to update the current stock for a certain toy at a particular store. You can also delete the inventory record for a selected toy at the current store.

- ◆ **Insert Toy Stock Page** (INSTOY). This page provides a fresh page where you can add a new toy to your store's inventory.

Figure 19-3 shows the relationship of the four pages.

Each of the four pages is a procedure in the database. In addition, two more procedures are needed to commit changes to the database. These are:

- ◆ COMMITUPDTOY. This procedure receives all data entered by the user in the UPDTOY Web page, creates an update statement, and commits the data to the database. If the user chooses to delete the row (using a radio button on the UPDTOY Web page), then this procedure deletes the row and commits the transaction.

- ◆ COMMITINSTOY. This procedure receives data and inserts one new row into a table. Then it commits the transaction.

Oracle8 added the HTML extensions to PL/SQL to support Web-enabled applications. To use the HTML extensions, you must Install Oracle WebServer (2.0 or later), an add-on to your Oracle database package. In addition, you must be running Net8 or SQL*Net.

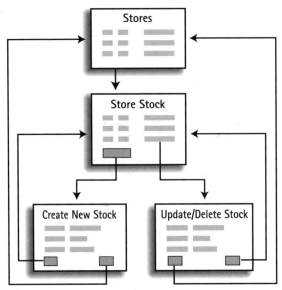

Figure 19-3: Four interconnected Web pages create our Toy Store application.

It is simpler to use the one HTML extension, *htm_print()*, to handle all the HTML. Learning the other extensions is equivalent to learning HTML and less useful. I recommend that you learn HTML instead of relying on the handful of HTML extensions created by Oracle. This affords much more flexibility in the long run.

To create a Web-enabled application, you must create a procedure in the database using PL/SQL. See Chapter 16 for basics on how to create a PL/SQL procedure.

The next sections break down the procedure for the first Web page, STORES, into logical pieces and then pull the entire procedure together.

Creating a cursor

The first step in creating the application involves creating a SQL query that retrieves a set of data to be displayed on the Web page. This section shows how to create the basic query within a PL/SQL procedure cursor and how to retrieve the data using a Cursor For loop.

The PL/SQL procedure we will build contains a cursor in the DECLARE section. This cursor contains the query used to find all the data we wish to place on the Web page. The basic syntax of the query cursor is:

```
CURSOR CURSORNAME IS
    SELECT COLUMN1, ...
    FROM ...
    WHERE ... ;
```

Replace CURSORNAME with the actual name of the cursor, which you use in the body of the procedure to retrieve records.

 Refer to the Quick Reference for examples of SQL queries.

The List Store page requires a query that shows three columns from the TOY_STORE table. Use the following cursor, ALLSTORES, for the List Stores Web page (the STORES procedure):

```
/* — get all stores, sorted by state and store name — */
CURSOR ALLSTORES IS
    SELECT STORE_ID, STORE_NAME, STATE_ABBR
    FROM TOY_STORE
    ORDER BY STATE_ABBR, STORE_NAME;
```

When you have the cursor, you must work with it in the body of the procedure. You can explicitly open, fetch, manipulate, and close the cursor. Alternatively, you can use a LOOP to do the work for you.

Using a loop to handle the cursor

By using a special loop construction for cursors (the Cursor For loop), you can avoid coding explicitly the OPEN, FETCH, and CLOSE commands to control the cursor. The loop handles these implicitly.

The basis syntax for the loop is:

```
FOR RECORDNAME IN CURSORNAME LOOP
    commands...
END LOOP;
```

Replace RECORDNAME with the name that prefixes each field when used inside the loop. Replace CURSORNAME with the name of the cursor you declared in the DECLARE section.

The List Stores page (STORES procedure) uses the following loop:

```
/* — loop through all store records here —— */
FOR CREC IN C1 LOOP
     /* -- print one HTML table row --- */
    HTP.PRINT('<TD>' || CREC.STATE_ABBR || '</TD>');
    HTP.PRINT('<TD>' || CREC.STORE_ID || '</TD>');
    HTP.PRINT('<TD>' || CREC.STORE_NAME || '</TD>');
END LOOP;
```

 TIP The loop opens the cursor, executes one time for each row retrieved by the query in the ALLSTORES cursor, and closes the cursor. The loop also builds the variables needed to store the values of each column retrieved by the cursor.

Writing a heading template for the Web page

To generate a consistent look and feel for the set of Web pages, you can use any of several tables that store template elements for your pages. Figure 19-2 (earlier in the chapter) shows the tables used for designing Web pages and user privileges. These tables are as follows:

◆ PAGE_TEMPLATE. Each row contains HTML commands and text used to build a portion of the Web page, such as a title or page heading.

◆ WEB_PAGE. Each Web page is identified in this table.

◆ WEB_PAGE_ELEMENT. Each Web page can pull in any number of template records to build the complete Web page.

◆ STAFF_PERSON. This table, which consists of a list of employees, comes into play when we build the Web pages for inserting, updating, and deleting data.

◆ PAGE_PRIVILEGE. If an employee is allowed to insert records, the PAGE_PRIVILEGE table contains a record to tell the application this information. See the section "Creating a Web Page for Modifying Data," later in this chapter.

Let's assume that each Web page contains three template element types:

◆ HEADER. This sets up the initial HTML for the page.

◆ BODY. This contains the HTML command BODY, which specifies the background and text colors. In addition, it establishes any other preliminary HTML commands or text that are standardized at the top of the Web page.

◆ FOOTER. This section adds any standard HTML, images, menu selections, and so on that are found at the end of the Web page.

There can be many different templates for all three of these template elements. To build a Web page, you choose one template element for the HEADER element, one for the BODY element, and one for the FOOTER element. These are used by the PL/SQL procedure to retrieve standardized Web page HTML and text.

Table 19-1 lists the rows in the PAGE_TEMPLATE table that define the HTML template elements for the Toy Store Web pages.

TABLE 19-1 DATA IN THE PAGE_TEMPLATE TABLE FOR USE IN THE TOY STORE WEB PAGE

Element name	Element type	HTML code	Description
HEADER1	HEAD	`<HTML><HEAD><TITLE>Busy Bee Toy Stores </TITLE></HEAD>`	Simple heading
BODY1	BODY	`<BODY BGCOLOR="FF0000" TEXT="33FF99">`	Body starter with red background color
BODY2	BODY	`<BODY BGCOLOR="3300FF" TEXT="33FF99" LINK="" VLINK="33FF66" ALINK="33FF33">`	Body with blue background
FOOTER1	FOOTER	`</BODY></HTML>`	No special additions in footer

Continued

TABLE 19-1 DATA IN THE PAGE_TEMPLATE TABLE FOR USE IN THE TOY STORE
WEB PAGE *(Continued)*

Element name	Element type	HTML code	Description
FOOTER2	FOOTER	`<P><img src ="line1.gif"> </BODY></HTML>`	Graphic line on bottom of page
HEADER2	HEAD	`<HTML><TITLE> Busy Bee Toy Stores, Inc. </TITLE>`	Another kind of heading for a Web page
BODY3	BODY	`<BODY BACKGROUND= "bg1.gif" TEXT ="000099" >`	Background with stripes on left

The STORES procedure uses the HEADER1, BODY1, and FOOTER1 template elements to build the List Stores Web page.

 The examples in this chapter use only three types of template elements. You can add as many types of template elements you need without any alteration to the table design.

The following cursor is added to the PL/SQL to retrieve the elements needed from the PAGE_ELEMENT table.

```
/* — get a template element as needed to build the Web page. —- */
CURSOR GETELEMENT IS
    SELECT HTML_CODE
    FROM PAGE_TEMPLATE PT,
              PAGE_ELEMENT PE
    WHERE PT.ELEMENT_NAME = PE.ELEMENT_NAME
    AND      PE.WEB_PAGE = V_WEB_PAGE_NAME
    AND      PT.ELEMENT_TYPE = V_ELEMENT_TYPE;
```

The variable V_WEB_PAGE_NAME is constant during the entire PL/SQL procedure and contains the name of the Web page being built, such as STORES (the name of the List Stores Web page). The variable V_ELEMENT_TYPE is modified at different stages during the procedure to build different parts of the Web page. For example, to build the beginning of the page, V_ELEMENT_TYPE contains the value "HEAD".

To build the Web page using template and custom code, use an interweaving of each element. Figure 19-4 shows the logical view of the resulting Web page that combines template and custom code.

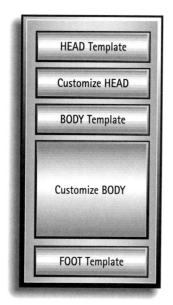

Figure 19-4: A Web page that combines template HTML commands and text with customized sections.

The PL/SQL to handle each section of the template can be generalized as follows:

```
/* ——— HEAD ——— */
    V_ELEMENT_TYPE := 'HEAD';
    OPEN GETELEMENT;
    FETCH GETELEMENT INTO V_TEMPLATE_HTML;
    CLOSE GETELEMENT;
    HTP.PRINT(V_TEMPLATE_HTML);
/* ——— begin custom code for Web page heading here ——- */
/* ——— end custom code for Web page heading here ——- */
/* ——— BODY ——— */
    V_ELEMENT_TYPE := 'BODY';
```

```
    OPEN GETELEMENT;
    FETCH GETELEMENT INTO V_TEMPLATE_HTML;
    CLOSE GETELEMENT;
    HTP.PRINT(V_TEMPLATE_HTML);
/* ————— begin custom code for Web page body here ——- */
/* ————— end custom code for Web page body here ——- */
/* ——— FOOT template ——— */
    V_ELEMENT_TYPE := 'FOOT';
    OPEN GETELEMENT;
    FETCH GETELEMENT INTO V_TEMPLATE_HTML;
    CLOSE GETELEMENT;
HTP.PRINT(V_TEMPLATE_HTML);
```

The final step is to add the customizing HTML for each of the Web pages. The next section shows how to accomplish this.

Handling errors

You can trap and handle errors using the exception clause. The general syntax is:

```
EXCEPTION WHEN exception_name THEN
    exception_block;
WHEN exception_name | OTHERS THEN
    exception_block;
END;
```

Replace *exception_name* with predefined exceptions or with user-declared exceptions. Replace *exception_block* with a set of PL/SQL commands.

The OTHERS exception handler traps any error conditions that raise an exception and are not explicitly handled with other exception handlers. It should always appear at the end of the exception handlers.

The List Stores Web page contains error handling of general errors. The PL/SQL code looks like this:

```
EXCEPTION WHEN OTHERS THEN
    DBMS_OUTPUT.PUT_LINE('Error encountered in STORES procedure:' ||
        SQLERRNO || ' ' || SQLERRMSG);
END;
```

SQLERRNO and SQLERRMSG are variables that any PL/SQL block can use because they are a part of the PL/SQL programming environment. The other Web pages in this chapter contain similar error handling routines. Refer to the CD-ROM for complete listings of all Web page procedures.

Designing the output body of the Web page

Now it's time to put all the elements together into one procedure. Listing 19-1 shows the complete procedure for the STORES procedure.

Listing 19-1: Complete PL/SQL script for STORES procedure

```
CREATE OR REPLACE PROCEDURE STORES AS
BEGIN
/* ——— DECLARE SECTION ————— */
DECLARE
 V_WEB_PAGE_NAME VARCHAR2(30) := 'STORES';
V_ELEMENT_TYPE VARCHAR2(10);
V_TEMPLATE_HTML VARCHAR2(2000);
/* — get a template element as needed to build the Web page. —- */
CURSOR GETELEMENT  IS
    SELECT HTML_CODE
    FROM PAGE_TEMPLATE PT,
                PAGE_ELEMENT PE
    WHERE PT.ELEMENT_NAME = PE.ELEMENT_NAME
     AND     PE.WEB_PAGE = V_WEB_PAGE_NAME
     AND     PT.ELEMENT_TYPE = V_ELEMENT_TYPE;
/* — get all stores, sorted by state and store name —- */
CURSOR C1 IS
    SELECT STORE_ID, STORE_NAME, STATE_ABBR
    FROM TOY_STORE
    ORDER BY STATE_ABBR, STORE_NAME;
/* ——————————————————— BODY OF PROCEDURE — */
BEGIN
/* ——— HEAD ——— */
    V_ELEMENT_TYPE := 'HEAD';
    OPEN GETELEMENT;
    FETCH GETELEMENT INTO V_TEMPLATE_HTML;
    CLOSE GETELEMENT;
    HTP.PRINT(V_TEMPLATE_HTML);
/* ——— begin custom code for Web page heading here ——- */
            HTP.PRINT('<H2>Choose one store by clicking the Store
ID#</H2>');
/* ——— end custom code for Web page heading here ——- */
/* ——— BODY ——— */
    V_ELEMENT_TYPE := 'BODY';
    OPEN GETELEMENT;
    FETCH GETELEMENT INTO V_TEMPLATE_HTML;
    CLOSE GETELEMENT;
    HTP.PRINT(V_TEMPLATE_HTML);
```

```
/* ——————— begin custom code for Web page body here ——- */
HTP.PRINT('<FORM ACTION="stock.htm" METHOD=POST>');
HTP.PRINT('<TABLE BORDER=4 BGCOLOR="3300FF">');
HTP.PRINT('<TR>');
HTP.PRINT('          <TD>State</TD>');
HTP.PRINT('          <TD>Store#</TD>');
HTP.PRINT('          <TD>Store Name</TD>');
HTP.PRINT('</TR>');
/* — loop through all store records here ——— */
FOR CREC IN C1 LOOP
    /* —- print one HTML table row —- */
    HTP.PRINT('<TR>');
    HTP.PRINT('<TD>' || SREC.STATE_ABBR || '</TD>');
    HTP.PRINT('<TD>' || SREC.STORE_ID || '</TD>');
    HTP.PRINT('<TD>' || SREC.STORE_NAME || '</TD>');
    HTP.PRINT('</TR>');
END LOOP;
        HTP.PRINT('</TABLE>');
/* ——————— end custom code for Web page body here ——- */
/* ——————— FOOT template ——————— */
    V_ELEMENT_TYPE := 'FOOT';
    OPEN GETELEMENT;
    FETCH GETELEMENT INTO V_TEMPLATE_HTML;
    CLOSE GETELEMENT;
HTP.PRINT(V_TEMPLATE_HTML);
EXCEPTION WHEN OTHERS THEN
    DBMS_OUTPUT.PUT_LINE('Error encountered in STORES procedure:' ||
        SQLERRNO || ' ' || SQLERRMSG);
END;
END;
```

Use SQL Worksheet or SQL*Plus to create the procedure in the database. To execute the procedure, you must be running Oracle WebServer. Then start your browser, and type the appropriate URL to call the WebServer listener and start the procedure in the database. Figure 19-5 shows the resulting Web page with sample data.

 The STOCK Web page contains elements similar to those in the STORES Web page just created. Therefore, by copying the procedure, renaming it, and making a few quick changes, we have created the second Web page in minutes.

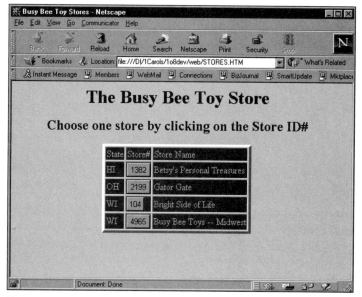

Figure 19-5: The output of the database procedure, STORES, is a Web page.

Copying the existing procedure

Here are step-by-step instructions for creating the STOCK procedure by modifying the STORES procedure:

1. Copy the source code to a new file.

2. Change the name of the procedure in the CREATE OR REPLACE command. This command is the first line in the file. The resulting line appears like this (changes are in **boldface**):

   ```
   CREATE OR REPLACE PROCEDURE STOCK AS
   (I_STORE_ID IN NUMBER, I_STORE_NAME IN VARCHAR2)
   ```

3. Modify the value of V_WEB_PAGE_NAME. Doing so enables you to reuse the core of the procedure that grabs Web-template elements.

   ```
   V_WEB_PAGE_NAME VARCHAR2(30) := 'STOCK';
   ```

4. Replace the CURSOR command in the DECARE section that queries the TOY_STORE table with a query of the STORE_STOCK table. The new CURSOR has the same name and different SQL code:

   ```
   /* — get all stock for one store, sorted by toy name —- */
   CURSOR C1 IS
       SELECT TOY_ID, TOY_NAME, TOY_DESCRIPTION
       FROM STORE_STOCK SS,
   ```

```
                    TOY_INVENTORY TI
            WHERE SS.TOY_ID = TI.TOY_ID
            ORDER BY TOY_NAME;
```

5. Modify the customized code for the HEAD section of the Web page. Replace the entire section of customized code with the following commands:

```
HTP.PRINT('<H2>Choose one Toy by clicking the Toy ID#</H2>');
HTP.PRINT('<H3> Store# ' || I_STORE_ID || I_STORE_NAME ||
'</H3>');
```

6. Modify the customized code for the BODY section of the Web page. The customized body should look like this:

```
/* ———— begin custom code for Web page body here ——- */
HTP.PRINT('<FORM ACTION="updtoy.htm" METHOD=POST>');
HTP.PRINT('<TABLE BORDER=4 BGCOLOR="3300FF">');
HTP.PRINT('<TR>');
HTP.PRINT('          <TD> Toy#</TD>');
HTP.PRINT('          <TD>Toy Name</TD>');
HTP.PRINT('          <TD>Description</TD>');
HTP.PRINT('</TR>');
/* — loop through all toy records here ——— */
FOR CREC IN C1 LOOP
    /* —- print one HTML table row —- */
    HTP.PRINT('<TR>');
    HTP.PRINT('<TD>' || CREC.TOY_ID || '</TD>');
    HTP.PRINT('<TD>' || CREC.TOY_NAME || '</TD>');
    HTP.PRINT('<TD>' || CREC.TOY_DESC || '</TD>');
    HTP.PRINT('</TR>');
END LOOP;
HTP.PRINT('</TABLE>');
/* ———— end custom code for Web page body here ——- */
```

Figure 19-6 shows the resulting Web page built by the STOCK procedure.

One important difference between the STORES procedure and the STOCK procedure is that the latter requires two incoming parameters to specify the store that should have its stock listed on the Web page.

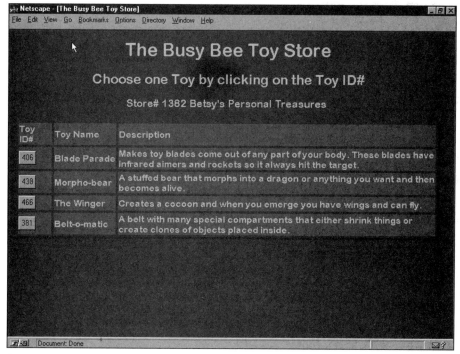

Figure 19-6: The STOCK Web page lists all toy stock in a single store.

Creating a Web Page for Modifying Data

The template-based procedure developed in the preceding sections can be used again to create a page for modifying table data. You can create Web pages for inserting, updating, and deleting a row in the table. The next section describes how to create a single Web page you can use to update or delete a row.

Making a combination update and delete Web page

The Web page to be developed must perform the following functions:

1. Query the database and retrieve one row of data.

2. Display the data in appropriately sized data entry fields.

3. Prevent the update of all primary key fields.

4. Call a procedure that either updates the row with changes or deletes the row.

Figure 19-7 shows the final Web page to be developed.

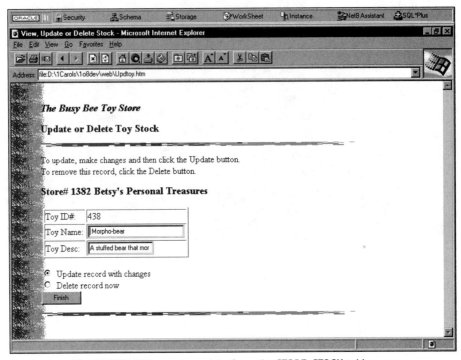

Figure 19-7: The UPDTOY Web page uses data from the STORE_STOCK table.

To create the appropriately sized textboxes for filling in data, we will use a query that looks at the Data Dictionary View called ALL_TABLE_COLUMNS. This view contains details such as the length and the order of the columns in a table.

```
CURSOR V1 IS
    SELECT COLUMN_ID,
            COLUMN_NAME,
            DATA_TYPE,
            DATA_LENGTH,
        DATA_PRECISION,
        DATA_SCALE,
            NULLABLE
    FROM ALL_TAB_COLUMNS
    WHERE TABLE_NAME = 'STORE_STOCK'
    ORDER BY COLUMN_ID;
```

Assuming we placed a PRIMARY KEY constraint on the table, it is easy to expand the original query to identify all columns in the primary key. The Data Dictionary View's USER_CONSTRAINTS and USER_CONS_COLUMNS are used to determine which columns are part of the table's primary key. The primary key of the table is displayed but not updateable. The query shown previously is built upon, and the resulting query is:

```
CURSOR V1 IS
SELECT COLUMN_ID,
               ATC.COLUMN_NAME,
               DATA_TYPE,
               DATA_LENGTH,
     DATA_PRECISION,
     DATA_SCALE,
               NULLABLE, UCC.COLUMN_NAME PRIMARY_KEY_COLUMN
   FROM ALL_TAB_COLUMNS ATC,
     USER_CONSTRAINTS UC,
     USER_CONS_COLUMNS UCC
   WHERE ATC.TABLE_NAME = 'STORE_STOCK'
   AND UC.CONSTRAINT_TYPE(+) = 'P'
   AND    UCC.CONSTRAINT_NAME = UC.CONSTRAINT_NAME(+)
   AND    UCC.TABLE_NAME(+) = ATC.TABLE_NAME
   AND    UCC.COLUMN_NAME (+) = ATC.COLUMN_NAME
   ORDER BY COLUMN_ID;
```

Next we set up a LOOP that builds each data entry field for the table. The loop uses the V1 cursor to loop through each column of the table and build one output line that is customized for data entry for that particular column. The following assumptions are made in this loop:

- Each column is displayed as a two-column row in the HTML table. The first column contains the column name, and the second column contains the current value of the column.

- All columns are displayed.

- The primary key column is displayed but not updateable. In addition, the primary key column is built into a hidden field.

- All other columns are updateable using a textbox.

- All dates are entered in the default Oracle format (DD-MON-YY).

- All columns that are more than 65 characters long are displayed as text areas with multiple rows and columns.

◆ The values for each column are in the varray V_COLARRAY in the same
order as the columns in the table.

The resulting loop is as follows:

```
/* — loop through all columns here —— */
FOR VREC IN V1 LOOP
    /* —- print one HTML table row —- */
    HTP.PRINT('<TR>');
    HTP.PRINT('<TD>' || VREC.COLUMN_NAME || '</TD>');
    HTP.PRINT('<TD>');
    /* —- handle primary key column —— */
    IF PRIMARY_KEY_COLUMN IS NOT NULL THEN
            HTP.PRINT(V_COLARRAY(COLUMN_ID));
    ELSE
        IF COLUMN_TYPE = 'DATE' then
                /* —- handle DATE TYPE column ——- */
                HTP.PRINT('<INPUT TYPE=TEXT SIZE=10' ||
                                        'MAXLENGTH=9' ||
                                        'NAME="'|| COLUMN_NAME ||
                                        '" VALUE="' ||
                                        V_COLARRAY(COLUMN_ID) || '"
>');
            ELSIF COLUMN_TYPE = 'NUMBER' then
                /* —- handle NUMBER TYPE column ——- */
                HTP.PRINT('<INPUT TYPE=TEXT SIZE=' ||
                                        DATA_PRECISION +
NVL(DATA_SCALE) +3 || '" ' ||
                                        'MAXLENGTH="' ||
                                        DATA_PRECISION +
NVL(DATA_SCALE) +2 || '" ' ||
                                        'NAME="'|| COLUMN_NAME ||
                                        '" VALUE="' ||
                                        V_COLARRAY(COLUMN_ID) || '"
>');
            ELSIF COLUMN_LENGTH < 66 THEN
                /* —- handle TEXT TYPE column less than 65
characters ——- */
                HTP.PRINT('<INPUT TYPE=TEXT SIZE=' ||
                                        DATA_LENGTH + 1 || '" ' ||
                                        'MAXLENGTH="' ||
                                        DATA_LENGTH || '" ' ||
                                        'NAME="'|| COLUMN_NAME ||
                                        '" VALUE="' ||
```

```
                                        V_COLARRAY(COLUMN_ID) || '"
>');
          ELSE
                    /* -- handle TEXT TYPE column more than 65
characters ------- */
                  HTP.PRINT('<INPUT TYPE=TEXTAREA COLS="' ||
                                ROUND((DATA_LENGTH + 1)
/65)+1 || '" ' ||

                                 'ROWS=65 ||
                                  'MAXLENGTH="' ||
                                  DATA_LENGTH || '" ' ||
                                  'NAME="'|| COLUMN_NAME ||
                                  '" VALUE="' ||
                                  V_COLARRAY(COLUMN_ID) || '"
>');
          END IF;
    END IF;
    HTP.PRINT('</TD>' );
    HTP.PRINT('</TR>');
END LOOP;
```

The series of IF-THEN-ELSE statements shown here handles numbers, dates, and character datatypes – for example, CHAR, VARCHAR, and VARCHAR2.

If you have other types of data, you can add to this structure to handle them according to your needs.

The final step for this Web page is adding two buttons on the page for the Update function and the Delete function. The code in the procedure appears at the end of the procedure BODY and looks like this:

```
HTP.PRINT('<INPUT TYPE="RADIO" NAME="SELECT_ACTION" ' ||
                  'CHECKED VALUE="Update">);
HTP.PRINT('<INPUT TYPE="RADIO" NAME="SELECT_ACTION"
VALUE="Delete">);
HTP.PRINT('<P><INPUT TYPE=SUBMIT VALUE="Finish">');
HTP.PRINT('</FORM>');
```

 See the CD-ROM for the complete text of the UPDTOY procedure.

Writing the Web page for insert

The Web page for inserting data is similar to the update Web page just completed in the previous section. The primary difference is that we place no data in the textboxes. To revise the LOOP shown in the previous section and remove the data, simply remove the parameter VALUE from the HTML code for each column.

For example, the portion of the loop for the DATE TYPE column looks like this in the updated Web page:

```
/* -- handle DATE TYPE column ----- */
              HTP.PRINT('<INPUT TYPE=TEXT SIZE=10' ||
                              'MAXLENGTH=9' ||
                              'NAME="'|| COLUMN_NAME ||
                              '" VALUE="' ||
                              V_COLARRAY(COLUMN_ID) || '"
>');
```

Next, to change the command so it displays no data, remove the last two lines as follows:

```
/* -- handle DATE TYPE column ----- */
              HTP.PRINT('<INPUT TYPE=TEXT SIZE=10' ||
                              'MAXLENGTH=9' ||
                              'NAME="'|| COLUMN_NAME || '"
>');
```

Creating supporting procedures

Now that you have created a set of Web pages to update, delete, and insert rows for a table, you must create two additional procedures that are called by the two Web pages. The procedures receive all the data entered into the Web page and apply it to the database.

THE SUPPORTING PROCEDURE FOR UPDATE AND DELETE

The procedure is called by the Web page when the user clicks a button on the Web page. The button sends all the data to the procedure named in the FORM command of the Web page. The FORM command looks like this for the UPDTOY Web page:

```
<FORM ACTION="COMMITUPDTOY" METHOD=POST>
```

The procedure COMMITUPDTOY is called when the user clicks the button labeled "Finish." This procedure is the one that actually updates or deletes the row in the database. All the textboxes, radio buttons, and hidden fields shown on the UPDTOY Web page serve as input parameters for the COMMITUPDTOY procedure.

The incoming parameters of a procedure for updating and deleting data look like this:

```
CREATE OR REPLACE PROCEDURE COMMITUPDTOY
(TOY_ID IN NUMBER, TOY_NAME IN VARCHAR2,
        TOY_DESC IN VARCHAR2, SELECT_ACTION) IS
```

Each of the parameters, except the SELECT_ACTION parameter, corresponds with a column in the table. The SELECT_ACTION parameter contains "Update" if the user has chosen to update the row. If the user chose to delete the row, this parameter contains "Delete." An IF-THEN-ELSE command determines which action to take.

The update command in the procedure is:

```
UPDATE STORE_STOCK
SET TOY_NAME = I_TOY_NAME,
        TOY_NAME = I_TOY_NAME
WHERE TOY_ID = I_TOY_ID;
```

The DELETE command in the procedure is:

```
DELETE FROM STORE_STOCK
WHERE TOY_ID = I_TOY_ID;
```

At the end of the procedure, all action is committed to the database with this command:

```
COMMIT TRANSACTION;
```

Putting it all together, the complete procedure appears as follows:

```
CREATE OR REPLACE PROCEDURE COMMITUPDTOY
(I_STORE_ID IN NUMBER, I_TOY_ID IN NUMBER,
  I_TOY_NAME IN VARCHAR2,
  I_TOY_DESC IN VARCHAR2, SELECT_ACTION IN VARCHAR2) IS
IF SELECT_ACTION = 'Update' THEN
    UPDATE STORE_STOCK
        SET TOY_NAME = I_TOY_NAME,
        TOY_NAME = I_TOY_NAME
    WHERE TOY_ID = I_TOY_ID
        AND STORE_ID = I_STORE_ID;
ELSIF SELECT_ACTION = 'Delete' THEN
    DELETE FROM STORE_STOCK
    WHERE TOY_ID = I_TOY_ID;
END IF;
```

```
COMMIT TRANSACTION;
     HTP.PRINT('Row for Toy# ' || I_TOY_ID || SELECT_ACTION ||
'ed.');
```

 See the CD-ROM for the complete procedure code in the subdirectory named Web.

THE SUPPORTING PROCEDURE FOR INSERT

When the user runs the INSTOY Web page and clicks the Save button, this Web page calls the COMMITINSTOY procedure, which inserts the row and commits the transaction.

The procedure COMMITINSTOY is similar to the COMMITUPDTOY procedure shown previously. The INSERT command uses incoming parameters, and it looks like this:

```
INSERT INTO STORE_STOCK
VALUES
     (I_STORE_ID,
      I_TOY_ID,
      I_TOY_NAME,
      I_TOY_DESC);
```

Figure 19-8 shows the Web page created by the COMMITINSTOY procedure after a successful insert is completed. See the CD-ROM for the complete procedure code in the subdirectory named Web.

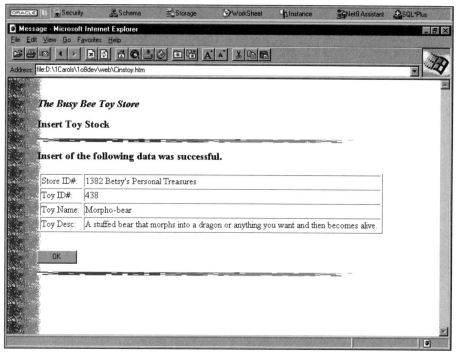

Figure 19-8: The CINSTOY Web page displays a message after inserting a row.

Summary

To create a set of interconnected Web pages using PL/SQL procedures, first be sure you have installed Oracle WebServer version 2.0 or later.

This chapter develops four Web pages that display, insert, update, and delete data.

The display data Web pages use a cursor to pull data from the tables. In addition, another query of the database retrieves data containing template HTML commands that format the Web pages consistently.

An exception handler traps errors encountered while running the procedure. The exception handler displays the Oracle error message on the Web page.

By using cursors and templates, a second Web page for querying data on a different table can be created by copying the first Web page and making some minor changes.

When modifying data using Web pages and procedures, you must create a pair of procedures. The first one displays the data and gives the user a place to type in information. The second procedure starts up when the user clicks the Submit button. This second procedure receives all the data fields as incoming parameters and then builds the appropriate insert, update, or delete command. The second procedure also commits the transaction and displays a Web page telling the user that the action was completed.

The next chapter of the book shows you how to use the Discoverer tool for both client/server and Web reports.

Chapter 20

Discoverer

Concepts

Discoverer has two components. A database administrator uses the administrator component to create a working environment for end-users. The user environment enables end-users to create their own reports.

A report is called a *sheet* in Discoverer. A collection of reports is called a *work-sheet*. An end-user must have access to the work area before creating reports. The work area is generated by the database administrator and contains tables, views, summary tables, and calculated fields.

The end-user does not require direct access to any database objects. All that he or she needs is access to business areas within Discoverer. The end-user creates his or her own workbooks. Workbooks contain one or more reports. Each report is a dynamic worksheet that the user can manipulate to change the level of detail, page layout, and so on. Figure 20-1 shows the architecture of Discoverer. The work area designed by the database administrator gathers related tables together in folders. There can be multiple work areas. Each one is customized for a different business function. For example, you might set up separate work areas for your inventory department and your sales department.

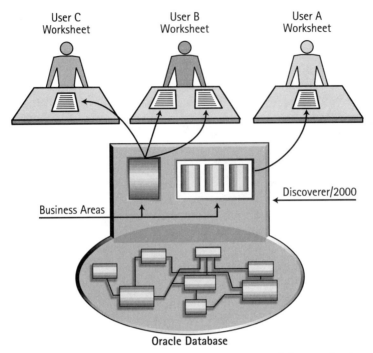

Figure 20-1: A buffer zone exists between end-users and the complex database structures.

One special feature of Discoverer is its capability to start other applications based on the file type. For example, Discoverer can start the Web browser for HTML documents and an Excel spreadsheet for spreadsheet documents.

Another great feature of Discoverer enables you to pregenerate summary tables that store the results of long-running summarizing queries. Summary tables save time indeed because 2000 substitutes data in a query for the users.

In the quick start section of this chapter, you learn how to quickly create a new work area for a set of related tables. In addition, you see how to grant end-users access to this new work area, and you create a report that drills out to a graphic.

Quick Start – Using Discoverer

Here we began working with the toy store sample tables. Figure 20-2 shows a database diagram of the four related tables in the toy store system.

The first step in setting up a work area for the toy store system is to create the work area containing all the tables.

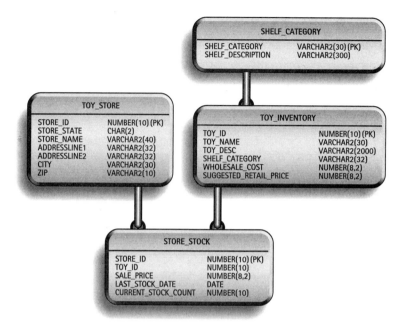

Figure 20-2: The toy store system tracks inventory of all the toy stores owned by the corporation.

Setting up the business area

You can easily create the business area using the Load Wizard. Start Discoverer Administrator, and choose File → New from the main menu. Figure 20-3 shows the first page of the Load Wizard.

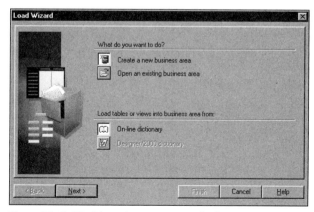

Figure 20-3: Start here to create a new business area.

Click Create a new business area, and select On-line dictionary to begin creating a new business area based on tables in the database.

Next, follow along with the wizard, and choose the tables your users need for reporting. In our example, we will choose all four of the tables owned by TOY-STORE. Figure 20-4 shows the business area after completing the wizard.

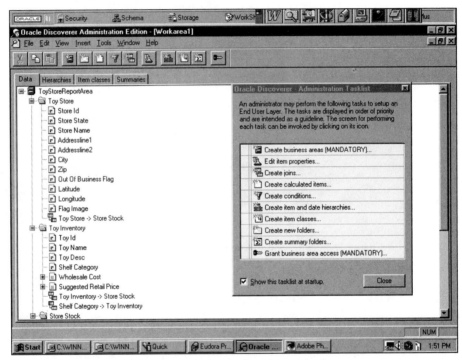

Figure 20-4: Four tables become four folders in the toy store business area.

 The Discoverer Administrator must have been granted SELECT privileges on all tables that he or she will use in any business area created.

When you open each of the folders, you will see that the foreign keys defined in the database follow into each folder as a Join.

Looking at the new work area, you'll see that it contains folders for each table. Click the plus sign (+) next to a folder to view the items (*columns*) within the table. Click the plus sign next to the Store Stock folder. Notice the Last Stock Date column has been broken into several time span columns. These columns are standard date *hierarchies*. This means you can summarize reports by year, month, quarter, and so on without any additional programming.

A *hierarchy* is a list of columns that contain data and subsets of data that allow the end-user to view details or summaries within the hierarchy. The date hierarchy is easy to picture. Figure 20-5 shows the date hierarchy used for all date columns by default. The end-user can view annual, quarterly, monthly, or daily summaries on a report that contains a date column. You can create your own hierarchy for columns that are not dates by using the Hierarchy Wizard. The next section shows how.

Figure 20–5: Discoverer has a default date hierarchy to simplify summarizing by date.

Customizing the work area

We will add a few additional items to the Toy Store Report Area business area.

First, rename the Store Id column. Call it **Store#**. Simply double-click the column name (as you would in Windows Explorer), and type the new name over the old name. You can also display the column properties (right-click the column, choose Properties) and type the appropriate name in the Name attribute.

Next, identify the Toy Photo column as a graphic. To do so, double-click the Toy Photo column to display its Properties window. Then simply modify the Content type property. Change it from NONE to FILE. Figure 20-6 shows the Content type property of the Toy Photo column. Click OK to save this change.

When the end-user clicks the Toy Photo column in a report, it will start a browser and display the photo.

ADDING A HIERARCHY

Let's also add a hierarchy of states, cities, and stores. To do so, choose Insert → Hierarchy from the menu. Figure 20-7 shows the first window of the Hierarchy Wizard.

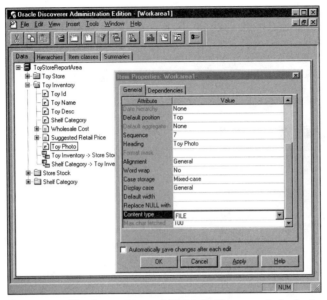

Figure 20-6: The Content type of FILE tells Discoverer to look at the contents of the column for a filename.

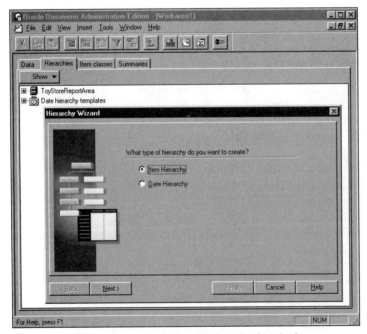

Figure 20-7: Begin a customized hierarchy by selecting the Item Hierarchy radio button.

Expand the Toy Store folder by clicking the plus sign to display items. Double-click the Store State item. Now double-click the City item. Finally, double-click the Store Name item. Click Finish to complete the hierarchy definition.

To view the hierarchy you created, click the Hierarchy tab, and then click the plus sign next to the new hierarchy. Figure 20-8 shows the hierarchy, which has been renamed State-City-Store hierarchy.

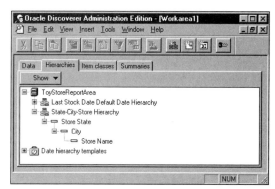

Figure 20-8: Create your own hierarchy to define how drill-down reports function.

When you have created a hierarchy, your end-users are free to expand and contract levels within their reports using the hierarchy. For example, a report created with a list of stores can show a summary of inventory costs for each state with the click of a button.

CREATING A COMPLEX FOLDER

Another handy feature for customizing your work area is the complex folder. This feature enables you to gather together related information into a single folder that hides the complexity of the data.

For example, users might want to list store names every time they work with the inventory table. To simplify the job for your users, create a complex folder containing both the Store Name, Store City, and Store State, along with all the items in the Store Stock table. Follow these steps:

1. Choose Insert → New → Folder from the main menu.

2. Next, open a new window to enable you to click and drag items into the new folder.

3. To do so, choose Window → New Window from the main menu. Figure 20-9 shows what the windows look like.

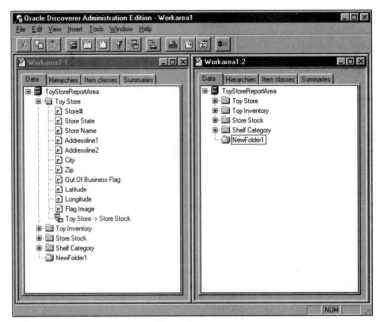

Figure 20-9: Two windows enable you to click and drag items into a complex folder.

Figure 20-10: The complex folder contains items that are related for convenience.

4. Now open and double-click columns to move them into the complex folder. Figure 20-10 shows the complex folder that contains all the data from the inventory table plus important data from the Toy Store folder. The complex folder was also renamed Toy Store Details.

5. Close the window on the right. To close the window, click the X in the top right corner of the window.

DEFINING DEFAULT CALCULATIONS AND DATA POINTS

Reports that use crosstab or page-detail crosstab need one or more items identified as data points. Usually, a data point is a column you can summarize, such as the number of toys in stock. Customized summaries and calculations are also good candidates for being data points. To make an item a data point, double-click the item to reveal the item properties. Next, click the Default position attribute. Select Data Point from the pull-down list. Figure 20-11 shows the location of the Default position attribute.

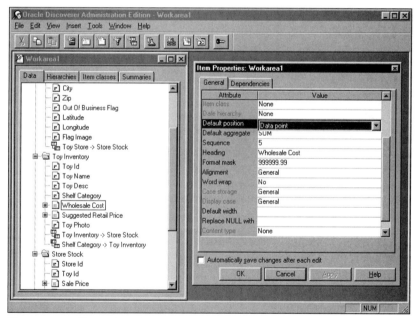

Figure 20-11: Choose Data Point as the Default position for numeric fields used in calculations.

Calculated items add more customization to the user's business area. To add a calculated item, click the folder that will hold the item. Then select Insert → Item from the main menu to access the New Item window. In this window you can name your new item, specify the calculation used to create it, and save the item. Figure 20-12 shows the Value of Stock calculated field. This item was created by double-clicking Store Stock.Current Stock Count in the left pane, clicking the X (for multiply) button at the base of the Calculation pane, and then double-clicking the Store Stock.Sale Price item.

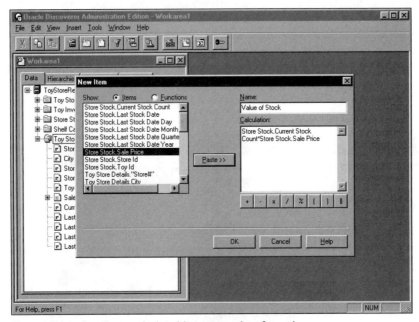

Figure 20-12: Creating a calculated item saves time for end-users.

Now that you have generated and customized the business area, you can enable end-users to use it.

Granting access to work areas

Users must already be Oracle users to use Discoverer. Assuming you have a set of existing Oracle users, granting these users access to Discoverer is simple.

Choose Tools → Security from the main menu. Doing so is the first step toward enabling two end-users to work with Discoverer using the toy store work area.

Choose the name of the user you wish to grant access to by double-clicking the user's name in the Available users/roles pane of the security window. In our example, we will double-click HARRY and then AMY. Figure 20-13 shows the Security window with both HARRY and AMY selected as valid users of the toy store work area. Click OK to save these changes.

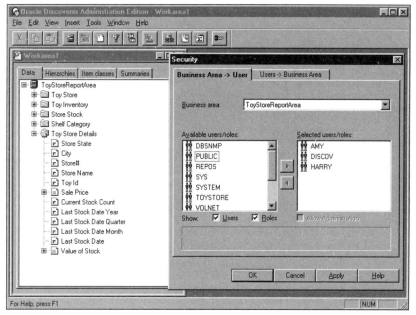

Figure 20-13: Harry and Amy are users designated to use the Toy Store Report Area.

Close the Discoverer Administrator window. This completes the first portion of our quick start section. The second portion shows you how to work as an end-user creating several reports.

Generating a quick and easy report

Start up Discoverer, and log in as HARRY. Harry's password is HIHARRY. Create a new workbook. Begin with a simple Table report.

Refreshing Your Business Area

If the database objects your business area uses contain changes, you must change the business area accordingly. To synchronize the business area with the database, right-click the business area file cabinet in the Administrator window. Next, choose Refresh from the pop-up menu. Finally, select on-line dictionary from the choices. Click OK, and you begin the process of updating your business area. Discoverer Administrator analyzes the changes and guides you through the process of modifying your business area.

Choose the entire contents of the Toy Inventory folder by clicking and dragging the folder from the left side to the right side of the window. Figure 20-14 shows what the Workbook Wizard window looks like at this point.

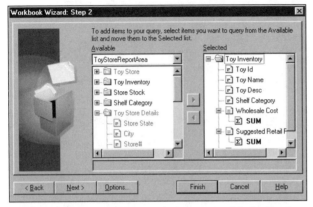

Figure 20-14: Create a simple tabular report with the Toy Inventory folder.

Click Finish to speed up the process.

 Although Discoverer offers many options to specify as you create your reports, the default settings get you to the meat of the report right away.

Figure 20-15 shows the resulting default report.

Notice that this report contains a drill-out component for the Toy Photo column. Double-click any of the cells in the Toy Photo column to see a picture of the toy.

Adjust the width of the columns, and add word wrap formatting to the Toy Description column using the mouse and the Format menu item.

After making these changes, save the file to your disk by selecting File → Save. Choose to save it on your computer or in the database.

Next, you can export the report to HTML format so you can view it using a Web browser.

EXPORTING REPORTS TO HTML FORMAT

To convert your finished report to an HTML report, simply select File → Export Data from the main menu. Choose HyperText Markup Language as your export format. Name the file, and save it as shown in Figure 20-16.

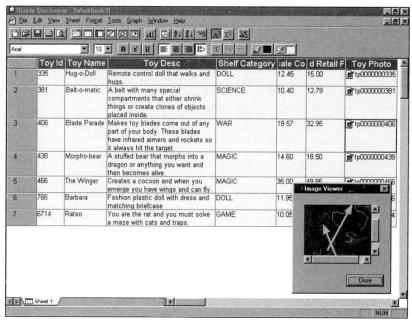

Figure 20–15: A simple report takes minutes to create.

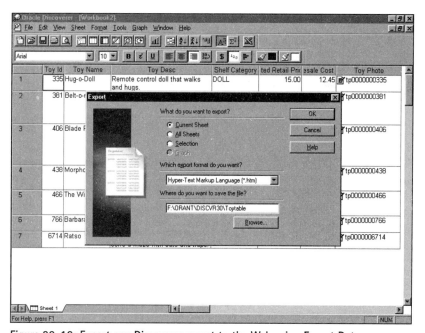

Figure 20–16: Export any Discoverer report to the Web using Export Data.

After saving the data in HTML format, open your browser, and open the file you saved. You will see links to the toy photos! Figure 20-17 shows what the default page looks like.

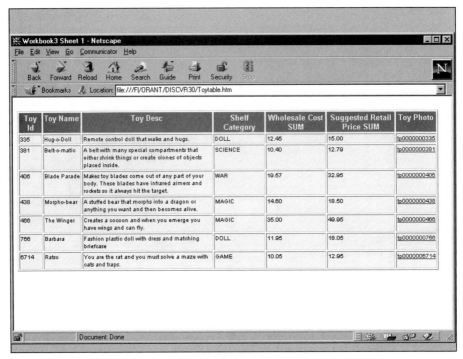

Figure 20-17: A finished Web report using the basics of Discoverer looks great.

The next section describes how to create a crosstab report.

Generating a crosstab report

This section shows how to generate a crosstab report using the toy store system. A crosstab report enables you to create multidimensional reports within a single report.

We will create a report that lists all the stores side by side. Each store's inventory is totaled and displayed with its dollar value. In addition, we will highlight the stock items that are worth more than $3,500.

TIP Discoverer has many special features you can take advantage of. These features are best used by designers to work with their end-users to determine what reports are most commonly needed. Without this information, it is difficult to design a reporting tool that an end-user will find easy to use.

Figure 20-18 shows the final report layout.

	Betsy's Personal Treasures	Bright Side of Life	Busy Bee Toys - Midwest	Gator Gate	The
Barbara					
# in stock	30		560	512	
$ Value	$285.00		$8400.00	$7674.88	
Belt-o-matic					
# in stock	157	88		272	
$ Value	$2008.03	$990.00		$3264.00	
Blade Parade					
# in stock	144	49		32	
$ Value	$1720.80	$1323.00		$849.60	
Hug-o-Doll					
# in stock	236	38	400	578	
$ Value	$3068.00	$511.10	$5220.00	$7392.62	
Morpho-bear					
# in stock	91	129	160	112	
$ Value	$1524.25	$2193.00	$2560.00	$1792.00	
Ratso					
# in stock	40			432	
$ Value	$340.00			$4860.00	
The Winger					
# in stock	136	255	240	192	
$ Value	$5909.20	$11217.45	$9720.00	$8256.00	

Figure 20–18: A crosstab report contains a lot of details.

To create this report, first choose the following items for the report:

◆ Store Stock.Current Stock Count

◆ Toy Inventory.Toy Name

◆ Toy Store.Store Id

◆ Toy Store.Store Name

Next, arrange the items on your report as shown in Figure 20-19. To move an item, use your mouse to click and drag the item up or down or left and right.

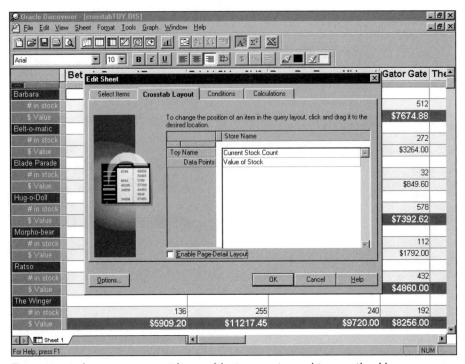

Figure 20-19: Arrange your report items with stores on top and toys on the side.

Now you must add a calculated item, called "Inventory Value," to your report. To add a calculation, click Tools → Calculations. Now define the calculation you need. In the Toy Store example, create an Inventory Value calculation that is calculated as follows:

```
Inventory Value = Store Stock.Current Stock Count * Toy
Inventory.Suggested Retail Price.
```

FORMATTING EXCEPTIONS

An exception is a condition that you wish to highlight in your report. For the example report, add red highlighting to the Store stock that has an inventory value greater than $3,500.

Add an exception by selecting Format → Exceptions from the main menu. The Exceptions window is displayed. Add a new exception by clicking the New button. Figure 20-20 shows how the exception for high valued inventories looks in the Format Exception window.

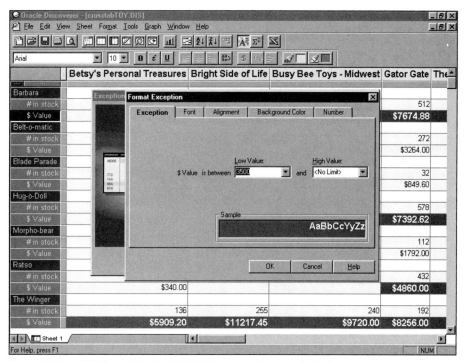

Figure 20-20: Add formatting to highlight an exception condition in your report.

Now you have completed a basic crosstab report. Such a report can be used for quickly spotting the higher or lower numbers. For example, you might highlight the highest priced toy in each store, or the toy with the lowest number in stock in each store.

Using Other Discoverer Features

Discoverer has so many features to choose from, your users may get confused at first. To give them some useful tools with which they can get started right away, show them the features described next.

Converting reports to other formats

Any reports generated in Discoverer can be exported to several different formats. For example, to convert a simple tabular report to an Excel spreadsheet, choose File Export from the main menu. Figure 20-21 shows the Export window. Type a filename, and then choose Excel as the format of the file.

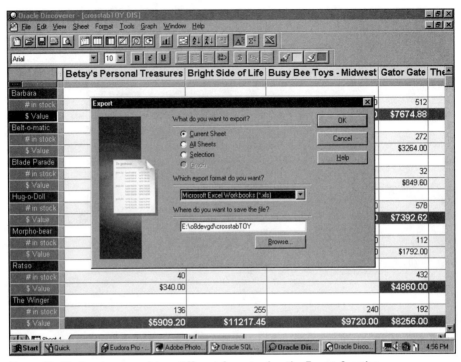

Figure 20-21: Save any report in a different format using the Export function.

Creating a Web-enabled report is simple. Generate the report using Discoverer, and then export the report into HTML format. Figure 20-17 (in the previous section) shows the drilled-down report created in the previous section when you export it to HTML format. The report even retains the links to the toy photos.

Making a graph

Discoverer has graph-making utilities. However, converting a simple report into a graph may cause unexpected results. As the DBA, you can ensure the predictability of graphs by adjusting the Default Position property of items you expect to use in graphs. You can define whether the item falls into the side, top, or page (vertical) axis of the chart.

Start the Discoverer Administrator, and open the create a report showing the inventory of toys by state. Figure 20-22 shows the default graph generated by Discoverer.

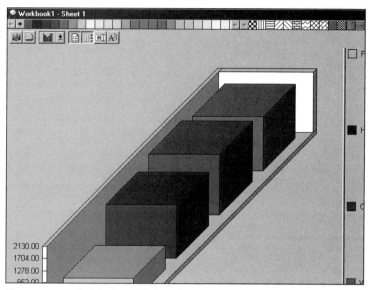

Figure 20-22: A default graph from Discoverer uses 3D blocks and color legends.

Changing a report's appearance

You can change the default appearance of report items using Discoverer Administrator. To do so, start Discoverer Administrator, open the work area, and work with the Item properties. You can adjust these attributes in the Discoverer Administrator:

◆ Upper/lower/mixed case

◆ Number formats

◆ Word wrapping

◆ Default column width

◆ Left/right/centered/general alignment of text

◆ Null value replacement text

◆ Heading text

◆ Visible/not visible to user

The end-user also can customize report appearance within Discoverer. You can change these attributes inside a report:

◆ Font, text color, background color, and alignment of Headings

◆ Font, text color, background color, and alignment of Data cells

◆ Title and background of Data sheet

When you change the attributes within a report, highlight the area you wish to alter.

Summary

Discoverer can help end-users create their own reports quickly. Initial setup requires that you, as administrator, create a business area and grant access to users. You can also add automatically joined tables (complex folders), calculations, and hierarchies to the business area.

Generate a report in minutes using default settings of Discoverer. Then export the report to HTML format just as easily.

A slightly more complex type of report, called the crosstab report, is illustrated with step-by-step instructions in this chapter.

You can highlight peaks and valleys in your data using the Exceptions property of a data item.

Other interesting features of Discoverer are described using several examples in this chapter, including:

◆ Converting reports to other formats

◆ Adding graphs to a report

◆ Changing report appearance

The next chapter describes another report generating tool: the Web Assistant found in the Enterprise Manager toolset.

Chapter 21

Web Publishing Assistant of Enterprise Manager

THE ENTERPRISE MANAGER IS A component of the client portion of Oracle8 Enterprise Edition. The Enterprise Manager provides a variety of interconnected tools that make life easier for the DBA.

This chapter zooms in on one interesting feature of Enterprise Manager: the Web Publishing Assistant. The Web Publishing Assistant is a tool for building reports in HTML format and scheduling them to refresh periodically. The tool communicates with the database using Net8 and handles scheduling on your native host.

You can explore the use of this tool to create a database report in a few minutes.

Concepts

The Web Publishing Assistant helps design static Web pages. You can design the pages to refresh themselves (by recreating the static pages) using the Web Publishing Assistant's menus. The basic steps for creating a Web page are:

1. Write a query that retrieves data needed for the Web page.

2. Design the Web page template.

3. Specify the location of the Web page, its name, and the frequency with which it regenerates.

After initially setting up a Web page using the Web Assistant Wizard, you can review and modify most of the components of the Web page.

TIP   If you want dynamic Web pages that interact with the database, you need a different tool, such as Forms Application Server.

Here are some examples of projects that can be created with the Web Publishing Assistant:

- ◆ A monthly report of sales that is posted on the intranet for the sales department.

- ◆ A "quick look" catalog showing the serial numbers and detailed descriptions of all the items available at an automotive parts store. The catalog is available on a Web site that has no database capability Customers who use the catalog can order parts by using a toll-free telephone number. The catalog is updated weekly.

- ◆ A weekly report for the DBA showing table fragmentation, table-space usage, and other storage-space indicators in the database.

- ◆ A daily report of certain lookup tables that are frequently used during the execution of routine tasks in a national real estate firm. The report is refreshed overnight and can be printed on remote sites via the Internet.

The quick start section of this chapter shows you how to create a Web-enabled report without knowing any HTML or SQL. You can generate a report listing any number of columns from a single table by using the Web Assistant Wizard.

Next, learn how to create a more complex series of interconnected reports using your own customized templates and SQL queries.

The sample tables used in this chapter are the Toy Store tables, shown in Figure 21-1.

The Busy Bee Toy Store chain has a centralized inventory system that all its stores use. Each store has its own stock of the toys. The main office purchases toys for all the stores, but each store can set the selling price of any toy as it sees fit.

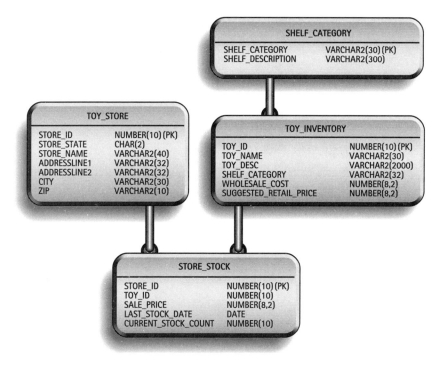

Figure 21-1: The toy store chain system has four relational tables.

Quick Start – Using Web Publishing Assistant

In this quick start section, you see how to create a simple Web report of a single table without any custom HTML or SQL.

Generating a quick and easy report

The report will be a list of all the toy stores with details about each store. You can easily generate this report by using the default settings of Web Publishing Assistant. Follow these steps:

1. Start the Web Publishing Assistant. On the NT, choose Start → Program → Oracle for NT → Web Publishing Assistant.

2. Choose New from the menu to start a new report.

3. Type the table owner and password. For the toy store example, use TOYSTORE (password TOYSTORE).

4. Using the graphical database hierarchy, choose the schema, table, and columns you wish to use on the report.

For this example, select the TOYSTORE schema, the TOY_STORE table, and the STORE_ID, STORE_NAME, and STORE_STATE columns.

Figure 21-2 shows the three columns selected.

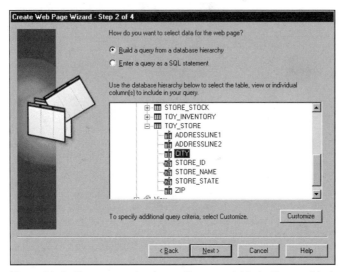

Figure 21-2: Choose report columns from one table in the graphical hierarchy.

5. Choose the frequency of generating the report.

6. Specify a file location and filename for the resulting report. In this example, use the filename SIMPLE.HTM.

7. Have Web Publishing Assistant generate a template for you.

Web Publishing Assistant generates the report and returns you to its main page, as shown in Figure 21-3.

To view the report, double-click the report name. Figure 21-4 shows the resulting Web report.

It doesn't get much simpler than that. However, the resulting report is pretty ugly. Later in this chapter, you'll see how to improve the appearance of your reports.

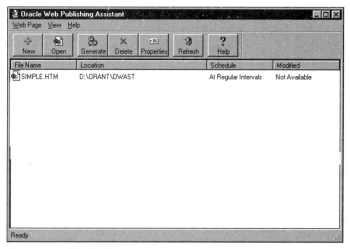

Figure 21-3: The SIMPLE report is now ready for viewing.

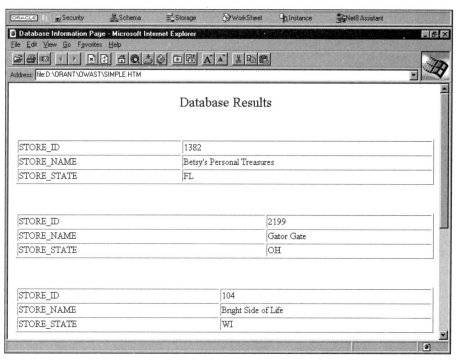

Figure 21-4: The SIMPLE report has all the toy stores, showing three columns for each one.

Using Web Publishing Assistant – What's easy and what's not

Web Publishing Assistant, even if you use no more than its basic capabilities, can make the following tasks easier:

- ◆ Generating a report with an existing query. Simply open the query in any text editor, select the entire query, copy it, and paste it into the Web Publishing Assistant window.

- ◆ Adding a WHERE clause and ORDER BY clause to the columns selected (when creating a new report). To do so, choose the Customize button after selecting the columns in the hierarchy (see Figure 21-2).

- ◆ Refreshing the report. Select the report, and click the Generate button.

- ◆ Viewing the report. Select the report, and click the Open button.

The following tasks require more careful attention:

- ◆ Adding the columns selected (using SQL). Select an existing report, and click the Properties button. Click the Query tab, and you now see the SQL that was generated for your report, as shown in Figure 21-5.

- ◆ You can modify this query as you would change any SQL query. However, you must modify the template associated with the report before the changes are displayed on the report.

- ◆ Changing a template. If you modify the template of a report, be careful to match the variables in the template with the column names in your report's query. To change a template, open the template (.htx file) with your favorite HTML editor or a text editor. Made the changes, and save the file.

 The Web Publishing Assistant does not issue error messages. If your variables don't match the column names, it simply displays your report with missing data.

- ◆ Deleting a report. To remove a report, select the report, and click the Delete button. This action takes the report off the schedule and "forgets" the SQL that was used to generate the report (unless you have saved it in a file). However, Web Publishing Assistant does not delete the template or the most recently generated version of the report that is on the Web. You must delete these two files yourself. They are the .htm and .htx files.

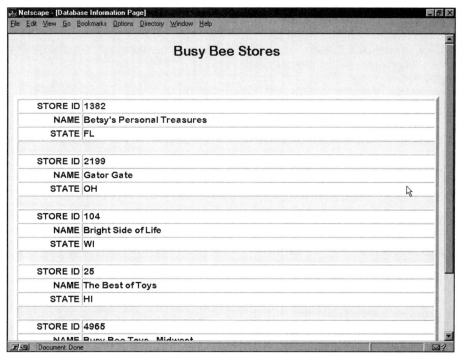

Figure 21–5: Customize a query in this window.

The following attributes can be viewed but cannot be changed; you must delete and recreate a report to make such changes:

◆ The frequency of regenerating the report

◆ The exact filenames of the report or the template

◆ The database login name, password, and database name

The limitations of the Web Publishing Assistant make it somewhat inconvenient to use. However, it can do more than what might initially seem obvious.

Using the Web Publishing Assistant for more complex tasks requires that you understand the keywords and variables used in the HTML template.

Understanding the HTML template

The HTML template used for the Web Publishing Assistant consists of three components:

◆ **Keywords** – Special markers, identified by a percent sign, control the generating process. These keywords are standard for HTML templates.

◆ **Variables** – Column names that are replaced by the actual value found in the query results column.

◆ **HTML tags and plain text** – These control the appearance of the Web page and standard text that is always displayed.

Looking at the default template (SIMPLE.HTX) generated for the report created in the previous section, we can see most of the variables used by Web Publishing Assistant.

The template begins with standard HTML for a header:

```
<html>
<head>
<meta http-equiv="Content-Type" content="text/html">
<title>Database Information Page</title>
</head>
```

The title is hard coded.

The next part of the template includes the HTML tag BODY, which defines the background color as white:

```
<body bgcolor="#FFFFFF">
```

Following the BODY tag are three lines for the page heading, and two blank lines:

```
<p align="center"><font size="5">Database Results</font></p>
<p align="center"> </p>
<div align="center"><center>
```

The next line shows the variable indicating the start of a repeated section that is executed once for each row returned from the query:

```
<%begindetail%>
```

In this example, a new HTML table is started with each query row:

```
<table border="1" width="100%">
```

The next four lines are the first row of the HTML table. The first column displays the column name (STORE_ID). The second column displays the value in the STORE_ID column using the variable <%STORE_ID%>:

```
<tr>
    <td width="50%">STORE_ID</td>
    <td width="50%"><%STORE_ID%></td>
</tr>
```

The next four lines generate the second row of the HTML table and display the STORE_NAME column using the variable <%STORE_NAME%>:

```
<tr>
    <td width="50%">STORE_NAME</td>
    <td width="50%"><%STORE_NAME%></td>
</tr>
```

The next four lines make a third row in the HTML table displaying the STORE_STATE data:

```
<tr>
    <td width="50%">STORE_STATE</td>
    <td width="50%"><%STORE_STATE%></td>
</tr>
```

Finally, the HTML table is completed with the following HTML tag:

```
</table>
```

Now a blank line is added:

```
<p> </p>
```

Next, the repeating section is closed:

```
<%enddetail%>
```

The final lines in the template are used only one time, after all query rows have been run through the repeating section.

These last five lines complete the body of the Web page and the Web page itself:

```
</center></div>
<p> </p>
</body>
</html>
```

This generates a single Web page with a title, heading, and series of tables. This short set of HTML template lines generates a Web page long enough to accommodate the number of rows in the query that generates the Web report.

THE IF CLAUSE: HANDLING CONDITIONAL LOGIC IN THE TEMPLATE

The IF keyword can serve to handle conditional logic in the template. The basic syntax of such an IF clause is as follows:

```
<%IF  condition %>
HTML statements
[<ELSE>
HTML statements ]
<%ENDIF%>
```

The IF clause enables you to execute the sections of your template selectively. For example, the following phrase prints only headings for the first row of the query results:

```
<%if CurrentRecord EQ 1%>
    <H1>Report Details</H1>
<%ENDIF%>
```

The following phrase prints a line only if the store is in Wisconsin:

```
<%if STORE_STATE CONTAINS "WI"%>
<P>This store is in Wisconsin!</P>
<%ENDIF%>
```

 The column name within the IF clause must not be enclosed in brackets.

You can use the following conditional operators with the IF clause:

◆ EQ. Equal to

◆ CONTAINS. Any portion of the left item equals the right item

◆ LT. The left item is less than the right item

◆ GT. The left item is greater than the right item

TIP You can use the special variable CURRENTRECORD only within an IF clause. The variable contains the record number of the current row being processed. The first row is 1, the next row is 2, and so on.

CUSTOMIZING YOUR TEMPLATE

Adding your own customized template to a Web page is easy if you let the Web Publishing Assistant create the basic template first. For example, take the Web report SIMPLE.HTM created in the previous section.

The Web Publishing Assistant created a template SIMPLE.htx that can now be customized. The original template results in a Web page shown earlier in Figure 21-4.

The code for the original SIMPLE.htx template follows:

```
<html>

<head>
<meta http-equiv="Content-Type" content="text/html">
<title>Database Information Page</title>
</head>

<body bgcolor="#FFFFFF">
<p align="center"><font size="5">Database Results</font></p>
<p align="center"> </p>
<div align="center"><center>

<%begindetail%>
  <table border="1" width="100%">
     <tr>
        <td width="50%">STORE_ID</td>
        <td width="50%"><%STORE_ID%></td>
     </tr>
     <tr>
        <td width="50%">STORE_NAME</td>
        <td width="50%"><%STORE_NAME%></td>
     </tr>
     <tr>
        <td width="50%">STORE_STATE</td>
        <td width="50%"><%STORE_STATE%></td>
     </tr>
  </table>
<p> </p>
<%enddetail%>

</center></div>
```

```
<p> </p>
</body>
</html>
```

Some easy changes can make your Web page more attractive. Try them out in the following steps.

1. First, modify the background color to light blue:

```
<html>
<head>
<meta http-equiv="Content-Type" content="text/html">
<title>Database Information Page</title>
</head>
<body bgcolor="#CCFFFF">
```

2. Next, replace the page heading with a meaningful title:

```
<p align="center"><font size="5">Busy Bee Stores</font></p>
<p align="center"> </p>
<div align="center"><center>
```

3. Next, modify the table layout so that a single table holds all the rows of data:

```
<table border="5" width="100%" BGCOLOR="FFFFFF">
```

4. Modify the headings slightly by making the width of the label 15% and the data 85% width. Add a blank row of light blue to mark where the store data ends:

```
<%begindetail%>
    <tr>
        <td width="15%" ALIGN=RIGHT><B>STORE ID</td>
        <td width="85%"><%STORE_ID%></td>
    </tr>
     <tr>
        <td width="15%" ALIGN=RIGHT><B>NAME</td>
        <td width="85%"><%STORE_NAME%></td>
    </tr>
     <tr>
        <td width="15%" ALIGN=RIGHT><B>STATE</td>
        <td width="85%"><%STORE_STATE%></td>
    </tr>
     <tr>
        <td COLSPAN="2" BGCOLOR="CCFFFF"> </td>
    </tr>
```

```
<%enddetail%>
```

5. Finally, close the table after completing the detail instead of after every row.

```
</table>
</center></div>
<p> </p>
</body>
</html>
```

Figure 21-6 shows the resulting Web page, which has a more appealing appearance while keeping the same data intact.

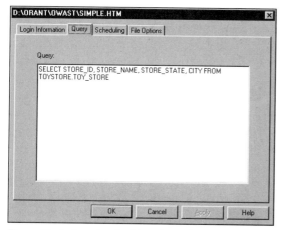

Figure 21-6: A customized template gives you flexibility in your report look and feel.

In the next section, you find more interesting reporting techniques to use.

Generating Drill-Down Reports

The Web Publishing Assistant is a simple tool, but with careful query and template designs it can do quite a lot of work. This section shows how to create three reports that are interconnected and can all be generated with the Web Publishing Assistant.

Figure 21-7 illustrates how the three reports connect to one another.

The three reports are as follows:

◆ **Webstore.htm.** This is the top-level report. It lists all stores in the Toy Store chain. The store's ID is an HTML link to the next report. By clicking a store ID, you go to the next report.

List of Stores

Webstore.htm

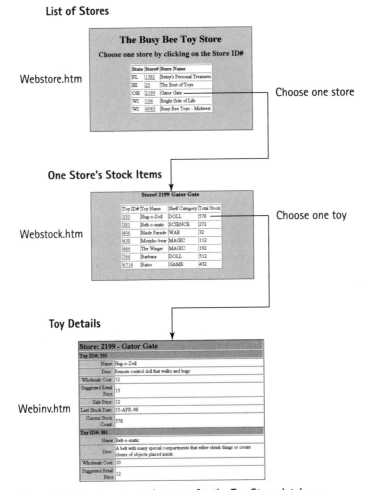

Choose one store

One Store's Stock Items

Webstock.htm

Choose one toy

Toy Details

Webinv.htm

Figure 21-7: Three generated reports for the Toy Store database

◆ **Webstock.htm.** This report lists all the stock (toys) in all stores in one Web page. All stock for one store is listed together. You arrive at the selected store's list of stock from the first page. The HTML tag NAME contains the toy store ID, which enables you to click the store in a previous Web report and arrive at the correct portion of the Webstock report page.

◆ **Webinv.htm.** The final report in the series, Webinv.htm lists all the details about each toy in all the stores. Again, the HTML NAME tag enables you to click one store's toy (on Webstock.htm) and go to the correct portion of the report displaying that toy on the Webinv.htm report page.

To build each report, create a query and a template. The next sections describe each report in detail.

Building the list of stores report

The list of stores report is named Webstore. It lists all the stores in the toy store chain. The database table containing this information is named TOY_STORE. The query for this report needs the following columns from the TOY_STORE table:

◆ STORE_STATE. State where the store is located. The list of stores is sorted by state name.

◆ STORE_ID. This ID number is the unique primary key of each store. This number helps us locate the correct position in the next report.

◆ STORE_NAME. Name of the store.

The following query retrieves all the data needed for the Webstore report:

```
SELECT STORE_STATE state,
       STORE_ID storeid,
       STORE_NAME storename
FROM TOY_STORE
ORDER BY STORE_STATE
```

The column alias listed in the query above must exactly match the column variable used in the template.

Now that the query is designed, the next step is to design the report page template. The top heading of the report page looks like this:

```
<HTML><HEAD><TITLE>Busy Bee Toy Stores</TITLE></HEAD>
<BODY BGCOLOR="FFCCFF" >
<CENTER>
<H1>The Busy Bee Toy Store</H1>
<H2>Choose one store by clicking the Store ID#</H2>
```

This results in a page with the title "Busy Bee Toy Stores" and heading "The Busy Bee Toy Store." The page has a lavender background. The last line is instructions on how to use the page.

Next, an HTML table is created that will hold the data from the query. To establish the table, its columns, and a heading row, the following HTML code is used:

```
<TABLE BORDER=4 BGCOLOR="FFFFFF">
<TR>
        <TD><B>State</B></TD>
        <TD><B>Store#</B></TD>
        <TD><B>Store Name</B></TD>
</TR>
```

Each row returned from the query creates a row in the HTML table on this report page. The first few lines start the table row and print the state abbreviation:

```
<%begindetail%>
<TR>
        <TD><%state%></TD>
```

The next line writes a link into the store ID column of the HTML table. The link calls the Web page Webstock.htm and tells the browser to go to a named location on the page.

```
        <TD>
        <A HREF="Webstock.htm#store<%storeid%>"><%storeid%></A>
        </TD>
```

For example, if the store ID is 1234, then the line looks like this in the final HTML:

```
        <TD>
        <A HREF="Webstock.htm#store1234"><1234></A>
        </TD>
```

Finally, the store name is printed in the last column of the HTML table:

```
<TD><%storename%></TD>
```

The row and the loop are ended:

```
</TR>
<%enddetail%>
```

After the loop, the final section of code is executed only one time. The HTML table and the Web page are closed:

```
</TABLE>
</BODY>
</HTML>
```

The complete HTML template looks like this:

```
<HTML><HEAD><TITLE>Busy Bee Toy Stores</TITLE></HEAD>
<BODY BGCOLOR="FFCCFF" >
<CENTER>
<H1>The Busy Bee Toy Store</H1>
<H2>Choose one store by clicking the Store ID#</H2>
<TABLE BORDER=4 BGCOLOR="FFFFFF">
<TR>
        <TD><B>State</B></TD>
        <TD><B>Store#</B></TD>
        <TD><B>Store Name</B></TD>
</TR>
<%begindetail%>
<TR>
        <TD><%state%></TD>
        <TD><A
HREF="Webstock.htm#store<%storeid%>"><%storeid%></A></TD>
        <TD><%storename%></TD>
</TR>
<%enddetail%>
</TABLE>
</BODY>
</HTML>
```

When creating this report in the Web Publishing Assistant, you follow the usual steps outlined in the first section of this chapter. When you are asked to define the query, choose the Enter a query as a SQL statement option, and then copy and paste the Webstore.sql query into the query window.

Figure 21-8 shows the resulting Web page after generating the page in Web Publishing Assistant.

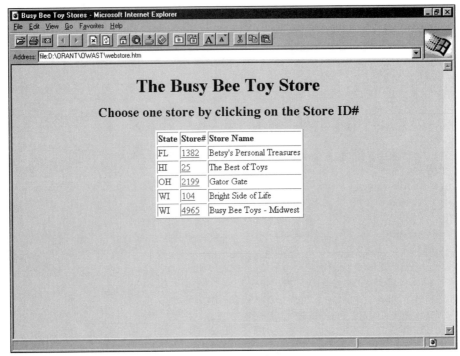

Figure 21-8: The Webstore.htm report has a link on each store's ID number.

When you view the report in your browser, you can click any store ID number. Doing so calls the next report we will create: Webstock.htm.

Building the list of store stock report

The list of store stock report is named "Webstock" and has an unusual design. You might expect to create separate report pages for each store. However, this would require that you the store ID numbers in advance and that you establish a separate report in Web Publishing Assistant for each store. The store stock report shown here is a single report containing all the stock for all the stores. If a new store is established, no changes are required of this report.

The query used for this report has two queries joined together with a UNION command. The first query retrieves only the first toy row for each store's inventory (the lowest TOY_ID). The column named "newstore" contains a literal value of "Y," indicating that this row is the first row for a store:

```
SELECT SS.STORE_ID storeid,
       TS.STORE_NAME storename,
       SS.TOY_ID toyid,
       TI.TOY_NAME toyname,
```

```
                TI.SHELF_CATEGORY shelf,
                SS.CURRENT_STOCK_COUNT currstock,
                'Y' newstore,
                TI.TOY_DESC toydesc,
                TI.WHOLESALE_COST wholesale,
                TI.SUGGESTED_RETAIL_PRICE srp,
                SS.SALE_PRICE sale,
                SS.LAST_STOCK_DATE stockdate
FROM TOY_STORE TS,
        STORE_STOCK SS,
        TOY_INVENTORY TI
WHERE TS.STORE_ID = SS.STORE_ID
AND     TI.TOY_ID = SS.TOY_ID
AND     SS.TOY_ID = (SELECT MIN(TOY_ID)
                        FROM STORE_STOCK SS2
                        WHERE STORE_ID = SS.STORE_ID)
```

Between the first and second queries, we add the UNION operator so that we create a single result set that combines both queries:

```
UNION
```

The second query returns all the remaining rows of stock data for the stores. The "newstore" column contains a literal value of N, indicating that this row is not the first row for a store:

```
SELECT SS.STORE_ID storeid,
        TS.STORE_NAME storename,
        SS.TOY_ID toyid,
        TI.TOY_NAME toyname,
        TI.SHELF_CATEGORY shelf,
        SS.CURRENT_STOCK_COUNT currstock,
        'N' newstore,
        TI.TOY_DESC toydesc,
        TI.WHOLESALE_COST wholesale,
        TI.SUGGESTED_RETAIL_PRICE srp,
        SS.SALE_PRICE sale,
        SS.LAST_STOCK_DATE stockdate
FROM TOY_STORE TS,
        STORE_STOCK SS,
        TOY_INVENTORY TI
WHERE TS.STORE_ID = SS.STORE_ID
AND     TI.TOY_ID = SS.TOY_ID
AND     SS.TOY_ID <> (SELECT MIN(TOY_ID)
```

```
FROM STORE_STOCK SS2
WHERE STORE_ID = SS.STORE_ID)
```

The following ORDER BY clause sorts the results of both queries together by STORE_ID and then by TOY_ID. The result is a list of all the stock for each store in order:

```
ORDER BY 1,3
```

As with all the Web reports, the next step is to design the report page template. The heading at the top of the report page looks like this:

```
<HTML><HEAD><TITLE> The Busy Bee Toy Store </TITLE></HEAD>
<BODY BGCOLOR="FFCCFF">
<CENTER>
<H1>The Busy Bee Toy Store</H1>
<H2>Choose one Toy by clicking the Toy ID#</H2>
```

The top heading is nearly identical to the one used in the report template for the Webstore report.

This report contains a separate HTML table to hold each row of the data from each store. Therefore, the initial table commands are found inside the looping structure of the template. An IF statement looks at the value of the "newstore" column to decide whether or not to start a new table. If the column has Y in it, the previous table is closed. Then a marker is laid down for the current store using the NAME tag. The NAME tag is the destination mark for the link on the previous report (Webstore). Finally, a new HTML table is started that contains a separate row for each stock record for this store.

```
<%begindetail%>
    <%if newstore EQ Y%>
        </TABLE>
        <P>
        <A NAME="store<%storeid%>"><BR>
        <H3> Store# <%storeid%> <%storename%> </H3>
        <TABLE BORDER=4 BGCOLOR="FFFFFF">
        <TR>
                <TD>Toy ID#</TD>
                <TD>Toy Name</TD>
                <TD>Shelf Category</TD>
            <TD>Total Stock</TD>
        </TR>
    <%endif%>
```

The next code executes for all rows, including the first row for each store. It creates a link to the toy details report in the same way that the Webstore report created a link to the Webstock report. It also lists the remaining details for each stock item:

```
<TR>
    <TD>
    <A
HREF="Webinv.htm#store<%storeid%>stock<%toyid%>"><%toyid%></A>
    </TD>
    <TD><%toyname%></TD>
    <TD><%shelf%></TD>
    <TD><%currstock%></TD>
</TR>
<%enddetail%>
```

After the loop, the final section of code is executed only one time. The final HTML table and the Web page are closed:

```
</TABLE>
</CENTER>
</BODY>
</HTML>
```

The complete HTML template (Webstock.htx) can be found on the CD-ROM in the back of the book.

Figure 21-9 shows the resulting Web page, Webstock.htm, after generating the page in Web Publishing Assistant.

You can click any of the toy ID numbers to drill down and view details on any particular stock item, using the Webinv.htm report you create next.

Creating the toy inventory detail report

This report is the final report of the three interconnected reports. This final report has no links. It uses the NAME tag to identify the location of each inventory record so that links from the Webstock report go to the correct area in this report.

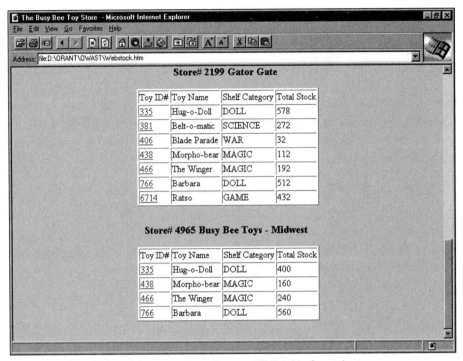

Figure 21-9: The Webstock.htm report creates one HTML table for each store.

The query for the toy inventory detail report has a UNION statement that combines two queries the same way that the previous Web report query (Webstock.sql) did:

```
SELECT SS.STORE_ID storeid,
       TS.STORE_NAME storename,
       SS.TOY_ID toyid,
       TI.TOY_NAME toyname,
       TI.SHELF_CATEGORY shelf,
       SS.CURRENT_STOCK_COUNT currstock,
       'Y' newstore,
       TI.TOY_DESC toydesc,
       TI.WHOLESALE_COST wholesale,
       TI.SUGGESTED_RETAIL_PRICE srp,
       SS.SALE_PRICE sale,
       SS.LAST_STOCK_DATE stockdate
FROM TOY_STORE TS,
     STORE_STOCK SS,
     TOY_INVENTORY TI
WHERE TS.STORE_ID = SS.STORE_ID
AND   TI.TOY_ID = SS.TOY_ID
```

```
AND    SS.TOY_ID = (SELECT MIN(TOY_ID)
                    FROM STORE_STOCK SS2
                    WHERE STORE_ID = SS.STORE_ID)
UNION
SELECT SS.STORE_ID storeid,
       TS.STORE_NAME storename,
       SS.TOY_ID toyid,
       TI.TOY_NAME toyname,
       TI.SHELF_CATEGORY shelf,
       SS.CURRENT_STOCK_COUNT currstock,
       'N' newstore,
       TI.TOY_DESC toydesc,
       TI.WHOLESALE_COST wholesale,
       TI.SUGGESTED_RETAIL_PRICE srp,
       SS.SALE_PRICE sale,
       SS.LAST_STOCK_DATE stockdate
FROM TOY_STORE TS,
     STORE_STOCK SS,
     TOY_INVENTORY TI
WHERE TS.STORE_ID = SS.STORE_ID
AND    TI.TOY_ID = SS.TOY_ID
AND    SS.TOY_ID <> (SELECT MIN(TOY_ID)
                    FROM STORE_STOCK SS2
                    WHERE STORE_ID = SS.STORE_ID)
ORDER BY 1,3
```

The query sorts toy inventory rows by STORE_ID and TOY_ID. It lists detailed information about the toy from the STORE_STOCK and TOY_INVENTORY tables. The name of the store is retrieved from the TOY_STORE table.

The template for the toy inventory report begins with a heading similar to those in the other two reports, using a background graphic instead of the lavender color. The graphic draws a line down the left of the page. The <UL> tags indent all the text to the right.

```
<HTML>
<TITLE>View Toy Stock Detail</TITLE>
<BODY BACKGROUND="bg1.gif" TEXT="000000" >
<CENTER>
<H3><I>The Busy Bee Toy Store</I>
<P>View Toy Stock
</CENTER>
<UL>
<UL>
<P><img src="line1.gif"></H3>
```

```
<UL>
<UL>
<UL>
```

The next part of the template begins the loop for each detail row:

```
<%begindetail%>
```

Next, an IF statement executes commands only when the first row of a store is found:

```
<%if newstore EQ Y%>
      </TABLE>
   <P>
     <TABLE BORDER=4 BGCOLOR="FFCCFF" WIDTH=80%>
   <TR>
      <TD ALIGN=LEFT BGCOLOR="FF99FF" COLSPAN="2">
       <H2> Store: <%storeid%> - <%storename%> </H2>
        </TD>
      </TR>
   <%endif%>
```

The NAME tag establishes the point of entry if you select this toy from the previous report Web page:

```
<TR>
        <TD ALIGN=LEFT BGCOLOR="FF99FF" COLSPAN="2">
         <A NAME="store<%storeid%>stock<%toyid%>">
         <B>Toy ID#:<%toyid%> 
        </TD>
   </TR>
```

The details of the toy inventory row are displayed in several rows of the HTML table:

```
<TR>
      <TD ALIGN=RIGHT>Name:</B></TD>
        <TD BGCOLOR="FFFFFF"><%toyname%>  </TD>
   </TR>
   <TR>
      <TD ALIGN=RIGHT>Desc: </B></TD>
        <TD BGCOLOR="FFFFFF"><%toydesc%>  </TD>
   </TR>
   <TR>
```

```
        <TD ALIGN=RIGHT>Wholesale Cost: </TD>
        <TD BGCOLOR="FFFFFF"><%wholesale%>  </TD>
    </TR>
    <TR>
        <TD ALIGN=RIGHT>Suggested Retail Price:</B></TD>
          <TD BGCOLOR="FFFFFF"><%srp%>  </TD>
    </TR>
    <TR>
          <TD ALIGN=RIGHT>Sale Price: </B></TD>
          <TD BGCOLOR="FFFFFF"><%sale%>  </TD>
    </TR>
    <TR>
        <TD ALIGN=RIGHT>Last Stock Date: </B></TD>
          <TD BGCOLOR="FFFFFF"><%stockdate%>  </TD>
    </TR>
    <TR>
        <TD ALIGN=RIGHT>Current Stock Count: </B></TD>
          <TD BGCOLOR="FFFFFF"><%currstock%>  </TD>
    </TR>
```

The repeating loop for rows ends here:

```
<%enddetail%>
```

The final section of code prints only one time on the bottom of the report:

```
<P><img src="line1.gif">
</BODY>
</HTML>
```

Now that you have created the template and the query, you can use Web Publishing Assistant to set up the frequency of when the report is refreshed.

The three report pages must be located in the same directory on the Web site. If they are not, modify the template to reflect the correct directory path in the links defined in the Webstore and Webstock pages.

TIP

To ensure that all reports properly reflect any changes to your data, establish the same reporting frequency for all three reports.

This set of reports is dependent on the correct naming of the links in the resulting HTML pages. In fact, Web Assistant really does not understand the relationship between the reports.

Figure 21-10 shows the resulting Web page for Webinv.htm, the Web report for details of all toys stocked in all stores. Zoom into the correct toy detail row using the previous two Web report page links.

Store: 2199 - Gator Gate	
Toy ID#: 335	
Name:	Hug-o-Doll
Desc:	Remote control doll that walks and hugs.
Wholesale Cost:	12
Suggested Retail Price:	15
Sale Price:	12
Last Stock Date:	15-APR-98
Current Stock Count:	578
Toy ID#: 381	
Name:	Belt-o-matic
Desc:	A belt with many special compartments that either shrink things or create clones of objects placed inside.
Wholesale Cost:	10
Suggested Retail Price:	12

Figure 21-10: The detail report has NAME tags to locate a particular toy in a selected store.

Summary

The Web Publishing Assistant has several components, including the query, the template, and the frequency of the report. Use the Web Publishing Assistant's GUI view of the database to create the query, if you wish. Combine your query with a template (which the Assistant can generate for you). When your page is on the Web, set the Web Publishing Assistant to refresh the Web report page at a specified frequency.

The fastest way to get results with this tool is to use the wizard to build a query and a template for you. When this process is complete, some modifications (such as refreshing the report on the Web) are easier to make. Other modifications – such as changing the query or the template – require careful attention to avoid errors. Still other report parameters, such as the filenames and frequency, cannot be modified at all.

Before you customize a template, first be sure you understand how to use the keywords and variables defined in the template file. These are standard to most HTML editors.

A more complex example of reporting is illustrated next. The toy store schema has several tables on which inter-related reports are created. By using customized queries and templates, it is possible to link all three reports using standard HTML link tags and standard HTML NAME tags. The trick is to create a single Web page that contains details for all stores and then to go to specific locations within the Web page using the NAME tag to point to a specific STORE_ID or TOY_ID or both.

Appendix A

What's on the CD-ROM?

The CD-ROM included with your Oracle8 Developer's Guide has several directories with a variety of information in each.

There are sample Designer and Developer applications, samples of PL/SQL procedures, packages, and triggers. You can view the list of directories and files in a section of this appendix.

The CD-ROM aids you in viewing the many examples shown throughout the book. I encourage you to install the sample tables and data and run the many sample applications yourself. You can explore them in your own Designer and Developer toolset.

 The entire text of the *Oracle8 Developer's Guide* is contained on the CD-ROM in PDF format. For your convenience in viewing these files, Adobe Acrobat Reader is also included on the CD.

Installing the Sample Tables and Data

There are three primary schemas that are used in the book:

◆ **OBJOWNER.** This schema contains the data for the Book Lending Library system. The schema is made up of Oracle8 Object Types, Object Tables, Nested Tables, and Varrays.

◆ **TOYSTORE.** This schema is referenced most often in the book and has the data for the Busy Bee Toy Stores system. The schema has relational tables connected by primary and foreign key constraints.

◆ **USRHELP.** The tables created here are used to collect data from your Designer Repository. Later, you use the tables to display help tips in your applications.

Install TOYSTORE

Figure A-1 shows the database diagram for the TOYSTORE schema.

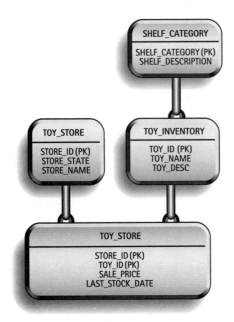

Figure A-1: The TOYSTORE schema has four relational tables.

Follow these steps to create the TOYSTORE user, all its tables and data.

1. Review the following code. This is the beginning lines of the toystore.sql file. Notice that there is a tablespace named USER_DATA and TEMPORARY_DATA. There is also a CONNECT command with no database path. If these items need to be changed, make a copy of the file, change the tablespace and connect information and continue with these instructions using your revised copy of the file.

   Here is the code to review:

   ```
   /* --------- create user TOYSTORE ------- */
   CREATE USER TOYSTORE IDENTIFIED BY TOYSTORE
   DEFAULT TABLESPACE USER_DATA
   TEMPORARY TABLESPACE TEMPORARY_DATA
   PROFILE DEFAULT ACCOUNT UNLOCK;
   GRANT CONNECT TO TOYSTORE;
   GRANT RESOURCE TO TOYSTORE;
   GRANT UNLIMITED TABLESPACE TO TOYSTORE;
   ```

```
ALTER USER TOYSTORE DEFAULT ROLE ALL;
/* --------- create tables for toy store chain ---- */
CONNECT TOYSTORE/TOYSTORE;
```

2. Log into SQLPLUS or SQL Worksheet (or any SQL tool you prefer to use).

3. Execute the following command (Replace D with your CD-ROM drive letter):

```
start D:\Make\toystore
```

4. Save the changes by executing the following command:

```
commit;
```

Install OBJOWNER

Figure A-2 shows the database diagram for the OBJOWNER object named PERSON_TABLE_T.

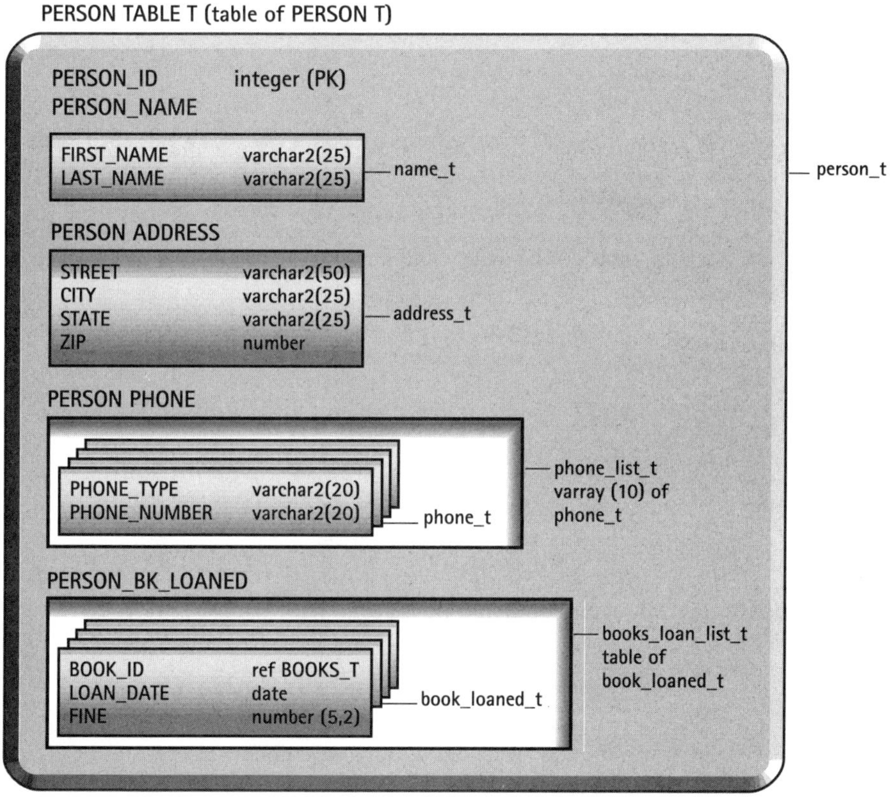

PERSON TABLE T (table of PERSON T)

Figure A-2: The PERSON_TABLE_T is an Object Table owned by OBJOWNER.

Figure A-3 shows a diagram of the object named BOOK_TABLE_T.

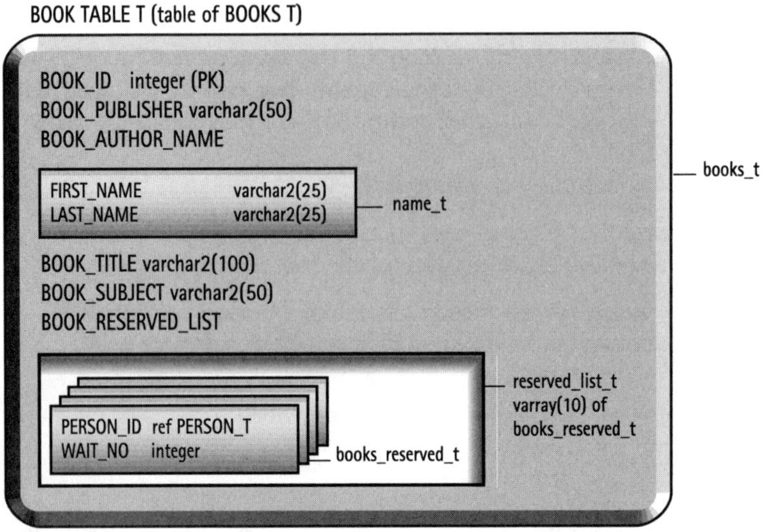

BOOK TABLE T (table of BOOKS T)

Figure A-3: The BOOK_TABLE_T Object Table contains a VARRAY and other object types.

Follow these steps to create the OBJOWNER user and its schema.

1. Log into SQL*Plus, SQL Worksheet, or your favorite SQL tool.

2. Create the user OBJOWNER with capability to create objects by executing these commands:

```
CREATE USER OBJOWNER IDENTIFIED BY OBJOWNER;
    GRANT CONNECT TO OBJOWNER;
    GRANT RESOURCE TO OBJOWNER;
```

3. Connect to OBJOWNER by typing this command (Replace dblink with your database link):

```
CONNECT OBJOWNER/OBJOWNER@dblink
```

4. Execute the following command (Replace D with your CD-ROM drive letter):

```
start D:\Make\makeobjects
```

5. Save the changes by executing the following command:

```
commit;
```

Install USRHELP

Follow these steps to create the USRHELP user and its schema.

1. Log into SQL*Plus, SQL Worksheet, or your favorite SQL tool.

2. Create the user USRHELP with capability to create objects by executing this command:

```
CREATE USER USRHELP IDENTIFIED BY USRHELP;
    GRANT CONNECT TO USRHELP;
    GRANT RESOURCE TO USRHELP;
```

3. Connect to USRHELP by typing this command (Replace dblink with your database link):

```
CONNECT USRHELP/USRHELP@dblink
```

4. Execute the following command (Replace D with your CD-ROM drive letter):

```
start D:\Make\User_help
```

5. Save the changes by executing the following command:

```
commit;
```

Directory Listings

The CD-ROM contains the following directories:

- ◆ **Forms.** This contains forms applications and additional objects such as menus, sample triggers, charts that are connected with forms, and so on.

- ◆ **Graphics.** Here you find several charts that are built in the chapters of Oracle8 Developer's Guide. There are also related SQL scripts here.

- ◆ **Make.** The tables and objects of the sample schemas are found here.

- ◆ **Pictures.** There are pictures needed to complete the applications and they are all found here.

- ◆ **Plsql.** This contains all the sample code found in the book. See Table C-1 in Appendix C for a complete listing of the files in this directory and a cross-reference of which chapter in the book uses each file.

- ◆ **Plsql_objects.** Here are all the Oracle8 object functions, packages, views, and procedures used in the book for manipulating ORacle8 Object tables, nested tables, and varrays. Table C-1 in Appendix C includes a description of these files.

- ◆ **Reports.** The Reports built in the Report Builder chapter are found here.

- ◆ **Tree.** This contains an executable file (setup.exe) to aid you in installing the ActiveX modules for tree navigation in forms. See Chapter 6 for more details.

- ◆ **Web.** This directory contains procedures that deliver Web pages using PL/SQL and the Web extensions. There are other miscellaneous Web pages here.

- ◆ **Webassistant.** The applications created using the Oracle WebAssistant tool can be found here.

 I will maintain a Web page for comments or additions to the sample database and applications. The URL is: `http://www.maui.net/ ~mcculc/ora8devgd`.

Watch this Web site for new information. You can also send comments or questions to me at this e-mail address:

`mcculc@maui.net`

Appendix B

Additional Resources

THIS APPENDIX LISTS AND describes Oracle- and database-related Web sites that you might want to check out. Here are a few of the hundreds of Web sites that cover Oracle- and database-related subjects. I avoided commercial sites for the most part. This list includes sites with information and with collections of similar Web sites. Most of the descriptions were gathered from search engines. Where I have reviewed a site myself, I've added comments to the description in italics.

 I have included an HTML format of this appendix on the CD-ROM for your convenience. Find it in the Web directory.

Oracle-Related Web Sites

◆ **Accessing Oracle**

Basic description of the Oracle relational database management system.

http://www.ecst.csuchico.edu/~morganm/oracle.html

◆ **All things Oracle**

http://www.mcs.net/~hugo/ftp/files.html

◆ **Converting Forms 3.0 to Forms 4.5**

Database Consultants Limited GUI*Converter – Converting Oracle Forms 3.0 to Oracle Forms 4.5.

http://www.hk.super.net/~dbc/convert.htm

◆ **Gary & Julie Piper's Oracle Tech Tips**

http://www.ozemail.com.au/~gpiper

◆ **Janet's Oracle Information**

http://pages.prodigy.com/janetb/2dba.htm

◆ **Ken Atkin's Oracle Database Tip of the Week**

   `http://www.arrowsent.com/oratip`

◆ **Kevin Looney's Oracle DBA FAQ**

   `http://www.osborne.com/oracle/dbafaq/dbafaq1.htm`

◆ **Oracle Assist**

   `http://www.oracleassist.com`

◆ **Oracle Books**

   `http://www.flash.net/~darcre/ors.htm`

◆ **Oracle Compile Utility for Forms 4.5 and Reports Shareware**

   Easy Oracle compile utility for Oracle Forms 4.5 Reports 2.5 (shareware).

   `http://www.geocities.com/SiliconValley/Way/1384/index.html`

◆ **Oracle Fans**

   `http://www.orafans.com`

◆ **Oracle FAQ and WWW Links**

   Great Oracle-related Web sites to visit. *This list will keep you busy for a couple of hours.*

   `http://infoboerse.doag.de/mirror/frank/faqlink.htm`

◆ **Oracle Forms FAQ**

   Oracle Developer/2000

   `http://www.dcr.co.jp/ORAC/faq/dev2000.htm`

◆ **Oracle Graphics SmartCharts within Oracle Forms**

   Oracle Forms developers can easily deliver powerful point-and-click applications by embedding graphical objects developed in Oracle Graphics 2.5.

   `http://www.oracle.com.sg/products/developer2000/smartcharts/html/index.html`

◆ **Oracle List Servers**

   `http://ns.netmcr.com/~rhubarb/oracle/index.html`

◆ **Oracle Links**

   `http://oralinks.home.ml.org`

◆ **Oracle Magazine Interactive**

http://www.oramag.com

◆ **Oracle Media Object Tips**

Tips and techniques for Oracle Media Objects developers.

http://www.ewg.com/OMO/tips.html

◆ **Oracle Overview**

http://www.rhic.bnl.gov/html/local/oracle/oracle_overview.html

◆ **Oracle Related Web Sites Compiled by Jerry Swisshelm**

An abundance of Oracle-related information is available over the Web.

http://www.stkma.com/images/ora_rel.html

◆ **Oracle Utilities Etc**

This page will be updated periodically, so come back often.

http://members.aol.com/jomarlen2/oraclesh.html

◆ **Oracle View**

http://www.oreview.com

◆ **OraWorld**

Oracle training, technical articles, news, tips, utilities, events, links, and product info.

http://www.oraworld.com/intervie.htm

◆ **PL/SQL Pipeline**

http://www.revealnet.com/plsql-pipeline/index.htm

Systems-Related Web Sites

◆ **Benchmarking Exchange and Best Practices Home Page**

A network for trading effective business practices.

http://www.benchnet.com/

◆ **Benchmarks FAQ**

The site is divided into general information, common benchmarks (for example, AIM and MUSBUS), terminology, and other sources of information.

`http://hpwww.epfl.ch/bench/bench.FAQ.html`

◆ **CCS Labs – Computer Science – University of Massachusetts**

`http://www-ccs.cs.umass.edu/`

◆ **Client/Server Labs**

This site offers plenty of useful information about the Atlanta, Georgia, independent testing lab that performs different kinds of testing, including performance, compatibility, and usability for end users, computer-related vendors, and resellers.

`http://www.cslinc.com/`

◆ **Computer Systems Authority**

Connections to Oracle-related sites and Oracle Corporation's connections maps to the Oracle Education Center.

`http://www.csac.com/oracle-sites.html`

◆ **Cybernetics and Systems Theory**

The links provide general background material on the field of cybernetics and systems theory. This material was collected and is provided in the context of the Principia Cybernetica Project but can be consulted independently of the rest of the project.

`http://pespmc1.vub.ac.be/CYBSYSTH.html`

◆ **NC World**

Product reviews, news, and links to the world of network computers.

`http://www.ncworldmag.com/`

◆ **PDS: The Performance Database Server**

Listings of performance databases, benchmark reports, papers, a bibliography, and related computer testing information at the University of Tennessee, Knoxville, site.

`http://performance.netlib.org/performance/html/PDStop.html`

◆ **System Optimization PC Hardware and Performance Guide**

`http://www.sysopt.com/`

◆ **Tool for Oracle Application Developers – SQL-TOAD**

TOAD – the tool for Oracle application developers is the most powerful and most developer-oriented tool available for testing queries and PL/SQL, viewing database objects and scripts, and more.

http://www.toadsoft.com/

◆ **Uncle Bobby's Oracle Play Korner**

Let's face it kids, SQL and RDBMS systems like Oracle are about as much fun as a root canal.

http://ugweb.cs.ualberta.ca/~beck/oracle/

General Database Web Sites

◆ **The Business Sight Framework**

An object-relational Java framework that enables Java objects to be easily saved and retrieved from relational databases.

http://www.objectmatter.com/

◆ **Database Concepts (GIS)**

http://www.utexas.edu/depts/grg/gcraft/notes/datacon/datacon.html#GIS\

◆ **DataModel.Org Home Page**

http://www.datamodel.org/

◆ **DBMS Magazine**

http://www.dbmsmag.com

◆ **DBA Mentor**

http://www.dba-mentor.co.uk

◆ **DBA Pipeline**

http://www.revealnet.com/dbapipe/index.htm

◆ **Web-Oracle Gateway**

Current version: 2.02: general information, news, bug complaints, and fixes.

http://oradb1.jinr.ru/Software/ORALink/

Internet and the Web Sites

◆ **Internet Hoax Pages**

Check out the latest email hoaxes

`http://ciac.llnl.gov/ciac/CIACHoaxes.html`

◆ **Internet Usage Surveys**

Georgia Tech's Graphic, Visualization, & Usability Center conducts the most comprehensive Internet usage reseach. This site gets you the results of all the annual surveys.

`http://www.cc.gatech.edu/gvu/user_surveys/`

◆ **Page Concepts: Frequently Asked Questions**

Frequently asked questions and answers about the Internet and Web site design

`http://www.page-concepts.com/faq/`

◆ **Search Engine Watch**

A resource to keep up on search engine technology

`http://searchenginewatch.com/`

◆ **WDVL: The Illustrated Encyclopedia of Web Technology**

Authoring, HTML, multimedia, and reference material

`http://www.stars.com/`

◆ **Web Page Design for Designers**

Good for going from hard copy to digital art design

`http://ds.dial.pipex.com/pixelp/wpdesign/wpdintro.htm`

◆ **WebGrrls International**

Great resource for all things Net-wise

`http://www.webgrrls.com`

Miscellaneous Web Sites

- ◆ **Comp Sci Singalong**

  Children's songs with computer terms

  http://www.sirius.com/~jmkohn/CKS/

- ◆ **Lexical FreeNet**

  A rich lexical tool box, this program enables you to search for rhymes and relationships between words and concepts that might never have occurred to you before.

  http://bobo.link.cs.cmu.edu/dougb/lexfn/

- ◆ **NIIT NetVarsity**

  Anytime, anywhere learning is here! NIIT NetVarsity uses the advantages of the Internet: flexibility, interaction, and access to unlimited resources.

  http://www.niitnetvarsity.com/

- ◆ **NSWCDD: Advanced Concepts Team (K61)**

  http://dias.nswc.navy.mil/

- ◆ **TechEncyclopedia**

  Find definitions to computer terms and concepts.

  http://www.techweb.com/encyclopedia/

Appendix C

Sample Code

SOMETIMES IT HELPS TO BROWSE through some code samples without all the detailed explanations to clutter up the page. This section is for readers who get inspiration from sample code just by reading through it.

The appendix is arranged in order by chapter, so that you can follow the code samples as you read the chapters. One exception is the final sections of the appendix, which is source code for creating and populating the sample tables and objects.

In addition, a cross-reference table helps you scan for functionality that you might want to review. Use the code here as a reference so you can study or copy the code into your own applications.

 All the code you see here is included in the CD-ROM in soft copy. See Appendix A for a listing of the contents of the CD-ROM.

The last part of this appendix has the creation scripts for all the sample users, tables, and objects used in the book.

Table C-1 has a cross-reference of all the PL/SQL scripts in this appendix by function.

Here is an explanation of the table's columns:

◆ **Application type.** The type of application in which the code is used or which is relevent to the code usage.

◆ **Feature.** A short description of the functionality of the code. This is also the heading (beneath the chapter heading) in which you will find this segment of code in this appendix.

◆ **Chapter #.** The chapter where the code is described fully. This is also the main heading under which you'll find the code in this appendix.

◆ **Code Name.** This is the directory and file name where you will find the same code on the CD-ROM.

TABLE C-1 CROSS-REFERENCE OF PL/SQL CODE BY TOOL AND FUNCTION

Application Type	Feature	Chapter #	Code Name
DESIGNER	Copy module role security across databases	4	`sqlplus/copy_module_roles.sql`
DESIGNER	Extracting module roles from repository	4	`Plsql/Extract_access.sql`
DESIGNER	Preparing database text for MS Word Macro	7	`Plsql/Headline_tag.sql`
FORMS	Dynamic security grants	4	`Forms/code4-1.sql`
FORMS	Function to Retrieve user's current roles	4	`Plsql/Getroles.sql`
FORMS	Function to update tool tip	19	`Forms/tooptip.sql`
FORMS	Package to access Objects in forms	13	`Plsql_objects/BOOK_HANDLING_PKG.sql`
FORMS	Procedure for form to check security	4	`Plsql/Chkform.sql`
FORMS	Reporting security violations	4	`Plsql/Report violations.sql`
FORMS	Running a progress bar	7	`Plsql/Update_progress.sql`
FORMS	Send query from form to chart	18	`Plsql/Load_query.sql`
FORMS	Send table as variant to ActiveX	20	`Forms/variant.sql`
FORMS	Set menu item attributes	21	`Forms/idnull.sql`
FORMS	Trigger to get last WHERE clause	18	`Forms/Save_where_clause.sql`
FORMS	Trigger to reset tool tip text	19	`Forms/load_tool_tip.sql`
FORMS	Using hidden items to control field placement	7	`Plsql/Loop_items.sql`

Application Type	Feature	Chapter #	Code Name
GRAPHICS	Button on chart calls report	18	`Graphics/Button` `_calls_report.sql`
GRAPHICS	Trigger to import image from filesystem	18	`Graphics/Format` `_template.sql`
REPORTS	Function to check user security	4	`Plsql/chkrpts.sql`
WEB	Display help text in Web	6	`Plsql/Showhelp.sql`
WEB	Function to add values from nested table	17	`Plsql_objects/` `Book_fine.sql`
WEB	Function to get one row from a varray	17	`Plsql/Home` `_phone.sql`
WEB	Procedure that creates HTML Insert page	22	`Web/Instoy.sql`
WEB	Procedure that creates HTML page using parameters	22	`Web/Stock.sql`
WEB	Procedure that creates HTML page	22	`Web/Store.sql`
WEB	Procedure that creates HTML Update page	22	`Web/Updtoy.sql`
WEB	Procedure to create HTML Commit Insert page	22	`Web/Commitins.sql`
WEB	Procedure to create HTML Commit Update/Delete page	22	`Web/Commit.sql`
WEB	Retrieve help text from Designer	6	`Plsql/cdsddl.pks`
WEBASSISTANT	Customized template for Webassistant	23	`Webassistant/` `template.htx`
WEBASSISTANT	Webassistant detail report template	23	`Webassistant/` `Webstock.htx`
WEBASSISTANT	Webassistant query for detail report	23	`Webassistant/` `Webstock.sql`
WEBASSISTANT	Webassistant query for third level detail report	23	`Webassistant/` `Webinv.sql`

Continued

TABLE C-1 CROSS-REFERENCE OF PL/SQL CODE BY TOOL AND FUNCTION
       (Continued)

Application Type	Feature	Chapter #	Code Name
WEBASSISTANT	Webassistant template for third level detail report	23	`Webassistant/ Webinv.htx`
WEBASSISTANT	Webassistant template for top drill-down page	23	`Webassistant/ Webstore.htx`

Chapter 4: Security

The code that follows relates to Chapter 4.

Dynamic security grants

```
/* ------- Forms/code4-1.sql --------------- */
PROCEDURE GRANT_TO_GLOBAL_ACCESS_ROLE
 (P_APPLICATION VARCHAR2
 )
 IS
-- Program Data
/* ID of application to update */
V_APPLICATION NUMBER;
/* Property list for Module access */
V_ACCESS CIODATABASE_OBJECT_GRANT.DATA;
/* Activity status */
V_ACT_STATUS VARCHAR2(1);
/* Activity warning flag */
V_ACT_WARNINGS VARCHAR2(1);
/* ID of the role GLOBAL_ACCESS_ROLE */
V_GLOBAL_ACCESS_ROLE NUMBER;

-- PL/SQL Block
/* Initiate API and get ID of application and GLOBAL_ACCESS_ROLE */
BEGIN
  BEGIN
  --
  -- Fetch application ID
    SELECT id
    INTO v_application
```

```
   FROM ci_application_systems
   WHERE
     name =p_application AND
     latest_version_flag='Y';
EXCEPTION
   WHEN NO_DATA_FOUND THEN
     raise_application_error
     (-20000,'Unable to find application:' ||p_application);
END;
--
-- Get ID for GLOBAL_ACCESS_ROLE
BEGIN
   SELECT id
   INTO v_GLOBAL_ACCESS_ROLE
   FROM ci_roles
   WHERE
     NAME = 'GLOBAL_ACCESS_ROLE';
EXCEPTION
   WHEN NO_DATA_FOUND THEN
     raise_application_error
       (-20000,'Unable to find GLOBAL_ACCESS_ROLE');
END;
--
-- Initialize API activity
BEGIN
   IF cdapi.initialized = FALSE THEN
   -- Initialize the API globals
   cdapi.initialize(p_application);
   END IF;
   -- Open API-activity
   cdapi.open_activity;
EXCEPTION WHEN OTHERS THEN
   raise_application_error
     (-20000,'Unable to initialize activity');
END;
       --
-- Create access for tables ***********************
BEGIN
   FOR tab IN (
     SELECT id, 'T'typ
     FROM ci_table_implementations t
     WHERE
       t.application_system_owned_by = v_application AND
       NOT EXISTS
```

```
              (SELECT id FROM ci_database_object_grants g
               WHERE g.ROLE_reference = v_GLOBAL_ACCESS_ROLE
               AND g.table_reference = t.id)
        UNION SELECT id, 'V'
        FROM ci_view_implementations v
        WHERE
          v.application_system_owned_by = v_application AND
          NOT EXISTS
            (SELECT id FROM ci_database_object_grants g
             WHERE g.ROLE_reference = v_GLOBAL_ACCESS_ROLE
             AND g.table_reference = v.id)
        UNION SELECT id, 'S'
        FROM ci_sequence_implementations s
        WHERE
          s.application_system_owned_by = v_application AND
          NOT EXISTS
            (SELECT id FROM ci_database_object_grants g
             WHERE g.ROLE_reference = v_GLOBAL_ACCESS_ROLE
             AND g.table_reference = s.id)
        )
    LOOP
      v_access.v.role_REFERENCE:= v_GLOBAL_ACCESS_ROLE;
      v_access.v.REMARK:=
       'Created by API-module ACCESS_TO_GLOBAL_ACCESS_ROLE';
      v_access.v.SELECT_FLAG:= 'Y';
      v_access.v.TABLE_REFERENCE:= tab.id;
      v_access.i.role_REFERENCE:= TRUE;
      v_access.i.REMARK:= TRUE;
      v_access.i.SELECT_FLAG:= TRUE;
      v_access.i.TABLE_REFERENCE:= TRUE;
      IF tab.typ IN('T', 'V') THEN
        v_access.v.DELETE_FLAG:= 'Y';
        v_access.v.INSERT_FLAG:= 'Y';
        v_access.v.UPDATE_FLAG:= 'Y';
        v_access.i.DELETE_FLAG:= TRUE;
        v_access.i.INSERT_FLAG:= TRUE;
        v_access.i.UPDATE_FLAG:= TRUE;
      END IF;
      -- do the grant ****************************************
      ciodatabase_object_grant.ins(NULL, v_access);
    END LOOP;
  EXCEPTION
    WHEN OTHERS THEN
      raise_application_error
```

```
        (-20000,'Unable to insert grant');
  END;
  -- ***************************************************
  --         End API activity
  BEGIN
    cdapi.validate_activity(v_act_status, v_act_warnings);
    --
    --         Display all violations and other messages
    --         regardless of the activity warnings flag
    REPORT_VIOLATIONS;
    -- Attempt TO CLOSE the activity
    cdapi.close_activity(v_act_status);
    --
    -- If the activity did not close successfully,
    -- roll back all changes made
    -- during the activity*/
    IF v_act_status != 'Y'THEN
      -- Could not close the activity
      cdapi.abort_activity;
      dbms_output.put_line
       ('Activity interupted by "constraint validations"');
      -- Otherwise, we're done
    ELSE
      -- Ok
      dbms_output.put_line
         ('Activity closed without errors');
    END IF;
  EXCEPTION WHEN OTHERS THEN
    raise_application_error(-20000,'Unable CLOSE activity');
  END;
  --
EXCEPTION WHEN OTHERS THEN
  raise_application_error
    (-20000,'Unable CREATE grants FOR GLOBAL_ACCESS_ROLE');
END GRANT_TO_GLOBAL_ACCESS_ROLE;
```

Reporting security violations

```
/* ------- Plsql/Reportviolations.sql -------- */
PROCEDURE REPORT_VIOLATIONS
 IS
-- Program Data
ARG3 VARCHAR2(64);
M_FACILITY VARCHAR2(3);
```

```
ARG4 VARCHAR2(64);
ARG5 VARCHAR2(20);
M_CODE NUMBER(38, 0);
ARG6 VARCHAR2(20);
ARG1 VARCHAR2(240);
ARG7 VARCHAR2(20);
ARG2 VARCHAR2(64);
ARG8 VARCHAR2(20);

-- PL/SQL Block
BEGIN
-- Report all violations regardless of the activity status
FOR viol IN (SELECT * FROM ci_violations) LOOP
  dbms_output.put_line(cdapi.instantiate_message(
     viol.facility, viol.code,
     viol.p0, viol.p1, viol.p2, viol.p3,
     viol.p4, viol.p5, viol.p6,viol.p7));
END LOOP;
--
-- Pop messages off the stack and format them
-- into a single text string
WHILE cdapi.stacksize > 0 LOOP
  rmmes.pop(m_facility, m_code, arg1, arg2, arg3,
            arg4, arg5, arg6, arg7, arg8);
  dbms_output.put_line
    (cdapi.instantiate_message(m_facility, m_code,
     arg1, arg2, arg3, arg4, arg5, arg6, arg7, arg8));
END LOOP;
END REPORT_VIOLATIONS;
```

Extracting module roles from repository

```
/* --------------- Plsql/Extract_access.sql ---------- */
CREATE OR REPLACE PROCEDURE EXTRACT_ACCESS
 (P_MODULE_SHORT_NAME IN MODULE_ROLES.MODULE_NAME%TYPE
 )
 IS
-- PL/SQL Block
--  Delete all access rights to modules being updated.
BEGIN

DELETE module_roles
WHERE
  module_name LIKE p_module_short_name;
```

```
IF (SQL%notfound) THEN
  NULL;
END IF;

-- Loop through all modules to be updated.
FOR r_modules IN
 (SELECT id , name, short_name
  FROM ci_modules
  WHERE short_name LIKE p_module_short_name)

LOOP
   -- Loop trough all roles granted to each module.
   FOR r_role_access IN
   (SELECT cg.name, cm.short_name
    FROM ci_role_module_accesses cma,
         ci_roles cg, ci_modules cm
    WHERE cma.general_module_reference=cm.id
    AND cm.id = r_modules.id
    AND role_reference = cg.id)

   LOOP
     BEGIN
        -- insert access row in MODULE_ROLES table.
        INSERT INTO module_roles(MODULE_NAME, ROLE_NAME)
        VALUES
           (r_role_access.short_name, r_role_access.name);
     EXCEPTION
        WHEN DUP_VAL_ON_INDEX
        THEN
        NULL;
     END;
   END LOOP;
END LOOP;
END EXTRACT_ACCESS;
```

Copy module role security across databases

```
/* ----------- sqlplus/copy_module_roles.sql -------------- */
accept table_owner    char prompt "Enter username of the table
owner: "
accept from_db        char prompt "Enter database conncet string to
copy from: "
accept pw_from char prompt "Enter password of repository_owner on
```

```
from database (&&from_db): "
accept to_db          char prompt "Enter database connect string to
copy to: "
accept pw_to   char prompt "Enter password of table_owner on to
database (&&to_db): "
connect &&table_owner/&&pw_to@&&to_db
drop database link moduleroles;
create database link moduleroles
  connect to &&table_owner identified by &&pw_from
  using '&&from_db';
prompt deleting old rows in module_roles
delete from &&table_owner.module_roles;
prompt Inserting new rows.
insert into &&table_owner.module_roles
select * from &&table_owner.module_roles@moduleroles;
drop database link moduleroles;
```

Procedure for form to check security

```
/* ------ Plsql/Chkform.sql -------- */
Procedure CHECK_FORMS_ACCESS IS
l_module_access vachar2(1);
l_dummy varchar2(1);
begin
  -- Find out if the current user is granted a role that
  -- gives access to the current form.
  begin
    select 'Y'
    into l_module_access
    from module_roles m, dba_role_privs r
    where
      m.module_name =
      get_application_property(current_form_name) and
      m.role_name = r.granted_role and
      r.grantee = USER and
      rownum = 1;
  exception when no_data_found then
    l_module_access:= 'N';
  end;
  if l_module_access = 'N' then
    message('You do not have access to this screen');
    synchronize;
    exit_form;
  end if;
```

```
-- activate the GLOBAL_ACCESS_ROLE (if it isn't already)
  begin
    select 'x' into l_dummy
    from session_roles
    where role = 'GLOBAL_ACCESS_ROLE';
  exception
    when no_data_found then
      dbms_session.set_role(
        get_default_roles||', GLOBAL_ACCESS_ROLE identified by
<password>');
  end;
```

Function to retrieve user's current roles

```
/* ----------- Plsql/Getroles.sql ----------- */
FUNCTION get_default_roles RETURN varchar2 IS
  default_roles varchar2(2000);
  -- All default roles, comma separated
  cursor get_system_role is
    select granted_role
    from user_role_privs
    where
      default_role = 'YES' and
      granted_role <> 'GLOBAL_ACCESS_ROLE';
BEGIN
  for def_role in get_system_role loop
    default_roles := def_role.granted_role||','||default_roles;
  end loop;
  default_roles := rtrim(default_roles,',');
  return(default_roles);
END;
```

Function to check user security

```
/* ------------- Plsql/chkrpts.sql ------------- */
Function CHECK_REPORTS_ACCESS (p_report in varchar2)IS
l_module_access vachar2(1);
l_dummy varchar2(1);
begin
  -- Find out if the current user is granted a role that
  -- gives access to the current report.
  begin
    select 'Y'
    into l_module_access
    from module_roles m, dba_role_privs r
```

```
    where
      m.module_name = p_report and
      m.role_name = r.granted_role and
      r.grantee = USER and
      rownum = 1;
  exception when no_data_found then
    l_module_access:= 'N';
  end;

if l_module_access = 'N' then
  return(FALSE);
end if;

  -- activate the GLOBAL_ACCESS_ROLE (if it isn't already)
  begin
    select 'x' into l_dummy
    from session_roles
    where role = 'GLOBAL_ACCESS_ROLE';
  exception
    when no_data_found then
      dbms_session.set_role(
        get_default_roles||', GLOBAL_ACCESS_ROLE identified by
<password>');
  end;

return(TRUE);
```

Chapter 6: WebServer Generator and WebForms

The code that follows relates to Chapter 6.

Retrieve help text from Designer

```
/* ------ plsql/cdsddl.pks ------- */
-- cdsddl.pks
--
-- Generated for Oracle 8 on Tue Aug 18  04:48:01 1998 by Server
Generator 2.1.19.5.0


PROMPT Creating Package 'HELPPACK'
```

```
CREATE OR REPLACE PACKAGE HELPPACK IS
-- Sub-Program Unit Declarations
PROCEDURE extract_help
 (P_APPSYS IN VARCHAR2
 );


END HELPPACK;
/
-- cdsddl.pkb
--
-- Generated for Oracle 8 on Tue Aug 18  04:48:02 1998 by Server
Generator 2.1.19.5.0


PROMPT Creating Package Body 'HELPPACK'
CREATE OR REPLACE PACKAGE BODY HELPPACK IS
cursor modules(v_app in number) is
  select id, application_system_owned_by, short_name from ci_modules
  where application_system_owned_by = v_app;

cursor module_components(v_app in number) is
  select id, application_system_owned_by, name from
ci_module_components
  where application_system_owned_by = v_app;

cursor texts(ref number) is
  select txt_seq, txt_text
  from cdi_text
  where
    txt_ref = ref and
    txt_type = 'CDIDSC';-- Program Data
/* The prefix of user/help text headers */
V_TYPE_PREFIX VARCHAR2(240) := 'USER_HELP$';

-- Sub-Program Unit Declarations
FUNCTION get_text
 (P_TEXT IN VARCHAR2
 ,P_TYPE IN VARCHAR2
 )
 RETURN VARCHAR2;

-- Sub-Program Units
FUNCTION get_text
```

```
(P_TEXT IN VARCHAR2
,P_TYPE IN VARCHAR2
)
RETURN VARCHAR2
IS
-- Program Data
/* The description text of p_text matching the p_type header */
V_TEXT VARCHAR2(2000);
/* Start position of matching text */
V_START NUMBER(4, 0);
/* End position of matching text */
V_END NUMBER(4, 0);

-- PL/SQL Block
BEGIN
v_text:=p_text;
    v_start:= instr(v_text,v_type_prefix||p_type);
    if v_start > 0
    then
      v_start:= v_start + length(v_type_prefix||p_type)+1;
      v_text:= substr(v_text,v_start,2000);
      v_end:= instr(v_text,v_type_prefix)-2;
      if v_end = -2 then v_end:= 2000; end if;
      v_text:= substr(v_text,1,v_end-1);
      return v_text;
    else
      return null;
    end if;
END get_text;

PROCEDURE extract_help
 (P_APPSYS IN VARCHAR2
 )
 IS
-- Program Data
/* Application system to extract */
V_APP NUMBER(38);
/* Text to be stored in help table */
V_TEXT VARCHAR2(2000);

-- PL/SQL Block
BEGIN
SELECT id INTO v_app
  FROM ci_application_systems
```

```
   WHERE name = p_appsys;

DELETE FROM user_help_text
WHERE
EXISTS (SELECT 1 FROM USER_HELP
WHERE user_help_text.help_ref = user_help.help_ref AND appsys =
v_app);
DELETE FROM user_help
WHERE appsys = v_app;

FOR m IN modules(v_app) LOOP
  INSERT INTO user_help (
    HELP_REF,
    APPSYS,
    MODULE_NAME)
  VALUES (
    m.id,
    m.application_system_owned_by,
    m.short_name);

  FOR t IN texts(m.id) LOOP
    v_text:=get_text(t.txt_text,'TEXT');
    IF v_text IS NOT NULL
    THEN
      INSERT INTO user_help_text (
        HELP_REF,
        SEQ,
        TEXT_LINE)
      VALUES (
        m.id,
        t.txt_seq,
        v_text);
    END IF;
    v_text:=get_text(t.txt_text,'KEYWORDS');
    IF v_text IS NOT NULL
    THEN
      UPDATE user_help
      SET keywords = v_text
      WHERE help_ref = m.id;
    END IF;
  END LOOP;

END LOOP;
```

```
FOR c IN module_components(v_app) LOOP
  INSERT INTO user_help (
    HELP_REF,
    APPSYS,
    MODULE_COMPONENT_NAME)
  VALUES (
    c.id,
    c.application_system_owned_by,
        c.name);

  FOR t IN texts(c.id) LOOP
    v_text:=get_text(t.txt_text,'TEXT');
    IF v_text IS NOT NULL
    THEN
      INSERT INTO user_help_text (
        HELP_REF,
        SEQ,
        TEXT_LINE)
      VALUES (
        c.id,
        t.txt_seq,
        v_text);
    END IF;
    v_text:=get_text(t.txt_text,'KEYWORDS');
    IF v_text IS NOT NULL
    THEN
      UPDATE user_help
      SET keywords = v_text
      WHERE help_ref = c.id;
    END IF;
  END LOOP;

END LOOP;
END extract_help;

-- PL/SQL Block

END HELPPACK;
```

Display help text in Web

```
/* ---------- Plsql/Showhelp.sql -------- */
PROCEDURE SHOWHELP
 (P_APPSYS IN USER_HELP.APPSYS%TYPE
```

```
 ,P_MODULE IN USER_HELP.MODULE_NAME%TYPE default null
 ,P_MODULE_COMPONENT default null
USER_HELP.MODULE_COMPONENT_NAME%TYPE default null
 ,P_COLUMN IN USER_HELP.COLUMN_NAME%TYPE default null
 )
 IS
-- PL/SQL Block
BEGIN
 wsgl.OpenPageHead('Help Screen');
 wsgl.ClosePageHead;
 wsgl.OpenPageBody(NULL);
 wsgl.DefaultPageCaption(NULL);
 FOR texts IN (
  SELECT text_line
  FROM user_help h, user_help_text t
  WHERE
  h.help_ref = t.help_ref AND
  p_appsys = h.appsys AND
  (p_module IS NULL OR p_module = h.module_name) AND
  (p_module_component IS NULL OR p_module_component =
h.module_component_name) AND
  (p_column IS NULL OR p_column = h.column_name)
  ORDER BY t.seq)
 LOOP
  htp.p(texts.text_line);
 END LOOP;
 wsgl.ClosePageBody;
END SHOWHELP;
```

Chapter 7: Making User-Friendly GUIs

The code that follows relates to Chapter 7.

Using hidden items to control field placement

```
/* ----------- Plsql/Loop_items.sql ----------- */
PROCEDURE Loop_Items is
  v_block_name varchar2(30) := get_form_property
               (name_in('SYSTEM.CURRENT_FORM'),first_block);
  v_item_name  varchar2(30);
  v_original_cursor_item  varchar2(70) :=
```

```
name_in('SYSTEM.cursor_item');
  v_original_cursor_record  number(10) :=
name_in('SYSTEM.cursor_record');
  v_original_top_record  number(10) := get_block_property
                (name_in('SYSTEM.cursor_block'),TOP_RECORD);
BEGIN
  -- loop through all blocks
  LOOP
        -- Loop through all items
        v_item_name := get_block_property (v_block_name,first_item);
        LOOP
              IF
get_item_property(v_block_name||'.'||v_item_name,item_type) =
                      'TEXT ITEM' and

get_item_property(v_block_name||'.'||v_item_name,hint_text) =
                                '$$HIDDEN_ITEM$$' THEN

set_item_property(v_block_name||'.'||v_item_name,
                                Visible, property_false);
                END IF;
                -- get next item
                v_item_name := get_item_property
                        (v_block_name||'.'||v_item_name, NextItem);
                -- exit if no more items
                EXIT WHEN v_item_name is null;
        END LOOP;        -- end of item loop
        -- get next block
        v_block_name := get_block_property (v_block_name,
NextBlock);
        -- exit if no more blocks
        EXIT WHEN v_block_name is null;
  END LOOP;                        -- end of block loop
  --
  -- return to the original cursor location
  go_item(v_original_cursor_item);           -- return to the
original block
  go_record(v_original_top_record);          -- return to the
original top record
  go_record(v_original_cursor_record);       -- return to the
original record
  go_item(v_original_cursor_item);           -- return to the
original item
END;
```

Running a progress bar

```
/* ---- Plsql/Update_progress.sql ------- */
PROCEDURE update_progress
    (p_progress in number, p_max in number default 100) IS
BEGIN

set_item_property('progress_block.progress',width,p_progress*250/p_m
ax);
  set_item_property('progress_block.progress',
                    label,to_char((p_progress/p_max)*100)||'%');
  synchronize;
END;
```

Preparing database text for MS Word macro

```
/* ----- Plsql/Headline_tag.sql ------- */
function HeadlineTag (
    p_headline in varchar2,
    p_level in number default 1,
    p_product in varchar2 default 'MSWORD') is
begin
    return(
        p_product||'$HEADLINE_'||to_char(p_level)||'_BEGIN'||
        p_headline||
        p_product||'$HEADLINE_'||to_char(p_level)||'_END');
end;
```

Chapter 12: Using Oracle8 Objects in Forms

The code that follows relates to Chapter 12.

Package to access Objects in forms

```
/* -------Plsql_objects/BOOK_HANDLING_PKG.sql ---- */
/* -------PACKAGE BOOK_HANDLING -------------------- */
CREATE OR REPLACE PACKAGE BOOK_HANDLING IS
    TYPE V_BOOK_REC IS RECORD
        (R_BOOK_ID NUMBER(10),
         R_BOOK_TITLE VARCHAR2(100),
         R_LOAN_DATE DATE,
```

```
        R_FINE NUMBER(5,2));
    TYPE BOOK_TBL IS TABLE OF V_BOOK_REC INDEX BY BINARY_INTEGER;
PROCEDURE GET_BORROWED_BOOKS
(
I_PERSON_ID          IN NUMBER,
O_BOOK_LIST          IN OUT BOOK_TBL
);
PROCEDURE LOAN_A_BOOK
(
I_PERSON_ID          IN NUMBER,
O_BOOK_LIST          IN OUT BOOK_TBL
);
PROCEDURE UPDATE_BOOK
(
I_PERSON_ID          IN NUMBER,
O_BOOK_LIST          IN OUT BOOK_TBL
);
PROCEDURE DELETE_BOOK
(
I_PERSON_ID          IN NUMBER,
O_BOOK_LIST          IN OUT BOOK_TBL
);

PROCEDURE LOCK_TABLE
(
I_PERSON_ID          IN NUMBER,
O_BOOK_LIST          IN OUT BOOK_TBL
);

END BOOK_HANDLING;
/
SHOW ERRORS PACKAGE BOOK_HANDLING;

/* ------------- PACKAGE BODY--------------------- */
CREATE OR REPLACE PACKAGE BODY BOOK_HANDLING  AS
    V_BOOK_LIST BOOK_TBL;
    V_PERSON_BK_LOANED BOOKS_LOAN_LIST_T;
    V_BOOK_LOANED BOOK_LOANED_T;
    V_BOOK BOOKS_T;
    V_REF_BOOK REF BOOKS_T;
PROCEDURE GET_BORROWED_BOOKS
(
I_PERSON_ID          IN NUMBER,
O_BOOK_LIST          IN OUT BOOK_TBL
```

```
) IS
BEGIN
   /* ---- REMOVE INCOMING (OLD) BOOK LIST -- */
   FOR V_CNT IN 1..O_BOOK_LIST.COUNT LOOP
       O_BOOK_LIST.DELETE(V_CNT);
   END LOOP;
   /* ----- GET CURRENT BOOK LIST -- */
BEGIN
   SELECT P.PERSON_BK_LOANED
      INTO V_PERSON_BK_LOANED
   FROM PERSON_TABLE_T P
   WHERE P.PERSON_ID = I_PERSON_ID;
   EXCEPTION
      WHEN NO_DATA_FOUND THEN
           V_PERSON_BK_LOANED := BOOKS_LOAN_LIST_T(NULL);
END;
FOR V_COUNTER IN 1..V_PERSON_BK_LOANED.COUNT LOOP
       /* --LOOP THROUGH EACH ROW IN THE NESTED TABLE.*/
       V_BOOK_LOANED := V_PERSON_BK_LOANED(V_COUNTER);
       V_REF_BOOK := V_BOOK_LOANED.BOOK_ID;
      /* ------- USE DEREF TO RETRIEVE THE
                   BOOK_TABLE_T ROW THAT IS REFERENCED
                   ------------------------ */
       SELECT DEREF(V_REF_BOOK) INTO V_BOOK
       FROM DUAL;
      /* -- ADDS THE BOOK ID INTO THE OUTPUT TABLE. --*/
       V_BOOK_LIST(V_COUNTER).R_BOOK_ID := V_BOOK.BOOK_ID;
       V_BOOK_LIST(V_COUNTER).R_BOOK_TITLE := V_BOOK.BOOK_TITLE;
       V_BOOK_LIST(V_COUNTER).R_LOAN_DATE :=
V_BOOK_LOANED.LOAN_DATE;
       V_BOOK_LIST(V_COUNTER).R_FINE := V_BOOK_LOANED.FINE;
END LOOP;
   O_BOOK_LIST := V_BOOK_LIST;
   RETURN;
END GET_BORROWED_BOOKS;


PROCEDURE LOAN_A_BOOK
(
I_PERSON_ID           IN NUMBER,
O_BOOK_LIST           IN OUT BOOK_TBL
)
AS
BEGIN
/* --- INSERT ROWS INTO BOOK LOANED NESTED TABLE ---- */
```

```
FOR V_COUNTER IN 1..O_BOOK_LIST.COUNT LOOP
    INSERT INTO THE(
    SELECT A.PERSON_BK_LOANED
    FROM PERSON_TABLE_T A
    WHERE A.PERSON_ID = I_PERSON_ID
    )
    SELECT REF(C),
    O_BOOK_LIST(V_COUNTER).R_LOAN_DATE,
    O_BOOK_LIST(V_COUNTER).R_FINE
    FROM BOOK_TABLE_T C
    WHERE C.BOOK_ID = O_BOOK_LIST(V_COUNTER).R_BOOK_ID;
END LOOP;
/* ----------- RETURN NULL TABLE -------- */
    FOR V_CNT IN 1..O_BOOK_LIST.COUNT LOOP
        O_BOOK_LIST.DELETE(V_CNT);
    END LOOP;
END LOAN_A_BOOK;
/* ---------- PROCEDURE LOCK_TABLE --------------- */
PROCEDURE LOCK_TABLE
(
I_PERSON_ID         IN NUMBER,
O_BOOK_LIST         IN OUT BOOK_TBL
)
IS
BEGIN
/* ------------- LOCK TABLE. ----------- */
LOCK TABLE PERSON_TABLE_T IN SHARE UPDATE MODE;
END LOCK_TABLE;
/* ---------- PROCEDURE UPDATE_BOOK --------------- */

PROCEDURE UPDATE_BOOK
(
I_PERSON_ID         IN NUMBER,
O_BOOK_LIST         IN OUT BOOK_TBL
)
IS
BEGIN
DECLARE
    V_X VARCHAR2(1);
BEGIN
    SELECT 'X' INTO V_X FROM DUAL;
END;
END UPDATE_BOOK;
/* -------- PROCEDURE DELETE_BOOK --------------- */
```

```
PROCEDURE DELETE_BOOK
(
I_PERSON_ID          IN NUMBER,
O_BOOK_LIST          IN OUT BOOK_TBL
)
IS
BEGIN
DECLARE
V_REF_BOOK REF BOOKS_T;
V_BOOK_RESERVED BOOK_LOANED_T;
V_PERSON_BK_LOANED BOOKS_LOAN_LIST_T;
V_ID NUMBER;
V_BOOK_ID NUMBER(10);
V_BOOK BOOKS_T;
V_DELETE_BOOK_SUBSCRIPT NUMBER;
CURSOR C1 IS
SELECT A.PERSON_ID, A.PERSON_BK_LOANED
      FROM PERSON_TABLE_T A
      WHERE PERSON_ID = I_PERSON_ID
      FOR UPDATE;
BEGIN
/* -- OUTER LOOP IS INCOMING TABLE OF DELETED BOOKS -- */
FOR V_DELCOUNTER IN 1..O_BOOK_LIST.COUNT LOOP
    V_BOOK_ID := O_BOOK_LIST(V_DELCOUNTER).R_BOOK_ID;
    V_DELETE_BOOK_SUBSCRIPT := -1;
    /* --INNER LOOP IS CURRENT PERSON
         (LOOPS ONE TIME) -- */
    FOR C1REC IN C1 LOOP
        V_PERSON_BK_LOANED := C1REC.PERSON_BK_LOANED;
        /* ---THIRD LOOP IS LIST OF BORROWED BOOKS --- */
        FOR V_COUNTER IN 1..V_PERSON_BK_LOANED.COUNT LOOP
            V_BOOK_RESERVED :=
              V_PERSON_BK_LOANED(V_COUNTER);
            V_REF_BOOK := V_BOOK_RESERVED.BOOK_ID;
            SELECT DEREF(V_REF_BOOK) INTO V_BOOK
              FROM DUAL;
            IF V_BOOK.BOOK_ID = V_BOOK_ID  THEN
                /* ---- SAVE THE SUBSCRIPT FOR
                        THIS BOOK -------- */
                V_DELETE_BOOK_SUBSCRIPT := V_COUNTER;
            END IF;
        END LOOP;
        IF V_DELETE_BOOK_SUBSCRIPT > 0 THEN
            V_PERSON_BK_LOANED.DELETE(V_DELETE_BOOK_SUBSCRIPT);
```

```
                    UPDATE PERSON_TABLE_T
                    SET PERSON_BK_LOANED = V_PERSON_BK_LOANED
                    WHERE CURRENT OF C1;
            END IF;
        END LOOP;
    END LOOP;
/* ----------- RETURN NULL TABLE -------- */
    FOR V_CNT IN 1..O_BOOK_LIST.COUNT LOOP
        O_BOOK_LIST.DELETE(V_CNT);
    END LOOP;
END DELETE_BOOKS;
END;
END;
/
SHOW ERRORS
```

Chapter 14: Report Builder and Web Reports

The code that follows relates to Chapter 14.

Function to add values from nested table

```
/* ------- Plsql_objects/Book_fine.sql --------- */
CREATE OR REPLACE FUNCTION BOOK_FINE
(I_PERSON_ID IN NUMBER)
RETURN NUMBER
IS
BEGIN
DECLARE
V_PERSON_BK_LOANED BOOKS_LOAN_LIST_T;
V_TOTAL_FINE NUMBER;
BEGIN
/* ------------- READ IN LOANED LIST ------------ */
BEGIN
    SELECT P.PERSON_BK_LOANED
    INTO V_PERSON_BK_LOANED
    FROM PERSON_TABLE_T P
    WHERE P.PERSON_ID = I_PERSON_ID;
  EXCEPTION
```

```
    WHEN NO_DATA_FOUND THEN
          V_TOTAL_FINE := 0;
          RETURN V_TOTAL_FINE;
END;
V_TOTAL_FINE := 0;
FOR V_COUNTER IN 1..V_PERSON_BK_LOANED.COUNT LOOP
     /* -- Add each new fine to the current total. --- */
      V_TOTAL_FINE  := NVL(V_PERSON_BK_LOANED(V_COUNTER).FINE,0) +
V_TOTAL_FINE;
END LOOP;
RETURN V_TOTAL_FINE;
END;
END;
/
show errors
```

Function to get one row from a varray

```
/* ------- Plsql/Home_phone.sql --------- */
CREATE OR REPLACE FUNCTION HOME_PHONE
(I_PERSON_ID IN NUMBER)
RETURN VARCHAR2
IS
begin
declare
V_PHONE VARCHAR2(20) := 'No home phone';
V_PHONE_LIST PHONE_LIST_T;
begin
SELECT PERSON_PHONE INTO V_PHONE_LIST
FROM PERSON_TABLE_T
WHERE PERSON_ID = I_PERSON_ID;
FOR V_COUNTER IN 1..V_PHONE_LIST.COUNT LOOP
  IF V_PHONE_LIST(V_COUNTER).PHONE_TYPE = 'HOME' THEN
      V_PHONE := V_PHONE_LIST(V_COUNTER).PHONE_NUMBER;
      EXIT;
  END IF;
END LOOP;
RETURN V_PHONE;
END;
END;
/
```

Chapter 18: Fast Graphics

The code that follows relates to Chapter 15.

Trigger to get last WHERE clause

```
/* -------- Forms/save_where_clause.sql --- */
/* placed in the KEY-EXEQRY trigger in the TOYCALLSFORM form. ----
*/
begin
execute_query;
/* Save the WHERE clause to build the chart */
IF instr(:system.last_query,'WHERE')= 0 then
    :CTRL.STORE_WHERE_CLAUSE := NULL;
ELSE
    :CTRL.STORE_WHERE_CLAUSE :=
      substr(:system.last_query,instr(:system.last_query,'WHERE'));
END IF;
end;
```

Send query from form to chart

```
/* ---- Forms/Load_query.sql ----- */
PROCEDURE LOAD_QUERY IS
BEGIN
DECLARE
parmlist  PARAMLIST;
recgroup  RECORDGROUP;
chartqry    VARCHAR(2000);
returncode   NUMBER;
grp_name VARCHAR(40) := 'CHARTQRY';
BEGIN
OG.CLOSE('valuechart','chartblk.chart_o_values');
/*Prepare a query in a string based on the last
 **WHERE clause issued.*/
chartqry := 'select ts.store_id, ts.store_name,  '
        || ' sum(nvl(sale_price,0)* '
        || ' nvl(current_stock_count,0)) TOTAL_VALUE '
        || ' from toy_store ts, '
        || ' store_stock ss '
        || ' where ts.store_id = ss.store_id '
        || ' and ts.store_id in '
        || ' (select store_id from toy_store '
        || :CTRL.STORE_WHERE_CLAUSE || ')'
        || ' group by ts.store_id, ts.store_name '
```

```
            || ' order by ts.store_id, ts.store_name';
recgroup := Find_Group( 'chart_group' );
IF Id_Null(recgroup) THEN
        recgroup := CREATE_GROUP_FROM_QUERY('chart_group',
chartqry);
        returncode := POPULATE_GROUP_WITH_QUERY
                        (recgroup, chartqry);
ELSE
    /* clear out and repopulate it based on
       the new query*/
    DELETE_GROUP('chart_group');
    recgroup := CREATE_GROUP_FROM_QUERY
                ('chart_group', chartqry);
    returncode := POPULATE_GROUP_WITH_QUERY
                (recgroup, chartqry);
END IF;
break;
/*Now create a parameter list*/

/*Add a data parameter with the same name
    as the query in the display*/
Add_Parameter(parmlist,'toystorecompare',
            DATA_PARAMETER,'chart_group');
/* Open display with the new data*/
OG.OPEN('valuechart', 'CHARTBLK.CHART_O_VALUES',
        TRUE, TRUE, parmlist);
/* Destroy the parameter list*/
DESTROY_PARAMETER_LIST('pl_chart_data');
END;
END;
```

Trigger to import image from filesystem

```
/* ----- Graphics/Format_trigger.sql -------- */
-- Chart Element Format trigger. Called for each member of a
-- specified chart element group (e.g., each bar in a group of
-- bars for a bar chart).
-- ARGUMENTS:
--   ELEM   The current chart element.
--   QUERY  The query associated with this chart. The current
--          row of the query is the one associated with ELEM.
--          Use OG_GET_xxxCELL to get at column values for the
--          current row.
PROCEDURE OGFORMATTRIGO(elem IN og_object,
```

```
                              query IN og_query) IS
BEGIN
DECLARE
image_name VARCHAR2(30);     -- file name of the image
image_pic OG_OBJECT;         -- image itself as an object
Location_point OG_POINT;     -- x,y coordinates

BEGIN
IMAGE_NAME := OG_GET_CHARCELL(query,'FLAG_IMAGE');
IMAGE_PIC := OG_Import_Image(IMAGE_NAME, OG_Filesystem,
     OG_Gif_Iformat);
LOCATION_POINT.X := (.1*OG_INCH);
LOCATION_POINT.Y := (4.2*OG_INCH);
OG_MOVE(IMAGE_PIC,LOCATION_POINT);
END;
END;
```

Button on chart calls report

```
/* ------ Graphics/Button_calls_report.sql ------ */
PROCEDURE OGBUTTONPROCO (buttonobj IN og_object,
                         hitobj IN og_object,
                         win IN og_window,
                         eventinfo IN og_event) IS
BEGIN
declare
piechart_in og_object;     -- the chart
piequery    OG_QUERY; -- the query for the chart
rows_count number;         -- use to save total number of rows in the
qeury
row_num number;            -- use to store the current row number
V_STORE_ID NUMBER;  -- variable for STORE_ID
rep_list  tool_int.paramlist;  -- parameter list sent to the report
begin
/* ------------ explode current pie slice ------ */
   piechart_in := OG_GET_OBJECT ('piechart');
   piequery := OG_GET_QUERY ('toystorecompare');
   OG_EXECUTE_QUERY(piequery);
rows_count := OG_NUMROWS(piequery, OG_NEWDATA);
   OG_START_FROM(piequery, OG_NEWDATA, 0);
        FOR I IN 0 .. rows_count -1 LOOP
            V_STORE_ID := OG_GET_NUMCELL
                piequery, OG_NEWDATA, 'STORE_ID');
            IF V_STORE_ID = :P_STORE_ID THEN
```

```
            row_num := i;
            exit;
         END IF;
         OG_NEXT_ROW(piequery, OG_NEWDATA);
      END LOOP;
 OG_Set_Explosion(piechart_in, row_num,
                 'TOTAL_VALUE', 25);
OG_UPDATE_CHART(piechart_in, OG_ALL_CHUPDA);
/* ----------- call a report now ---------- */
/*call Report Builder to display the report*/
/*add the USERID executable option to the list  */
  rep_list:=TOOL_INT.CREATE_PARAMETER_LIST('list2');
TOOL_INT.ADD_PARAMETER (rep_list, 'userid',
       TOOL_INT.TEXT_PARAMETER, 'TOYSTORE/TOYSTORE');
/*add the STORE_ID parameter to the list */
  TOOL_INT.ADD_PARAMETER (rep_list, 'P_STORE_ID',
       TOOL_INT.TEXT_PARAMETER, :P_STORE_ID);
/*call Report Builder batch mode to print the report*/
  TOOL_INT.RUN_PRODUCT(TOOL_INT.REPORTS, 'toyinv.rdf',
       TOOL_INT.SYNCHRONOUS, TOOL_INT.RUNTIME,
       TOOL_INT.FILESYSTEM,rep_list);
TOOL_INT.DESTROY_PARAMETER_LIST('list2');
END;
END;
```

Chapter 16: Procedure Builder

The code that follows relates to Chapter 16.

Function to update tool tip

```
/* ---- Forms/tooptip.sql ----- */
FUNCTION DOIT
(ITEMNAME IN varchar) RETURN VARCHAR2 IS
BEGIN
  declare
      v_tooltip varchar2(50);
  begin
   IF ITEMNAME = 'TOY_ID' THEN
       V_TOOLTIP := ' Unique ID ';
ELSIF ITEMNAME = 'TOY_NAME' THEN
       V_TOOLTIP := ' Name ';
ELSIF ITEMNAME = 'TOY_DESC' THEN
```

```
                    V_TOOLTIP := ' Description ';
ELSIF ITEMNAME = 'SHELF_CATEGORY' THEN
        V_TOOLTIP :=
' Location for shelving this item in the store ';
ELSIF ITEMNAME = 'WHOLESALE_COST' THEN
        V_TOOLTIP := ' Cost to the home office (per unit) ';
ELSIF ITEMNAME = 'SUGGESTED_RETAIL_PRICE' THEN
        V_TOOLTIP :=
         ' Suggested Retail Price -- usually too high ';
ELSIF ITEMNAME = 'TOY_PHOTO' THEN
        V_TOOLTIP := ' File name of photograph of toy ';
ELSIF ITEMNAME = 'OUT_OF_BUSINESS_FLAG' THEN
        V_TOOLTIP := ' Y = closed; N = in business ';
ELSIF ITEMNAME = 'STORE_ID' THEN
        V_TOOLTIP := ' Unique id for each store ';
ELSIF ITEMNAME = 'STORE_STATE' THEN
        V_TOOLTIP := ' Two digit state, such as NY ';
ELSIF ITEMNAME = 'STORE_NAME' THEN
        V_TOOLTIP := ' Store name (40 chars max) ';
ELSE  V_TOOLTIP := 'Where am I?';
END IF;
return V_TOOLTIP;
  end;
END;
```

Trigger to reset tool tip text

```
/* ----- Forms/load_tool_tip.sql ---- */
begin
declare
V_TIP varchar2(100);
V_FIRST_ITEM VARCHAR2(30);
begin
   V_FIRST_ITEM := :SYSTEM.CURRENT_ITEM;
LOOP
   V_TIP := DOIT(:SYSTEM.CURRENT_ITEM);
   set_item_property(:SYSTEM.CURRENT_ITEM,TOOLTIP_TEXT,V_TIP);
 IF GET_ITEM_PROPERTY(:SYSTEM.CURRENT_ITEM,NEXTITEM) IS NULL THEN
      GO_FIELD(V_FIRST_ITEM);
      EXIT;
   ELSE
      GO_FIELD(GET_ITEM_PROPERTY(:SYSTEM.CURRENT_ITEM,NEXTITEM));
   END IF;
END LOOP;
end;
end;
```

Chapter 17: ActiveX and Forms

The code that follows relates to Chapter 17.

Send table as variant to ActiveX

```
/* ------ Forms/variant.sql ---- */
DECLARE

  control    OleObj;
  record number;

    /* Table */
  type    sample_table_type is
    table of  database_tbl%type index by binary_integer;
  sample_table    sample_table_type;
  cursor    sample_cursor  is
  select * from  database_tbl;

BEGIN

  control := :item('ActiveX').interface;

  /* Load Table */
  record := 0;
  open  sample_cursor;
     loop
         record := record + 1;
         fetch  sample_cursor into sample_table(record);
         exit when sample_cursor%NOTFOUND;
     end loop;
  close  sample_cursor;

ATLMYCONTROL..SetTable(control, o_variant(sample_table));

END;
```

Chapter 18: Practical Applications Libraries, Menus, and Tab Canvases

The code that follows relates to Chapter 18.

Set menu item attributes

```
/* ---- Forms/Idnull.sql ----- */
DECLARE
V_MENU_ITEM_ID MENUITEM;
BEGIN
V_MENU_ITEM_ID := FIND_MENU_ITEM('DEPTAMNU.SAVERECORD');
/* ----- check for item: does it exist. --- */
IF NOT(ID_NULL(V_MENU_ITEM_ID)) THEN
        /* ------- set VISIBLE to FALSE ----- */
        SET_MENU_ITEM_PROPERTY
          (V_MENU_ITEM_ID, VISIBLE, PROPERTY_FALSE);
END IF;
END;
```

Chapter 19: PL/SQL and HTML Extensions

The code that follows relates to Chapter 19.

Procedure that creates HTML page

```
/* ------ Web/stores.sql ------- */
CREATE OR REPLACE PROCEDURE STORES AS
BEGIN
/* ----------- DECLARE SECTION ----------------- */
DECLARE
 V_WEB_PAGE_NAME VARCHAR2(30) := 'STORES';
V_ELEMENT_TYPE VARCHAR2(10);
V_TEMPLATE_HTML VARCHAR2(2000);
/* ---- get a template element as needed
        to build the web page. --- */
CURSOR GETELEMENT  IS
    SELECT HTML_CODE
    FROM PAGE_TEMPLATE PT,
             PAGE_ELEMENT PE
    WHERE PT.ELEMENT_NAME = PE.ELEMENT_NAME
     AND    PE.WEB_PAGE = V_WEB_PAGE_NAME
     AND    PT.ELEMENT_TYPE = V_ELEMENT_TYPE;
/* ---- get all stores, sorted by state
        and store name --- */
```

```
CURSOR C1 IS
    SELECT STORE_ID, STORE_NAME, STATE_ABBR
    FROM TOY_STORE
    ORDER BY STATE_ABBR, STORE_NAME;
/* ---------------------- BODY OF PROCEDURE ---- */
BEGIN
/* ---------- HEAD ---------- */
    V_ELEMENT_TYPE := 'HEAD';
    OPEN GETELEMENT;
    FETCH GETELEMENT INTO V_TEMPLATE_HTML;
    CLOSE GETELEMENT;
    HTP.PRINT(V_TEMPLATE_HTML);
/* --- begin custom code for web page heading here --- */
            HTP.PRINT('<H2>Choose one store by clicking on the Store
ID#</H2>');
/* --- end custom code for web page heading here ---- */
/* ---------- BODY ---------- */
    V_ELEMENT_TYPE := 'BODY';
    OPEN GETELEMENT;
    FETCH GETELEMENT INTO V_TEMPLATE_HTML;
    CLOSE GETELEMENT;
    HTP.PRINT(V_TEMPLATE_HTML);
/* --- begin custom code for web page body here ---- */
HTP.PRINT('<FORM ACTION="stock.htm" METHOD=POST>');
HTP.PRINT('<TABLE BORDER=4 BGCOLOR="3300FF">');
HTP.PRINT('<TR>');
HTP.PRINT('          <TD>State</TD>');
HTP.PRINT('          <TD>Store#</TD>');
HTP.PRINT('          <TD>Store Name</TD>');
HTP.PRINT('</TR>');
/* ---- loop through all store records here ------ */
FOR CREC IN C1 LOOP
    /* --- print one HTML table row --- */
    HTP.PRINT('<TR>');
    HTP.PRINT('<TD>' || SREC.STATE_ABBR || '</TD>');
    HTP.PRINT('<TD>' || SREC.STORE_ID || '</TD>');
    HTP.PRINT('<TD>' || SREC.STORE_NAME || '</TD>');
    HTP.PRINT('</TR>');
END LOOP;
        HTP.PRINT('</TABLE>');
/* ---- end custom code for web page body here ------- */
/* ---------- FOOT template ---------- */
    V_ELEMENT_TYPE := 'FOOT';
    OPEN GETELEMENT;
```

```
        FETCH GETELEMENT INTO V_TEMPLATE_HTML;
        CLOSE GETELEMENT;
HTP.PRINT(V_TEMPLATE_HTML);
EXCEPTION WHEN OTHERS THEN
        DBMS_OUTPUT.PUT_LINE('Error encountered in STORES procedure:' ||
             SQLERRNO || ' ' || SQLERRMSG);
END;
END;
```

Procedure that creates HTML page using parameters

```
/* ---- Web/Stock.sql ----- */
CREATE OR REPLACE PROCEDURE STOCK AS
(I_STORE_ID IN NUMBER, I_STORE_NAME IN VARCHAR2)
V_WEB_PAGE_NAME VARCHAR2(30) := 'STOCK';
/* ---- get all stock for one store,
        sorted by toy name --- */
CURSOR C1 IS
    SELECT TOY_ID, TOY_NAME, TOY_DESCRIPTION
    FROM STORE_STOCK SS,
             TOY_INVENTORY TI
    WHERE SS.TOY_ID = TI.TOY_ID
    ORDER BY TOY_NAME;
HTP.PRINT('<H2>Choose one Toy by clicking on the Toy ID#</H2>');
HTP.PRINT('<H3> Store# ' || I_STORE_ID || I_STORE_NAME
         || '</H3>');
/* --- begin custom code for web page body here ----- */
HTP.PRINT('<FORM ACTION="updtoy.htm" METHOD=POST>');
HTP.PRINT('<TABLE BORDER=4 BGCOLOR="3300FF">');
HTP.PRINT('<TR>');
HTP.PRINT('         <TD> Toy#</TD>');
HTP.PRINT('         <TD>Toy Name</TD>');
HTP.PRINT('         <TD>Description</TD>');
HTP.PRINT('</TR>');
/* ---- loop through all toy records here ------ */
FOR CREC IN C1 LOOP
     /* --- print one HTML table row --- */
    HTP.PRINT('<TR>');
    HTP.PRINT('<TD>' || CREC.TOY_ID || '</TD>');
    HTP.PRINT('<TD>' || CREC.TOY_NAME || '</TD>');
    HTP.PRINT('<TD>' || CREC.TOY_DESC || '</TD>');
    HTP.PRINT('</TR>');
END LOOP;
```

```
HTP.PRINT('</TABLE>');
/* ---- end custom code for web page body here ------- */
END;
END;
```

Procedure to create HTML Update page

```
/* ----- Web/Updtoy.sql ---- */
CREATE OR REPLACE PROCEDURE UPDTOY AS
BEGIN
DECLARE
CURSOR V1 IS
SELECT COLUMN_ID,
               ATC.COLUMN_NAME,
               DATA_TYPE,
               DATA_LENGTH,
       DATA_PRECISION,
       DATA_SCALE,
               NULLABLE, UCC.COLUMN_NAME PRIMARY_KEY_COLUMN
     FROM ALL_TAB_COLUMNS ATC,
        USER_CONSTRAINTS UC,
        USER_CONS_COLUMNS UCC
    WHERE ATC.TABLE_NAME = 'STORE_STOCK'
     AND UC.CONSTRAINT_TYPE(+) = 'P'
     AND    UCC.CONSTRAINT_NAME = UC.CONSTRAINT_NAME(+)
     AND    UCC.TABLE_NAME(+) = ATC.TABLE_NAME
     AND    UCC.COLUMN_NAME (+) = ATC.COLUMN_NAME
    ORDER BY COLUMN_ID;
BEGIN
/* ---- loop through all columns here ------ */
FOR VREC IN V1 LOOP
    /* --- print one HTML table row --- */
    HTP.PRINT('<TR>');
    HTP.PRINT('<TD>' || VREC.COLUMN_NAME || '</TD>');
    HTP.PRINT('<TD>');
    /* --- handle primary key column -------- */
    IF PRIMARY_KEY_COLUMN IS NOT NULL THEN
            HTP.PRINT(V_COLARRAY(COLUMN_ID));
    ELSE
        IF COLUMN_TYPE = 'DATE' then
            /* --- handle DATE TYPE column --------- */
            HTP.PRINT('<INPUT TYPE=TEXT SIZE=10' ||
                  'MAXLENGTH=9' ||
                  'NAME="'|| COLUMN_NAME ||
```

```
                              '" VALUE="' ||
                              V_COLARRAY(COLUMN_ID) || '" >');
               ELSIF COLUMN_TYPE = 'NUMBER' then
                  /* --- handle NUMBER TYPE column --------- */
                  HTP.PRINT('<INPUT TYPE=TEXT SIZE=' ||
                  DATA_PRECISION + NVL(DATA_SCALE) +3 || '" ' ||
                     'MAXLENGTH="' ||
                  DATA_PRECISION + NVL(DATA_SCALE) +2 || '" ' ||
                     'NAME="'|| COLUMN_NAME ||
                     '" VALUE="' ||
                     V_COLARRAY(COLUMN_ID) || '" >');
               ELSIF COLUMN_LENGTH < 66 THEN
                  /* --- handle TEXT TYPE column less than
                         65 characters --------- */
                  HTP.PRINT('<INPUT TYPE=TEXT SIZE=' ||
                     DATA_LENGTH + 1 || '" ' ||
                     'MAXLENGTH="' ||
                     DATA_LENGTH || '" ' ||
                     'NAME="'|| COLUMN_NAME ||
                     '" VALUE="' ||
                     V_COLARRAY(COLUMN_ID) || '" >');
               ELSE
                  /* --- handle TEXT TYPE column more than
                         65 characters --------- */
                  HTP.PRINT('<INPUT TYPE=TEXTAREA COLS="' ||
                     ROUND((DATA_LENGTH + 1) /65)+1 || '" ' ||
                     'ROWS=65 ||
                     'MAXLENGTH="' ||
                     DATA_LENGTH || '" ' ||
                     'NAME="'|| COLUMN_NAME ||
                     '" VALUE="' ||
                     V_COLARRAY(COLUMN_ID) || '" >');
               END IF;
          END IF;
          HTP.PRINT('</TD>' );
          HTP.PRINT('</TR>');
     END LOOP;
     HTP.PRINT('<INPUT TYPE="RADIO" NAME="SELECT_ACTION" ' ||
               'CHECKED VALUE="Update">');
     HTP.PRINT('<INPUT TYPE="RADIO" NAME="SELECT_ACTION" ' ||
               'VALUE="Delete">');
     HTP.PRINT('<P><INPUT TYPE=SUBMIT VALUE="Finish">');
     HTP.PRINT('</FORM>');
     END;
END;
```

Procedure that creates HTML Insert page

```
/* ----- Web/Instoy.sql ---- */
CREATE OR REPLACE PROCEDURE UPDTOY AS
BEGIN
DECLARE
CURSOR V1 IS
SELECT COLUMN_ID,
                ATC.COLUMN_NAME,
                DATA_TYPE,
                DATA_LENGTH,
        DATA_PRECISION,
        DATA_SCALE,
                NULLABLE, UCC.COLUMN_NAME PRIMARY_KEY_COLUMN
      FROM ALL_TAB_COLUMNS ATC,
        USER_CONSTRAINTS UC,
        USER_CONS_COLUMNS UCC
    WHERE ATC.TABLE_NAME = 'STORE_STOCK'
     AND UC.CONSTRAINT_TYPE(+) = 'P'
     AND    UCC.CONSTRAINT_NAME = UC.CONSTRAINT_NAME(+)
     AND    UCC.TABLE_NAME(+) = ATC.TABLE_NAME
     AND    UCC.COLUMN_NAME (+) = ATC.COLUMN_NAME
    ORDER BY COLUMN_ID;
BEGIN
/* ---- loop through all columns here ------ */
FOR VREC IN V1 LOOP
    /* --- print one HTML table row --- */
    HTP.PRINT('<TR>');
    HTP.PRINT('<TD>' || VREC.COLUMN_NAME || '</TD>');
    HTP.PRINT('<TD>');
    /* --- handle primary key column -------- */
    IF PRIMARY_KEY_COLUMN IS NOT NULL THEN
          /* ------ assume that Database will assign the primary
key --- */
          HTP.PRINT(' ');
    ELSE
        IF COLUMN_TYPE = 'DATE' then
            /* --- handle DATE TYPE column --------- */
            HTP.PRINT('<INPUT TYPE=TEXT SIZE=10' ||
                'MAXLENGTH=9' ||
                'NAME="'|| COLUMN_NAME || '" >');
        ELSIF COLUMN_TYPE = 'NUMBER' then
            /* --- handle NUMBER TYPE column --------- */
            HTP.PRINT('<INPUT TYPE=TEXT SIZE=' ||
```

```
                    DATA_PRECISION + NVL(DATA_SCALE) +3 || '" ' ||
                    'MAXLENGTH="' ||
                    DATA_PRECISION + NVL(DATA_SCALE) +2 || '" ' ||
                    'NAME="'|| COLUMN_NAME || '" >');
            ELSIF COLUMN_LENGTH < 66 THEN
                /* --- handle TEXT TYPE column less than
                       65 characters --------- */
                HTP.PRINT('<INPUT TYPE=TEXT SIZE=' ||
                    DATA_LENGTH + 1 || '" ' ||
                    'MAXLENGTH="' ||
                    DATA_LENGTH || '" ' ||
                    'NAME="'|| COLUMN_NAME || '" >');
            ELSE
                /* --- handle TEXT TYPE column more than
                       65 characters --------- */
                HTP.PRINT('<INPUT TYPE=TEXTAREA COLS="' ||
                    ROUND((DATA_LENGTH + 1) /65)+1 || '" ' ||
                    'ROWS=65 ||
                    'MAXLENGTH="' ||
                    DATA_LENGTH || '" ' ||
                    'NAME="'|| COLUMN_NAME || '" >');
            END IF;
        END IF;
        HTP.PRINT('</TD>' );
        HTP.PRINT('</TR>');
END LOOP;
HTP.PRINT('<INPUT TYPE="RADIO" NAME="SELECT_ACTION" ' ||
          'CHECKED VALUE="Insert">');
HTP.PRINT('<P><INPUT TYPE=SUBMIT VALUE="Finish">');
HTP.PRINT('</FORM>');
END;
END;
```

Procedure to create HTML Commit Update/Delete page

```
/* ---- Web/Commit.sql ---- */
CREATE OR REPLACE PROCEDURE COMMITUPDTOY
(I_STORE_ID IN NUMBER, I_TOY_ID IN NUMBER,
  I_TOY_NAME IN VARCHAR2,
  I_TOY_DESC IN VARCHAR2, SELECT_ACTION IN VARCHAR2) IS
IF SELECT_ACTION = 'Update' THEN
    UPDATE STORE_STOCK
        SET TOY_NAME = I_TOY_NAME,
```

```
        TOY_NAME = I_TOY_NAME
    WHERE TOY_ID = I_TOY_ID
        AND STORE_ID = I_STORE_ID;
ELSIF SELECT_ACTION = 'Delete' THEN
    DELETE FROM STORE_STOCK
    WHERE TOY_ID = I_TOY_ID;
END IF;
COMMIT TRANSACTION;
      HTP.PRINT('Row for Toy# ' || I_TOY_ID || SELECT_ACTION ||
'ed.');
END;
```

Procedure to create HTML Commit Insert page

```
/* ---- Web/Commitins.sql ---- */
CREATE OR REPLACE PROCEDURE COMMITINSTOY
(I_STORE_ID IN NUMBER, I_TOY_ID IN NUMBER,
  I_TOY_NAME IN VARCHAR2,
  I_TOY_DESC IN VARCHAR2, SELECT_ACTION IN VARCHAR2) IS
IF SELECT_ACTION = 'Insert' THEN
INSERT INTO STORE_STOCK
VALUES
    (I_STORE_ID,
      I_TOY_ID,
      I_TOY_NAME,
      I_TOY_DESC);
END IF;
COMMIT TRANSACTION;
      HTP.PRINT('Row for Toy# ' || I_TOY_ID || SELECT_ACTION ||
'ed.');
END;
```

Chapter 21: Web Assistant

The code that follows relates to Chapter 21.

Customized template for Webassistant

```
/* ---- Webassistant/template.htx ---- */
<html>
<head>
<meta http-equiv="Content-Type" content="text/html">
<title>Database Information Page</title>
```

```
</head>
<body bgcolor="#CCFFFF">
<p align="center"><font size="5">Busy Bee Stores</font></p>
<p align="center"> </p>
<div align="center"><center>
 <table border="5" width="100%" BGCOLOR="FFFFFF">
<%begindetail%>
    <tr>
       <td width="15%" ALIGN=RIGHT><B>STORE ID</td>
       <td width="85%"><%STORE_ID%></td>
    </tr>
     <tr>
       <td width="15%" ALIGN=RIGHT><B>NAME</td>
       <td width="85%"><%STORE_NAME%></td>
    </tr>
     <tr>
       <td width="15%" ALIGN=RIGHT><B>STATE</td>
       <td width="85%"><%STORE_STATE%></td>
    </tr>
     <tr>
       <td COLSPAN="2" BGCOLOR="CCFFFF"> </td>
    </tr>
 <%enddetail%>
</table>
</center></div>
<p> </p>
</body>
</html>
```

Webassistant template for top drill-down page

```
/* --- Webassistant/Webstore.htx
QUERY that is needed for this template is:
       SELECT STORE_STATE state,
              STORE_ID storeid,
              STORE_NAME storename
       FROM TOY_STORE
                       ORDER BY STORE_STATE
--- */
<HTML><HEAD><TITLE>Busy Bee Toy Stores</TITLE></HEAD>
<BODY BGCOLOR="FFCCFF" >
<CENTER>
<H1>The Busy Bee Toy Store</H1>
<H2>Choose one store by clicking on the Store ID#</H2>
```

```
<TABLE BORDER=4 BGCOLOR="FFFFFF">
<TR>
        <TD><B>State</B></TD>
        <TD><B>Store#</B></TD>
        <TD><B>Store Name</B></TD>
</TR>
<%begindetail%>
<TR>
        <TD><%state%></TD>
        <TD><A
HREF="Webstock.htm#store<%storeid%>"><%storeid%></A></TD>
        <TD><%storename%></TD>
</TR>
<%enddetail%>
</TABLE>
</BODY>
</HTML>
```

Webassistant query for detail report

```
/* --- Webassistant/Webstock.sql
    Query for creating the Webstock report using Web Publishing
Assistant.
    Each column's alias is matched with the variable name in
Webstock.htx (template).
*/
SELECT SS.STORE_ID storeid,
       TS.STORE_NAME storename,
       SS.TOY_ID toyid,
       TI.TOY_NAME toyname,
       TI.SHELF_CATEGORY shelf,
       SS.CURRENT_STOCK_COUNT currstock,
       'Y' newstore,
       TI.TOY_DESC toydesc,
       TI.WHOLESALE_COST wholesale,
       TI.SUGGESTED_RETAIL_PRICE srp,
       SS.SALE_PRICE sale,
       SS.LAST_STOCK_DATE stockdate
FROM TOY_STORE TS,
     STORE_STOCK SS,
     TOY_INVENTORY TI
WHERE TS.STORE_ID = SS.STORE_ID
AND    TI.TOY_ID = SS.TOY_ID
AND    SS.TOY_ID = (SELECT MIN(TOY_ID)
```

```
                        FROM STORE_STOCK SS2
                        WHERE STORE_ID = SS.STORE_ID)
UNION
SELECT SS.STORE_ID storeid,
       TS.STORE_NAME storename,
       SS.TOY_ID toyid,
       TI.TOY_NAME toyname,
       TI.SHELF_CATEGORY shelf,
       SS.CURRENT_STOCK_COUNT currstock,
       'N' newstore,
       TI.TOY_DESC toydesc,
       TI.WHOLESALE_COST wholesale,
       TI.SUGGESTED_RETAIL_PRICE srp,
       SS.SALE_PRICE sale,
       SS.LAST_STOCK_DATE stockdate
FROM TOY_STORE TS,
     STORE_STOCK SS,
     TOY_INVENTORY TI
WHERE TS.STORE_ID = SS.STORE_ID
AND   TI.TOY_ID = SS.TOY_ID
AND   SS.TOY_ID <> (SELECT MIN(TOY_ID)
                        FROM STORE_STOCK SS2
                        WHERE STORE_ID = SS.STORE_ID)
ORDER BY 1,3
```

Webassistant detail report template

```
/* ---- Webassistant/Webstock.htx ----- */
<HTML><HEAD><TITLE> The Busy Bee Toy Store </TITLE></HEAD>
<BODY BGCOLOR="FFCCFF">
<CENTER>
<H1>The Busy Bee Toy Store</H1>
<H2>Choose one Toy by clicking on the Toy ID#</H2>
<%begindetail%>
    <%if newstore EQ Y%>
        </TABLE>
        <P>
        <A NAME="store<%storeid%>"><BR>
        <H3> Store# <%storeid%> <%storename%> </H3>
        <TABLE BORDER=4 BGCOLOR="FFFFFF">
        <TR>
                <TD>Toy ID#</TD>
                <TD>Toy Name</TD>
                <TD>Shelf Category</TD>
```

```
                <TD>Total Stock</TD>
            </TR>
        <%endif%>
<TR>
    <TD>
    <A
HREF="Webinv.htm#store<%storeid%>stock<%toyid%>"><%toyid%></A>
    </TD>
    <TD><%toyname%></TD>
    <TD><%shelf%></TD>
    <TD><%currstock%></TD>
</TR>
<%enddetail%>
</TABLE>
</CENTER>
</BODY>
</HTML>
```

Webassistant query for third level detail report

```
/* Webinv.sql
    Query for creating the Webinv report using Web Publishing
Assistant.
    Each column's alias is matched with the variable name in
Webinv.htx (template).
*/
SELECT SS.STORE_ID storeid,
       TS.STORE_NAME storename,
       SS.TOY_ID toyid,
       TI.TOY_NAME toyname,
       TI.SHELF_CATEGORY shelf,
       SS.CURRENT_STOCK_COUNT currstock,
       'Y' newstore,
       TI.TOY_DESC toydesc,
       TI.WHOLESALE_COST wholesale,
       TI.SUGGESTED_RETAIL_PRICE srp,
       SS.SALE_PRICE sale,
       SS.LAST_STOCK_DATE stockdate
FROM TOY_STORE TS,
     STORE_STOCK SS,
     TOY_INVENTORY TI
WHERE TS.STORE_ID = SS.STORE_ID
AND   TI.TOY_ID = SS.TOY_ID
AND   SS.TOY_ID = (SELECT MIN(TOY_ID)
```

```
                        FROM STORE_STOCK SS2
                        WHERE STORE_ID = SS.STORE_ID)
UNION
SELECT SS.STORE_ID storeid,
       TS.STORE_NAME storename,
       SS.TOY_ID toyid,
       TI.TOY_NAME toyname,
       TI.SHELF_CATEGORY shelf,
       SS.CURRENT_STOCK_COUNT currstock,
       'N' newstore,
       TI.TOY_DESC toydesc,
       TI.WHOLESALE_COST wholesale,
       TI.SUGGESTED_RETAIL_PRICE srp,
       SS.SALE_PRICE sale,
       SS.LAST_STOCK_DATE stockdate
FROM TOY_STORE TS,
     STORE_STOCK SS,
     TOY_INVENTORY TI
WHERE TS.STORE_ID = SS.STORE_ID
AND    TI.TOY_ID = SS.TOY_ID
AND    SS.TOY_ID <> (SELECT MIN(TOY_ID)
                        FROM STORE_STOCK SS2
                        WHERE STORE_ID = SS.STORE_ID)
ORDER BY 1,3
```

Webassistant template for third level detail report

```
/* ---- Webassistant/Webinv.htx ---- */
<HTML>
<TITLE>View Toy Stock Detail</TITLE>
<BODY BACKGROUND="bg1.gif" TEXT="000000" >
<CENTER>
<H3><I>The Busy Bee Toy Store</I>
<P>View Toy Stock
</CENTER>
<UL>
<UL>
<P><img src="line1.gif"></H3>
<UL>
<UL>
<UL>
<%begindetail%>
    <%if newstore EQ Y%>
            </TABLE>
        <P>
```

```
              <TABLE BORDER=4 BGCOLOR="FFCCFF" WIDTH=80%>
          <TR>
            <TD ALIGN=LEFT BGCOLOR="FF99FF" COLSPAN="2">
             <H2> Store: <%storeid%> - <%storename%> </H2>
              </TD>
          </TR>
      <%endif%>
<TR>
          <TD ALIGN=LEFT BGCOLOR="FF99FF" COLSPAN="2">
            <A NAME="store<%storeid%>stock<%toyid%>">
            <B>Toy ID#:<%toyid%> 
          </TD>
    </TR>
<TR>
        <TD ALIGN=RIGHT>Name:</B></TD>
          <TD BGCOLOR="FFFFFF"><%toyname%>  </TD>
    </TR>
    <TR>
        <TD ALIGN=RIGHT>Desc: </B></TD>
          <TD BGCOLOR="FFFFFF"><%toydesc%>  </TD>
    </TR>
    <TR>
        <TD ALIGN=RIGHT>Wholesale Cost: </TD>
        <TD BGCOLOR="FFFFFF"><%wholesale%>  </TD>
    </TR>
    <TR>
        <TD ALIGN=RIGHT>Suggested Retail Price:</B></TD>
          <TD BGCOLOR="FFFFFF"><%srp%>  </TD>
    </TR>
    <TR>
          <TD ALIGN=RIGHT>Sale Price: </B></TD>
          <TD BGCOLOR="FFFFFF"><%sale%>  </TD>
    </TR>
    <TR>
        <TD ALIGN=RIGHT>Last Stock Date: </B></TD>
          <TD BGCOLOR="FFFFFF"><%stockdate%>  </TD>
    </TR>
    <TR>
        <TD ALIGN=RIGHT>Current Stock Count: </B></TD>
          <TD BGCOLOR="FFFFFF"><%currstock%>  </TD>
    </TR>
<%enddetail%>
<P><img src="line1.gif">
</BODY>
</HTML>
```

Creating Oracle8 Objects for Sample Applications

Here is the SQL script for creating the Oracle8 objects used in the book. Run this in SQL Worksheet, SQL*Plus, or any tool that executes SQL. You must run this script while logged in as the owner of the objects.

Initiating the object types

```
-- CREATE OBJECTS AND TYPES AND OBJECT TABLES, NESTED TABLES .
--
--
/* ------------------------ Object Type    PERSON_T
        initial partial definition
*/
CREATE TYPE PERSON_T;
/* ---------------------- Object Type    BOOK_T
          initial partial definition
*/
CREATE TYPE BOOKS_T;
/* -------------------------- Object Type    NAME_T    */
CREATE TYPE NAME_T AS OBJECT(
FIRST_NAME  VARCHAR2(25),
LAST_NAME   VARCHAR2(25));
/* -------------------------- Object Type    ADDRESS_T    */
CREATE TYPE ADDRESS_T AS OBJECT(
STREET      VARCHAR2(50),
CITY        VARCHAR2(25),
STATE       VARCHAR2(2) ,
ZIP         NUMBER);
/* -------------------- Object Type    BOOK_LOANED_T    */
CREATE TYPE BOOK_LOANED_T AS OBJECT
(BOOK_ID         REF        BOOKS_T,
 LOAN_DATE       DATE,
 FINE            NUMBER(5,2)
);
/* -------------------- Object Type    BOOKS_RESERVED_T    */
CREATE TYPE BOOKS_RESERVED_T AS OBJECT
(PERSON_ID REF PERSON_T,
 WAIT_NO   INTEGER
);
/* --------------------- Object Type    RESERVED_LIST_T
          varray
```

```
*/
CREATE TYPE RESERVED_LIST_T AS
VARRAY(10) OF BOOKS_RESERVED_T;
/* -------------------------- Object Type     PHONE_T      */
CREATE TYPE PHONE_T AS OBJECT
(
PHONE_TYPE          VARCHAR2(20),
PHONE_NUMBER        VARCHAR2(20)
);
/* ---------------------- Object Type    PHONE_LIST_T
          varray
 */
CREATE TYPE PHONE_LIST_T AS
VARRAY(10) OF PHONE_T;
/* ------------------- Object Type    BOOKS_LOAN_LIST_T
          nested table
*/
CREATE TYPE BOOKS_LOAN_LIST_T AS
TABLE OF BOOK_LOANED_T;
```

Creating object table ADDRESS_TABLE_T

```
/* -------------------- Object Table    ADDRESS_TABLE_T
*/
CREATE TABLE ADDRESS_TABLE_T OF
ADDRESS_T;
/* ------------------ Object Table Index   IDX_ADDRESS_ZIP
CREATE INDEX IDX_ADDRESS_ZIP ON
ADDRESS_TABLE_T(ZIP);
```

Creating STUDENT table

```
/* ----------------------- Relational Table    STUDENT
*/
CREATE TABLE STUDENT
(
 STUDENT_ID              INTEGER       NOT NULL,
 STUDENT_FIRST_NAME    VARCHAR2(25)    NULL    ,
 STUDENT_LAST_NAME     VARCHAR2(25)    NULL    ,
  STUDENT_ADDRESS         ADDRESS_T,
 CONSTRAINT PK_PERSON_1 PRIMARY KEY (STUDENT_ID)
);
```

Completing object type definitions

```
/* ------------------------- Object Type    PERSON_T
            complete definition
 */
CREATE OR REPLACE TYPE PERSON_T AS OBJECT
(
    PERSON_ID           INTEGER,
    PERSON_NAME         NAME_T,
    PERSON_ADDRESS      ADDRESS_T,
    PERSON_PHONE        PHONE_LIST_T,
    PERSON_BK_LOANED    BOOKS_LOAN_LIST_T,
    PERSON_BL_STATUS    CHAR
);
/* ----------------------- Object Type    BOOKS_T
            complete definition
 */
CREATE OR REPLACE TYPE BOOKS_T AS OBJECT
(
    BOOK_ID             INTEGER,
    BOOK_PUBLISHER      VARCHAR2(50),
    BOOK_AUTHOR_NAME    NAME_T,
    BOOK_TITLE          VARCHAR2(100),
    BOOK_SUBJECT        VARCHAR2(50),
    BOOK_RESERVED_LIST  RESERVED_LIST_T
);
```

Creating PERSON_TABLE_T object table

```
/* -------------------- Object Table    PERSON_TABLE_T   */
CREATE TABLE PERSON_TABLE_T OF PERSON_T
(PRIMARY KEY(PERSON_ID))
NESTED TABLE PERSON_BK_LOANED
STORE AS BOOK_LOANS_TABLE;
```

Creating BOOK_TABLE_T object table

```
/* ----------------------- Object Table    BOOK_TABLE_T      */
CREATE TABLE BOOK_TABLE_T OF BOOKS_T
(PRIMARY KEY(BOOK_ID));
```

Adding data to BOOK_TABLE_T object table

```
/* ------------- Data for Object Tables --------------- */
```

```
INSERT INTO BOOK_TABLE_T VALUES
    (1,'IDG',
    NAME_t('Amy', 'Chandi'),
    'Rough Guide to Vancouver', 'Travel',
    RESERVED_LIST_t()
);
INSERT INTO BOOK_TABLE_T VALUES
    (2,'IDG',
    NAME_t('Iolani', 'Kalani'),
    'Hiking Maui', 'Travel',
    RESERVED_LIST_t()
);
INSERT INTO BOOK_TABLE_T VALUES
    (3,'SCIFI Press',
    NAME_t('Isaac', 'Asimov'),
    'Foundation', 'Science Fiction',
    RESERVED_LIST_t()
);
INSERT INTO BOOK_TABLE_T VALUES
    (4,'SCIFI Press',
    NAME_t('Isaac', 'Asimov'),
    'Best of Science Fiction', 'Science Fiction',
    RESERVED_LIST_t()
);
INSERT INTO BOOK_TABLE_T VALUES
    (5,'SCIFI Press',
    NAME_t('Ray', 'Bradbury'),
    'The Illustrated Man', 'Science Fiction',
    RESERVED_LIST_t()
);
INSERT INTO BOOK_TABLE_T VALUES
    (6,'Time Life',
    NAME_t('Joe', 'Banks'),
    'The Technical Drummer', 'Music',
    RESERVED_LIST_t()
);
INSERT INTO BOOK_TABLE_T VALUES
    (7,'Time Life',
    NAME_t('Joe', 'Dieter'),
    'Slide Guitar', 'Music',
    RESERVED_LIST_t()
);
```

Adding data to PERSON_TABLE_T object table

```
INSERT INTO PERSON_TABLE_t
VALUES
(1,
NAME_t('Tony', 'Prem'),
ADDRESS_t('11316 Jollyville','Austin', 'TX', 78759),
PHONE_LIST_T(PHONE_t('Home', '512-555-1212')),
BOOKS_LOAN_LIST_T(),
'Y'
);
INSERT INTO PERSON_TABLE_t
VALUES
(2,
NAME_t('Amy', 'Chandi'),
ADDRESS_t('100 West Main St','Austin', 'TX', 78759),
PHONE_LIST_T(PHONE_t('Home', '522-212-2222')),
BOOKS_LOAN_LIST_T(),
'Y'
);
INSERT INTO PERSON_TABLE_t
VALUES
(3,
NAME_t(' Cortney', 'Dumas'),
ADDRESS_t('215 E Dewey St','Dallas', 'TX', 78799),
PHONE_LIST_T(PHONE_t('Home', '529-112-2322')),
BOOKS_LOAN_LIST_T(),
'Y'
);
INSERT INTO PERSON_TABLE_t
VALUES
(4,
NAME_t('Patrick', 'Mohyde'),
ADDRESS_t('80 Kealani St','Honolulu', 'HI', 12345),
PHONE_LIST_T(PHONE_t('Home', '689-198-7567')),
BOOKS_LOAN_LIST_T(),
'Y'
);
/* ---- update person's first name --------------------- */
update person_table_t a
set  A.PERSON_NAME.FIRST_NAME = 'Cortney'
where A.PERSON_NAME.FIRST_NAME = ' Cortney';
/* --------------- update book table ----------- */
UPDATE BOOK_TABLE_T A
```

```
SET A = BOOKS_T(
1, 'IDG',
NAME_t('Amy', 'Chandi'),
'Rough Guide to British Columbia',
'Travel',
RESERVED_LIST_t()
)
where a.book_id = 1;
```

Creating ID_SEQ sequence

```
/* - sequence for Person_TABLE_t and Book_TABLE_t --- */
CREATE SEQUENCE ID_SEQ
INCREMENT BY 1 START WITH 10 NOMAXVALUE
MINVALUE 1 NOCYCLE CACHE 20 NOORDER;
```

Creating Relational Tables Used in the Book

This section has the script for creating and populating the relational tables for the TOYSTORE schema.

Creating the TOYSTORE user

```
/* -------------- create user TOYSTORE -------------- */
CREATE USER TOYSTORE IDENTIFIED BY TOYSTORE
DEFAULT TABLESPACE USER_DATA
TEMPORARY TABLESPACE TEMPORARY_DATA
PROFILE DEFAULT ACCOUNT UNLOCK;
GRANT CONNECT TO TOYSTORE;
GRANT RESOURCE TO TOYSTORE;
GRANT UNLIMITED TABLESPACE TO TOYSTORE;
ALTER USER TOYSTORE DEFAULT ROLE ALL;
```

Creating SHELF_CATEGORY table

Run this script and the other table create scripts as the user TOYSTORE.

```
/* --- SHELF_CATEGORY -------------------------- */
CREATE TABLE TOYSTORE.SHELF_CATEGORY
   (SHELF_CATEGORY VARCHAR2(30) NOT NULL,
    SHELF_DESCRIPTION VARCHAR2(300) NULL,
  PRIMARY KEY (SHELF_CATEGORY)) ;
```

Creating TOY_STORE table

```
/* --- TOY_STORE ------------------------------ */
CREATE TABLE TOYSTORE.TOY_STORE
    (STORE_ID NUMBER(10,0) NOT NULL,
     STORE_STATE CHAR(2) NULL,
     STORE_NAME VARCHAR2(40) NULL,
     ADDRESSLINE1 VARCHAR2(32) NULL,
     ADDRESSLINE2 VARCHAR2(32) NULL,
     CITY VARCHAR2(30) NULL,
     ZIP VARCHAR2(10) NULL,
   PRIMARY KEY (STORE_ID)) ;
```

Creating TOY_INVENTORY table

```
/* --- TOY_INVENTORY ----------------------- */
CREATE TABLE TOYSTORE.TOY_INVENTORY
    (TOY_ID NUMBER(10,0) NOT NULL,
     TOY_NAME VARCHAR2(30) NULL,
     TOY_DESC VARCHAR2(2000) NULL,
     SHELF_CATEGORY VARCHAR2(32) NULL,
     WHOLESALE_COST NUMBER(8,2) NULL,
     SUGGESTED_RETAIL_PRICE NUMBER(8,2) NULL,
   PRIMARY KEY (TOY_ID)) ;
```

Creating STORE_STOCK table

```
/* --- STORE_STOCK ---------------------- */
CREATE TABLE TOYSTORE.STORE_STOCK
    (STORE_ID  NUMBER(10,0) NOT NULL,
     TOY_ID NUMBER(10,0) NOT NULL,
     SALE_PRICE NUMBER(8,2) NULL,
     LAST_STOCK_DATE DATE,
     CURRENT_STOCK_COUNT NUMBER(10,0),
   PRIMARY KEY (STORE_ID,TOY_ID)) ;
```

Inserting Data into TOY_STORE table

```
/* --------------------------------------- TOY_STORE DATA ----- */
INSERT INTO TOY_STORE
    (STORE_ID,STORE_STATE, STORE_NAME, ADDRESSLINE1, ADDRESSLINE2,
CITY, ZIP, OUT_OF_BUSINESS)
 VALUES
    (1382,'FL', 'Betsy''s Personal Treasures', '34988 East Main
Blvd',null,'Miami','87654','N')
```

```
/
INSERT INTO TOY_STORE
     (STORE_ID,STORE_STATE, STORE_NAME, ADDRESSLINE1, ADDRESSLINE2,
CITY, ZIP, OUT_OF_BUSINESS)
 VALUES
     (2199,'OH', 'Gator Gate', 'Charlotte Mall','80 South
Ave','Cincinatti','84001','Y')
/
INSERT INTO TOY_STORE
     (STORE_ID,STORE_STATE, STORE_NAME, ADDRESSLINE1, ADDRESSLINE2,
CITY, ZIP, OUT_OF_BUSINESS)
 VALUES
     (104,'WI', 'Bright Side of Life', 'Gateway Mall','1005 Gammon
Road','Madison','54321','N')
/
INSERT INTO TOY_STORE
     (STORE_ID,STORE_STATE, STORE_NAME, ADDRESSLINE1, ADDRESSLINE2,
CITY, ZIP, OUT_OF_BUSINESS)
 VALUES
     (25,'HI', 'The Best of Toys', '411 Front
Street',null,'Lahaina','96781','N')
/
INSERT INTO TOY_STORE
     (STORE_ID,STORE_STATE, STORE_NAME, ADDRESSLINE1, ADDRESSLINE2,
CITY, ZIP, OUT_OF_BUSINESS)
 VALUES
     (4965,'WI', 'Busy Bee Toys - Midwest', '100 North Central
Ave','Suite 4510','Chicago','14822','N')
/
```

Inserting data into SHELF_CATEGORY table

```
/* --------------- SHELF_CATEGORY DATA ------------- */
INSERT INTO SHELF_CATEGORY VALUES ( 'DOLL','Dolls, doll clothing,
doll accessories');
INSERT INTO SHELF_CATEGORY VALUES ( 'GAME','All board games, video
games, computer games');
INSERT INTO SHELF_CATEGORY VALUES ( 'MAGIC','Magic supplies, books,
kits');
INSERT INTO SHELF_CATEGORY VALUES ( 'SCIENCE','Science kits and
books');
INSERT INTO SHELF_CATEGORY VALUES ( 'WAR','Guns, weapons, action
figures and accessories');
```

Inserting data into TOY_INVENTORY table

```
/* -------------- TOY_INVENTORY DATA ------------ */
INSERT INTO TOY_INVENTORY
   (TOY_ID, TOY_NAME, TOY_DESC, SHELF_CATEGORY, WHOLESALE_COST,
SUGGESTED_RETAIL_PRICE)
VALUES
   (406,'Blade Parade','Makes toy blades come out of any part of
your body. These blades have infrared aimers and rockets so it
always hit the target.',
    'WAR',19.57,32.95)
/
INSERT INTO TOY_INVENTORY
   (TOY_ID, TOY_NAME, TOY_DESC, SHELF_CATEGORY, WHOLESALE_COST,
SUGGESTED_RETAIL_PRICE)
VALUES
   (438,'Morpho-bear','A stuffed bear that morphs into a dragon or
anything you want and then becomes alive.',
    'MAGIC',14.60,18.50)
/
INSERT INTO TOY_INVENTORY
   (TOY_ID, TOY_NAME, TOY_DESC, SHELF_CATEGORY, WHOLESALE_COST,
SUGGESTED_RETAIL_PRICE)
VALUES
   (466,'The Winger','Creates a cocoon and when you emerge you have
wings and can fly.',
    'MAGIC',35.00,49.95)
/
INSERT INTO TOY_INVENTORY
   (TOY_ID, TOY_NAME, TOY_DESC, SHELF_CATEGORY, WHOLESALE_COST,
SUGGESTED_RETAIL_PRICE)
VALUES
   (381,'Belt-o-matic','A belt with many special compartments that
either shrink things or create clones of objects placed inside.',
    'SCIENCE',10.40,12.79)
/
INSERT INTO TOY_INVENTORY
   (TOY_ID, TOY_NAME, TOY_DESC, SHELF_CATEGORY, WHOLESALE_COST,
SUGGESTED_RETAIL_PRICE)
VALUES
   (335,'Hug-o-Doll','Remote control doll that walks and hugs.',
    'DOLL',12.45,15.00)
/
INSERT INTO TOY_INVENTORY
```

```
   (TOY_ID, TOY_NAME, TOY_DESC, SHELF_CATEGORY, WHOLESALE_COST,
SUGGESTED_RETAIL_PRICE)
VALUES
   (6714,'Ratso','You are the rat and you must solve a maze with
cats and traps.',
    'GAME',10.05,12.95)
/
INSERT INTO TOY_INVENTORY
   (TOY_ID, TOY_NAME, TOY_DESC, SHELF_CATEGORY, WHOLESALE_COST,
SUGGESTED_RETAIL_PRICE)
VALUES
   (766,'Barbara','Fashion plastic doll with dress and matching
briefcase',
    'DOLL',11.95,18.05)
/
```

Inserting data into STORE_STOCK table

```
/* --------------------- STORE_STOCK DATA ----- */
INSERT INTO STORE_STOCK
   (STORE_ID, TOY_ID, SALE_PRICE, LAST_STOCK_DATE,
CURRENT_STOCK_COUNT)
VALUES
   (1382,766,9.50,'04-JUN-98',30)
/
INSERT INTO STORE_STOCK
   (STORE_ID, TOY_ID, SALE_PRICE, LAST_STOCK_DATE,
CURRENT_STOCK_COUNT)
VALUES
   (1382,6714,8.50,'12-MAY-98',40)
/
INSERT INTO STORE_STOCK
   (STORE_ID, TOY_ID, SALE_PRICE, LAST_STOCK_DATE,
CURRENT_STOCK_COUNT)
VALUES
   (1382,406,11.95,'15-APR-98',144)
/
INSERT INTO STORE_STOCK
   (STORE_ID, TOY_ID, SALE_PRICE, LAST_STOCK_DATE,
CURRENT_STOCK_COUNT)
VALUES
   (1382,438,16.75,'04-JUN-98',91)
/
INSERT INTO STORE_STOCK
```

```
    (STORE_ID, TOY_ID, SALE_PRICE, LAST_STOCK_DATE,
CURRENT_STOCK_COUNT)
VALUES
    (1382,381,12.79,'15-APR-98',157)
/
INSERT INTO STORE_STOCK VALUES
    (2199,335,12.79,'15-APR-98',578)
/
INSERT INTO STORE_STOCK VALUES
( 25, 335, 13.69, '11-JUL-98',394)
/
INSERT INTO STORE_STOCK VALUES
( 25, 381, 12, '11-JUL-98',204)
/
INSERT INTO STORE_STOCK VALUES
( 25, 406, 28.99, '11-JUL-98',64)
/
INSERT INTO STORE_STOCK VALUES
( 25, 466, 44, '11-JUL-98',224)
/
INSERT INTO STORE_STOCK VALUES
( 25, 766, 15.55, '11-JUL-98',543)
/
INSERT INTO STORE_STOCK VALUES
( 25, 6714, 12, '11-JUL-98',460)
/
INSERT INTO STORE_STOCK VALUES
( 104, 335, 13.45, '11-JUL-98',38)
/
INSERT INTO STORE_STOCK VALUES
( 104, 381, 11.25, '11-JUL-98',88)
/
INSERT INTO STORE_STOCK VALUES
( 104, 406, 27, '11-JUL-98',49)
/
INSERT INTO STORE_STOCK VALUES
( 104, 438, 17, '11-JUL-98',129)
/
INSERT INTO STORE_STOCK VALUES
( 104, 466, 43.99, '11-JUL-98',255)
/
INSERT INTO STORE_STOCK VALUES
( 1382, 335, 13, '11-JUL-98',236)
/
```

```
INSERT INTO STORE_STOCK VALUES
( 1382, 466, 43.45, '11-JUL-98',136)
/
INSERT INTO STORE_STOCK VALUES
( 2199, 381, 12, '11-JUL-98',272)
/
INSERT INTO STORE_STOCK VALUES
( 2199, 406, 26.55, '11-JUL-98',32)
/
INSERT INTO STORE_STOCK VALUES
( 2199, 438, 16, '11-JUL-98',112)
/
INSERT INTO STORE_STOCK VALUES
( 2199, 466, 43, '11-JUL-98',192)
/
INSERT INTO STORE_STOCK VALUES
( 2199, 766, 14.99, '11-JUL-98',512)
/
INSERT INTO STORE_STOCK VALUES
( 2199, 6714, 11.25, '11-JUL-98',432)
/
INSERT INTO STORE_STOCK VALUES
( 4965, 335, 13.05, '11-JUL-98',400)
/
INSERT INTO STORE_STOCK VALUES
( 4965, 438, 16.00, '11-JUL-98',160)
/
INSERT INTO STORE_STOCK VALUES
( 4965, 466, 40.50, '11-JUL-98',240)
/
INSERT INTO STORE_STOCK VALUES
( 4965, 766, 15, '11-JUL-98',560)
/
```

Building foreign keys

```
/* ---------- ADD FOREIGN KEY NOW ---------- */
ALTER TABLE STORE_STOCK
 ADD( FOREIGN KEY (STORE_ID)
REFERENCES TOY_STORE(STORE_ID));
/* ---------- ADD FOREIGN KEY NOW ---------- */
ALTER TABLE STORE_STOCK
 ADD( FOREIGN KEY (TOY_ID)
REFERENCES TOY_INVENTORY(TOY_ID));
```

```
/* -------- ADD FOREIGN KEY NOW ----------- */
ALTER TABLE TOY_INVENTORY
 ADD( FOREIGN KEY (SHELF_CATEGORY)
REFERENCES SHELF_CATEGORY(SHELF_CATEGORY));
```

Building comments on TOYSTORE tables

```
/* -------------- add comments ---------------- */
    COMMENT ON COLUMN TOY_STORE.STORE_ID IS
 'Unique id for each store';
    COMMENT ON COLUMN TOY_STORE.STORE_STATE IS
 'Two digit state, such as NY';
    COMMENT ON COLUMN TOY_STORE.STORE_STATE IS
 'Two digit state, such as NY';
    COMMENT ON COLUMN TOY_STORE.STORE_NAME IS
 'Store name (40 chars max)';
    COMMENT ON COLUMN TOY_STORE.OUT_OF_BUSINESS_FLAG IS
 'Y = closed; N = in business';
    COMMENT ON COLUMN TOY_STORE.STORE_STATE IS
 'Two digit state, such as NY';
    COMMENT ON COLUMN TOY_INVENTORY.TOY_ID IS
 'Unique ID';
    COMMENT ON COLUMN TOY_INVENTORY.TOY_NAME IS
 'Name';
    COMMENT ON COLUMN TOY_INVENTORY.TOY_DESC IS
 'Description';
    COMMENT ON COLUMN TOY_INVENTORY.SHELF_CATEGORY IS
 'Location for shelving this item in the store';
    COMMENT ON COLUMN TOY_INVENTORY.WHOLESALE_COST IS
 'Cost to the home office (per unit)';
    COMMENT ON COLUMN TOY_INVENTORY.SUGGESTED_RETAIL_PRICE IS
 'Suggested Retail Price -- usually too high';
    COMMENT ON COLUMN TOY_INVENTORY.TOY_PHOTO IS
 'File name of photograph of toy';
```

Creating USER_HELP table

```
/* ----- make/User_help.sql ------ */
PROMPT Creating Table 'USER_HELP'
CREATE TABLE USER_HELP
 (HELP_REF NUMBER(38) NOT NULL
 ,MODULE_NAME VARCHAR2(20)
 ,MODULE_COMPONENT_NAME VARCHAR2(50)
 ,TABLE_NAME VARCHAR2(50)
 ,COLUMN_NAME VARCHAR2(50)
```

```
 ,KEYWORDS VARCHAR2(2000)
 )
/
PROMPT Creating Table 'USER_HELP_TEXT'
CREATE TABLE USER_HELP_TEXT
 (HELP_REF NUMBER(38) NOT NULL
 ,SEQ NUMBER(10,0) NOT NULL
 ,TEXT_LINE VARCHAR2(2000)
 )
/
PROMPT Creating Primary Key on 'USER_HELP'
ALTER TABLE USER_HELP
 ADD CONSTRAINT USER_HELP_PK PRIMARY KEY
  (HELP_REF)
/
PROMPT Creating Primary Key on 'USER_HELP_TEXT'
ALTER TABLE USER_HELP_TEXT
 ADD CONSTRAINT USER_HELP_TEXT_PK PRIMARY KEY
  (HELP_REF
  ,SEQ)
/
PROMPT Creating Foreign Keys on 'USER_HELP_TEXT'
ALTER TABLE USER_HELP_TEXT ADD CONSTRAINT
 USER_HELP_TEX_USER_HELP_FK FOREIGN KEY
  (HELP_REF) REFERENCES USER_HELP
  (HELP_REF) ON DELETE CASCADE
/
```

Quick Reference

IN THIS QUICK REFERENCE

◆ Finding the SQL syntax quickly

◆ Writing HTML easily

◆ Creating JSQL syntax

Common SQL Syntax

This section has very brief syntax examples of all the most common SQL commands. Use it to quickly find the exact code you need.

TIP Another book by this author has a complete SQL reference manual built in. The book is titled *Oracle8 Bible* (IDG Books Worldwide, 1998).

In this section, lowercase terms represent variables that you fill in. Words in all capitals are part of the command. Square brackets represent portions of the command that are optional. Vertical bars divide choices of which you select one. Curved parentheses () are part of the command.

Creating database objects

CREATE USER

```
CREATE USER username
    IDENTIFIED [BY password |
        EXTERNALLY | GLOBALLY  AS 'external_name']
            [ DEFAULT TABLESPACE tablespace]
            [TEMPORARY TABLESPACE tablespace]
            [QUOTA {n [K | M] | UNLIMITED} ON tablespace]
            [PROFILE profile]
            [ACCOUNT [LOCK | UNLOCK]
            [PASSWORD EXPIRE]
```

CREATE TABLE

```
CREATE TABLE [user.]tablename
                ( column1 datatype [DEFAULT expn]
                                [column_constraint] |
table_constraint
                [, column1 datatype [DEFAULT expn]
                                [column_constraint] |
table_constraint] ... )
                [CLUSER cluster (column1 [,column2] ...) ]
                [PCTFREE n]
                [PCTUSED n]
                [INITRANS n]
                [MAXTRANS n]
                [STORAGE n]
                [TABLESPACE tablespace]
                [ ENABLE | DISABLE]

CREATE TABLE [user.]tablename [ AS query]
```

CREATE INDEX

```
CREATE INDEX [user.]indexname
      ON [user.]tablename (columnname [ASC | DESC]
     [,columnname [ASC | DESC] ] ... )
                [CLUSTER [user.]cluster]
                [INITRANS n]
                [MAXTRANS n]
                [PCTFREE n]
                [STORAGE storage]
                [TABLESPACE tablespace]
                [NO SORT]
```

CREATE VIEW

```
CREATE [OR REPLACE] [FORCE/NO FORCE] VIEW [user.]viewname
[column_name1, column_name2] AS query
[WITH OBJECT OID | DEFAULT]
[WITH CHECK OPTION [CONSTRAINT constraint]
      [WITH READ ONLY]
```

CREATE OBJECT TYPE AND MEMBER

```
CREATE OR REPLACE Type [schema.]type_name AS OBJECT
(
attribute_name  datatype [, attribute_name datatype].......
| [{MAP|ORDER} MEMBER function specification]
| [MEMBER {procedure_specification |function_specification}
```

```
[,MEMBER {procedure_specification |function_specification}]...]
| [PRAGMA RESTRICT_REFERENCES (method_name, constraints)
[, Pragma RESTRICT_REFERENCES (method_name, constraints)]....]
);
```

CREATE OBJECT TABLE
```
CREATE TABLE table_name of type_name
```

CREATE OBJECT VIEW
```
CREATE OR REPLACE VIEW
object_view_name OF object_type_name WITH OBJECT
OID(unique_object_column) AS
SELECT Statement
```

CREATE SYNONYM
```
CREATE [PUBLIC] SYNONYM [user.] synonym
                FOR [user.] table [@database_link]
```

CREATE SEQUENCE
```
CREATE SEQUENCE [user.]sequence
                [ INCREMENT BY n]
                [ START WITH n]
                [ MAXVALUE n | NOMAXVALUE]
                [ MINVALUE n | NOMINVALUE]
                [ CYCLE | NO CYCLE]
                [CACHE n | NO CACHE]
                [ORDER | NO ORDER]
```

Altering database objects

ALTER TABLE
```
ALTER TABLE [user.] table
                { [ ADD ( { column1 | table_constraint }
                  [, column2 | table_constraint} ] ... ) ]
                [ MODIFY ( column1, column2) ]
                [ DROP drop_constraint]
                [PCTFREE n]
                [PCTUSED n]
                [INITRANS n]
                [MAXTRANS n]
                        [STORAGE n]
                        ALLOCATE EXTENT
                        [ SIZE n [K | M]]
                        [DATAFILE file]
```

```
                              [INSTANCE n]
                              [ ENABLE | DISABLE]
```

ALTER TYPE

```
ALTER TYPE schema.type_name
        { COMPILE { SPECIFICATION | BODY } |
          REPLACE AS | AS TABLE | AS OBJECT }
        { VARRAY (size) | VARYING ARRAY (size) }
            { OF datatype}
            { REF object_type_name}
            { MAP | ORDER MEMBER function_specification }
            { PRAGMA RESTRICT_REFERENCES
                    function_specification restriction}
```

ALTER TABLESPACE

```
ALTER TABLESPACE tablespace
                [ ADD DATAFILE file_definition [,file_definition] |
                        RENAME DATAFILE file [,file] ... TO file [,
file] |
                        DEFAULT STORAGE storage |
                        ONLINE | OFFLINE [NORMAL | IMMEDIATE] |
                        [ BEGIN | END] BACKUP ]
```

Dropping database objects

```
DROP TABLE [user.] table [CASCADE CONSTRAINTS]

DROP [PUBLIC] SYNONYM [user.]synonym

DROP SEQUENCE [user.]sequence

DROP INDEX [user.]index

DROP TYPE [schema.] type_name [FORCE]

DROP USER user [CASCADE]

DROP VIEW [user.]view
```

Selecting from table

```
SELECT [DISTINCT | ALL]   * | column1[, column2]...
FROM { table_1 | (subquery)}  [alias]
        [, {table_2 | (subquery) } [alias]]...
[WHERE condition]
```

```
[CONNECT BY condition [START WITH condition]
[GROUP BY expn] [HAVING expn]
[ {UNION [ALL] | INTERSECT | MINUS } SELECT ... ]
[ ORDER BY [expn ] [ ASC | DESC]
[ FOR UPDATE [OF [user.]table | view] column ]
[NOWAIT]
```

Modifying data

DELETE FROM TABLE OR OBJECT

```
DELETE [FROM] {table | object | (sub_query)} [alias]
[WHERE {search_condition | CURRENT OF cursor_name}];
```

INSERT INTO TABLE

```
INSERT INTO {table | (sub_query)}
[(column_1[, column_2,...column_n)]
{VALUES (sql_expression_1[,sql_expression_2,…,sql_expression_n ]) |
sub_query);
```

INSERT INTO OBJECT

```
INSERT INTO object_table_name VALUES
    (  object_type([value, value, ...]),
      [value [, value, ... ]] );
```

UPDATE TABLE

```
UPDATE {table | (sub_query)} [alias]
SET { column_name = {sql_expression | (sub_query)}
| (column_name[, column_name]...) = (subquery)}
[, {  column_name = {sql_expression | (subquery)}
        | (column_name[, column_name]...) = (subquery)}]...
[WHERE {search_condition | CURRENT OF cursor_name}];
```

UPDATE OBJECT TABLE

```
UPDATE tablename alias
SET { object_name = object_type(
value, value, object_type(value, value, ... ), .... ) }
where alias.object_name = value
```

Pseudocolumns

```
USER
ROWNUM
ROWID
SYSDATE
```

```
[user.]sequence.CURRVAL
[user.]sequence.NEXTVAL
```

Character functions

TABLE Q-1 CHARACTER FUNCTIONS

Function	Example
TO_DATE (column [pattern])	TO_DATE('4/1/98','mm/dd/yy')
TO_NUMBER (column)	TO_NUMBER(TO_CHAR(birth_date,'YYYY'))
DECODE (n, if1, then1, if2, then2 ......, else)	DECODE(approved_flag,'Y','Approved','N', Rejected','Unknown')
INSTR (column,'pattern' [,'startpos', occurencenum'])	INSTR(full_name,'Har',1,2)
SUBSTR (column [,startpos, length])	SUBSTR(full_name,instr(full_name, ')+1)
RPAD (column, totallength [,'padchar'])	RPAD(PAGE_NUM,36,'-')
LPAD (column, totallength [,'padchar'])	LPAD(PAGE_NUM,36,'-')

Group functions

```
SUM | COUNT | AVG | MAX |  MIN | STDDEV | VARIANCE
( [DISTINCT | ALL] expn)
```

Number functions

TABLE Q-2 NUMBER FUNCTIONS

Function	Example
TO_CHAR(number)	TO_CHAR(area_code)
TRUNC (column [, decimals])	TRUNC(annual_sales/365,2)
ROUND (column [, decimals])	ROUND(annual_sales,0)

Date functions

TABLE Q-3 DATE FUNCTIONS

Function	Example	Comment
TO_CHAR (date,['pattern'])	TO_CHAR(birth_date, Day, Month dd, YYYY')	Converts date to VARCHAR2
TRUNC (date ['pattern'])	TRUNC(birth_date, MMYYYY')	Removes time, days, or months from date
ADD_MONTHS(date, nummonths)	ADD_MONTHS (birth_date,6)	Adds number of months to date
MONTHS_BETWEEN (d1, d2)	MONTHS_BETWEEN (birth_date, death _date)	Returns a number
NEXT_DAY(date, weekday)	NEXT_DAY(sysdate, MONDAY')	Returns date of the first MONDAY (for example) after the specified date
LAST_DAY (date)	LAST_DAY(sysdate)	Returns the date of the last day of the month for specified date
date+ | - numdays	sysdate+10 = date	Returns date after adding or subtracting specified days

TABLE Q-4 DATE FORMATTING CODES

Code	Description
D	Number of days in week
DAY	Day fully spelled out in all capital letters
Day	Day fully spelled out with first letter capitalized
DD	Number of days in month
DDD	Number of days in year, since Jan 1
DY	Three-letter abbreviation of the day
AM	Meridian indicator without punctuation

Continued

TABLE **Q–4 DATE FORMATTING CODES** *(Continued)*

Code	Description
A.M.	Meridian indicator with punctuation
PM	Meridian indicator without punctuation
P.M.	Meridian indicator with punctuation
HH	Hours of day
HH12	Hours of day
HH24	Hours in the 24-hour clock format
J	Julian -days since December 31, 4713 B.C.
MI	Minutes of hour
MM	Number of month
MON	Three-letter abbreviation of month in all capitals
Mon	Three-letter abbreviation of month with first letter capitalized
MONTH	Month fully spelled out
Month	Month fully spelled out with first letter capitalized
RM	Roman numeral month
Q	Number of quarter
RR	Last two digits of year relative to current date
RRRR	Four digits of the year relative to current date (This returns year 2000 dates in the year 2000.)
SS	Seconds of hour
SSSSS	Seconds of hour past midnight
IW	Weeks in year from ISO standard
W	Number of weeks in month
WW	Number of weeks in year
I	One-digit year from ISO standard
IY	Two-digit year from ISO standard
IYY	Three-digit year from ISO standard

Code	Description
IYYY	Four-digit year from ISO standard
SYYYY	Signed year (minus sign displayed for B.C.)
YEAR	Year fully spelled out in all capitals
Year	Year fully spelled out with first letters capitalized
Y	Last digit of the year
YY	Last two digits of the year
YYY	Last three digits of the year
YYYY	Full four-digit year

HTML Reference

If you use HTML every day, you probably have memorized the tags you like to use. This section of the Quick Reference helps you find HTML tags without digging through a long manual. It is intended as a reminder, not a tutorial.

 TIP The best way to find examples of good HTML code is to surf the Net and view the source code of Web pages you like. In Netscape, choose View → Page Source. In Internet Explorer, choose View   Source.

In this section, lowercase terms represent variables that you fill in. Words in all capitals are part of the command. Square brackets represent portions of the command that are optional. Vertical bars divide choices of which you select one. Angled parenthesis (<>), double quotes ("), the number sign (#), and the percent sign (%) are part of the command.

Head

This tag is optional.

```
<HEAD>
      [<TITLE>write title here</TITLE>]
</HEAD>
```

Lines (horizontal rule)

```
<HR
        [ALIGN=LEFT | RIGHT | CENTER]
        [SIZE=numpixels]
        [WIDTH=numpixels | "n%"]
        [NOSHADE] >
```

Graphics (images)

```
<IMG SRC="url"
        [ALIGN=TOP | BOTTOM | MIDDLE | LEFT | RIGHT]
        [ALT="image description here"]
        [WIDTH=numpixels]
        [HEIGHT=numpixels]
        [BORDER=numpixels]
        [HSPACE=numpixels]
        [VSPACE=numpixels]
        [LOWSRC="url"] >
```

Link

```
<A HREF="url[#targetname]|#targetname">
write link description here
</A>
```

The URL can be listed with or without a target name. The URL can be omitted if the target name points to a target in the same document.

Target

```
<A NAME="targetname">
        [write target description here]
</A>
```

The target description is optional. This means that you can mark a target location without any obvious notations in the text.

Tables

Figure Q-1 shows examples of tables.

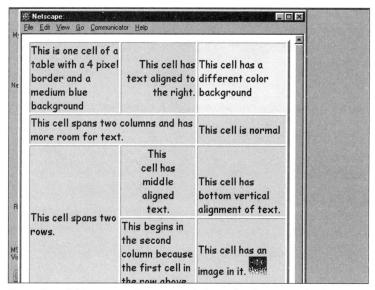

Figure Q-1: Tables are used to present information in rows and columns.

The basic syntax for HTML tables is laid out below.

TABLE CAPTION
```
<CAPTION ALIGN=TOP|BOTTOM >write caption here</CAPTION>
```

TABLE BODY
```
<TABLE
        [BORDER=numpixels]
        [BGCOLOR="hexnumber"]
        [CELLSPACING=numpixels]
        [CELLPADDING=numpixels]
        [WIDTH=numpixels | "num%" ] >
Place table row here
</TABLE>
```

TABLE ROW
```
<TR
        [BGCOLOR="hexnumber"]
        [ALIGN=LEFT | RIGHT | CENTER | MIDDLE | BOTTOM ]
        [ VALIGN=TOP | BOTTOM | MIDDLE ] >
[Place table header here optional]
Place table cells here
</TR>
```

TABLE HEADER

The table header is the same as the table cell, except by default the words in this row are bolded and centered. Table header is an optional tag.

```
<TH
        [BGCOLOR="hexnumber"]
        [ALIGN=LEFT | RIGHT | CENTER | MIDDLE | BOTTOM ]
        [ VALIGN=TOP | BOTTOM | MIDDLE ]
        [NOWRAP ]
        [COLSPAN=numcols]
        [ROWSPAN=numrows]
        [WIDTH=numpixels | "num%"] >
write header text here
</TH>
```

TABLE CELL

```
<TD
        [BGCOLOR="hexnumber"]
        [ALIGN=LEFT | RIGHT | CENTER | MIDDLE | BOTTOM ]
        [ VALIGN=TOP | BOTTOM | MIDDLE ]
        [NOWRAP ]
        [COLSPAN=numcols]
        [ROWSPAN=numrows]
        [WIDTH=numpixels | "n%"] >
write cell text here
</TD>
```

List (ordered)

LIST BODY

```
<OL
        [COMPACT ]
        [TYPE=A | a | I | I | 1]
        [START=num] >
place list items here
</OL>
```

ORDERED LIST ITEM

```
<LI
        [TYPE= A | a | I | I | 1] >
write list text here
[</LI>]
```

List (unordered)

LIST BODY
```
<UL>
        [COMPACT]
        [TYPE=DISC | CIRCLE | SQUARE]
place unordered list items here
</UL>
```

UNORDERED LIST ITEM
```
<LI
[TYPE=DISC | CIRCLE | SQUARE]
write list text here
[</LI>]
```

Form

The form is a complex structure that contains many components within it. Figure Q-2 illustrates the different features of a form that are described in this section.

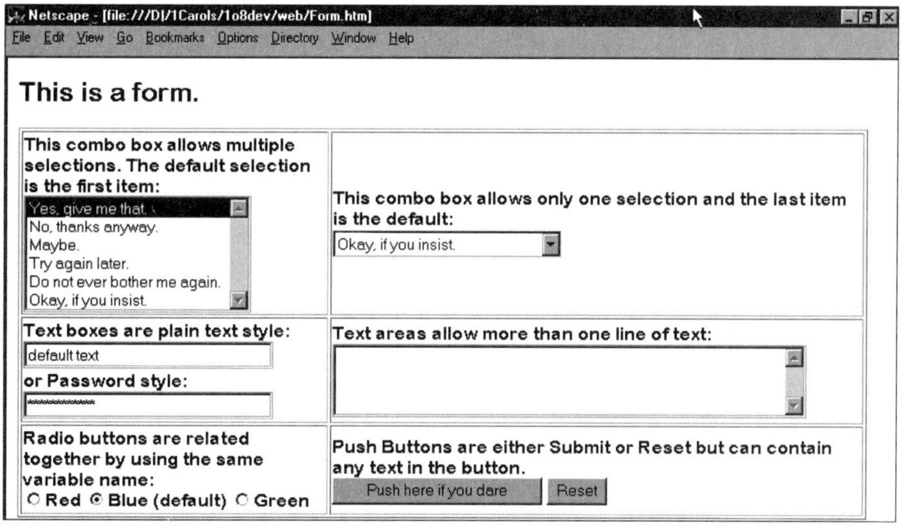

Figure Q-2: The HTML form defines ways to gather information from a user and pass it to a computer process.

FORM BODY

```
<FORM ACTION="url"
       METHOD=GET|POST>
Place other tags, input items, text here
</FORM>
```

COMBO BOX

```
<SELECT NAME="variablename" [SIZE=num]  [MULTIPLE ]>
       <OPTION[SELECTED] [VALUE="selected data"]> Place description
here
      [<OPTION[SELECTED] [VALUE="selected data"]> Place description
here] ...
</SELECT>
```

TEXT BOX

```
<INPUT TYPE="TEXT|PASSWORD
       [SIZE=num]
       [MAXLENGTH=num]
       [NAME="variablename"]
       [VALUE="default text"] >
```

TEXT AREA

```
<TEXTAREA ROWS=n COLS=n
       [NAME="variablename"]
       [VALUE="default text"]
       [WRAP=OFF|VIRTUAL|PHYSICAL] >
</TEXTAREA>
```

RADIO BUTTONS

```
<INPUT TYPE="RADIO"
       [NAME="variablename"]
       [VALUE="button text"] >
```

PUSH BUTTONS

```
<INPUT TYPE="SUBMIT|RESET"
       [NAME="variablename"]
       [VALUE="button text"] >
```

JSQL Reference

This new addition to SQL combines Java and SQL to simplify the job of writing applications. When you use JSQL (Java SQL), you do not write (Java Database Connectivity) commands. The JSQL translator transforms your JSQL clauses into standard Java code that accesses the database through a JDBC call interface. The output of a JSQL translator is a generated Java program that can then be compiled by any Java compiler.

This section is not a complete syntax guide, but highlights the basics.

Embedding a query

```
#sql { SELECT ... };
```
   Begin all JSQL statements with #sql.
   Enclose SQL in curly brackets.
   Example:
```
#sql { SELECT STORE_ID, STORE_NAME
           FROM STORE
           WHERE STORE_STATE = :state };
```

Insert, update, delete

Insert variable values:

```
void m (int var1, String st1, float fl1) throws SQLException {
      #sql { INSERT INTO SHELF_CATEGORY VALUES (:var1, :st1, :fl1)
};}
```

   Delete rows from table:
```
#sql { DELETE FROM STORE_STOCK };
```
   Update with cursor:
```
{
    iterator_type c;
    #sql c = { SELECT TOY_ID, SUGGESTED_RETAIL_PRICE
                   FROM TOY_INVENTORY };
    ...
    #sql { UPDATE TOY_INVENTORY
               SET SUGGESTED_RETAIL_PRICE =
                       SUGGESTED_RETAIL_PRICE*1.05
               WHERE CURRENT OF :c };
}
```
   Set columns to null values:
```
    String s1 = null;
    Double d1 = null;
    #sql { UPDATE TOY_INVENTORY
               SET SHELF_CATEGORY = :s1,
               WHOLESALE_COST = :d1 };
```

Select . . . into

```
{
    ByPos getit; // declare iterator object
    String storename;
    int toyid;
    int laststockmon;
    #sql getit = { SELECT STORE_NAME,
                                    TOY_ID,

TO_CHAR(LAST_STOCK_DATE,'MM')
                            FROM TOY_STORE TS, STORE_STOCK SS
                            WHERE TS.STORE_ID = SS.STORE_ID }; //
populate it
    while (true) {
      #sql { FETCH :getit INTO :storename, :toyid, :laststockmon };
      if (getit.endFetch()) break;
      System.out.println(storename + " — toy " + toyid +
                              " was last stocked in " +
laststockmon);
    }
  }
```
Positional column fetch:
```
#sql iterator toyrec (int, String, float);
 toyrec p;
  #sql p = { SELECT * FROM SHELF_CATEGORY };
  #sql { FETCH :p INTO :x, :y, :z };
```
You must explicitly close the query after the fetch.

Function call

```
{ int x;
    #sql x = { VALUES( fname(:parm1) ) };
  }
```
Replace fname with function name.

Login

```
#sql (CONNECT username/password@dblink)
```

Procedure call

```
#sql {CALL procedure_name( parameter1, ... )}
```
You can use IN, OUT, and INOUT parameters.
Example:

```
#sql {
        CALL OBJOWNER.BOOK_HANDLING.LOAN_A_BOOK
                (:personid, :booklist)
    };
```

SQL blocks

```
#sql { BEGIN
            sql stmt;
            sql stmt;
        END
    };
```

Glossary

4GL A fourth generation language (4GL) such as SQL is a high-level language with English-like commands. Such languages are easier to use, presumably, than third generation languages such as C.

abstract datatype See user-defined datatype.

alias A nickname or alternative name for a table or column that is used in SQL.

applet Small Java program that runs within the browser environment.

Application Program Interface An API is a standard language used by a program to communicate with other programs that provide services to it.

attribute A feature or characteristic. For example, the datatype and size of a column are two of the column's attributes.

backup A copy of all or some part of the database. There are several different methods of creating a backup, including operating system file backups, database exports, and using the Backup Manager.

Binary Large Object A large nontext file such as a color graphic file or sound file.

BLOB See Binary Large Object.

block A unit of storage for data and other information in the database.

Boolean operator Boolean operators such as AND and OR are used in queries to link other sets of operators together. For example, a SQL statement with Boolean operators is: select name from artist where school = 'ABSTRACT' AND medium = 'WATERCOLOR'.

browser A client for a Web server. A browser is a program that enables a user to view Web documents.

buffer cache A segment of the System Global Area (SGA) that maintains copies of all data blocks read from data files by user processes requesting data.

built-in datatype Datatype used in relational tables. VARCHAR2 and LONG are built-in datatypes. See also user-defined datatype.

Cartesian join   An unconditional join between two tables resulting in a match between every row in one table and every row in another table.

cartridge   Prebuilt application that plugs into your Oracle8 database and provides additional functionality that you can incorporate into your own applications.

chain   A block of database data that contains overflow information from another data block.

class   In object-oriented systems, a method of grouping similar objects. A class of objects has similar attributes, such as color, shape, or mathematical function.

client   The client portion of the Oracle8 package includes utilities, assistant programs, and tools that can be run remotely using a network. The client portions usually include a graphical user interface (GUI) that makes them easier to use.

client/server   A network system that features a server computer that provides digital services to other computers (clients) on the network. Client/server software consists of a network server program that provides specific digital services to other programs (clients) on the network.

cluster   A schema object that contains a group of tables that share one or more common columns (cluster key) and are stored on the same data block.

cold backup   A backup that is taken while the database is shut down.

column   A component of a database table. A column contains the definition of what kinds of data are to be collected and stored in the rows of the table.

comma-delimited file   A format for extracting data out of a database and placing it into a plain text file. Each line in the file contains one row, and each column is separated from the following column by a comma.

commit   To permanently save all changes since the last commit was executed on the database.

constraint   A rule applied to a table or a column that restricts the data that is allowed in any row in the table. For example, a primary key constraint defines the primary key for a table. All rows must have unique values in the columns included in the primary key constraint.

constructor method   A default system-generated method for each object type that helps create an instance of that object type.

control file A binary file used by Oracle8 to store its configuration parameters.

correlated sub-query A subquery that references the outer query.

cursor for loop A form of LOOP in PL/SQL. The loop opens a specified cursor, executes one time for each row retrieved by the query in the cursor, and closes the cursor. The loop also builds the variables needed to store the values of each column retrieved by the cursor.

DAD See Database Access Descriptors.

database As used in this book, database is an adjective that means having to do with database technology. The word is otherwise avoided because it is so generic that it's confusing to use it as a noun in a book about database technology.

Database Access Descriptors The DADs are Oracle-specific elements. They let you define a set of environment values to be used when executing a client request.

database application An application involving data designed to run with a database engine.

database development tools Programs that create database applications.

database engine The set of programs that run the database, keeping track of all the information, monitoring usage, checking security, checking for errors, and so on.

datatype In relational databases, the characteristic of a column. For instance, a column storing dates has the date datatype. A column storing your age has the number datatype.

datatype Defines the type of information that can be stored, such as dates, numbers, or characters.

DBA The database administrator.

derived data Data that can be calculated, summarized, or otherwise extracted entirely from other data in the database.

dialog A pop-up window where the user is either receiving new information, asked to take action, or both.

display An application created in Developer's Graphics Builder tool.

entity A table or group of tables. Used interchangeably with table in this book.

Entity Relationship Diagram A style of drawing a relational database model that uses boxes, text, lines, and a few simple symbols to represent the entities and relationships in the model.

explicit data conversion The user controls conversion of a column or expression from one datatype into another. This controls the data conversion in a predictable manner. See also implicit data conversion.

export Retrieve information from a database into a file to use in another application (such as a spreadsheet), another database engine, or a word processor (mail merge).

expression A column, a literal, or a column with some function applied to it, such as addition. In SQL queries, expressions can be used almost anywhere a column can be used.

extent A secondary allocation of space for a tablespace, table, or physical data file.

field See column.

foreign key A column or a group of columns in one table that refer to the primary key of another table.

form Fill-in-the-blank screen for gathering information in an organized way. Created with HTML. The information can then be used in e-mail or a database application.

fragmented table A table that contains wasted space in the form of empty blocks and chained blocks.

front-end The portion of a computer program that is designed to interact with a human being.

GRANT SQL command for granting security privileges for a table, view, or synonym.

GUI A user interface for a program that is graphical and uses icons, buttons, and a mouse.

hierarchy A relationship of tables where a parent table has a child table and that child table has its own child table and so on.

hot backup A backup taken while the database is open and in use.

HTML See HyperText Markup Language.

hybrid As used in this book, it means a hybrid object-oriented relational database engine or application.

HyperText Markup Language The primary language used to create Web pages. HTML consists of normal text and special codes, called tags, that tell a Web browser how to display the text. Tags determine the size of the font, color of the background, and other formatting details.

identity In object-oriented systems, a complex formula that can be attached to a class or subclass of objects.

implicit data conversion Oracle8 converts a column or expression from one datatype into another using its own internal logic. This is unpredictable and subject to change with new releases. See also explicit data conversion.

import Add information into a database or software tool from an external source such as a file or nondatabase application.

incremental space In a table definition, incremental space specifies the amount of space reserved if the table runs out of room and needs more space. It is repeated again if the table again needs more space, until the table hits the maximum space limitation.

index A sorted map of selected columns in a table or object. It makes searching on that column much faster.

initial space In a table definition, initial space sets the starting size of the table.

input Any information that is entered by a user into the computer such as a person's name typed into a database row and column.

INSERT A command to add a new row into a table.

instance A single complete Oracle database. Each instance has its own name, number, and initilization parameters. Multiple instances can run on one computer.

intelligent key An intelligent key is a primary key that has meaning for the row of data.

interactive Any process where the computer asks for information from the user and then acts on it.

Internet A global, public network of computers linked with telephone lines and network software. See also World Wide Web.

intranet A network of computers connected via phone or cable lines that is inside one organization for internal use only.

Java A high-level language especially adapted for use on the Web.

Java Database Connectivity A protocol for connecting Java programs to ODBC databases.

JDBC See Java Database Connectivity.

join A type of query in which two or more tables are connected, or joined, together.

key A column or set of columns in a table that identifies a unique row of data. See also primary key and foreign key.

LAN See Local Area Network.

legacy system A set of tables (schema) that have been brought into your Oracle8 system from an older source, such as Oracle7, or another database system.

literal A word or phrase, number, or letter that is used at its face value (exactly as it is written) in a query or in a SQL*Plus command. A literal is always surrounded by single quotes.

local area network A network connecting computers, printers, and other equipment. The connections do not use telephone lines and are usually restricted to equipment located in a single building, such as an office building.

local database A database that resides on the computer the user is logged into.

logical operator A connection between two columns or expressions in a WHERE clause. Examples are = (equal), <> (not equal), like, between, < (less than), > (greater than).

master site In database replication, the site that is the primary source of new data for a table. See also snapshot site.

method Programmed behavior for manipulating an object. A function or procedure attached to an Object type.

named routine   In Designer, a procedure, function, or package that is stored within the generated module (that is, a form, report, and so on). A named routine translates into a program unit in a form.

native driver   A Dynamic Link Library (DLL) that provides an interface between an application and a specific database run-time library for the database server. See also ODBC driver.

nested table   A table contained within a single object column. See also varray.

Net8   Formally known as SQL*Net, it is a software layer that exists between Oracle8 clients and servers, which uses the Transparent Network Substrate (TNS) to establish and maintain connections, and most importantly, it enables the exchange of data messages between them.

Non-intelligent key   A key that is unique and does not change, even when information in the row changes. A sequential ID number is an example of a non-intelligent key.

object   Any of several kinds of elements in a database, such as indexes, tables, packages, views, and synonyms. Another definition for object is the instantiation of a class in an object-oriented data structure.

object identifier   An indexed column that you use when referencing one object to another using the REF parameter.

object oriented   A system of logic where everything is defined as groups of objects, or "behavior matrices," that interact with one another in predictable ways.

Object-Oriented Database Management System   A form of database consisting of objects that are classified into categories and subcategories to define special traits. Commonly used in scientific applications to predict how two objects interact, such as in a chemical compound or a mechanical device. Often abbreviated as OODBMS.

object table   A database construction made up of user-defined datatypes and built-in datatypes that stores data.

object view   Object-oriented view. Use object views to abstract data from relational or object tables.

object-relational database   A database that combines features of a relational database with features of an object-oriented database. Oracle8 is an object-relational database. As an object-relational database, Oracle8 supports all the familiar relational database concepts of tables, columns, rows, and relationships. It also supports a subset of the object-oriented features of types, methods, and attributes.

ODBC See Open Database Connectivity.

ODBC driver Cross-platform programming interface that provides a language to access database applications on a network. See also Open Database Connectivity.

OID See object identifier.

OODBMS See Object-Oriented Database Management System.

Open Database Connectivity A set of standards that defines communication methods to be used when sending and receiving data and commands to and from a database.

operator Used in queries to evaluate columns. For example, < (less than), <= (less than or equal to), > (greater than), >= (greater than or equal to), and <> (not equal to).

optimizer Oracle8 uses its optimizer to evaluate every command that is run in the database. The optimizer has rules that tell it what the most efficient path to the data might be. The optimizer reviews the WHERE clause of a command and determines how to use indexes, table scans, partial indexes, and so on. From this information, the optimizer comes up with a plan.

Oracle Names Server A directory service that provides name-to-address resolution for each Net8 service on the Oracle8 network.

overhead Information about tables, columns, rows, indexes, and other structures in the database.

outer join A table join that enables mismatches between the joined columns. One of the tables is chosen as the primary table. Any row in this table that has no matches in the other table stays in the results set of the join.

owner The user who creates a table.

package A database program consisting of one or more procedures. A package executes when called using SQL or a programming language interface.

physical data file A database requires physical storage space, and Oracle8 allocates storage space using physical data files. You can assign physical data files for use in the database. You can also design a file to grow in predetermined increments to avoid causing the database to run out of space.

plan Access path that the Oracle8 optimizer determines is the most cost-effective method to execute a command.

precompiler A compiler program that enables C/C++, COBOL, and Fortran visual or nonvisual applications to be developed with embedded SQL statements to access the database.

preference set In Designer/2000, the preference set enables you to identify standard, named ways to generate a form.

primary key A column or set of columns that is used to uniquely identify a row of data in a table.

private synonym A synonym that can be used only by the synonym creator, unless the creator grants privileges to others.

procedure A database program that contains PL/SQL commands. A procedure can be contained within a package or can stand alone. A database procedure executes when called using SQL or a programming language interface.

project In Personal Oracle8 Navigator, a collection of tables, views, users, or other items. Projects can be exported and imported.

pseudocolumn A column defined by Oracle8 that you can use in a query. For example, USER is a pseudocolumn that always contains the Oracle8 user ID of the current user.

public synonym A synonym created by a database administrator (DBA) that can be used by anyone.

query A question posed in SQL to look at data in the database.

record See row.

relational database A collection of tables connected in a series of relationships so that they model some small part of the real world.

remote database A database that does not reside on the computer the user is logged into.

reorganize To rebuild the internal physical structure of a table by dropping it and recreating it. Data must be removed and restored using export and import.

REVOKE A SQL command for removing security privileges.

role A set of privileges that can be assigned to or removed from a user.

ROLLBACK A command that removes all changes since the last commit.

row A component of a database table. It contains the actual data, compartmentalized in columns.

row ID A pseudocolumn that contains the exact physical address of a row. Retrieving a table row using its row ID is the fastest method available.

schema A set of tables, views, and other objects that are all created by one user is called a schema. A schema is not given a unique name; it inherits the name of the user who created the objects.

script A file that contains more than just a single SQL or SQL*Plus command.

server The server portion of the Oracle8 package includes the core database itself (the background processes that keep the entire database functioning) and some rudimentary tools that enable basic processes, such as starting and stopping the database.

snapshot site In database replication, a site that receives identical updates to keep it synchronized with the master site. See also master site.

SQL See Structured Query Language.

Structured Query Language Programming language developed to manipulate relational database objects.

synonym An alternate name for a table or view. Synonyms can be private (for use only by its creator) or public (for use by any user).

table A set of related columns and rows in a relational database.

tablespace A tablespace is a logical allocation of space within the database. A tablespace can span more than one data file. Only objects assigned to the tablespace can use the available space in a data file.

third normal form A set of rules specifying how tables and columns in a relational database relate to one another.

tree diagram See Entity Relationship Diagram.

user A unique login name in Oracle8. A user's capabilities inside the database are determined by the user's roles, privileges, and profiles.

user-defined datatype Datatypes that are defined by the user as combinations of built-in datatypes and other user-defined datatypes. They are used as building blocks for objects. See also built-in datatype.

user ID See user.

variable A placeholder in an equation, an HTML command, or a computer program that is replaced by some value when the equation is solved or when the command or program is run.

varray A repeating set of columns contained within one object column. See also nested table.

view A query that is named in the database so that it can be used as if it were a table. Views can be used anywhere tables can be used, except some restrictions apply to adding, removing, or changing rows from views that join tables.

WAN See wide area network.

Web See World Wide Web.

Web Database Development Tools Software tools that develop applications for retrieving and manipulating database objects via Web pages.

Web page A screen of data, graphics, music, and so on that appears on the World Wide Web (Internet) or on an intranet. This is a general term referring to any document on the Web. It may be an order entry form, a database report, a video, a text document, or any number of other possibilities. The length of one page is totally flexible, and the document contains HTML tags.

Web server Software that delivers Web pages and their accompanying files (imagery, sounds, multimedia, and so on). The Web server delivers Web pages to the client, which is also called the Web browser.

wide area network A network connecting computers, printers, and other equipment. The connections use telephone lines. There are no restrictions on where the equipment is located. A WAN can reach around the world or just next door.

wizard A software tool that can do one specialized task.

World Wide Web A text-based, hyperlinked, multimedia publishing system enabled by the HyperText Transport Protocol (HTTP), which is an Internet protocol. The Web, as it is often referred to, is a versatile, colorful, and highly interactive area.

WWW See World Wide Web.

WYSIWYG Acronym for "what you see is what you get." Used to describe editors and other tools that display information in output format.

Index

IDG BOOKS WORLDWIDE, INC. END-USER LICENSE AGREEMENT

4. <u>Restrictions on Use of Individual Programs</u>. You must follow the individual requirements and restrictions detailed for each individual program in the "What's on the CD?" section of this Book. These limitations are also contained in the individual license agreements recorded on the Software Media. These limitations may include a requirement that after using the program for a specified period of time, the user must pay a registration fee or discontinue use. By opening the Software packet(s), you will be agreeing to abide by the licenses and restrictions for these individual programs that are detailed in the "What's on the CD?" section and on the Software Media. None of the material on this Software Media or listed in this Book may ever be redistributed, in original or modified form, for commercial purposes.

5. <u>Limited Warranty</u>.

(a) IDGB warrants that the Software and Software Media are free from defects in materials and workmanship under normal use for a period of sixty (60) days from the date of purchase of this Book. If IDGB receives notification within the warranty period of defects in materials or workmanship, IDGB will replace the defective Software Media.

(b) IDGB AND THE AUTHOR OF THE BOOK DISCLAIM ALL OTHER WARRANTIES, EXPRESS OR IMPLIED, INCLUDING WITHOUT LIMITATION IMPLIED WARRANTIES OF MERCHANTABILITY AND FITNESS FOR A PARTICULAR PURPOSE, WITH RESPECT TO THE SOFTWARE, THE PROGRAMS, THE SOURCE CODE CONTAINED THEREIN, AND/OR THE TECHNIQUES DESCRIBED IN THIS BOOK. IDGB DOES NOT WARRANT THAT THE FUNCTIONS CONTAINED IN THE SOFTWARE WILL MEET YOUR REQUIREMENTS OR THAT THE OPERATION OF THE SOFTWARE WILL BE ERROR FREE.

(c) This limited warranty gives you specific legal rights, and you may have other rights that vary from jurisdiction to jurisdiction.

6. <u>Remedies</u>.

(a) IDGB's entire liability and your exclusive remedy for defects in materials and workmanship shall be limited to replacement of the Software Media, which may be returned to IDGB with a copy of your receipt at the following address: Software Media Fulfillment Department, Attn.: *Oracle8 Developer's Guide*, IDG Books Worldwide, Inc., 7260 Shadeland Station, Ste. 100, Indianapolis, IN 46256, or call 1-800-762-2974. Please allow three to four weeks for delivery. This Limited Warranty is void if failure of the Software Media has resulted from accident, abuse, or misapplication. Any replacement Software Media will be warranted for the remainder of the original warranty period or thirty (30) days, whichever is longer.

(b) In no event shall IDGB or the author be liable for any damages whatsoever (including without limitation damages for loss of business profits, business interruption, loss of business information, or any other pecuniary loss) arising from the use of or inability to use the Book or the Software, even if IDGB has been advised of the possibility of such damages.

(c) Because some jurisdictions do not allow the exclusion or limitation of liability for consequential or incidental damages, the above limitation or exclusion may not apply to you.

7. <u>**U.S. Government Restricted Rights**</u>. Use, duplication, or disclosure of the Software by the U.S. Government is subject to restrictions stated in paragraph (c)(1)(ii) of the Rights in Technical Data and Computer Software clause of DFARS 252.227-7013, and in subparagraphs (a) through (d) of the Commercial Computer – Restricted Rights clause at FAR 52.227-19, and in similar clauses in the NASA FAR supplement, when applicable.

8. <u>General</u>. This Agreement constitutes the entire understanding of the parties and revokes and supersedes all prior agreements, oral or written, between them and may not be modified or amended except in a writing signed by both parties hereto that specifically refers to this Agreement. This Agreement shall take precedence over any other documents that may be in conflict herewith. If any one or more provisions contained in this Agreement are held by any court or tribunal to be invalid, illegal, or otherwise unenforceable, each and every other provision shall remain in full force and effect.

my2cents.idgbooks.com

Register This Book — And Win!

Visit **http://my2cents.idgbooks.com** to register this book and we'll automatically enter you in our fantastic monthly prize giveaway. It's also your opportunity to give us feedback: let us know what you thought of this book and how you would like to see other topics covered.

Discover IDG Books Online!

The IDG Books Online Web site is your online resource for tackling technology — at home and at the office. Frequently updated, the IDG Books Online Web site features exclusive software, insider information, online books, and live events!

10 Productive & Career-Enhancing Things You Can Do at www.idgbooks.com

- Nab source code for your own programming projects.

- Download software.

- Read Web exclusives: special articles and book excerpts by IDG Books Worldwide authors.

- Take advantage of resources to help you advance your career as a Novell or Microsoft professional.

- Buy IDG Books Worldwide titles or find a convenient bookstore that carries them.

- Register your book and win a prize.

- Chat live online with authors.

- Sign up for regular e-mail updates about our latest books.

- Suggest a book you'd like to read or write.

- Give us your 2¢ about our books and about our Web site.

You say you're not on the Web yet? It's easy to get started with IDG Books' *Discover the Internet,* available at local retailers everywhere.

Installation Instructions

The CD-ROM that accompanies this book includes sample tables and data, the complete book in PDF files, and Adobe Acrobat Reader.

Place the CD in your CD-ROM drive. To install:

- ◆ Acrobat Reader, double-click on the .exe file and follow the prompts.

- ◆ Sample files, copy the files to your hard drive. (Complete instructions for using the sample tables and data are found in Appendix A.)

- ◆ PDF files, open the folder and choose the file name you wish to view. Note: Acrobat Reader should be installed on your computer at this point.